D1118734

N

JAZZ

AMERICAN POPULAR MUSIC ON ELPEE:

Jazz

Other volumes:

- *Black Music*
- *Grass Roots Music*
- *Contemporary Popular Music*

Dean Tudor

Chairman
Library Arts Department
Ryerson Polytechnical Institute
Toronto, Canada

Nancy Tudor

Assistant Head
Cataloguing Department
Metropolitan Toronto Public Library Board
Toronto, Canada

Libraries Unlimited, Inc. - Littleton, Colo. -1979

LIBRARIES UNLIMITED, INC.
P.O. Box 263
Littleton, Colorado 80160

Library of Congress Cataloging in Publication Data

Tudor, Dean.
    Jazz.

    (American popular music on Elpee)
    Includes index.
    1. Jazz music--Discography. 2. Phonorecord
collecting. I. Tudor, Nancy, joint author.
II. Title. III. Series.
ML156.4.J3T73   016.7899'12   78-11737
ISBN 0-87287-148-7

PREFACE

This book is a survey of and buying-guide to one aspect of American commercial popular music on discs: jazz. The other three modes—black, contemporary popular, and grass roots—are detailed through three companion books, all published by Libraries Unlimited. Coverage of the four volumes of "American Popular Music on Elpee" extends to all worthwhile discs since the advent of recorded sound that are presently available on long-playing records or tapes. Recently deleted items are included when they are still available from specialist stores, and the labels are international in scope, for many reissued records of American music are currently available in France, Scandinavia, West Germany, Japan, and in other countries.

For this book, approximately 1,300 recordings have been pre-selected and annotated, representing relatively current thought expressed through thousands of reviews and articles, plus hundreds of books, that we have read. This is fully explained in the section "What This Book Is All About. . . ." Thus, the recordings selection librarian can base his or her choice upon informed evaluation rather than random choice. In some respects, then, *Jazz* is to recordings what the H. W. Wilson *Standard Catalog* series are to books, or what Bill Katz's *Magazines for Libraries* is to periodicals. Our criteria have been noted through discographic essays and comments, mainly emphasizing musical development, "popularity," repertoire indexes, artistic merits of discs, and extra-musical developments.

Arrangement includes a division by anthologies, different stylings, different time periods, diverse instrumentation and vocal techniques, etc., along with explanatory narrative essays that present short musicological descriptions, definitions, brief histories, roots of development and progressions, and a discussion on the written literature (reviews, articles, books). Each album is numbered, and sometimes a few are grouped together for ease of discussion. All relevant order information is included: name of artist, title, label, last known serial number, and country of origin. A directory of specialty stores and label addresses appears at the rear of the book, also. Each annotation averages 300 words and specifically states why that record and/or material is significant. In each grouping, anthologies have been presented together, "innovators" have been carefully separated into their own section, and important discs have been starred to indicate a "first purchase."

This book can be used by both libraries and individuals to build a comprehensive record collection reflective of jazz, within the constraints noted in each section. Other uses include tracing the background of musical interactions in the explanatory notes and annotations, gaining an overview of the jazz field in general, and establishing criteria on which to base *future* purchases. Obviously, this aid is only as current as are clearly defined musical developments; thus, while the physical discs are, for the most part, "in-print," the actual performed music is

BELLINGHAM PUBLIC LIBRARY
BELLINGHAM, WASHINGTON

5

293642

lagging behind this book's printing date, because no one knows what "fresh" music of 1977 or 1978 will be the leader in the years to come. Other limitations include the placement of discs within the four books.

Our intent has been to select recordings indicative of a style, regardless of convenient popular (and often simplistic) classifications of an artist or group. The over-riding condition for each selection has been its manner of presentation—whether a pop or a jazz item, a country or a rock item—with serious consideration given to its ultimate placement. (But all classification schemes seem to have their exceptions.) However, we are confident that in our four books, viewed as a whole, no important available material has been overlooked.

For *Jazz*, this meant deciding what is jazz-oriented mood music (or is it mood-oriented jazz music?) and listing that music either here or in *Contemporary Popular Music*. Thus, the lyrical works of Ben Webster and Stan Getz, plus the pre-1950 "big bands" and "dance bands" are in that other book. Yet, Benny Goodman, for instance, worked in a number of styles, and he too can be found in both books. "Blues" presented difficulties, and we opted for "big band vocal blues" (but *not* the "jump blues") and instrumentals for *Jazz*, while all other forms went into *Black Music*. "Modern jazz," while arguably black music, is located in *Jazz*. Some thematic jazz discs based on the musical stage (Porter, Gershwin, *My Fair Lady*, et al.) are in *Contemporary Popular Music*, as are "jazz-rock" discs issued primarily to the rock world. (Note, though, that "pop jazz" released first to the jazz world is included here at J6.125-138.) The marketing patterns of cross-overs and fragmentation in the music world are, as indicated in the introduction, further examples of regional breakdowns in musical styles.

ACKNOWLEDGMENT AND THANKS

While this book is basically a summation and synthesis of existing thought about jazz (as revealed through books, periodical articles, record reviews, and the music itself), we sought guidance from collectors in the field through letters and conversations. All are knowledgeable critics; some are even librarians. In no way did they comment on the text itself; that was our responsibility alone. Our thanks, then, go to: John Arpin (ragtime, piano jazz), Harald Bohne (European jazz, modern jazz), Paul Copeland (swing), Dave Done, Baron McCormick (piano jazz, ragtime), John Norris (pre-War jazz), Ed Popoff, Jim Ross (Chicago jazz), Joe Showler, Bill Smith (modern jazz), and Ralph Tapp (British jazz).

Our gracious thanks also to Nan Ward, who typed a good part of the manuscript.

Dean Tudor
Nancy Tudor

1978

"Popular music in America never was taken seriously by anyone
other than the people who produced it or bought it."
—Mike Jahn, *Rock* (1973)

TABLE OF CONTENTS

WHAT THIS BOOK IS ALL ABOUT
AND HOW TO USE IT

"Of all the arts, music has always been nearest
to the hearts of Americans and the most expressive of their
essential needs, fears, and motivations."
—William O. Talvitie

"Music is music and that's it. If it sounds good,
it's good music and it depends on who's listening
how good it sounds."
—Duke Ellington

"It's all music, no more, no less."
—Bob Dylan (1965)

This reference tool offers a complete pre-selected evaluative guide to the best and most enduring of recorded jazz music (largely American) available on long-playing discs and tapes. It can be used by both libraries and individuals to build up a comprehensive collection reflective of every area of jazz (except black music, which has a separate volume in this set of four). About 1,300 discs are annotated within a space of 300 (average) words each indicating musical influences, impact, and importance. This represents about a $7,500 investment. However, about 220 key albums are identified and suggested as a "first purchase" (about $1,000). These are seminal recordings. The interested individual can use the selection guide to buy first, for instance, the key ragtime albums followed by the balance. Then this person could start purchasing all other discs by favorite ragtime performers, or perhaps move on to a related field such as Chicago style or modern jazz. The approach is by ever-widening circles.

This book also is concerned with the preservation of recorded popular music through the long–playing disc. The commercial disc, even though it does not adequately reflect the total characteristics of musical genres, is a very convenient way to scrutinize popular music and audience reactions in an historical perspective. A disc preserves exactly the manner of a performance, with absolutely no chance of change through future progression—except for the most recent materials that have been altered by remixing or tape dubbing (e.g., Hank Williams with strings or Simon and Garfunkel's "Sounds of Silence" with a soft rock background). Records are constantly available around the country; some may be difficult to acquire, but the waiting is worth the aggravation. By the 1970s, audiences for all types of music have been fully catered to in some form or another. However, at some point in the development of a genre, musical minorities can become cult fanatics who insist on having every single note a particular artist performed. At this point, the cult audience must seek out bootleg records, taped concerts, airshots, and so forth, most of which are outside the mainstream of the recording industry.

The discographic essays in this book provide information on the basic elements of musical genres, criticisms, and analysis, as well as literature surveys for book and magazine purchases. The introductory essay presents an overview of popular music generally; the bibliography lists core books and magazines dealing with popular music that were especially chosen to show broad historical trends of importance and influence. The narrative discographic essays head each category, beginning with musicological descriptions, definitions, and continuing with brief histories and roots of development, reasons why it succeeded, musical hybrids, recording company policies, leading proponents in the field, criteria for inclusion of records, a discussion on record critics, and the tendencies of specialist review magazines. A useful by-product of this mechanism is that significant data and criticism are presented on which the record librarian can base popular music phonodisc selection for future recorded issues and reissues. The *Annual Index to Popular Music Record Reviews* can serve to update this book for record purchasing.

ARRANGEMENT AND FORMAT

All records in this volume are arranged under such categories as anthologies, stylings, time periods, instrumentation, vocal techniques, and so forth, as laid out in the table of contents. Narrative essays not only introduce the world of jazz music (see page 29), but also head each category within. These essays include short musicological descriptions, definitions, brief histories, roots of development and progressions, the leading proponents in the field, general criteria for inclusion of the specific records that follow, and a discussion of relevant books and existing periodicals (plus some detail on record reviewing and critics).

Each album discussed is entered in abbreviated discographic style: an internal numbering scheme to pinpoint its location within the book; entry by group, individual or title (if anthology) with commonalities collected for comparison purposes; album title, the number of discs in the package, label and serial number; country of origin if *not* American. Prices have been omitted because of rapid changes, discounts, and foreign currencies. Annotations, which average 300 words, specifically state why the record and/or material is significant, with references to personnel and individual titles.

There are three clear special indications: one, the "innovators" have been carefully separated into their own section; two, important discs have been starred (*); and three, the anthologies have been collected (see the short essay on the anthology, page 25). In terms of budgets, the suggested order of purchasing is: 1) within each genre desired, the starred anthologies (approximately $250 total for each genre); 2) within each genre desired, the other anthologies (approximately $750); 3) within each genre desired, the starred recordings of the innovators (approximately $500); 4) within each genre desired, the rest of the innovators (approximately $500); 5) within each genre desired, the balance of the starred items (approximately $750); 6) within each genre desired, the rest of the recordings (approximately $4,750).

The repackaged anthology represents the best choice for even the smallest of libraries. This maximizes the dollar so that libraries can get a reasonable "flavoring" of the widest repertoires or themes in an attempt to manage on the smallest of budgets. Larger libraries which, for whatever reason, prefer not to collect in a particular genre could still supplement their collection by purchasing the worthwhile anthologies in those genres for about $250 a grouping. These books will not include "classical" music, spoken word and humor, children's, marching bands, foreign language, religious (except for gospel and sacred music, both exceptionally popular religious music), and non-commercial items such as instructional recordings, educational records if the commercial form co-exists on album, and field trips (except for significant folk music).

Additional information is provided after the text: a directory of latest known addresses for record companies, plus an indication of their albums that we have starred in label numerical order; a short list of specialist record stores; a bibliography of pertinent books and periodicals; and an artist index with entries for both musical performances in diverse genres and musical influences.

METHOD OF RATING

Written materials about important popular music phonodiscs exist in a variety of forms: scattered discographic essays; scattered citations as footnotes; short biographic essays of leading performers; books with lists of records; discographic "polls"; annual "best of the year" awards; "tops of the pops" lists and chart actions; and passing references in ordinary reviews. Written material about popular music genres in general—at an introductory level—exists mainly in books, but such books were not written with the intention of assembling a representative historical core collection of phonodiscs.

The basic method we have used is a manual version of citation analysis by consensus. Through the 1965-1976 period, we studied about 60 popular music periodicals, which contained over 50,000 relevant reviews and over 10,000 articles. We also read more than 2,000 books on popular music, some dating from the 1920s, and we actually listened to 14,000-plus long-playing albums. Although we didn't know it at the time, work began on this book in 1967—a decade ago. We started out by identifying, for personal use, *all* the important performers in popular music, and we then read widely and bought all of that person's material *before* going on to anyone else. The rationale here was that, since these performers are acknowledged as the *best*, even their "off" material might be considerably better than a second-generation or derivative imitator. By moving in ever-widening circles (somewhat akin to a Venn diagram), we then began to investigate influences, impacts, and importance—for whatever reasons. At the same time we began to categorize performers so that we could make some sense out of the profusion of records by time, place, and influence. Generally, the slotting of performers by genre does not really affect one's appreciation of them at all but rather produces common groupings for the novice listener. What has developed is the categorization of available records rather than of the performers. Thus, this book is about significant recordings rather than significant artists (although the two do coincide fairly often). By *not* first choosing artists and then seeking out important discs (which is what we started to do) but instead seeking important recordings first, we have neatly avoided the "star" approach, which has two main disadvantages: first, that individual reputations may rise and fall without reference to artistic merit; and second, that styles of performance rapidly change from fashionable to unfashionable.

Reading and listening widely, we developed several criteria for evaluation:

1. Musical development
    a) musical quality of the recording
    b) importance in relation to music history
    c) musical standards of musicians (soloists, sidemen, session artists)
    d) musical creativeness, inventiveness, devotion, drive
    e) each musical genre is considered on its own terms as being equally important

2. "Popularity"
    a) airplay listings since 1920s
    b) reviews of records
    c) purchases
    d) critics' notes
    e) amount of material available
    f) longevity of the artist
    g) music itself (words and/or melodies)
    h) indication of "influence on" and "influenced by"—the links in a chain

3. Index to repertoires
    a) the favorite tunes of the performers
    b) the tunes most recorded and performed constantly
    c) what was re-recorded and why
    d) what was best remembered by fans and friends
    e) sheet music and songbook availability
    f) the tunes still being performed by others

4. Artistic merit of a record
    a) the way the song or tune is structured
    b) the relation between its structure and meaning
    c) the manipulation of the medium
    d) the implications of its content
    e) art criticism

5. Extra-musical developments
    a) the record industry and media manipulation
    b) the concept album or one with a thematic or framing device (both original, long-playing recordings and reissued collections of singles)
    c) the impact of radio and regional breakdowns

5.   Extra-musical developments (cont'd)
    d)   the folklore process of oral transmission
    e)   consideration of differences in listening appreciation between singles (78 and 45 rpm) and albums (33-1/3 rpm)

Citation analysis revealed that certain artists and tunes keep appearing, and hence any important record is important by virtue of its historical worth, influence, best-selling nature, trend setting, and so forth. We have deliberately restricted ourselves to long-playing discs, believing that most of the major records of the past (available only as single plays before 1948) are now available in this format.

We would not be honest, though, if we stated that we personally enjoyed every single album. Each individual's cultural upbringing places limits on what he can enjoy completely, and these restrictions can be overcome only by an extensive immersion into the society that created the genre of music. Attempting to understand what the artist is saying will help build a vocabulary of listening. For example, modern jazz has less impact on the Dixieland fan, while Dixieland has little impact on the "modern" fan. Thus, we must treat each musical genre as being equally important in terms of what it attempts to do, with an eye to cross-fertilization among different horizontal structures. It must be recognized that we are *not* rating a swing recording against a "New Orleans" recording. Rather, we are comparing similar genre recordings against each other, such as a New York style recording against another New York style recording.

One difficulty we faced was that there is no historical perspective for the recordings of the past decade; this is particularly noticeable for "fusion" jazz. We have no idea how this music will be accepted ten years from now, but we certainly know that these recordings should have a prominent place because of their current importance. It was a different world fifty, forty, thirty years ago; of course, the artists of a prior generation seem funny-strange today. Let us hope that the future will still remain kind.

PROBLEMS IN SELECTING FOR A COLLECTION

The selection of better pop recordings poses a problem because of the profusion of unannotated "best listings," the current trend toward reissuing and repackaging, and the unavailability of some records due to sudden deletions. Record librarians, most of whom lack a subject knowledge of popular music, usually select the most popular recordings without turning to evaluations. With the impact of the music and its general availability at low prices, the record librarians may end up with a current collection without an historical core. Where can record librarians turn for the back-up record evaluations of older discs? The same problems of continuity and historical perspective exist with respect to best-selling books. A disc that received rave reviews a decade ago might be consigned to the wastebasket today.

There is another reason that libraries end up with purely contemporary collections of popular music. Records do wear out and get lost or stolen; replacements may be sought. However, the original record could be deleted and the librarian lacks a source for locating an appropriate and perhaps better record by the same artists. For lack of a better alternative, the selector usually chooses an artist's latest recording, if that artist is still to be represented in the collection. This means a continually contemporary collection with no historical perspective.

The problem of choosing older records (or new reissues of older records) becomes one of selecting blindly from the *Schwann−1* or *Schwann−2* catalogs, or else hunting for the occasional discographic essay or lists in whatever periodicals are at hand. Fortunately, the librarian can also turn to *Popular Music Periodicals Index, 1973-* (Scarecrow, 1974-) or *Annual Index to Popular Music Record Reviews, 1972-* (Scarecrow, 1973-), but these are indexes only to the substance. Our book is a selection tool of that substance, enabling selectors to base their choices on informed evaluation rather than on random choice.

The balance of material in these books is not always in proportion to the importance of a genre or an artist, and this is mainly because there are so many examples of *good* music—"a good song is a good song." A greater proportion of materials is included for the minority offerings in blues, bluegrass, rockabilly, etc.—the same forms of music that laid the foundations for more commercial offerings in soul, country, rock music, respectively.

THE MARKET PLACE—IN BRIEF

The year 1977 was a very significant anniversary year for records. In 1877, Edison invented the phonograph by embossing sound on a piece of tinfoil wrapped around a *cylinder* and reproduced that sound through an acoustic horn. (Marie Campbell, the girl who recited "Mary Had a Little Lamb," died in 1974 at the age of 103.) Ten years after Edison's success, in 1887, Emile Berliner invented the gramophone for *flat* discs. In 1897 the first shellac pressings were created, and in 1907, the first double-sided record was created by Odeon, the record company. In 1917, the first jazz disc was recorded by Victor (original Dixieland Jazz Band, January 30), and ten years later, in 1927, the first modern country music was recorded (Jimmie Rodgers and the Carter Family, August 2). That same year saw two inventions: the first sequential recording device (magnetic paper tape, by J. A. O'Neill) and Edison's development of the long-playing record. Also in 1927 came the first record changer, the first transmission of television, and the first feature-length talking picture. This book, then, is about some of those events and the impact on modern popular music of today and it appears at a time in which more discs from the past are currently available than in any other previous year.

Records have always been popular purchases, despite their original high costs. And the market has always been flooded with as many discs as it could hold. For instance, in 1929, about 1,250 old-time music 78 rpm discs were released; by 1976, this number was about 850 for 45 rpm discs (the modern equivalent of country and bluegrass music). In terms of 1929 dollars, though, this music now costs less than a dime. At that time, there were 10 million phonographs; now, there are about 70 million phonographs. In 1929, there were about 100 record companies, but by 1976, the industry numbered over 1,500.

During those years, four types of companies have developed. First, there are the *majors* (CBS, MCA, RCA, UA, Capitol, Mercury, etc.), who have shared the bulk of the market. The *independents* (King, Imperial, Arhoolie, Savoy, etc.) arose as an alternative source of music, catering to musical minorities; these companies were interested not in getting rich but in promoting good music. A third category is the quasi-legal *bootleg* outfits. Some of these are sincere companies interested in reissuing treasures of the past by performers long since dead or missing (e.g., Biograph, Yazoo, Old Timey), while some are dubious operations that issue taped concerts and other unpublished items they feel should not be withheld from fans (e.g., Bob Dylan's *White Wonder* set, Rolling Stones' concerts, jazz and dance music airshots). The fourth grouping consists of *pirates*, who reproduce in-print records and tapes in the lucrative rock and country fields, and who, by false and misleading claims, make a high profit since they pay no royalties and no studio costs are collected. The records included in this book were produced by an uncommonly high percentage of independent and bootleg labels. This is because the roots of each musical genre lie in the beginning steps taken by independent companies and by the innovative performers themselves, who first recorded for these labels early in their careers.

It should certainly be noted that the historical worth of disc recordings will increase even more in the years to come. One reason that older recordings have not been popular is that modern higher fidelity equipment amplifies the poorer reproduction of bygone years. An early compensation from the late 1950s was the "electronically processed stereo" disc, in which the highs went to one channel and the lows to the other. This suited stereo consoles but not the hi-fi components market. By 1976, though, RCA had developed its "sound stream" process, in which a computer reduces not only surface scratch from older discs but also faulty resonance and reverberation. This computer "justification" works on the same principles as NASA's clarification of the 1976 pictures of the surface of Mars. RCA's first such disc was of Caruso recordings; within the next few years, certain forms of popular music may be added.

POST-1974 RECORDINGS: POTENTIAL CLASSICS

Although the discographic information and availability of albums are current with this book's imprint, *most* of the music described here had been recorded before 1974. This lead time of five years allows for settling/detecting trends rather than fads and letting the jury, as it were, have sufficient time to arrive at decisions. Recognizing, however, that certain modern discs just *might* be significant in the long run, we list those recent innovative records that have drawn exceptionally fine current reviews.

Mainstream

George Barnes. Swing Guitar. Famous Door HL 100

Count Basie. Basie Jam. Pablo 231o.718

Count Basie and Zoot Sims. Basie and Zoot. Pablo 2310.745

Ruby Braff and George Barnes. Chiaroscuro CR 121

Bobby Hackett and Vic Dickenson. Live at the Roosevelt Grill. Chiaroscuro
 CR 105

Dick Hyman. Scott Joplin; The Complete Works for Piano. five discs. RCA
 CRL5-1106

Joe Pass. Portraits of Duke Ellington. Pablo 2310.716

Joe Pass. Virtuoso. Pablo 2310.708

Oscar Peterson and Stephane Grappelli. two discs. Prestige PR 24041

Dick Wellstood and Kenny Davern. Famous Orchestra. Chiaroscuro CR 129

Bob Wilbur and Kenny Davern. Sporano Summit. World Jazz 5

Modern Jazz

Anthony Braxton. Creative Orchestra Music, 1976. Arista AL 4080

Anthony Braxton. Town Hall, 1972. two discs. Trio PA 3008/9 (Japanese issue)

Dollar Brand. African Piano. Japo 60002

Don Cherry and the Jazz Composers Orchestra. Relativity Suite. JCOA 1006

Billy Cobham. Spectrum. Atlantic SD 7368

Jan Garbarek and Keith Jarrett. Belonging. ECM 1050

Jim Hall and Ron Carter. Alone Together. Milestone MSP 9045

Jones-Lewis Big Band. Potpourri. Philadelphia International KZ 33152

Spontaneous Music Ensemble. So, What Do You Think? Tangent TGS 118
 (British issue)

Cecil Taylor. Indent (Mysteries, 1972-1973). Unit Core 30555

Cecil Taylor. Solo. Trio PA 7067 (Japanese issue)

Cecil Taylor. Spring of Two Blue J's. Unit Core 30551

McCoy Tyner. Atlantis. two discs. Milestone M 55002

Weather Report. Tale Spinnin'. Columbia PC 33417

Mike Westbrook. Metropolis. RCA Neon NE 10 (British issue)

REFERENCES AND INDEX

In the introductory comments to each section, reference will be made to the
literature on the topic of jazz. When a name appears followed by a number in
parentheses—e.g., Gitler (41)—the reader should consult "Book Citations" for a full
entry and a description of the book. When a title is followed by a number—e.g., *Jazz
Journal* (10)—the "Periodical Citations" should be consulted.

The alphanumeric code preceding each entry first locates that item in the overall
classification used for the four volumes (J here denotes *Jazz*; B is used for *Black Music*,
etc.). The number immediately following the letter code then indicates the major
section of this book in which an item/artist can be found. Additionally, the Artists'
Index references all of the recordings listed in this book by that code number.

INTRODUCTION TO POPULAR MUSIC

> "Time has a way of making the style stick out,
> rather than the music, unless
> that music is exceptional."
> —Joe Goldberg

Popular music is a twentieth century art form made available to the masses through records, radio and, to a lesser extent, nightclubs, concerts, festivals, and television. As an art form, it is in a state of constant evolution in which each generation redefines its own music. One's perception of popular music is based only on what is heard or what is available to be heard. "Access," then, becomes a key word that was not found before either the breakdown of regional barriers or the advent of mass media. Previous to bulk production of commercial recordings (about 1920), different styles had arisen to meet the moods of geographic areas and of the times. All that these diverse styles had in common were the elements of rhythm, melody, harmony, and form; each style went its separate way in emphasizing one of these elements over the other. Sorting out the musical strains and streams is confusing, then, because of the vast number of musical and extra-musical influences shaping the styles. Some of these will be explored in the introductions to the various volumes on specific musical genres, but it should be noted that there are five general statements that appear to be incontrovertible when discussing styles of popular music:

1) Styles persist past their prime, and often they are revived by a new musical generation, perhaps in a series of permutations.

2) One development in a style leads to another development through constant evolution.

3) Each style and stream of music influences the other styles and streams through the artists' awareness of trends in all areas, this caused by the exposure that the mass media give to such a variety of artists.

4) Styles are as much shaped by extra-musical influences (such as the recording industry and radio) as by other styles themselves.

5) To the novice, all music performed in one particular style may sound the same, but each stream is a language or form of communication, and to become familiar with it, the listener must consciously learn this new language.

Each of these statements will be further explored in this section and with the appropriate genres of popular music.

Schoenberg once wrote (in a different context): "If it is art it is not for all; if it is for all it is not art." Popular music relates to the existing mores of an era, and it falls in step with a current culture by reflecting popular tastes. In this sense, popular music is relevant to its audience's interests. But listeners evolve with time, for society never stands still. Popular music changes in response to audience manipulation or demand; consequently, *all* popular music styles of the past may make little sense to a modern audience. There appears to be little need *today* for the sentimental ballads of the late nineteenth century, the New Orleans jazz sound, the Tin Pan Alley pop music of the 1920-1950 period, and so forth, in terms of what that music meant to *past* generations. However, it is important to note the older styles of popular music because these styles have revivals that show an interest in the past (for stability or nostalgia) and also show the evolution of modern streams of music. In recordings, for each genre there exist at least three types of similar music: the original recordings of by-gone days; a revival of the style reinterpreted in modern terms; and the modern equivalent that evolved from that early style. An example would be the slick group singing of the 1930s and 1940s, as exemplified by the Andrews Sisters (in the original form), the Pointer Sisters (in the revival), and the Manhattan Transfer (in the modern equivalent). Through the phonograph record, all three co-exist, and future singers in this genre could borrow a different emphasis from each of the three closely-related styles to project a fourth synthesis of, to continue the example, the vocal group singing slick, catchy lyrics.

Over a period of years, each style of popular music loses much of the original drive, mood, and inventiveness that came from its roots in tradition. As a minority music style catches on with wider audiences, and as this style becomes influenced by both other genres and urban cultures, the original excitement of the innovation becomes diminished considerably. This is inevitable as styles evolve and as performers add something "a little different" to distinguish themselves from the increasing number of other similar musicians interpreting the same genre. This creates permutations and sub-genres, resulting in the creation of yet other musical streams. As these styles become commercially successful, performers self-consciously appraise their music as found in shows, concerts, or on record, and they become concerned over their image and saleability. They are frightened that they might fall into a rut (or, more appropriately, a groove). However, seeking reappraisal by becoming observers defeats both the spontaneity and the emotional impact of the music, and no emerging musical sub-genre would long survive if it stayed with a narrow conception of its style. This is what happened to the Beatles, and, to their credit, they split up when they recognized that they could no longer develop musically as a group. An emerging style at its beginnings can offer real excitement, emotion, and exuberance, all of which tend to fade (or be jaded or tired) in its mature years. This, then, is a prime rationale for the preservation and retention of early and historical recordings that helped to produce fanatical enthusiasm among both the performers and the audiences who knew and recognized new, emerging popular music styles.

It was David Reisman who identified two groups of performers and listeners as early as 1950 ("Listening to Popular Music," *American Quarterly* 2:359-71). There was the majority audience, which accepted the range of choices offered by the music industry and made its selections from this range without considering anything outside of it. And there were also the "cults," or minority audiences, more active and less interested in words and tunes than in the arrangement, technical virtuosity, and elaborate standards for listening and analysis. This audience (now scattered among the forms of early country music, jazz, blues, musical shows, rockabilly, etc.) preferred "personal discovery" of the music, and usually arrived at such listening pleasures by painstakingly searching for the roots of modern popular music. Their outlook was international, and they had a sympathetic attitude to black musicians, whom they considered to be the prime source of material. It was the cults that promoted "early music," wrote the books and magazines, and produced reissues of original recordings and issues of rediscovered early performers. The latter were past their prime but still active and often better in the musical style than current interpreters. The recordings cited in this book are based on both the cult image and the emerging musical stylings.

On a personal basis, as members of the cult, we have found that one of the most maddening things about loving minority musical styles is the frustration we feel when we try to share that love with others who are both ignorant of the form and apathetic towards it ("I don't know and I don't care"). In addition, there is an equally disheartening feeling—when that favorite minority musical style either changes into another form of expression which becomes more popular than the original while still being imitative, or when it gets raped by enterprising producers and performers who then try to pass it off as theirs alone. The circle becomes complete and the frustrations compounded when we try to convince others that this more "popular" music is but a pale imitation of the originals. We admit, therefore, that there is a proselytizing tone to the construction of this book.

The most dramatic influence upon the popular music of the twentieth century has been black African music. Its characteristics have pervaded all forms (except perhaps most musical comedies). Jazz, blues, and soul, of course, have direct roots. But the important innovators in other fields have had direct contact with black musicians and had assimilated black sounds, such as Bill Monroe (bluegrass music), Woody Guthrie (folk and protest music), Bob Wills (western swing), Jimmie Rodgers and the Carter Family (country music), Benny Goodman (big bands), Elvis Presley (rockabilly), the Yardbirds and the Beatles (blues rock), and Led Zeppelin (heavy metal music). Without this assimilation, there would have been no popular music as we know it today.

All of this relates to the essential differences between European (Western) and African (black) music. Black music, in its components, prefers an uneven rhythm but in strict time, and with a loose melody that follows the *tone* of the words. This tone is explained by the fact that the same syllable of a word can connote different things depending on whether it is sung in a high, medium, or low pitch of voice. For the African singer or instrument, beauty resides in the *expression* of music (the *how* of performance). Western music, on the other hand, prefers an even rhythm (which explains why rhythm is the weakest element here) in loose time, with a strict melody that follows the *stress* of the words. For the Western performer, the music stands or falls on its own merits (the *what* of performance), and, ideally, the performance could be perfectly duplicated by others in another place and time.

Much has been written about the differences between Western and black music (see the bibliography section), but little about why white audiences did not accept black music. Three assumptions, however, have arisen. One involves social barriers denying white access to black music; that access was a phenomenon brought about by mass media. Another relates to the musical traditions of black music that were foreign to white audiences (e.g., sexuality, ghetto life). A third assumption is that basic differences in musical cultural upbringing produce preconceptions of what is music and what is not (for example, the white listener defines a tune by its melody, whereas a black listener thinks of it in terms of its chord progressions; white song lyrics are either sentimental or sophisticated, while black song lyrics are experiential and improvised).

As an incidental note, it appears that the state of Texas is actually the well-spring of much of today's popular music. Most of the significant innovators were born and raised in Texas, where they perfectly assimilated the diverse musical stylings of the blues, ethnic materials (Chicano, Caribbean, Cajun), jazz, and so forth, to create and fashion swing jazz, western swing, urban blues, country music, troubador songs, rhythm 'n' blues, rock and roll, and country rock music. No appropriate written materials have yet emerged to explain this complex cross-fertilization of musical ideas, but it is important to remember that the vertical separation of white and black music did not exist in Texas (i.e., both groups shared a common heritage) and that literally all kinds of musical influences were at work virtually simultaneously—a true melting pot.

It is not our intention to present a history of the recording industry or of radio (elementary surveys can be found in Schicke's *Revolution in Sound* [104] for records, and in Passman's *The Dee Jays* [82] for radio), but we view these industries as being equally important as the music itself towards the shaping of popular music. Both recordings and radio had the power to encourage and to deny by their manipulation of public tastes. A brief overview of the highlights follows:

1917-1925—limited retention of sound through the acoustic recording method. Many companies formed.

1925-1931—electric recordings begin, capturing the sounds of a piano and larger groups. 1929 was a peak year, with different markets for different recording styles of regional characteristics (largely ignored outside the geographic areas of marketing; no cross-fertilizations except by musicians who borrowed from other records).

1931-1934—The Depression meant fewer sales (in 1933, these were 7 percent of the 1929 peak), fewer recordings, and the rise of recorded sound on radio. This was the beginning of regional breakdowns.

1934-1941—This period saw cheaper records ($0.25 to $0.35), more recording activities, and the beginning of *professional* musicians who aided in the shifting of the geographic centers of recording activities (pop moved to Hollywood, swing jazz to the West and Midwest, western swing to the Midwest, folk to New York, etc.).

1942-1945—Musicians were drafted, shortage of shellac appeared, there was the ASCAP ban, and the musicians' union went on strikes. Very little new music recorded here, but this was also the beginning of independent companies.

1946-1950—The post-War era saw the establishment of hit parades, the popularity of juke boxes, records becoming full-time radio programming, a complete break in regional stylings, and expenses rising for touring groups.

1950-1959—This period brought a resurgence of *different* forms of music existing simultaneously for diversified but separate markets (blues, jump music, rhythm 'n' blues; jazz, swing, bop, cool; rock and roll; folk, country, bluegrass, etc.), this because of many competing independent companies. The situation is similar to the 1920s.

1959-1963—An age of imitation and derivative music, this was highlighted by a watered-down folk revival, the beginnings of soul music, and the decline of specialized markets in bluegrass, jazz, and rock 'n' roll.

1964-1970—An age of cross-overs, this period sees country music go pop and rock music emerge as a symbiotic co-existent through country-rock, blues-rock, jazz-rock, theatre-rock, soul-rock, folk-rock, etc.

1970-   —Now there is the simultaneous co-existence not only of separate musical styles, but also of merging styles and "roots" music. All three are widely known to a mass audience for the first time *ever*.

Recordings have had a troubled history, and it is a wonder at all that historically important recordings still remain. Many basic conflicts shaped audience appeal. First, it was the cylinder versus the disc, and then the conflict about early playing speeds that ranged from 60 to 85 revolutions per minute. Then, there were different types of materials used for the physical product (metal, shellac, paper, etc.). The method of reproduction varied from the "hill and dale" of the vertical groove cutting to the horizontal cutting, being compounded by the outward playing groove as against the inward playing groove. After World War II, further technological conflicts had to be resolved: tape versus disc; 45 rpm versus 33-1/3 rpm; ten-inch disc versus seven-inch disc; ten-inch disc versus twelve-inch disc; stereophonic sound versus monophonic sound; quadrophonic sound versus stereophonic sound; different configurations of quadrophonic sound (discrete, matrixed, compatible) and tapes (reel-to-reel, cartridge, cassette), and so forth. If an audience was expected to hear everything available and make judgments, then it would have to purchase a wide variety of equipment far too expensive for all but radio stations. Thus, unless recordings were issued and reissued in a variety of configurations, there would be music that people would simply never hear because they lacked the necessary play-back equipment.

Beyond the shape of the prime listening document, there were other conflicts. Various musician unions' strikes against the industry precluded hearing first-hand evidence of aural changes in music at crucial times. The various licensing bans called by ASCAP in the 1940s precluded listening to new records on radio and on the juke box. The rise of the disc jockey on radio led to an influence over what records the public could hear, which in turn resulted in scandals of "payola" and "drugola" for bribes that ensured that certain records were played (and others thus denied air time). And from time to time, there were various shortages of materials for reproducing the record, such as the wartime shellac crisis (to buy a new record, the customer had to turn in an old one for recycling) and the vinyl crisis of the 1970s. All of these slowed down the rate at which new music became acceptable.

The practices of the recording industry are also illuminating when trying to understand the popular music performer. The big schism in the industry occurred during World War II. Previous to this time, the type of singer the industry looked for was one who coupled low cost with better-than-average returns. Later, when the industry learned that it took money to make money, the shift would be to turn a fairly high investment into an astronomical return. Thus, the pre-war performers were largely middle-aged people who had already established for themselves a loyal fandom. These people were self-accompanied, and wrote or modified their own materials. Indeed, their major employment was not in records, or even in music. They were *not* "professional musicians," but simply better than adequate performers who were paid a flat recording fee and given no promotional tours for emphasizing any regional characteristics of their music. At this time, radio was viewed as a competitor, and each record was usually about 50 percent sold out within a year (and left in the catalog for up to 10 years or more). Post-war developments, taking into account the young returning servicemen and the later "war baby boom," concentrated on the under-30 performer, who then broke new ground with a solid financial investment behind him.

These singers and musicians usually performed other people's materials (except for the 1970s rock movement) and relied on great accompaniment from major studio session men. Their prime occupation was in music, especially records; they were "professionals" with a high profile from tours and promotions. They were paid royalties instead of a flat rate, no doubt as a result of collecting funds from radio stations that were now heavily dependent on records as a source of programming. As national markets were aimed for (there was obviously more money to be made here than in just one geographic or minority audience), the music's consistency became blander and more stylized. Tours and national exposure meant that record sales would peak in the first three months, and many records were generally withdrawn after a year. Economically, this meant that, of all elpees released in 1977, 85 percent *lost* money, with the remaining 15 percent being monster sellers that created the corporate profits.

Record companies are always quick to discover new audiences. The fast pace of the industry, plus the high failure rate, indicate which records sell and which do not. Whether they are *good* records or not is largely immaterial. Playlists of radio stations, and best-selling lists of trade magazines, provide an *index* to popular music rather than a *criterion*. This is in much the same way as lists of best-selling books, in that both reflect the interests of the time. Whether they are enduring or not is up to "history" to decide, and by tracing the development of musical styles, any record's impact and influence can be ascertained. As Robert Shelton (*Country Music Story*) has said: "Few popular music styles remain pure for long. Nothing can spread quite so quickly as a musical style that is selling." On this basis, each and every modern record must be regarded as a one-shot attempt. No matter what its popularity, just three months after its release few people appear to buy it. And if the record is successful, then it will generate hybrids and derivative imitations (in addition to making its originators duplicate their success with an exact follow-up copy). This is the determining factor in the preservation and continuation of music, despite the poor side effects caused by records.

There is a distinction that can be made between a *record*, a *broadside*, and the *oral tradition*. The latter is very limited, being based on one-to-one contact in a community, and changes in the music are prone to develop. The broadside, on the other hand, presents words only (it might have been sung at the time of sale), and the later "sheet music" added piano versions of the music. With a broadside, one had to find a tune. With sheet music, one had to find an accompanying instrument. Both, though, stabilized the texts. A record, on the other hand, has not only the words and melody but also the performance style: the text, tune, and style are together in one package, from one particular moment in time. It can be replayed and memorized, and the listener can learn from it—perhaps indicating variants in later performances—and also, of course, duplicate any of its success.

Not everybody could possibly buy all records. Originally, it was up to radio to provide a "free" service, which meant random selection until the days of "Top 40" playlists. Radio was the medium that not only transmitted older songs but also created the regional breakdown in styles, as one geographic area began to hear the songs of other adjoining areas. Radio used a lot of material, and because of its random nature, it created a demand for more and newer material. This was furnished by both new records and live performances. The latter were very important, for many programs were recorded off the air at home, and are now available via small reissue labels. Disc recordings have certainly never reflected any artist's entire repertoire, and it is questionable as to how many discs were actually favorites of the performer. It was up to the a. and r. men and producers to select the tunes for marketing, yet this interfered with the artist's natural choice of songs. This was the case with Uncle Dave Macon, who also never felt at home in the studio. With radio work, the performer could program what he or she liked to sing and usually (in the early days) performed in front of an audience. "Airshots," as they are called, could determine more about a performer's repertoire than discs, and they also plugged the gaps that existed when there were recording bans. This was absolutely crucial during the development of bop jazz because few people outside of New York were aware of the music (in its early period, it was not recorded because of the recording bans).

A graphic conceptual display of diverse major Western musical influences in the twentieth century is shown on page 24. There are, of course, many, many minor variations. (Relative size of boxes is not indicative of influence or importance.)

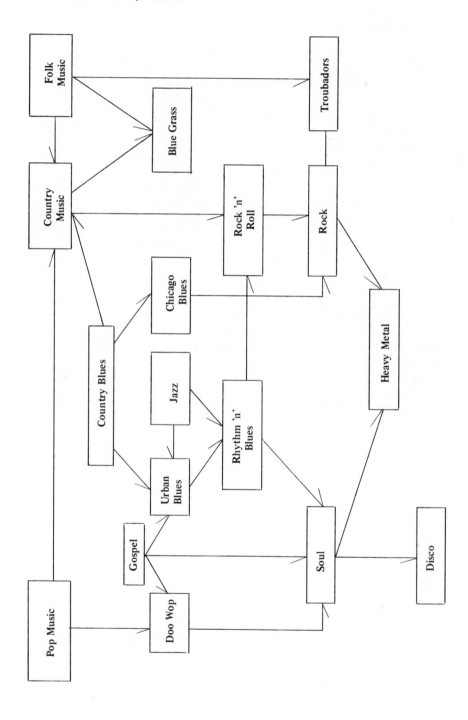

THE BEST OF THE BEST:
Anthologies of Popular Music on Records

"Anthology" is derived from Greek words meaning "flower gathering." Presumably, this means either the best that is available or a mixed bag, with some parts showing off the rest by means of contrast. Certainly the display should be stunning, for why else anthologize? In the music world, anthologies serve either as samplers or as introductions to a company's products. These collections of the works of popular performers sell to a captured audience that is used to having pre-selected convenience items before their eyes. At the same time, anthologies are invaluable for rapidly building up a music record library, or for fleshing out an area of music not already covered in the library. There will also be little duplication among the items in collections if the library does not already have the originals.

Within the past three years, aided by the soaring costs of studio time and performers' fees plus the recognized nostalgia fad, more anthologies and collections than ever before have been released. From a manufacturer's point of view, they are cheap to produce: the material has virtually paid for itself already; the liner notes are few (if any) or standardized; there is uniform packaging and design; a ready market exists, which the rackers and jobbers love, so little advertising is necessary; and anthologies act as samplers of the performer or to the catalog, hence promoting future sales. However, selection of the program depends on the cooperation of music publishers in granting reduced rates.

Personally, we are quite partial to anthologized performances. For a pure musical experience, there has been nothing quite like, say, on a hot and humid night, throwing on a pile of 45 rpm singles and sitting back guzzling beer while tapping to the rhythms. At this point, our attention span is about three minutes; thus a new record with a new voice comes on just as minds start to wander. With older records, the effect is one of familiarity, evoking fond, past memories. For the sake of convenience and better musical reproduction, though, a stack of anthologized long-play records makes this easier. Most new records today can be quite boring between the highlights, and it is not uncommon for a group to have an album with one hit single, fleshed out with nine duds. You really wouldn't want to hear it all again. Too, while most people might all like or remember one or two particular numbers, they also like other tracks individually. An anthology or "best" album attempts to take those most popular selections that we all enjoy and market them so that the most people might like the whole reissue album. One man's meat is not another man's poison in the case of the anthology.

Many reservations exist about compilations, especially with regard to trickery, motives, and shoddy packaging. Some of these are discussed here, but a few general comments are also necessary. In many instances, anthologies have only 10 tracks to a disc. This may be fewer tracks than the original albums had, and certainly it makes each number more expensive at a per selection cost. Yet, there are distinct advantages for a certain market that has low-fidelity equipment: the wider grooves give a full range of sound and increase the bass proportionately, thus making this particular type of disc virtually ideal for home stereo consoles and for older, heavier needle cartridges. Since these wider grooves don't wear out as quickly as compressed ones, the records may be played over and over again with less wear than on an "original" disc. In other instances, some "best" collections (especially multi-volume sets) almost equal the catalog material from which they are drawn and, hence, cost more in the long run.

Trickery involves a number of gimmicks, such as "electronic enhancement" for stereo, with its vast echoing sound being reminiscent of a train station lobby. These types are dying out, as it costs money to re-channel, some of the public are demanding original monophonic sound, and—the biggest marketing blow of all—these discs have been relegated to the semi-annual *Schwann–2* catalog with the mono discs. Sometimes the informative print is very small, or was printed say, yellow on orange, and the consumer virtually couldn't read the notice "enhanced for stereo." Some tricks are not solely for deception, though. Cute tricks include the title "The Worst of the Jefferson Airplane"—an obvious collection of best material. But what about an original first record by an unknown group that is titled "The Best of . . ." just to attract sales?

Another problem with the vinyl product is that anthologies are mostly regional pressings. Duplicate masters are used in factories not as careful as the home plant and are shipped directly to the regional distributor. Of course, a careless pressing sounds worse than a skillfully crafted product. And the polyvinyl chloride content can drop to below 85 percent. This is important, for the extender in a disc can be exposed to the stylus riding on the otherwise soft plastic and great harm can occur. Classical records are generally 95-99 percent vinyl, with pop recordings being around 90 percent. Anything lower than 90 percent can be detrimental to sound reproduction.

The material included in anthologies is another concern. It is usually selected by the producer or company, so that it may have no relation to what the performers themselves think is their best material. Many groups are anthologized *after* they leave one company for greener pastures, and the original manufacturer can keep churning out the reissues year after year, relying on the groups' future success to advertise the old reissued product. Some anthologies are shoddily passed off as memorials after a performer's death; others are issued if performers cannot produce an album in any one particular year, whether through accident (as in Bob Dylan's case), personal problems, laziness, or personnel changes. This keeps the name in front of the record-buying public, but too often the album is at full list price and the cover only mentions in passing that it is a reissue.

With the new packaging gatefold, is it likely that *all* notes on anthologies (as well as many others) will be inside the shrink-wrapped cellophane parcel. Thus, the consumer will not know what he is supposed to buy until he reads a review, ad, or opens the package (thus forfeiting a "return" if he already has the item). As these records rarely get reviewed or advertised, there is no certain way of knowing what is on them; Schwann does not often give track listings for them.

Anthologies are also notable for what they do not contain. The biggest performers are rarely anthologized while they are still under contract, and if they are, then the discs are sold at full price. There is no inexpensive introduction to the best material of Hank Snow, Charlie Pride, Elvis Presley, or the Rolling Stones.

When the latter group left Decca/London, the company released two anthologies at a full price of $10.98. Presley is available on a set of four discs, if you want virtually *all* of his better product. England is the best place to go for inexpensive reissues in all fields, particularly so if the reissue is not available on the North American market.

Mail order houses are a direct development from the recording companies, and some of the latter have gone into the business themselves. Being leased only for such a one-shot appearance, the selected items are pure gravy for the companies. Thus, with groove compression, 18 to 24 titles (2½ minutes long) can appear on some of these albums. Usually these discs are promoted only by television commercials or direct mail. Other reissue companies (prevalent in England) lease material from the original companies and repackage it as they see fit. Pickwick International is most successful at this, drawing on the large Capitol and Mercury catalogs (which is one reason why these two companies do not reissue many discs).

The anthologies listed in the musical genres herein consist of reissued material, either in the form of anthologies, "best" collections, or "live" versions of studio tracks that enjoy reasonably good sound. They are set apart as subsections entitled "anthologies." These records are offered as a pre-selected guide to really good performances, or as material that may lie outside of a library's main interest or collecting policy. For instance, a recorded sound library may want to capture a flavoring of the blues without exceptional expense and without culling lists of basic records, discographic essays, or even Schwann (which splits blues among "current popular" and "jazz"). Determining what records may be basic, essential, or important is not always an enjoyable listening experience; it is certainly expensive. What is being stressed here is quantity *with* quality: to get the best and most available at the cheapest price possible. In many instances, a well-rounded collection will result from buying anthologies, but not necessarily an in-depth collection.

Basic recordings are something else again—interesting for the derivative performers that will follow in the style, but mainly useful in a historical context. Such a collection is one to build on—to use the "basic" in its literal sense. These selections are listed to capture the whole field at once. The demise of the record shop's listening room has meant that the informed consumer can no longer hear an album before purchase; others might not have any real knowledge of music other than somewhat vague personal interests. How can they hear the "best" in another field? The same reasons for anthology production that are advanced by recording companies can be applied when libraries acquire such records: to introduce people to new listening pleasures (despite all the gimmicks of hard sell). Also, nearly all these records are also available on tape (except for most of the mono reissues).

JAZZ MUSIC:
An Introduction

"One reason jazz has never been a great
success is because it is improvisational, and the
public loses the melody. It takes a well-trained ear
to enjoy jazz."
—Chet Akins,
country music producer.

"An excessive rate of stylistic change has forced
jazz to bypass areas of possible major growth,
leading it repeatedly to fall short of its full potential."
—Max Harrison,
music critic.

This book discusses material of diverse origins: New Orleans, Dixieland, rag-time, instrumental blues, swing, modern, and so forth. Music of a light "cocktail jazz" texture (usually performed by non-jazz musicians) will be found in the companion volume, *Contemporary Popular Music*; similarly, the employment of jazz in **rock** will be found in the "rock" category of that book for the most part. **Blues** has its own section in the *Black Music* volume, although the 12-bar construction and "blues" notes are employed extensively in jazz. Of all the areas in popular music, jazz is the best documented. There are sufficient discographies, journals, exchange markets, record stores, and mail-order outlets to meet the demand, but work continues into the esoteric reaches of descriptive writing and performance. Unfortunately, measured against "classical music" standards, jazz is far behind in critical and scholarly writing ventures. Articles and books thus far have been of the survey type, employing biographies and personal experiences, histories of ventures, discographic information, and photography; but while there have been a great many words written on the subject of jazz, little has been written about actual jazz music. Many jazz writers and critics do not play any instrument, and some cannot even read or write music, a situation completely opposite from that prevailing with writers in folk and blues music.

Jazz is basically an aural music; written scores represent only a skeleton of what actually takes place during a performance. Thus, there appears to be no need for the "classical music" approach. Yet it cannot be denied that written transcriptions are valuable for both instructional purposes and structural analysis. Such data are usually not available in published form, and the demand at the present time is slight. For educational purposes, people are limited to original transcriptions, often not yet published. Often, too, critics and reviewers will argue against systematic analysis of jazz, for then, they say, the music would not be enjoyable anymore. This visceral reaction, also common to rock music writers, is negated by the continual enjoyment that people derive from classical music, which is the subject of intense systematic study. What is really meant usually is that the writers would not be able to understand the musicological terms for they cannot play jazz. Reaction of this kind is missing in folk and blues, for the use of the solo instrument enables detailed study by the listener, often in order to emulate his favorite performers. One reason advanced for musicological discussions within jazz is that such writings will enhance the level of jazz criticism and thereby make jazz more acceptable to classical music writers. The other side of the coin is that the performers themselves cannot usually read or write music; they play only by ear and by a feel for the music. Both arguments are specious.

Within the limits of this book, we could furnish no more than a *brief* outline of *some* of the characteristics of jazz. Historically, jazz began as black music, blending three elements: the qualities of blue notes (flatted thirds and sevenths; later, a flatted fifth in bop music); the distinctive rhythmic elements of percussive African music (and, later, collective improvisation from the same source); and the instrumental imitation of vocalizing (with a basis in such vocals as spirituals, gospels, work-songs, children's songs, etc.). Instrumentation for groups became fixed by the turn of the century, utilizing percussion from Africa and discarded brass instruments from military bands. New Orleans music retained the essential marching band lineup of brass, reeds, and rhythm that later evolved (at least in the studio) to cornet/trumpet, trombone, clarinet, guitar/banjo, drums, and bass of some sort (brass—such as tuba—for marching; a bass violin in the studio when recording techniques were developed that could capture the sound).

We have no idea what "early jazz" sounded like, for no recordings exist from before the January 30, 1917, version of "Darktown Strutters Ball" by the (white) Original Dixieland Jazz Band. Various black bands had been asked to record their music, but the leaders declined because they felt that their styles and techniques then would be stolen by others. The ODJB felt no such concern, for the Dixieland variant of New Orleans music was essentially of a smooth ensemble texture with no soloists and nothing to steal. We do have some sheet music of ragtime, orchestrated rags, and early jazz, but this music was subject to widely varying improvisation that changed with each performance. Oral history projects have revealed—in words—the styles of some early jazzmen such as Buddy Bolden, Louis Armstrong, Jelly Roll Morton; and other performers have commented on how they arrived at their respective styles, so that it must be assumed that the earlier jazzmen sounded something like the later ones. But even so, such conversations are suspect, especially those of Morton, which have yet to be substantiated.

A valid school of jazz criticism states that jazz music is different at each performance, and that each tune is thereby distinctive, which is quite evident from listening to many alternate takes of the same number. It is a performer's art, one utilizing the element of surprise as an individual's style is imposed on the basic music. The history of jazz, as seen in this context, is thus one of individual musicians developing their own unique modes of expression and *influencing* others. This can be traced, in a chronological sense, through recordings. In many instances, there is the continuation of the craft-guild tradition of legitimization through the "laying on of hands" by master performers upon younger musicians. This not only indicates quality, but also shows "arrival" in the jazz world. By extension, then, there is some merit to the "school" theory, wherein styles are said to have certain elements in common. Thus, it can be safely argued that while *not all* of jazz "came up the Mississippi," at least New Orleans jazz did go up the river to Chicago to become "New Orleans in

Chicago" music, then the Chicago style, and later the New York style. Jazz had to travel because there was no jazz on radio and no recorded jazz. The musicians themselves had to travel, and with them came the sound. But the journeys were sudden; there was no steady territorial erosion. The musicians first traveled to the jobs and only later to the recording studios. Early jazz was also related to widely different streams of popular music that did travel via *sheet music*. Thus occurred simultaneous instances of great variety among local arrangements of a single written score; certainly, nineteenth century American music was treated this way. For instance, "High Society" was a college campus composition for the Yale Mandolin Club, yet its superb melody turned up in jazz music.

Perspectives on jazz music change with time, and jazz criticism has gone through several different stages, involving the roots of jazz (and whether it did indeed travel up the Mississippi), the nature of black versus white big bands, New Orleans music and Dixieland, jazz solos and the star cult, traditional music and bop (which was the first big schism), and the directions of modern jazz. The evidence, of course, is on disc, and any stance may be taken by closely documenting the recorded legacy. One thing we can say, though, is that jazz is very flexible, which makes jazz criticism very difficult. It is relatively easy to attack different styles and attempt to destroy them, rather than to highlight the importance of a beloved style and to show why that style is important or influential. Also, critics have distinctly avoided writing on the social, economic, and moral roots of jazz.

Another common ploy by jazz critics (and one that will affect any evaluation of this book) is *not* to criticize those musicians chosen as "great" but to point to some equally valid jazzmen who were left out. The ultimate test for purposes of this book, though, will be the artist's importance in the jazz tradition: some were obviously more influential than others. For these and other reasons, many general introductory comments on jazz music and its facets have been truncated here, but the salient points and issues have been reinserted under the name of particular innovators.

The scope and number of materials in jazz writings is truly awesome. Gregor (45) and Merriam (73) provide bibliographic data through 1953 for periodical articles and 1968 for books, while Kennington (59) critically assesses significant publications (biographies, reference works, periodicals, films, clubs, etc.) through 1969. It is interesting to note that the first serious writing on jazz was a 1919 article by Ernst Ansermet about Sidney Bechet (reprinted in Toledano [116]). Current survey materials, significantly better than older works because of hindsight, include Berendt (4; one of the best-selling of all jazz books), Feather (28), Gleason (42), Fox (37), Hodeir (48, 49, 50), Lang (61), Larkin (62), Longstreet (65), Paul (83), Stearns (111), Ulanov (118), Vian (120), Wells (121), Martin Williams (124, 127), and Peter Williams (129). Good text and superb illustrations can be found in three pictorial works from *Esquire* Magazine (26), Keepnews (58), and Wilmer (130). Some introductory texts are also useful in establishing musicological bases. A reading knowledge of music is usually necessary for the two Coker books (16, 17) on improvising, as well as for Dankworth (23) and Ostransky (80). Less seriously inclined listeners can get by with the Collier (19) and Martin Williams (128) guides.

Biographical details are relatively easy to secure but may not be up to date. Feather's (29, 30) two encyclopedias (= biographies) cover the basic period up to 1964; Ira Gitler is at work on a similar book to extend this period through 1975. Feather (31) also has a collection of biographical essays (thirteen total), as does

Blesh (5) (eight essays). Chilton's (15) "who's who" covers 1,000 American jazz musicians born before 1920; a similar arrangement is found in Panassie (81). Accounts of American jazz through the autobiographical details of the men who created it can be found in Ramsey (89) and Shapiro (106, 107). Good details can be found in Kinkle (60) for obscure jazzmen. From time to time, significant biographies are published, written in such a way that a musical genre and/or innovation is described in terms of its creator. Such recent books have included those by Allen (1) concerning Fletcher Henderson, Chilton's (14) story of Billie Holiday, Cole's (18) musical analysis of Davis and his sidemen, Pops Foster's (36) autobiography, which also details New Orleans life, and Lomax's (64) study of Jelly Roll Morton. Other books of a biographical survey, or analytic nature will be noted in the discussions of individual subgenres.

For record and discographic information, two basic sets of volumes exist. Rust (100) arranges all artists alphabetically and provides full data for all (title, personnel, dates, instrumentation, matrix numbers, release numbers, etc.). His time period is 1897-1942. He is updated (correction and additions) by articles in *Jazz Journal* (10) and *Storyville* (18). Jepsen (56) takes over for post-war jazz (mainly 1942-1962), but with some volumes going through to 1969; he is updated by reader contributions to *Jazz Journal* (10). A number of specialized discographies are devoted to only one artist, and these contain air check information. Selective discographies can be found through Feather (29, 30) and Kinkle (60). Other selective lists include Boretti (10), which is a guide to reissues and an analysis of anthologies and is continued somewhat by *Micrography* (13) magazine, and Van Eyle (119), who surveys essential jazz recordings of 3,102 tunes. McCarthy (68) and *Modern Jazz, 1945-1970* (74) discuss selective records that are the "best" in jazz. Meeker (70) traces film appearances made by jazzmen.

Periodicals come and go in jazz. Kennington (59) and Merriam (73) have documented most of the titles from the past. The key periodicals still publishing in English include *Coda* (4), noted for its coverage of modern jazz; *Downbeat* (7), now largely concerned with the jazz-rock-pop fusion; *Jazz Journal* (10), a high-caliber British magazine covering all fields of jazz; *Journal of Jazz Studies* (11), from Rutgers and devoted to scholarly musical analysis and sociological factors; *Micrography* (13), concerned both with tracing reissued materials in jazz and blues and with discographical studies; *Mississippi Rag* (14), devoted to New Orleans and ragtime music; and *Storyville* (18), specializing in blues, traditional, and New Orleans music, along with discographic research. And there are many others in French (*Jazz Hot*), German, Swedish, Italian, etc. A newer entry from 1976 is *Cadence* (3), an excellent source for interviews that also attempt to review every single jazz and blues album released in the world. Other magazines with some jazz content include *Black Music* (1), for modern black jazz; *Contemporary Keyboard* (5), for piano jazz; *Guitar Player* (8), for guitar jazz; *High Fidelity* (9), with John S. Wilson; *Melody Maker* (12), with Max Jones, and *Stereo Review* (17), with Chris Albertson.

Record reviews can be located through the *Annual Index to Popular Music Record Reviews* (2); periodical citations and books through *Popular Music Periodicals Index* (85), under name of artist or genre (**Jazz, Big Bands, Bop**, etc.).

Anthologies

ANTHOLOGIES

GENERAL ANTHOLOGIES

J1.1   **Americans in Europe.** Fontana SFJL 916. (English import).

J1.2   **Americans in Europe, v.1/2.** two discs. Impulse AS 36/7.

J1.3   **Americans in Europe, 1933/1938.** Tax m8008 (Danish import).

J1.4*   **Jazzmen in Uniform, Paris, 1945.** Harmony HEL 6004 (Canadian import).

J1.5*   **Swing Sessions, 1937-1950.** ten discs. EMI Pathe C 54-16021/16030.
These 15 records do an able job of documenting a phenomenon in American jazz: "Americans in Europe." Many American jazz performers have traveled to Europe, and most decided to remain for a long period of time or to reside permanently. Temporaries include Stan Getz and Sonny Rollins; permanents included Champion Jack Dupree, Memphis Slim, Dexter Gordon, Don Byas. The Fontana and Impulse sets are recent, from the 1960s, with Bud Freeman, Jimmy Witherspoon, Earl Hines, Wild Bill Davison, Ben Webster, Kenny Clarke, Bud Powell, Albert Nicholas, Don Byas. The first volume in the Impulse series was in a modern mode, while the second is more in the traditional vein. Recordings are made either in concert or in studios, sometimes with "native" help. The two most popular places seem to be Paris and London for studio work; concerts turn up from everywhere. Almost every major American artist has recorded in Europe sometime, and the reason is not hard to find. There is an adoration in Europe for American jazz artists—so much so that the performer plays better in response to the audience. He or she also has an easier time getting around, and there is no racial discrimination (which was a big help before 1965). Billie Holiday and Charlie Parker usually enjoyed their sojourns abroad.
Going further back, the Paris sessions here were with great soloists of the Glenn Miller band, and 1945 was certainly appropriate, as this was the liberation of Europe, and Paris in particular. The French were wildly ecstatic about anything American, and musician-soldiers had a chance to perform and to record while still in Europe through 1946. The 12 selections here were recorded by the Jazz Club Français, and include standards that made the French go wild. There is a companion volume on CBS 63052, from France, that features these same musicians with Django Reinhardt (Ray McKinley, Peanuts Hucko, Mel Powell, et al.). The Tax reissue goes back to the swing period's beginnings, and its 16 tracks feature such minor jazz figures as Arthur Briggs, Freddy Johnson, Bill Coleman, and Herman Chittison, with their respective orchestras or as solos. Most of it was recorded in Paris, but there are two tracks from Hilversum. The Swing record label was founded in Paris in 1937, by the two pioneering jazz critics of all times: Charles Delaunay and Hugues Panassié. There are some 140 tracks here, covering a mere 14 years but embracing all styles of jazz, from swing through soft bop. Americans played a prominent part, of course, and they were often recorded with accompaniment from native Frenchmen. Some

of Dickie Wells's best records are here (he has half of v.1, shared with pianists Joe
Turner and Teddy Weatherford in solo performances); pianist Garland Wilson solos,
Freddy Johnson and Herman Chittison are back, as well as Louis Armstrong, Benny
Carter, Gene Cedric, Billy Taylor, Jonah Jones, Don Byas, Sidney Bechet, the Amer-
icanized Stephane Grappelli, Bill Coleman, Duke Ellington, Johnny Hodges, Kenny
Clarke, James Moody, Fats Navarro, Bud Powell, Howard McGhee, and John Lewis
(the latter few from the bop period). Most of the recordings with Americans were
in 1937-1938 or 1946-1950. Some of the middle volumes in this series contain
French jazzmen, of necessity because the war intruded. But the prime purpose of
the label was to record "Americans in Europe" whenever they toured.

J1.6*   **Blue Note's Three Decades of Jazz, 1939-1969**. v.1/3. six discs. United
          Artists BN LA 158/160-G2.
          Blue Note was owned, operated, produced, and run by the Wolff brothers
before it was taken over by Transamerica and then United Artists. Since the Wolff
brothers sold out, the label has, quite frankly, gone downhill, concentrating on commercial jazz and pop plus a series of reissues and unissued recordings. In its time,
Blue Note was *the* important jazz label. It was always current with the times and
innovative in its approach to new music, because it never featured just one "brand"
of jazz. It was one of the first of the independents. The first two discs here cover
1939-1949, and feature some of the first of the boogie woogie records, with Albert
Ammons's "Boogie Woogie Stomp" and Meade Lux Lewis's "Honky Tonk Train
Blues." The important 1939 recording of Bechet's "Summertime" (the one that
catapulted him back to fame in the small combo frame) is here, as well as Edmund
Hall's "Profoundly Blue," George Lewis's "Climax Rag" (one of the first of the
New Orleans revival records, from 1943), material by Ike Quebec, Sidney De Paris,
James P. Johnson, Benny Morton ("Limehouse Blues"), Bunk Johnson ("Milen-
berg Joys"), the important bop statements of Thelonious Monk ("Round about
Midnight" and "Epistrophy"), and Tadd Dameron and James Moody. The 1949-
1959 period introduced Bud Powell ("A Night in Tunisia"), Milt Jackson ("Bags'
Groove"), Clifford Brown, Miles Davis, Horace Silver, Jimmy Smith, John Col-
trane ("Blue Train"), Sonny Rollins, and Art Blakey's interpretation of
"Moanin' ." Material slowed down in the 1959-1969 period, but impressive were
Jimmy Smith's pop "Back at the Chicken Shack," Donald Byrd's "Christo
Redentor," the immensely successful "Sidewinder" by trumpeter Lee Morgan, Eric
Dolphy's important "Out to Lunch," and Ornette Coleman's "European Echoes."
These are very good, quite often superb, collations of important recordings from the
Blue Note catalog.

J1.7   **History of Classic Jazz**. five discs. Riverside SDP 11.

J1.8   **The History of Jazz**. four discs. Capitol T 793/6.
          Both of these sets have been out-of-print for some time, but may still be
found in certain record stores or the second-hand market. In their time, they had
considerable impact, although not as strong as the Folkways anthology (J1.9). Bill
Grauer and Orrin Keepnews produced the Riverside anthology. It contains a
20,000 word essay by C. E. Smith, with many illustrations of early jazz and blues
musicians. Side one contains the historical material of African drums, Charleston
street cries, Blind Lemon Jefferson, Rev. J. M. Gates, some military bands, and

Fred Van Eps (a ragtime banjo soloist). The second side investigates ragtime, with some Joplin rolls, Scott, Lamb, and early jazz styles of Jelly Roll Morton. The blues are covered on the third side, with representation from largely the "classic" singers: Ma Rainey, Ida Cox, Chippie Hill, and Bessie Smith. Other sides detail New Orleans, boogie woogie, Chicago jazz (both black and white styles), New York (again, both black—from Harlem—and white), and an area not too well covered on other anthologies—the Dixieland-traditional revival of Kid Ory, Bunk Johnson, George Lewis, Lu Watters, et al.

Capitol records was founded in 1942; thus, jazz styles here that were current before that date have been recreated or early performers re-recorded in later styles. Through mass marketing, this set became one of the most successful in sales of the jazz anthologies. The first record covers New Orleans origins, with diverse representation from Sonny Terry, Leadbelly, Zutty Singleton, Lizzie Miles, Wingy Manone, and Nappy Lamare. The twenties are presented next, with Paul Whiteman, Sonny Greer, Jack Teagarden, Bud Freeman, Red Nichols, et al. The swing period, and the later bop and cool, are displayed on the last half: Glen Gray, Benny Goodman, Duke Ellington, Art Tatum, Coleman Hawkins, Dizzy Gillespie, Miles Davis, Stan Kenton, Lennie Tristano, et al.

J1.9*   **Jazz. v.1/11.** eleven discs. Folkways FJ 2801/2811.

This important jazz anthology came out between 1950 and 1953, when reissues of material from the past were unheard of, from a wide selection of record companies as well. Over the past 25 years or more, it has itself been included in many college courses on jazz and popular music, and is probably one of the most "popular" and important of the instructional music discs. No comprehensive coverage can be given in this annotation. In his notes to the *Addenda* volume (v.11), Frederick Ramsey, Jr., the collator, presents a brief history of the set, developing his criteria for selection of the 162 tracks, which encompass every category of jazz and jazz-related music up through the post-war years of bop (and stopping, naturally, before 1950). The *Addenda* includes some overlooked material, and an index of artists and titles. Briefly, volume one, *The South*, covers original records of black folk music related to jazz: hollers, blues, work songs, church meetings, rags, Creole music, breakdowns, and boogie woogie, with notes by Charles Edward Smith. Volume 2 concentrates on *The Blues*, and includes seminal recordings of Blind Willie Johnson, Blind Lemon Jefferson, Ma Rainey, Bessie Smith, etc. This is the weakest album of the set, as country blues are virtually ignored in favor of the "classic" songs. *New Orleans* is the third volume, displaying the few styles within a constricted framework. Volume 4 is *Jazz Singers*, with Louis Armstrong, Ivie Anderson, Ella Fitzgerald, Jimmy Rushing, and also some country bluesmen. *Chicago* is the concern of volumes 5 and 6, showing the New Orleans character created by migration (Armstrong, Ladnier, Noone, Dodds, Oliver, Keppard, Ory, etc.). *New York* (the 1922-1934 period) is covered with volume 7, contrasting both black and white performers. Volume 8 is *Big Bands before 1935*, such as Fletcher Henderson, Bennie Moten, Duke Ellington, etc., in the immediate pre-swing period. Volume 9 is *Piano*, with Morton, Hines, Stacy, Waller, etc., while volume 10 is *Boogie Woogie, Jump, and Kansas City* (Ammons, Lewis, Basie, Moten, McShann, etc.). Throughout, there are short notes, reasonably good sound, and discographical sourcing.

J1.10   **Leonard Feather Presents Encyclopedia of Jazz on Records, v.1/4.** four discs. MCA 2-4061/2.

These records originally came out in the mid-fifties to accompany Feather's *Encyclopedia of Jazz*. All of the offerings beyond 1934 come from the MCA-Decca archives; pre-1934, from a variety of sources that Decca had access to. Thus, it is limited in that it presents contracted personnel only, or later re-interpretations by the original artists, or even a cover (different version from the original) by someone else. The set is well annotated by Feather (MCA has wisely retained the original liner notes), and one disc is devoted to each decade. From the twenties, there is King Oliver's "Aunt Hagar's Blues" (recorded late in his career in 1928, not 1923), the New Orleans Rhythm Kings' "Tin Roof Blues" (from 1934, not the 1923 original version), Pine Top Smith's "Pine Top's Boogie Woogie," the first mention of the term on a piano record, and some white New York jazz with Red Nichols, Benny Goodman, Venuti-Lang. The thirties quite properly belong to the big bands, so here are Glen Gray, the Dorsey brothers, Andy Kirk, Chick Webb, Basie, Lunceford, etc. The forties are represented by Nat King Cole, Stan Kenton, Coleman Hawkins, Jay McShann, Roy Eldridge, Billie Holiday, Art Tatum, Eddie Condon, Lionel Hampton, and Woody Herman. The 1950s drop off, with some warmed-over Louis Armstrong, Red Norvo, Jimmy McPartland, and others—none of which are important recordings. However, this was one of the first anthology sets to emerge from a major recording company.

J1.11   **The Smithsonian Collection of Classic Jazz.** Collated by Martin Williams. six discs, boxed. Division of Performing Arts, Smithsonian Institution, Washington, DC. P6 11891 (distr. by Norton).

Musical revivals of any kind always seem to create a demand for anthologies or overviews. Jazz and "nostalgia" are currently being anthologized by a variety of record companies. The Smithsonian set is an excellent one that very handily supplements the Folkways "Jazz" series of years ago (see entry J1.9). The Folkways material went up to 1943 and concentrated on roots, unknown persons, and territory bands, with a smattering of big names. Williams here presents the big names and extends the coverage up to the present day. In time, the Folkways/Williams overlap is about half (but the selections do not overlap).

Williams has written a 46-page booklet with black and white illustrations, musical examples, some description of the work, and the current album (if such is the case) from which the selection is derived. Also here are a brief overview of jazz history and hints on how to use the recordings for an educational purpose. Like the Folkways set, the tracks—all 86 of them; some edited, some long (as recent tapings permit length denied when using shellac)—are representative for educational use. Accordingly, Norton has run off about 20,000 pressings for the educational market alone. A few complaints about coverage: while it is difficult to cull works satisfactory to everyone, only three blues are items here (two Bessie Smiths and one R. Johnson). This is insufficient, and they should have been either removed or expanded. Apparently, seventeen companies who hold the rights had to give their permissions; even so, Columbia, which did the pressing, seems to have contributed the most items.

CONCERT ANTHOLOGIES

[Note: Several other significant concerts may be found under the annotation of an individual or group.]

J1.12*   **Jazz at the Philharmonic, 1944-1946.** two discs. Polydor 2610.020. (British issue).
The concept of the jam or blowing session was extended by Norman Granz to the concert hall. He formed the "Jazz at the Philharmonic" touring group to bring that music to a wider audience. British Polydor is reissuing the whole lot (which may be too much of a good thing), and the citation above is for the very first concerts that were recorded. All were from the Philharmonic Auditorium in Los Angeles, beginning on July 2, 1944, with J. J. Johnson, Illinois Jacquet, Nat Cole, Les Paul, and others ("Blues," "Body and Soul," "Bugle Call Rag," "Tea for Two," etc.). From 1946, there are three tracks, with a boppish beat supplied by Dizzy Gillespie, Willie Smith, Charlie Parker, Lester Young, and Howard McGhee: "Crazy Rhythm," "Sweet Georgia Brown," and "After You've Gone." It has illustrations, and the good notes are from Steve Voce.

J1.13   **The Exciting Battle: J.A.T.P.** Stockholm '55. Pablo 2310 .713.

J1.14   **The Greatest Jazz Concert in the World.** four discs. Pablo 2660 .109.

J1.15   **Jazz at the Santa Monica Civic '72.** three discs. Pablo 2625 .701.
Norman Granz once created the "Jazz at the Philharmonic" series (usually abbreviated to JATP) to create a "package" of performers who would tour the country for a set period (and even go abroad), creating "jazz" along the way. Instead of having one or two "stars," they were all lumped together and played with each other in both small and large configurations. All of the JATP albums for Verve have been deleted in America, but, in 1973, Granz came back with new funds and founded the Pablo label to continue where Verve left off. One of the many tapes he had was of a JATP set from Stockholm in 1955, about a decade after JATP began. Heard are Roy Eldridge, Dizzy Gillespie, Flip Phillips, Bill Harris, and a rhythm section of Oscar Peterson, Louis Bellson, Herb Ellis, and Ray Brown. The two sides here are mainly cutting sessions, with long solos by each of the performers. The second set listed above is pretentious in its title, but it is a superb collection of 40 in-concert works (performed on June 28, 29, and July 1, 1967) by Duke Ellington and his band (and different configurations), the Oscar Peterson Trio, Ella Fitzgerald, and many others. There is included an over-sized booklet with pictures, text, data, and notes by Benny Green. One of Granz's modern products is the Civic set, recorded at the Santa Monica Civic Auditorium in 1972, with Ella Fitzgerald, the Count Basie Band, and several "guests" such as Oscar Peterson, Ray Brown, Stan Getz, Roy Eldridge, Eddie "Lockjaw" Davis, Harry Edison, and Al Grey. The result was a virtual JATP issue from 25 years back. The huge jam session gets underway with the Basie Orchestra in fine form, then switches to the rechristened JATP All Stars "In a Mellow Tone," "I Surrender Dear," and so forth. The order of solos is indicated. The third disc of this last set concerns a revitalized Ella Fitzgerald, who sings with the Basie outfit, with her own trio led by Tommy Flanagan, with them both together, and with the JATP All Stars for Ellington's "C Jam Blues."

J1.16   **George Wein and the Newport All-Stars.** Impulse AS 31.

J1.17   **George Wein Is Alive and Well in Mexico.** Columbia CS 9631.

J1.18   **Newport Jazz Festival All-Stars.** Odyssey 32 16 0296.
George Wein is the organizer of the Newport festivals, which have now moved to New York City. He is also a jazz pianist and arranger. For the festivals, he has had to assemble house bands to back up any vocalists and to perform when called upon (as warm-ups or fill-in for missing stars and bands). Occasionally, performers would go into the studio and on the road both. The Impulse set has Ruby Braff (cornet), Pee Wee Russell, Bud Freeman, and others performing outstanding versions of such warhorses as "At the Jazz Band Ball," "Ja-Da," "Lulu's Back in Town," etc. The Columbia album was recorded in 1967 in Mexico at three concerts, and the musicians here are basically the same, with such songs as "All of Me," "Take the 'A' Train," and "The World Is Waiting for the Sunrise." The Odyssey recording provides a more modern sound. It has the "House" band comprising Clark Terry, Howard McGhee, Coleman Hawkins, Zoot Sims, et al. on one side, with "Undecided" and "Stardust." The Newport All-Stars—with the same line-up as on the other two discs but adding Al Grey to Trombone—are modern with "Lester Leaps In" and "When Your Lover Has Gone." Good, solid blowing.

J1.19*   **The First Esquire All-American Jazz Concert, January 18, 1944.** two discs. Radiola 2MR 5051.
In 1944, *Esquire* released the results of its first jazz poll, which brought the names of the musicians before a wider audience, not just those fans and collectors who read music magazines. A concert was arranged for the winners, and the initial series, the proceedings of which are contained on these two discs, was the first jazz performance ever staged at the Metropolitan Opera House. Although acetates were made for re-broadcasting at a later date, no commercial recordings ever ensued, and it fell to quasi-legal pirates to issue the present set. All of the music here is fairly spontaneous, with some solos predominating, and as with the Carnegie Hall concerts, it certainly helped to popularize jazz among non-fans. Timings are generous, and the complete concert is on this set. Long jams include "I Got Rhythm," "Mop Mop," "Tea for Two," and others. Different configurations were used, such as solo work by Art Tatum or small group productions. Louis Armstrong has a few vocals, as well as Billie Holiday singing "Do Nothin' 'Till You Hear from Me" and Jack Teagarden singing "I Gotta Right to Sing the Blues." Other performers include Roy Eldridge, Barney Bigard, Coleman Hawkins, Al Casey, Oscar Pettiford, and Sid Catlett.

J1.20   **Hot Jazz on Film. v.1/2.** two discs. Extreme Rarities 1002 and 1004.
The 28 tracks on these two records were lifted from the optical soundtracks of various films, 1933-1959. Jazz has never been treated well in the movies as a story line, but often the music has been excellent. The soundtracks were better than studio recordings because of the fidelity of the 16mm optical system. This hodgepodge includes such interesting items as "Bugle Call Rag" by Benny Goodman, from *The Big Broadcast of 1937*; his quartet version of "I've Got a Heartful of Music," from *Hollywood Hotel* (1937); Art Tatum, who appeared in *The Fabulous Dorseys* (1947); Ethel Waters and Count Basie from the 1943 *Stagedoor Canteen*,

and even the soundtrack from a 1932 Betty Boop cartoon, with Louis Armstrong performing in a medley of "High Society," "I'll Be Glad When You're Dead, You Rascal You" (the title of the cartoon), and "Chinatown, My Chinatown." The good variety of jazz here could appeal to both the jazz collector and the sound track buff.

J1.21   **The Blue Angel Jazz Club. Proceedings, 1968-**. Blue Angel BAJC 1, 505- (two discs a year).

Every year, from Pasadena, California, the Blue Angel Jazz Club has a meeting, the bulk of which is devoted to hearing favorite musicians from the swing era and small group period. The recordings are lively, and while there are crowd noises, they do not intrude and, in fact, they add color to the club meeting. A variety of musicians, as in 1968, might include Dick Cary, Nappy Lamare, Matty Matlock, George Van Eps, and Joe Venuti, among others, in a variety of settings and configurations. Every year, two discs are released, and the tunes include such standards as "Blues My Naughty Sweetie Taught Me," "Blue Room," "Lazy River," and so forth. Some updating of modern tunes, such as "Stella by Starlight" or the "Shadow of Your Smile" deserve comment as gems of swing interpretation. Occasionally, there are originals, such as "Ballad for Eddie" by Dick Cary or "Blues in 5/4" by Johnny Guarnieri. Other musicians from other years include (from 1969) Clancy Hayes, Jess Stacy, and (from 1970) Red Norvo, Peanuts Hucko, Nick Fatool, and Flip Phillips. The club is carrying on its activities to preserve swing music.

J1.22   **The Sound of Jazz.** Columbia CL 1098.

This record conveys one of the great jazz meetings of all time. On Sunday, December 8, 1957, CBC aired the television show of the same name. It was *the* prototype of how a jazz program should be. It begins with Henry "Red" Allen performing "Wild Man Blues." Allen on trumpet takes the first chorus, while Coleman Hawkins and Vic Dickenson (sax and trombone, respectively) compete on the second. Then it's a battle between Pee Wee Russell (clarinet) and Rex Stewart (trumpet) in the third chorus. Most of the album goes on like this. The track "Rosetta" follows, and then comes later Billie Holiday with Mal Waldron. She is in superb form, although in the twilight of her troubled career. The absolute stunner of the event is "Blues," an open-ended jam featuring the twin clarinets of Jimmy Giuffre and Russell, with only drums and guitar accompaniment (by Jo Jones and Danny Baker). The clarinet was made for the blues (and vice versa) and here are two of the best licorice sticks ever trading off licks. Side two is virtually all Count Basie, in what must be reckoned as his last great band, especially assembled for the occasion. Jimmy Rushing takes four soaring choruses on "I Left My Baby." The other great piece, "Dickie's Dream," goes on and on for twelve choruses.

Ragtime

RAGTIME

INTRODUCTION

Ragtime is a musical form that contributed to jazz, even though it is outside the mainstream of American black music. In some respects, it can be linked to the nineteenth century ministrel shows (which were usually the work of white entertainers), but these shows were themselves parodies of "coon" songs and tap dances. A suspicion that ragtime was a response to a white demand for a form of black music is very valid, as its essence was the incorporation of black rhythms into European musical forms. "Classic" ragtime is piano ragtime—and nothing more. As it is heavily syncopated and highly formal (i.e., all notes are written), it allows little scope at all for improvisation, although Max Morath has said, "One of the most elusive qualities of classic piano ragtime is its grace and charm; perhaps 'felicity' is the word."

As it is written, ragtime piano music is notated and derived from European influences. The pattern is based on the *rondo* form of the minuet and scherzo. The "Maple Leaf Rag," for instance, has four different parts, each 16 bars long (AA BBA CC DD), in which the third part (CC) is the featured tune. The distinctive polyrhythms are lilting syncopations, where the weak beats are accented, coupled with an unsyncopated major beat at the same time. The steady beat (2/4, or "march," time) lies in the left hand, while the syncopated beat is in the right hand. The latter thus plays eight beats in the same interval, with the third beat taking the accent. This is sometimes called the "secondary rag," and it was perhaps taken from minstrel banjo techniques.

Robert Kimball, in his liner notes to Eubie Blake's double album (Columbia C2S 847), describes these musicological devices in social terms: "In its piano music, which drew inspiration from the folk melodies once heard on the plantation banjo, the left hand, with its precise rhythms, was an articulation of the unyielding presence of the system, while the right hand, which sharply and often gaily accented the normally unaccented beats of the measure, conveyed a release from inhibition, a joyous affirmation of man's individuality. The juxtaposition of the two helped create a music whose depth of feeling and variety of mood reflected the agony of the past but spoke directly to the quickening of future hopes at the start of the twentieth century."

In style, ragtime was an extension of the cakewalk and early minstrel tunes. In format, it developed from the march or quick-step played by brass bands of the era, as funeral marches in duple time. Early rags were often noted as *tempo di marcia* ("in slow march time"); later rags were simply noted as "marches." Significantly, ragtime developed in the Midwest, where marches still are popular. Piano rags are easy to play if one can read music, but straightforward playing usually lacks expressiveness while being confined to the tempered scale. The better compositions are tricky, and a sense of rhythm is needed. Toward this end, a better-than-average pianist will improvise a variety of "rhythmic suspensions," unusual accents, and between-the-beat effects. The better pianists around the turn of the century did this, and rhythm predominated, forcing the music into the jazz stream and later into commercial fields. The heavy march two-beat in the left hand declined and was replaced by four beats in the same interval, all evenly accented. Virtuosity crept in with complicated accents in the right hand, and the music became more danceable.

While piano ragtime may be limited in itself, it is possible to "rag" any tune. Indeed, it became apparent that ragtime was one of several approaches to music, and for this reason, it became popular as material for piano rolls and jazz bands. Different instruments can also be "ragged." However, although ads exist for guitar rag arrangements, no actual sheet music appears to have survived. The drawback of guitar rags is that all the necessary notes cannot be played with the strings (12-string guitars suit the medium better, and duets are best of all). But opportunities arise with guitar to use glissando, vibrato, and various tone colours to give the music a better lilt or melodic flow than the original piano pieces. Three black bluesmen of the East Coast area were the leaders in this field—Blind Willie McTell, Rev. Gary Davis, and Blind Blake.

Other variants, parallel to the development of ragtime piano into stride, include the society dance band arrangements. Joseph Robichaux's band in New Orleans orchestrated hundreds of rags, cakewalks, and minstrel tunes. His outfit included violins and performed music that appealed to the fashionable white audiences of the period. Similarly, Vess Ossman's banjo band and W. C. Hardy's society band played orchestrated rags.

In 1896 or 1897, Tom Turpin, a Negro saloon owner and piano player, arranged for his "Harlem Rag" to be published. "Ragtime" was used for the first time as a musical term in 1898 with Fred Stone's sheet music for "Ma Ragtime Baby." That same year saw the first Scott Joplin published work, "Original Rags," a medley of American Negro folk tunes. Then, in 1899, he wrote "The Maple Leaf Rag" (named after the Maple Leaf Club in Sedalia, Missouri), which quickly sold over a million copies. In 1902, Hughie Cannon published the first rag song: "Bill Bailey."

Scott Joplin (1868-1917), the father of ragtime music, took courses in harmony and composition in Sedalia. His interest in music led him to assimilate American and African Negro folk music with European devices into a city-folk music flavor, and urban sound with country banjo and minstrel roots (not all of them "rags"). Over his lifetime, he composed 504 piano pieces of all types and styles. He even published a book in 1908, detailing the secrets of playing ragtime. Joplin believed that ragtime would be the classical music of America, and he was once styled the "American Chopin." James Scott (1886-1938) and Joseph Lamb (1887-1960), Joplin's two most famous disciples, were perhaps better composers in the piano medium than Joplin himself. Scott, in particular, had a filigree treble that called for incredible technical skill and discipline.

It is difficult to say precisely why ragtime blossomed. Certainly a major factor was the fact that anyone could play it at home, and sheet music was available to everyone at a cheap price, long before the phonograph. John Stark and Son, of St. Louis, published Joplin plus anyone else who had Joplin's endorsement. Soon after "The Maple Leaf Rag" was printed, quadrilles and marches were republished with the word "ragtime" hastily overprinted on the cover or title page. Ragtime thus became featured in virtually all forms of entertainment. It was played at the various World Fairs of seventy-odd years ago: Chicago, St. Louis, Buffalo, and Omaha. It carried the "Cakewalk" with it, and this part-shuffle, part-dance became incorporated into the ragtime milieu, sweeping the nation and taking London and Paris by storm. Sousa featured the music on his post-1900 European tours (e.g., the "At a Georgian Camp Meeting" cakewalk). Debussy wrote "Golliwog's Cakewalk," and Stravinsky wrote "Piano-Rag-Music" and "Ragtime for 11 Instruments." Even now, when the musical director of a film sequence wants to emulate the mood at the turn of the century, he will invariably write or use "raggy music." And, of course, there was the movie "The Sting."

None of the pioneers of ragtime ever made phonograph records. Although they cut numerous piano rolls, many of these rolls were subjected to post-cutting changes (such as added embellishments); thus, it is difficult to envision how exponents such as Turpin, Joplin, and Scott really sounded. The closest we can come is either in the recorded works of Luckey Roberts, Jelly Roll Morton, and James P. Johnson, or in the later recorded works of Joseph Lamb and Eubie Blake. The former group were not ragtime exponents, but they did use the idiom, expanding and improvising on themes; Blake and Lamb were recorded late in their lives, at a time when both memories and fingers can so often fail.

Classic piano ragtime disappeared when Joplin died in 1917. The happy spirit of the early part of the century had dissipated, and over-commercialization by Tin Pan Alley exploited uptempo rags designed to give play to their melody and to their pianistic virtuosity. As a result, "novelty rags" were composed, published, and recorded; these were turned into dances, stomps, and fast blues.

Commenting on ragtime, John Norris, editor of *Code*, wrote (December 1971): "The original exponents were black musicians and their special qualities helped make the music unique. When the music passed into the hands of the general population it changed considerably. What was originally a sophisticated, complex piano music became a brittle, flashy—indeed raggy—music. It was orchestrated, it was played by brass bands, it was interpreted by banjoists and eventually, in a much simplified manner, was bashed out on out-of-tune uprights by pianists who could hardly stumble through the simplest of material. The subtlety of the original modulations, delightful melodic twists and underlying harmonic patterns was replaced by a glorified jollity."

The odd resurgence of ragtime, such as that of the mid-forties West Coast, tended to emphasize the honky-tonk-rinky-tink tone, and often pianos were deliberately put out of tune to give it that cheap, characteristic "piano roll" sound. It was this sound that led Johnny "Crazy Otto" Maddox to the top of the hit parade in the mid-fifties and influenced other pianists.

Literature

Ragtime is such a precise idiom that a few books cover the whole area. Most jazz surveys will comment on ragtime, but Schuller (105), who deals with early jazz, is the best, with Stearns (111) presenting basic materials for a musicological study. Blesh and Janis (17), the classic history of ragtime, has gone through four revisions. Schafer and Riedel (7) is a more formal book that duplicates Blesh and Janis to some extent, but it does provide a stronger musical analysis (which was first attempted by Waterman in 1940; this essay is reprinted in Williams [124]). Gammond (39) not only considers Scott Joplin but the whole milieu of the ragtime era. Sandberg and Weissman (102) treat ragtime as folk music and thus indicate books, records, songbooks, societies, etc., where more detail can be found. Jasen (55) has indexed recorded ragtime from 1897 through 1958 and presents relevant discographic data. Periodicals treat ragtime slightly, but it is to be found in *Jazz Journal* (10) or the more traditional magazines such as *Storyville* (18). The *Mississippi Rag* (14) is about two-thirds ragtime. Two societies operate in North America—the Maple Leaf Club in Los Angeles and the Ragtime Society Inc. in Toronto, Canada—and both publish newsletters. More citations to articles can be found through the *Popular Music Periodicals Index* (85) under **Ragtime** or under the name of the artist. Record reviews can be located through the *Annual Index to Popular Music Record Reviews* (2).

ANTHOLOGIES

J2.1 **Black and White Ragtime, 1921-1943.** Biograph BLP 12047.
Covering much the same period as Herwin 402 (J2.2), and again with programming and notes by David Jasen, this set presents substantial documentation of the ragtime era. Jasen notes that the commercial availability of the phonograph record coincided with the popularity of ragtime. Thus, it was the first time that technology provided original examples of the development of a music form. Three types of music are presented here: the New York Stride School, with Eubie Blake (a *sixth* alternate take of his "Charleston Rag"), James P. Johnson and Fletcher Henderson—all from 1921; the Chicago mixture of rags and blues, with Alonzo Yancey, Jimmy Blythe, and others; and novelties or Tin Pan Alley creations such as Zez Confrey's "Kitten on the Keys" or a novelty version of "Maple Leaf Rag." As indicated by the anthology title, the musicians were racially different, but in ragtime solo piano work, that seemed to matter little.

J2.2 **Piano Ragtime of the Teens, Twenties & Thirties.** Herwin 402.
These are 16 sterling examples of the various shapes that piano ragtime assumed during a twenty-year span after Scott Joplin's death (and the so-called death of "classic ragtime" at the same moment). The versatility on the album lies in the fact that many classical examples are given alongside Tin Pan Alley novelties and a few blues or stride piano tunes. The gamut goes from Ray Spangler's 1917 "Red Onion Rag" to Willie "The Lion" Smith's 1939 "Finger Buster." In between are James P. Johnson, Jelly Roll Morton, Clarence Williams, Cow Cow Davenport, and Joe Sullivan. As ragtime anthologies go, this is one of the very best to be assembled, and with the superb notes by ragtime scholar (and former librarian) Dave Jasen, it is probably one of the most informative surveys.

J2.3 **The Piano Roll.** RBF 7.

J2.4 **Picture Rags.** Transatlantic SAM 26 (British import).

J2.5 **They All Play Ragtime.** Jazzology JCE 52.
These three records illustrate different approaches to ragtime music. The RBF compilation, edited by Trebor Tichenor (himself a noted performer in the genre), has extensive liner lines. It is a hodge-podge collection of different styles found on some piano rolls, all with normal tempos. Rags include "Starburst Rag" and "Something Doing," the latter by Joplin. Side one has rolls cut by machine,

and side two has rolls played by hand. The Transatlantic effort is subtitled "A Rag-time Guitar Sampler." All of the artists are available on various albums of their own, but it is handy to have a compilation reflecting just ragtime. Of the 10 tracks, two are by John James (including an inspired Joplin-written "Original Rags"), two by Laibman and Schoenberg, two by Rev. Gary Davis, and others by Stefan Grossman, Ralph McTell, and Peter Berryman. The Jazzology set is basically a sampling of the leading ragtime pianists of the past 15 years. Joseph Lamb plays his "Alaskan Rag" (which was recorded shortly before his death), Tom Shea does "Brun Campbell Express," Trebor Tichenor has a rag, while John Arpin has two and Max Morath has three. Other pianists include Peter Lundberg from Sweden (before his New Orleans Ragtime Orchestra days) and Donald Ashwander. Rudi Blesh has written the sterling notes.

J2.6   Ragtime 1: The City. RBF 17.

J2.7   Ragtime 2: The Country. RBF 18.
  Compiled and annotated by Sam Charters, each disc offers 14 rags in two distinct stylings. The city features "nickel" pianos, banjos, and brass bands, such as those of Charles Prince. Many of the recordings were made before 1920, but the remastering is good. This disc is illustrative of the spread of ragtime from St. Louis to other regions. Included are Jelly Roll Morton's "Frog-I-More Rag," Ves Ossman's banjo on "Buffalo Rag," the "Notoriety Rag" of Fred Van Ep, and a novelty from the Tin Pan Alley pen of Arthur Collins ("Railroad Rag"). The country disc features strong bands, guitars, and pianos. As a collection, it shows the influence of ragtime in popular and country music. Included are the Carolina Tar Heels ("No Use Work-ing So Hard"), Dallas String Band ("Dallas Rag"), the pianist Cow Cow Davenport ("Atlanta Rag"), and the bluesman Blind Boy Fuller and his "Rag Mama Rag."

J2.8   They All Played the Maple Leaf Rag. Herwin 401.
  Here are 15 versions in largely remastered sound of the most famous ragtime composition of all times (excepting, perhaps, the latter-day popularity of Joplin's "The Entertainer" from the score of *The Sting*). While "The Maple Leaf Rag" lacked the rhythmic felicities of "The Magnetic Rag" or "The Entertainer," it was perhaps the least formalized of Joplin's rags, and hence lent itself most to impro-visation and to jazz popularity. All 15 tracks are of the same tune, but interpreted differently. While it is good to have different versions collated, Herwin could also have made Joplin's piano roll version available so that listeners could have a refer-ence point established by the composer. Pianists are well represented here: Jelly Roll Morton (with two versions—one in New Orleans style, and the other in St. Louis style), Eubie Blake, James P. Johnson, Willie Eckstein, Hank Duncan, Paul Lingle, Don Ewell, Willie "The Lion" Smith, and Ralph Sutton. Swinging versions from the thirties, mainly by big bands, include those of Sidney Bechet, Earl Hines, and Tommy Dorsey. There are also two novelties: Vess Ossman's banjo band from 1907 and W. C. Handy's society band of 1917. The latter shows the deterioration of ragtime into commercialism.

PIANO

Innovators

J2.9* **Eubie Blake. The Eighty Six Years of Eubie Blake.** two discs. Columbia C2S 847.

J2.9a **Eubie Blake. Rags to Classics.** Eubie Blake Music. EBM 2.

Blake was just under ninety when he recorded these three discs. He was one of the innovators of ragtime (and a major force in the musical theatre). He created some of the most original rags, including "Chevy Chase" (1914), "Tricky Fingers," and "Charleston Rag" (1899), the latter heard on both sets as recorded in 1921, 1968, and 1971. He has done a lot of adaptive work, and the roots of ragtime are clearly shown in the two Sousa marches "Semper Fidelis" and "Stars and Stripes Forever." One disc of the Columbia twofer is ragtime piano, the other is of his theatre work with (in most cases) Noble Sissle, such as "Memories of You" and "Wild about Harry." Both are superb discs of solo piano. His own company's records, one of a half dozen, present some new and old creations, such as "Junk Man Rag" and "Pork and Beans" from the great Luckeyth Roberts, and his own "Capricious Harlem" and "You're Lucky to Me."

J2.10 **Scott Joplin. Ragtime, v.2.** Biograph BLP 1008 Q.

These classic rags were re-recorded from Joplin piano rolls cut between 1900 and 1910. Mike Montgomery, noted ragtime performer, was in charge of the transcription and he has provided good sound, correct speeds, and excellent notes. Of all the Joplin rolls, these are amongst the best because ragtime was at its peak during these years. Joplin took ill after 1910, and his decline started, both in health and in creativity. Included here are his definitive versions of "The Cascades," "The Gladiolus Rag," "Swipsey Cake Rag," "Stop Time Rag," and ten others.

J2.11 **Joseph Lamb. A Study in Classic Ragtime.** Folkways FG 3562.

This disc was recorded at Lamb's home in Brooklyn in 1959. Lamb was a white man who everybody thought was black because of his ragtime compositions. He has been ranked with Joplin and Scott as being one of the three most productive, interesting geniuses of ragtime music. Once a protégé of Joplin, he reminisces here in interviews concerning James Scott and Scott Joplin. Also included are his versions of his own material: "Cottontail Rag," "Sensation Rag," "Contentment Rag," "Alaskan Rag," and others. Lamb played with unusual depth, despite faltering because of his age. His overall music is usually characterized by rich, warm chords and harmonics.

Standards

J2.12 **John Arpin. Concert in Ragtime.** Scroll LSCR 101 (Canadian issue).

J2.13 **John Arpin. The Other Side of Ragtime.** Scroll LSCR 103 (Canadian issue).

Both of these discs provide a wealth of variety among their 24 items. Each set has two rags by Joplin, Lamb, and Scott (the big three) plus others by Jelly Roll Morton. There are a few originals such as the "Centennial Rag" (1964).

Arpin's light and airy touch is ideally suited for performing ragtime as it was written, and this is no doubt a result of his classically trained background.

J2.14   **William Bolcom. Heliotrope Bouquet; Piano Rags, 1900-1970.** Nonesuch H 71257.

J2.15   **William Bolcom. Pastimes and Piano Rags.** Nonesuch H 71299.
    James Scott created pyrotechnical ragtime works, the most demanding in all of ragtime; a good example is "Efficiency Rag." Artie Mathews, on the other hand, created dance tempos with some Latin influences and rhythms, most notably the tango. These are revealed in "Pastime Rags, No. 1-5 (A Slow Drag)," where other devices include   stop time, slow drags, and barrelhouse movements. Bolcom plays these five Mathews works plus five Scotts with his usual felicity. The *Heliotrope Bouquet* record encompasses the diverse styles of the main ragtime composers. As a serious musician and composer himself, Bolcom presents literal stylings of Turpin's "A Ragtime Nightmare" and Lamb's "Ethiopia Rag." He also contributes two original rags, "Graceful Ghost" and "Seabiscuit," as well as playing a contemporary selection by William Albright ("Brass Knuckles") and three Joplin pieces that do not duplicate the offerings by Rifkin, also on the Nonesuch label.

J2.16   **Dave Jasen. Fingerbustin' Ragtime.** Blue Goose 3001.
    There are eight originals by Jasen here, such as "Festival—A Ragtime Cakewalk," "Dave's Rag" (perhaps derived from Morton), a bouncy "Raymond' Rag" and "That American Ragtime Dance," this latter being indicative of the type of commercialism that surrounded ragtime in its declining years. From the eight others are two novelty rags—Zez Confrey's "Kitten on the Keys" and Herbert Ingraham's "Poison Ivy Rag," plus the obligatory "Maple Leaf Rag" and Eubie Blake's "Charleston Rag." The album's title is indicative of the contents, as these are all stomping versions.

J2.17*   **Max Morath. The Best of Scott Joplin and Other Rag Classics.** two discs. Vanguard VSD 39/40.

J2.18   **Max Morath. Plays Ragtime.** Vanguard VSD 83184.
    These four discs contain diverse materials. The first record of the first set is a concert of ragtime piano from its flowering, 1897-1917. There are seven rags from Joplin, three from Lamb, two from Scott, Turpin's "St. Louis Rag" (written to celebrate the St. Louis Louisiana Purchase Exposition of 1904), and Joe Northup's "The Cannonball," an early example of the novelty rag. Joplin's "Silver Swan" was only discovered in 1970 and is here given a sterling interpretation. The second record of the set is a major document, lovingly performed and nicely recorded in spacious stereo. This is the serious side of Morath, with the expertise of Jim Tyler on banjo plus added guitar and bass. Fantastic renditions of "Slippery Elm," "A Real Slow Drag," "Ragtime Nightingale," and "The Cascades." Of particular interest is George L. Cobb's "Russian Rag" (1918), a syncopated treatment of one of Rachmaninoff's *Preludes.* There are excellent liner notes contributed by Rudi Blesh. The second set was a follow-up effort. There are some little-known rags here, and not all of them are by Joplin. James Scott and Joseph Lamb are also

included. Some of the originals are in styles, such as Morath's "Golden Hours" and the dedication to Joseph Lamb's wife, "One for Amelia."

J2.19   **Knocky Parker. The Complete Works of Scott Joplin.** two discs. Audiophile AP 71/2.

J2.20   **Knocky Parker. The Complete Works of James Scott.** two discs. Audiophile AP 76/7.

J2.21   **Knocky Parker. Golden Treasury of Ragtime, v.1/4.** four discs. Audiophile AP 89/92.

J2.22   **Knocky Parker. Old Rags.** Audiophile AP 49.
     Dr. John W. ("Knocky") Parker is now an English professor who plays ragtime piano for fun and relaxation. During the era of "Western Swing," he was the pianist for a number of Southwest jazz-infused country bands, where he developed a flowing style and a solid regimen. In these discs, he has come up with definitive editions of ragtime works by the masters. He has even recorded the complete piano works of Jelly Roll Morton, the man responsible for transforming the ragtime piano into the stride variety. The James Scott collection is from his 1903-1922 writing period, and it embraces 34 rags, all warmly recorded. The Joplin set has 50 tracks, including some rag marches. Recent discoveries indicate that this was not all of Joplin's material; thus, the appellative "complete" is no longer exact. Both sets have strong notes. The *Treasury* is a collection of rag music and rag-type tunes (such as cakewalks) from 1899-1913, arranged in chronological order. Parker is not alone this time, for he has good support from a combination of banjo, bass, brushes, and tuba. In some cases, he performs on the celeste and harpsichord, in a quite enchanting manner. Volume 1 covers 1899-1901 and includes "At a Georgia Camp Meeting," "Tickled to Death," and "Dusty Dudes" among its 16 selections. The 14 tracks from volume 2 cover 1902-1908 (the greatest time span in the set), and include "St. Louis Rag," "Hiawatha," "Tennessee Tantalizer," and "Florida Rag." Volume 3 is from 1908-1909, with "Dusty," "The Peach," "Poison Ivy Rag," and "Porcupine Rag" among the 15 tracks. Of particular interest is volume 4, 1910-1913, which illustrates the beginning of the decline of ragtime. Here are "Tar Babies," "Silver Bell," "Live Wires," and "Chatterbox Rag." These 16 cuts show signs of the commercial embellishments and ornamentations that began to intrude as Tin Pan Alley took over with what are known as "novelty rags." The last disc is mainly pre-1900 and rounds out the four-disc set. Parker's sensitive fingering does justice to such "old" rags as Joplin's "Fig Leaf" and Scott's "Froglegs" and "Climax Rag."

J2.23*   **Joshua Rifkin. Joplin Piano Rags, v.1/3.** three discs. Nonesuch HB73026 and H71305.
    Rifkin's first volume here was the disc that probably started the latest revival of ragtime. Credibility for ragtime was gained because Nonesuch is a respected "classical" label, and it was once instrumental in spreading the baroque vogue of more than a decade ago. The label is accessible for it has national distribution, and it is widely discounted at inexpensive prices. Rifkin was Juilliard-trained, and here he displays superb touch and control. There is little variance from the original scores, and, in fact, he gives a very carefully balanced interpretation. These rags are played

as they were meant to be played—in march time, rather than in dance time. Thus, there are no flashy displays of speed or dexterity as was once interpreted by the stride pianists. It was a shock to some people that "ragtime" was originally *not* equated to "ragged" or "honky tonk" music, but that it was a viable miniature art form that was scored and played as was any other "classical" piano music. In his time, Joplin was known as the Chopin of America. Included on these discs are "The Maple Leaf Rag," "The Entertainer," "Ragtime Dance," "Euphonic Sounds," "Magnetic Rag," "Original Rags," and "The Cascades," among others. There are excellent liner notes by Rifkin. These are essential records, and the series may be in progress to re-record all of Joplin's piano works.

ORCHESTRATED/TRANSPOSED RAGTIME

J2.24   **Ken Colyer. Ragtime Revisited.** Joy JOYS 194 (British issue).
Colyer was a pioneer figure in British jazz of the post-war era. He once studied "traditional" music first-hand on an extended visit to New Orleans, and he had since acquired a respect for original compositions, as is reflected on this disc. Here are tightly arranged band versions of ragtime selections, including "Pineapple Rag" and "Ragtime Oriole." The tempos are moderate, but the sound is crisp.

J2.25*   **Rev. Gary Davis. Ragtime Guitar.** Kicking Mule 106.
Although better known as a bluesman and as a gospel singer, Davis has equal strength as a guitarist. Coming from the East Coast, along with Blind Boy Fuller, Brownie McGhee, Blind Blake, etc., he had much exposure to rags and ragtime tunes. This "region" of the blues has long been known for the dexterity of its guitarists: long, fluid lines and intricate finger-picking. Rags are a natural adaptation of this. Among the many who claim to be influenced by Davis are Larry Johnson, Ry Cooder, Dave Van Ronk, and Taj Mahal. These recordings are derived from a series of tapes made between 1962 and 1970 in various circumstances and settings. The ten selections have very good sound quality. Traditional rags include "West Coast Blues" (the Blind Blake tune, played here on a six-string banjo), "St. Louis Tickle" (done in an old-time mould), "Italian Rag," and a retitled "C Rag." There are also two versions of Davis's most popular song, "Candyman." On the first, "Two Step Candyman," the tempo is, of course, in two step time. The "Waltz Time Candyman" is in 3/4 rhythm.

J2.26*   **Turk Murphy. The Many Faces of Ragtime.** Atlantic SD 1613.
Every now and then, a record appears that can be termed "delightful"—and this is one of them. It is more "jazzy" (obviously) than either the New Orleans Ragtime Orchestra or Gunther Schuller's New England ensemble. Breaking out of San Francisco's Earthquake McGoon for this set, Turk has assembled sterling arrangements of 12 ragtime pieces (including his dusted off "Little John's Rag," unheard lo these 25 years). With his septet (including Leon Oakley, cornet, and Phil Howe, clarinet), the trombonist leader runs through five Joplins (the lush "Euphonic Sounds," the swinging "Cascades," etc.), two James Scotts, and four pop or novelty ditties. Except for his original, all the tunes here were written before 1910, still well within ragtime's classic years. Much of the load falls on Pete Clute, the pianist, as ragtime is essentially a piano form. He is featured on all the breaks

and solos, so much so that the ensemble accompanies the piano, as in a concerto.

J2.27   **New England Conservatory Ragtime Ensemble. More Scott Joplin.** Golden Crest CRS 31031.

J2.28*   **New England Conservatory Ragtime Ensemble. Scott Joplin: The Red Back Book.** Angel S 36060.

Gunther Schuller, an expert on early jazz developments and a creator in Third Stream jazz, leads the ensemble through brisk paces in two definitive programs embracing the scope of ragtime. The material in the Angel collection was selected from Joplin's *Fifteen Standard High Class Rags* (the "Red Back Book"), a work comprised of the most successful of his rags, arranged for a combination of eleven instruments, equally suitable for dance floors, theatre pits, or park bandstands. Heard are "The Cascades," "The Chrysanthemum," "The Entertainer," "The Easy Winners," and "The Maple Leaf Rag." The Golden Crest record, made a half year later, extends to include four hitherto unorchestrated works, heard for the first time in arrangements by Schuller. Consistent scoring and a verve in attack make these two discs outstanding examples of small ensemble ragtime playing.

J2.29   **Tony Parenti.** Jazzology J 15.

J2.30   **Tony Parenti. Ragtime Jubilee.** Jazzology J 21.

Parenti had led or performed with many groups, playing a mean clarinet. On J 15, he is supported on one side by a 1947 group featuring Wild Bill Davison (cornet), Ralph Sutton (piano), Baby Dodds (drums), and others. These play "Hysterics Rag," "Sunflower Slow Drag," "Grace and Beauty," etc. Sutton lends solid support with his ragtime piano work, and Davison really puts vigor into the cornet obbligatos. Both Sutton and Parenti are part of a trio on side two (from 1949) with "Cataract Rag," "Entertainers Rag," "Lilly Rag," and "Nonsense Rag." With Knocky Parker's piano and a group of lesser-known musicians on J 21, Parenti deals quite admirably with "Sapho Rag," "Erratic Rag," "Patricia Rag," "Dynamite Rag," plus six others. Liner notes are by the ubiquitous ragtimer, Rudi Blesh. While there is a small amount of good fun and hokum here, there is definitely little commercialism. Of all the jazzed-up ragtime performances by small units (or ragged-up jazz performances), these Parenti-led groups are among the best.

Geographic Origins and Stylings

GEOGRAPHIC ORIGINS AND STYLINGS

INTRODUCTION

The New Orleans influence in jazz has been thoroughly researched and documented. It is commonly thought of as being the "home" of jazz, but there are also non-believers who say that jazz occurred at other places at this same time. Whatever the case, the atmosphere of New Orleans promoted interracial musical developments—a pleasing contact between French Creoles, Latins (South America, Mediterranean), Africans, and Caribbean Islanders. Ideas were exchanged, ragtime and blues worked into the music, and social functions acquired entertainment. One of the prime ancestors of "jazz" is the New Orleans brass band which not only performed at dances but also established the funereal marching patterns of playing a dirge on the way to the graveyard and a swinging, happy number (related to gospel) on the way back. Of those that recorded, the Eureka and the Tuxedo Bands stand out, the latter contributing clarinetist Alphonse Picou to jazz music.

By the turn of the century, musical developments in "jazz" were struck at St. Louis (ragtime oriented), Memphis (blues dominated), Atlanta, Baltimore, and so forth—mainly in urban centers located in or near the South, where blacks still remained. During World War I, and for years afterwards, New Orleans jazz actually did travel to New York and Chicago, following the industrial boom that came with munitions factories and the 1917 closing of New Orleans's tenderloin district, Storyville, by the U.S. Navy. Musicians were not professionals. Most worked at other jobs, and when these jobs collapsed, they moved with other blacks out of the South to the large urban North. Their music went with them, especially after the red light district in New Orleans was closed. A highly simplistic statement would be that jazz moved from New Orleans to Chicago, and then to New York. Different variations certainly did, and the leaders here were King Oliver and Louis Armstrong, both of whom did travel that route.

New Orleans Style

The New Orleans style of playing evolved largely from French and African backgrounds. In style, it was basically free counterpoint played by the three melody instruments. The cornet (later, trumpet) always played lead because of its brilliant tone; the trombone provided bass harmony and contrast because of its weighty tone; the clarinet (the main Creole instrument, in the French woodwinds tradition) played the melody, interweaving an ornamentation of notes. Thus, the first real jazz improvisors were the clarinetists. Rhythm was furnished by a mixture of strings (bass, guitar, banjo), brass (tuba), and percussion (piano, drums). The "front line" were the three melody instruments; "rhythm" changed depending on circumstances. A *marching* band would have two or three of tuba, drums, guitar, or banjo; a *recording/performing* band that didn't have to walk could have the same sort of instrumentation, or use a stand-up bass, piano, and a drum set. Acoustic recordings could not pick up piano and strings very well; consequently, the initial recordings of New Orleans bands include a rhythm of brass, bass, and drums. New Orleans music was "hot," with great emotion through a blistering attack on the cornet, plus vibrato and phrasing from the rest of the front line. European march rhythms and ragtime predominated, with syncopation and the emphasized 1 and 3 beats. Overall, it was social music.

Dixieland Style

Dixieland was often called a "white" style, as it was music divorced from traditional New Orleans roots and played anywhere. It was less expressive, but better in a technical sense, as all performers were polished, professional musicians working at their music as a full-time job. The melodies were smoother, and pure harmony was emphasized. Leading proponents such as the Original Dixieland Jazz Band and the New Orleans Rhythm Kings did not feature soloists. Thus, there were fewer emphatic statements, as vibrato was rarely used, orthodox sonorities predominated, and glissandi (sliding notes) or growls were employed for comic effects only.

Over the years, New Orleans music and Dixieland styles fused. In New Orleans itself, the music remained static: it is played today in much the same fashion as 75 years ago. Elsewhere, the permutations and development of New Orleans styles in Chicago and New York led to a more sophisticated jazz (as country blues led to urban blues), and the earlier music was largely forgotten. Recording studios closed in New Orleans because of a lack of business; others there retained segregation, so blacks could not play with whites. In a search for "roots" and early developments in jazz in the 1940s, New Orleans music was rediscovered and offered as an alternative to the then crystalizing "bop" music. Polarization was created between the traditional "mouldy figs" and the new sound; purists insisted on the "real" music. Quite often, apart from early Bunk Johnson and George Lewis, this meant black and white musicians playing together in the New Orleans-Dixieland fusion. The black musician was in the front line as a soloist in New Orleans fashion; the others were harmonizing in Dixieland fashion. Some white groups, learning from the soloists, adopted the same musical stance and utilized a featured soloist (as in the Lu Watters bands). As this music was relatively simple and structured within certain rules, many amateurs gathered to play for fun. By 1950, the New Orleans Revival had run its course in North America; however, it did not come into full bloom in Britain until the 1950s. Black musicians then shifted their place of employment to Europe, and several of them embarked on world-wide tours (especially George Lewis).

Chicago Style

To return to the 1920s in Chicago: the blacks from the South migrated, New Orleans musicians especially after 1917. The events related to the closing of the Storyville district in New Orleans are unclear, but soon afterwards, King Oliver's Creole Jazz Band—the best at the time—turned up in Chicago. This began the style of "New Orleans in Chicago"; most of the recorded legacy of New Orleans music was done in Chicago studios, not in New Orleans. Oliver later asked Louis Armstrong to join him, and from that date (1922) onward, the style of the music drastically changed. For one thing, there was more interaction among the musicians, which later developed into featured soloists (as in Armstrong's case). For another thing, the proximity of Memphis and St. Louis plus migratory blues singers helped to develop the boogie woogie piano style (blues-based but rougher than New York's stride piano). Other significant musicians at this time included Jelly Roll Morton and Johnny Dodds.

Ultimately, "New Orleans in Chicago" was a transitory stage; the musicians moved on to New York, where lay the fatter contracts. However, they left a legacy behind in the form of the so-called Austin High Gang (Chicago-area and Midwest youngsters who supposedly went to Austin High School; but few of them did). This group was profoundly affected by cornetist Bix Beiderbecke's records, who, along with saxist Frank Trumbauer, was then exploring new sounds in jazz beyond the tight strictures of his normal job with Paul Whiteman's dance orchestra. Coupled with New Orleans and Dixieland, Beiderbecke's music provided a fusion point for what was subsequently called "Chicago style" (this, too, spread to New York). This style began as a blatant imitation of blacks by white performers, far beyond the harmonically cohesive early Dixieland. Soloists predominated, admidst a series of parallel voicings and slick ensemble work.

Here began the concept of the "jam," with each member soloing in turn, while the rest of the group performed a few melodic lines in rhythm accompaniment. The most influential man in this group was Eddie Condon, whose banjo and guitar are barely audible on the recordings. But as the leader, arranger, and assimilator, he personified the Chicago style. The most significant contributions of the Chicago style lay in the rise of the saxophone (a multi-faceted instrument, more versatile than the New Orleans clarinet) to preeminence through Bud Freeman, the early notion of the jam, and the groundwork for the swing period through the group's ensemble work. Other members working in this style included clarinetists Benny Goodman and Frank Teschemacher, pianists Joe Sullivan and Jess Stacy, drummers Gene Krupa and Dave Tough, plus Mezz Mezzrow and Jimmy McPartland. Many moved to New York to become studio musicians in the late 1920s before assembling the swing bands of the early 1930s.

New York Style

Early jazz in New York was in sad shape. Apart from the success of the original Dixieland Jazz Band, jazz was mainly theatrical music with a touch of vaudeville. This was expressed through the work of Ted Lewis, the Goofus Five, etc., and this situation existed simply because few blacks had emigrated to New York from the South. The few who did headed for Harlem. There the concept of the "classic blues" developed, a form of urban blues singing by women with a sparse jazz accompaniment varying from piano to a quintet's normal lineup. But certain black musicians (Oliver, Armstrong, etc.) moved to New York, and they were followed by the white "Chicago style" musicians. The music in New York was segregated, with black music in Harlem and white music "uptown." But the whites could visit the blacks and learn from them; consequently, many such visits were made, and modifications occurred in the white jazz scene of New York.

The one local form of jazz produced in New York was the "stride" piano. The swinging atmosphere of St. Louis quickly produced the even four-beat left hand. Jelly Roll Morton added melody to the bass (called a "walking bass") and further refined the accents between the right hand beats. In Harlem, the house party (or "rent party"; a device used to help pay off the rent by charging admission) picked up the syncopation and the walking bass; and, through cutting competitions to determine who was the best piano player that night, there evolved the "stride" piano of James P. Johnson, Lucky Roberts, Willie "The Lion" Smith, and Fats Waller. Johnson and Morton employed ragtime and blues in a heavily percussive style of performing (to get the music heard over the crowd's noise) that also had European roots in its harmony and counterpoint. The one characteristic of stride is that the left hand is entirely concerned with striking single notes in the low register, either an octave or tenth, on the first and third beats of the 4/4 measure, plus a middle register chord on the second and fourth beats. Thus, all of the left arm is always in motion, traveling back and forth at least 13 inches. This momentum was pegged by someone as "striding." With the left hand furnishing the rhythm, the right hand can work on the melody in the treble—the entire range of the piano is used in this fully "orchestrated" music.

Increasingly sophisticated piano music began to work its way into bands. The larger clubs could afford a larger band, and many incorporated the piano. Quite often, the "piano player" was the leader, as was the case with Duke Ellington. Such "orchestrated" pianos led to more sophisticated arrangements for the band plus coloration for newer instruments such as the saxophone. The basic front line was doubled—with two trumpets, two trombones, two clarinets, and two saxophones. Material was specially written or borrowed from dance bands.

New Orleans and Chicago made their substantial contributions; New York put it all together for the "roaring twenties." But other areas also had jazz in diverse forms. Regional centers throughout the United States provided clubs and bars for local versions of ragtime and early jazz. During the 1920s and 1930s, different aggregations played big band jazz and served as training grounds for new performers, who would then make the trek to New York. And, of course, it was Kansas City and the Southwest that provided the big band riff and the elements of swing.

Literature

Besides the books and periodicals mentioned in the general literature survey of jazz, many specialized studies can be located through Gregor (45), Kennington (59), and Merriam (73). On New Orleans and its style, Williams (126) has a good overview. Blesh (6) analyzes performances, while Buerkle and Barker (11) and Rose (94) present fascinating historical data on Storyville and a sociological analysis of the early black jazzman. Two biographies of note: Lomax's (64) study of Jelly Roll Morton also examines the whole ramifications of influences and styles at the time, while Pops Foster's (36) autobiography looks at musicians' relationships and the studios. Hadlock (46) provides commentary on the 1920s in New York and Chicago, while Condon (20) reminisces about the white Chicago school. Schuller (105) discusses the roots and musical development of early jazz to 1932. *Storyville* (18) is the important jazz magazine that covers this whole period.

NEW ORLEANS

Anthologies

J3.1   **Jazz Odyssey: v. 1: New Orleans, 1917-1947.** three discs. Columbia C3L 30.

J3.2*   **New Orleans, v.1/5.** Folkways 2461/5.

J3.3*   **New Orleans, v.1/2.** two discs. RCA 741.107 and FPM 1-7003 (French issue).

J3.4   **New Orleans Jazz Men.** Saga 8011 (British issue).
    While the style of Dixieland has been exceptionally popular, providing the thrust behind Chicago jazz, the actual recordings of many bands from the twenties have never been successful in the hearts of jazz collectors, perhaps because of the sameness of the music: the equal instrumentation of the front line, countered with the simple marching of the rhythm. The Folkways set, volumes 4 and 5 in particular (dealing with the birth of jazz and New Orleans jazz), illuminates the many diverse styles and characteristics of the different bands, including society orchestras. The Columbia set is the weakest of the three (other Columbia sets concern Harlem and Chicago), despite its glorious texts, discography, notes, and photographs in the booklet. Columbia simply did not have the resources nor the catalog to draw on. What does remain are the 1917 Original Dixieland Jazz Band recording of "At the Darktown Strutters' Ball" (which is paradoxical, as the composer was Canadian, the band all white, and the recording done in New York), through various groups who took the *sound* of New Orleans such as Clarence Williams, Louis Armstrong, Wingy Manone, Noble Sissle, King Oliver, Jelly Roll Morton, Jimmy Noone, latter-day N.O.R.K. (New Orleans Rhythm Kings), and Sam Morgan.
    The Saga disc anthologizes three bands that took the N.O. revival to heart: Kid Ory, George Lewis, and Oscar "Papa" Celestin, from 1945 to 1953. This is the type of music favored by the fans today: revivalism, with a touch of "jazz," and clear recording sound. One of the earlier problems was, of course, the fact that N.O. and Dixieland music, like ragtime, had just about run its course by 1925; thus, few electrical recordings are by the original innovators, and few recordings exist at all.
    In the case of Buddy Bolden, a prime innovator, there are no recordings because he did his work before recording gained prominence. Often, recordings were thought of as a means for people to set down improvisations and then have them stolen by someone simply duplicating the passage at a later date. Many N.O. groups were highly suspicious of records, and this meant that the O.D.J.B. was the first to record "jazz," even though they were a white group. The RCA set is interesting in that it captures the feel of New Orleans through such diverse styles as A. J. Piron's group, the rag-infected style of Tony Parenti, and the blues of John Hyman—everything recorded 1923-1927. The second volume here presented the New Orleans Rhythm Kings, Louis Dumaine, Ann Cook, Geneviève Davis, and the Boswell Sisters (who were originally from New Orleans), and of course, a heavy

predominance of vocal music. [Note: To complete the picture of New Orleans music *in general*, please see the Ragtime section herein and the Rhythm 'n' Blues section in the *Black Music* volume.]

J3.5*   **New Orleans Jazz: The Twenties.** two discs (boxed). RBF 203 (distr. by Folkways).

This was compiled and edited by Sam Charters, with the usual erudite notes, texts, and discographies. New Orleans comes across in 28 reissued selections by various bands (usually playing only one tune each), among which are: Original Tuxedo Jazz Orchestra, Piron's New Orleans Orchestra, Original New Orleans Rhythm Kings, Fate Marable's Society Syncopators, Punch Miller, Papa Celestin, the Owls—truly *crème de la crème*. These working bands, often playing for high society but rarely outside of New Orleans, were accustomed to doing the likes of "Everybody Loves Somebody," "Dirty Rag," "Frankie and Johnny," "Maple Leaf Rag," "Creole Blues," "Meat on the Table," and "Panama." This is a superb collection that neatly identifies the trends that the music was taking and what was left behind as "jazz went up the river."

Innovators

J3.6*   **Freddie Keppard.** Herwin 101.

Keppard was the first New Orleans musician to take his music to the rest of the United States. He had established a great reputation before World War I, playing, for example, in New York with his Original Creole Orchestra in 1912 at the various vaudeville houses. He was also a loud cornet player, never using a mute and possessing iron lungs. The seventeen recordings here come from the early 1920s and highlight his solo ability with four groups: The Jazz Cardinals, Jimmy Blythe and His Ragmuffins, Jasper Taylor and His State Street Boys, and the Cookie Gingersnaps. "Stockyard Strut" is a march from New Orleans; "Salty Dog" is a good blues performance. On two numbers, he has good solos and interplays with clarinetist Johnny Dodds: "Messin' Around" and "Adams Apple." The sound has been superbly remastered, and there are good, extensive notes.

J3.7*   **King Oliver. The Great 1923 Gennetts.** Herwin 106.

Here are 13 of the tracks that preceded the 1923 Paramount sessions, and all include Louis Armstrong (second cornet), Honore Dutrey (trombone), Johnny Dodds (clarinet), Lil Hardin—later Louis's wife—(piano), "Baby" Dodds (drums), and Bill Johnson, or Johnny St. Oyr (banjo). This was authentic black New Orleans music, in this instance recorded at Richmond, Indiana, a short hop from Chicago where Oliver was playing. Later, the band was to become one of Louis's Hot Fives and Sevens. If there is a star here, it is the woody, emotional sound of Dodds's clarinet (heard effectively on solos in "Canal Street Blues," "Mandy Lee Blues," and "Dipper Mouth Blues"). Oliver has been restrained as a soloist, but his best spots are on "Dipper Mouth Blues" and "Working Man Blues." Armstrong shines on "Chimes Blues" and "Froggie Moore." These acoustic recordings have been remastered as well as possible on today's equipment, but they are still a little rough.

At this time, Oliver had created the Creole Jazz Band (Armstrong joined in late 1922) and worked around the combination of *two* cornets plus the exciting Dodds brothers—Jimmy on clarinet with perfect shading and "Baby" Warren on swinging drums. By using pails, glasses, and rubber plungers to get sounds from his cornet, Oliver developed the plunger mute, which was to significantly alter the course of jazz through Bubber Miley. Despite being an innovator on cornet and a good bandleader, Oliver's music declined in the middle twenties, providing fragments of shapes and no real directions, but a minor comeback for Victor in 1929 had some commercial success with pop tunes. Sadly, these latter recordings are very uneven and old-fashioned, even for that time period.

Standards

J3.8   **Eureka Brass Band. Jazz at Preservation Hall, v. 1.** Atlantic S 1408.
This brass band—so characteristic of the New Orleans development—was led by Percy Humphrey (trumpeter) and his brother Willie on the clarinet. Typical tunes assembled included "Whoopin' Blues," "Panama," "Joe Avery's Blues," and "Down in Honky Tonk Town." This disc is a good representative sample of a New Orleans band in stereo, during a live performance by second generation musicians who were still in touch with the past.

J3.9   **Bunk Johnson.** Storyville SLP 152 (Danish issue).

J3.10*   **Bunk Johnson. Superior Jazz Band.** Good Time Jazz 12048.
Bunk Johnson was the second cornet in the last Buddy Bolden band; thus, he was a direct link to perhaps the finest New Orleans ensemble that existed (but unfortunately never recorded). The revival of New Orleans music in the 1940s led to his rediscovery, and the revival steamrollered onwards (assisted by the violent negative reaction to bop music). Johnson was first recorded in 1943. The Storyville reissue comes from the American Music discs of 1944 and includes the exhilarating "See See Rider" plus numerous conversations. His storytelling, while interesting, was directly responsible for many myths and legends of New Orleans, as his mind tended to wander and he made up stories and garbled others. The Good Time Jazz record is a better-produced item, clearly showing his good ensemble work (where he passes the lead very subtlely) and giving more credence to the development of New Orleans as *ensemble* music, and not just three soloists in the front line (as was Dixieland). Selections here include "Make Me a Pallet on the Floor," "Panama," "Down By the Riverside," and "Balling the Jack."

J3.11   **George Lewis. v.1.** Blue Note BLP 1205.

J3.12*   **George Lewis. Doctor Jazz.** Delmark 202.

J3.13   **George Lewis. In New Orleans.** Storyville 671.127. (Danish issue).

J3.14*   **George Lewis. Memorial Album.** Delmark 203.

J3.15   **George Lewis. On Parade.** Delmark 201.

Clarinetist George Lewis was perhaps the best and most consistent Dixie-lander to record (until his death in 1968). Through his European travels, he became a very heavy influence on the British traditional jazz; similarly, he influenced patterns in Japan as well. In 1941, he came up with Bunk Johnson, and together they were directly responsible for the revival in the 1940s, occasionally called "West Coast Revival" or "Yerba Buena," after the Lu Watters band. In any case, Lewis was responsible for at least three different revivals of Dixieland music. He had a simple blues style, utilizing both the upper and lower register of the clarinet, and employed a little bit of swing occasionally. In 1943, he began to record under his own name. The Danish Storyville reissue includes 10 tracks from 1944-1945, formerly on the Master label. With Kid Shots Madison, Jim Robinson, and Baby Dodds in the band, Lewis set the pattern for the rest of his life: 1/2 blues (such as "Bucket's Got a Hole in It," with moving solo work) and 1/2 religious marches (such as "Old Rugged Cross," "Glory Land," and "Lead Me Savior").

The next highlight in his recording career was for Antone Records in 1953. With Kid Howard (trumpet), Jim Robinson (trombone), Alton Purnell (piano), and Joe Watkins (drums and vocals), Lewis had assembled perhaps the best Dixie-land band to ever leave New Orleans. These have been reissued on the Delmark label and contain careful contributions to the musical scene, maintaining the religious-secular balance. Delmark 201 is mainly marches and spirituals, including "Just a Closer Walk with Thee," "Down By the Riverside," and "Just a Little While to Stay Here." The 202 offering is spirited with "Doctor Jazz," "Mama Don't Allow It," "High Society," and "Ice Cream." The *Memorial Album* contains the slow blues of Lewis, as on "Careless Love," "Tin Roof Blues," and "Dippermouth Blues." These are all extended pieces, totaling 20 tracks on three discs. The Blue Note collection from 1955 adds further items to the repertoire, including the important "Lord, Lord You Sure Been Good to Me." These five discs contain virtually all of the selections that Lewis was to play at concerts outside of New Orleans.

J3.16   **Billie and DeDe Pierce. New Orleans Music.** Arhoolie 2016.

Billie and DeDe are a good team for these 12 selections. DeDe has apparently been influenced by the legendary Chris Kelly, and thus provides good backing for Billie's vocals. His own voice is light but rough, and he appears on "Eh, La-Bas" and "Peanut Vendor" singing in Creole French. Billie is a rough-and-ready pianist who once worked with Bessie Smith (hence, the Bessie-type renditions of "Gulf Coast Blues" and "Nobody Knows You When You're Down and Out"), Buddy Petit, Picou, and George Lewis. "Jelly Roll" features her singing the lyrics of the great Butterbeans and Susie to the music of Jelly Roll Morton. There is an excellent washboard rhythm on "Mama Don't 'Low," a sort of combination of tap dancing and drumming.

NEW ORLEANS INFLUENCES

Innovators

J3.17*   **Louis Armstrong. Very Special Old Phonography.** eight discs. CBS 88001/4 (French Issue).

Louis Armstrong has been written about more than any other jazzman except for Duke Ellington, and most of that concerned his "classic" recordings for OKeh, all of which (under his own name) may be found on this CBS set. Others are available in various collections, such as *Rare Blues Singers of the Twenties*, a four-volume set from CBS (annotated in the Blues section of *Black Music*), or with King Oliver and Clarence Williams. These recordings have been analyzed so often throughout the 40 years of jazz criticism that it would be pointless to even present a summary here. Some random thoughts, however, might be that Louis's melodic lines represented new discoveries about alternative chord progressions in these tunes (and this predated the bop movement). He led jazz out of the New Orleans-Dixieland period into the "hot" jazz era. Even the names of his groups reflected this: the Hot Five and Hot Seven. He made several significant contributions to the vocabulary of jazz, and, of course, *every* trumpet player began to imitate him and assimilate his musical characteristics. Technically, many of his solos were difficult to emulate, as on "Struttin' with Some Barbecue," because he was so brilliant and advanced. His affectations—rips, tears, vibratos, half-valve effects, bent notes up and down, etc.— were (and still are) very difficult to duplicate. His vocals were models of the day, with a not displeasing voice that injected humor into almost anything. Louis could not sing a sad song. Some important selections include "Gilt Bucket Blues," "Cornet Chop Suey," "Muskrat Ramble," "Weary Blues," "A Monday Date," "West End Blues," "Sugarfoot Stomp," "Square Me," "Basin Street Blues," "Weather Bird," "St. Louis Blues," "Tiger Rag," "Shine," and "When It's Sleepy Time Down South." Diverse personnel over the years included Kid Ory, Johnny Dodds, Baby Dodds, Jimmie Noone, Zutty Singleton, Don Redman, Jack Teagarden, Henry Allen, et al. Perhaps his best association was with pianist Earl Hines (as on "Weather Bird"). This exceptionally innovative musician chased Louis on to greater heights, which resulted in many superb performances. The total number of tracks here is 127.

J3.18   **Sidney Bechet. Master Musician.** two discs. RCA AXM 2-6516.

J3.19*   **Sidney Bechet. Concert à l'Exposition Universelle de Bruxelles, 1958.** Vogue SB1 (French issue).

J3.20*   **Sidney Bechet. Jazz Classics, v.1/2.** two discs. Blue Note BST 81201/2.

J3.21   **Sidney Bechet and "Mezz" Mezzrow. King Jazz Story, v.1/5.** five discs. Storyville SLP 136/7, 141/2, and 153. (Danish issue).
Bechet was the first true jazz improviser who played consistently. His style was organized and projected by 1924, when he made his first records with Clarence Williams. Originally a clarinetist, he later dominated the soprano saxophone. His was a highly personalized development of New Orleans jazz, and he was equally famous abroad and at home. The soprano sax, of which he was a master, clearly showed his vibrant emotional power and sinuosity. Some of his earliest recordings under his own name are on the RCA discs. On the clarinet, he fashioned definitive trios before Goodman even thought of them, such as "Blues in Thirds," with Earl Hines on piano and Baby Dodds on drums, where there was early use of counterpoint between the clarinet and the piano. Some of his material here was definitely characterized as violent or threatening, such as "Shag," "Lay Your Rocket," "Maple Leaf Rag" or "Ain't Misbehavin' ." This would later turn into harsh, over-powering

statements of reality, such as on the Brussells disc. Accompanied by Buck Clayton, Vic Dickenson, George Wein and Arvell Shaw—almost as a "Newport in Europe"— Bechet turns in virtually nasty performances of "Indiana" and "Swanee River," as if he was vitriolic towards America; the most stunning of all is "In a Sentimental Mood," where his dirtiness is teamed with the almost copyrighted obscene growl of Dickenson's trombone. Between these two periods, there was a succession of American and foreign records (mostly the latter). The best were done for Blue Note and King Jazz.

The Blue Note discs developed when Bechet came out of semi-retirement in 1939 to perform his conception of "Summertime." The sensuous nature of this song as played on soprano sax has since become one of the few real classics of jazz. Another such trio item was "Blue Horizon," performed on the clarinet. Up to 1951, Bechet recorded for Blue Note off and on, and the best are pulled together here, support coming from Vic Dickenson, Pops Foster, Art Hodes, Meade Lux Lewis, and others. All reveal a certain lyricism that indicated Bechet was happy. When temperamental or sick, though, his playing was nasty. In 1945, he recorded four Blue Note tracks with Bunk Johnson, the leader of the New Orleans revivalists, and these utilized completely different approaches and attacks.

King Jazz was Mezz Mezzrow's label from 1945-1947. This clarinetist had received little critical acclaim, yet his sidemen were always of the highest calibre: Hot Lips Page, Pops Foster, Sammy Price, Baby Dodds, Sid Catlett, and, of course, Bechet. They recorded both as a septet and as a quintet, emphasizing largely the blues repertoire and standards. These were the best of Bechet's small label recordings, and include "Really the Blues," "Minor Snow," "Sheik of Araby," "Gone Away Blues," and the emotional climaxes of "Out of the Gallion."

J3.22*   **Johnny Dodds**. RCA Vintage LPV 558.

J3.23   **Johnny Dodds. Clarinet King**. Ace of Hearts AH 169 (British issue).

J3.24*   **Johnny Dodds and Kid Ory**. Epic LN 24269 (French issue).
Dodds's clarinet music is characterized by an aggressiveness that was almost unknown among the New Orleans school. His style was directly opposite that of the lyrical Jimmie Noone. In 1923, he recorded with King Oliver's Creole Jazz Band (q.v.), and later, he made good solos and ensembles with Armstrong. His greatest work was with the blues and he made numerous records with his Black Bottom Stompers, Lovie Austin, and washboard bands. The RCA album covers 1926-1929, with marvelous trio versions of "Indigo Stomp," "Blue Clarinet Stomp," and "Blue Piano Stomp." Musicians around this time included various jug performers and washboard experts, as well as the New Orleans front line. The Ace of Hearts set, from 1927-1929, shows him in a more relaxed vein, even humorous, as in "Oh Lizzie" or "When Erastus Plays His Old Kazoo." Definitely, his style tended to lean lines, with a broad, full tone, strong vibrato, and sharp attack. Having little ornamentation, he was carefully listened to by Benny Goodman, Pee Wee Russell, Frank Teschemacher, and others of the so-called "Chicago" school. Despite his death in 1940, his music was recalled by the New Orleans revival, and his records were played over and over again. Together with Jimmie Noone, he fashioned the jazz clarinet. The Epic reissue covers a similar period, 1926-1928, but with a more interesting line-up. With George Mitchell on trumpet, this was basically the Louis

Armstrong Hot Five without Louis Armstrong—and it appeared to be a little more relaxed. Just hear "Gate Mouth," "Too Tight Blues," "I Can't Say," "Mad Dog," or "Perdido Street Blues." Certainly his best low register work was on the 1927 septet's outing, "Come On and Stomp, Stomp, Stomp."

J3.25*   **Jelly Roll Morton. v.1/8.** eight discs. RCA 730.549/605; 731.059, 741.040/054/070/081/087. (French issue).

J3.26*   **Jelly Roll Morton. King of New Orleans Jazz.** RCA LPM 1649.

J3.27*   **Jelly Roll Morton. Library of Congress Recordings.** nine discs. Classic Jazz Masters. CJM 2/10 (Swedish issue).

J3.28   **Jelly Roll Morton. New Orleans Memories and Last Band Dates.** two discs. Atlantic SD 2-308.

Morton's talents lay in three distinct fields: composing, organizing and arranging, and playing the piano. His earlier work was annotated previously. The records here must be thought of as an extension of predetermined patterns. With his Red Hot Peppers of 1926-1928, he may have produced the greatest music in all of jazz. These were items of solo and creative improvisation, in a New Orleans creative period similar to that of King Oliver and Sidney Bechet. The RCA LPM 1649 set adequately covers this period, with ten items from 1926 such as "Black Bottom Stomp," "The Chant," "Steamboat Stomp," and "Doctor Jazz." Other fertile selections include "Jelly Roll Blues," "Grandpa's Spells," "Sidewalk Blues," "Deadman Blues," and "Wildman Blues." The organizational character of all of this music was superb (many were revised versions of earlier recordings or of solo piano works). There was complete solo and ensemble integration; masterful timing for the riffs and breaks, stop time, call and response patterns; and much harmony and polyphony. Some of his great sidemen of this period included clarinetist Omer Simeon, trombonist Greechy Fields, and trumpeter George Mitchell.

All of their RCA material may be found on the French Black and White imports. There are 123 tracks here, which include important alternate takes, his 1929 piano solos and trios, and some air checks. The period is mainly 1926-1932, with some after 1938 until his death in 1942. These later recordings (including the Atlantic set) all came about from his "rediscovery" through the Library of Congress recordings. Classic Jazz Masters has done a superb job in cleaning up the sound. These 1938 sessions are a gold mine about early jazz, even discounting Morton's ability to pad his life. Alan Lomax asked Morton questions, and Morton answered about himself, others, and jazz in general. Of course, he also played and sang. Included in the repertoire are "Mr. Jelly Lord," "Alabama Bound," "Aaron Harris," "Buddy Bolden," "See See Rider," "Kansas City Stomps," and so forth. His piano style had not deteriorated through the years, and it included elements of ragtime, stride, and "Spanish tinge," which Morton claimed was New Orleans style (thus he plays the "Maple Leaf Rag" in two fashions—New Orleans style and St. Louis style). The ten 1939 piano solos were done for Commodore as a follow-up to the LC sessions. These are on the Atlantic twofer, and despite his failing health, they include an excellent "Mamie's Blues" and "Michigan Water Blues." The twelve 1940 band sides are quite similar to the later RCA recordings (with Sidney Bechet). These were done on request for a commercial venture, and contain a great deal of pop material and vocals. Featured in this latter half are Red Allen, Albert Nicholas, and Zatty Singleton. This was his last great effort and Morton was pushing himself to lay down as many tracks as possible before he died.

J3.29   **Jimmie Noone.** International Association of Jazz Record Collectors No. 18.

J3.30*   **Jimmie Noone. At the Apex Club, 1928, v.1.** MCA Decca DL 79235.

J3.31*   **Jimmie Noone. Chicago Rhythm, 1928-1930, v.2.** MCA 510.110 (French issue).

J3.32*   **Jimmie Noone and Kid Ory.** Folklyric 9008.

Jimmie Noone was considered the very best of all the clarinet players in the 1920s. His New Orleans clarinet was a strong influence on Benny Goodman, Omer Simeon, Darnell Howard, Jimmy Dorsey, and Irving Fazola. A technician of the highest skills, with a great tone and trills in solo work, Noone had unique phrasing and control over all the registers. Like Louis Armstrong, he could build a solo in an architectural sense, with complete unity. Unfortunately, he was not too well represented on disc. His best overall period was undoubtedly 1928, when he performed at the Apex Club in Chicago. Earl Hines was his pianist and Joe Poston, his altoist. Several alternate takes are presented here (with some more on the French MCA disc) to explore the diversity of the solo work. "I Know That You Know" and "Four or Five Times" are strong in a cohesive sense, with Noone contrasting solos with Hines. Both are at ease. "Sweet Lorraine" is a masterpiece of interpretation. At this time, Noone was doing some high-level experimenting that would have profound effects in the jazz world. The instrumentation here was a quintet. To expand the sound, he had the reeds *and* piano play in unison; he encouraged instruments to drop in and out of the melody at will to create shifting textures and new shades of development. Fifteen of the sixteen tracks on the French MCA are without Hines, but the same logical development occurs. The IAJRC record, for collectors, presents more alternate takes from this period, as well as four tracks from 1934 and 1940. Noone got passed by in the Depression, but resurged briefly before his death by appearing on Orson Welles's radio jazz program in 1944, the one that began the Dixieland revival. Air checks are on the Folklyric album, with co-leader Kid Ory. Apart from "Jimmie's Blues," the material is of the traditional New Orleans type, and, while worthwhile in itself, it is not Jimmie Noone in the sense of the 1920s' architect.

Standards

J3.33*   **Henry "Red" Allen. v.1/3, 1929.** three discs. RCA FXM1-7060, 7090, 7192 (French issue). In progress.

Allen was a trumpet master, somewhat affected by Louis Armstrong but developing an intensely rhythmic style that strayed away from what Louis was doing. He performed with King Oliver in 1927, and then made a series of recordings with Luis Russell's outfit (all will be on the RCA Black and White series). These sets reveal that his rhythmic flexibility increased as time progressed; the recordings on these compilations will go through 1957. Improvisation became a dominating technique for him. His early recordings with Russell show that almost every solo he did was outstanding: "Swing Out," "Patrol Wagon Blues," and "Feelin' Drowsy." Throughout his long career, he recorded with several blues singers (blowing the obbligatos behind their vocals) and studio units, such as King Oliver, Jelly Roll Morton, Fletcher Henderson, Spike Hughes, and Sidney Bechet. (References to these are all found under the relevant jazzman's name in this book.) In the late forties, and for about a decade, he made many more recordings under his own name, including the brilliant 1957 rendition of "I Cover the Waterfront" (making effective use of controlled dynamics).

J3.34   **Louis Armstrong. At the Crescendo.** two discs. MCA 2-4013.

J3.35   **Louis Armstrong. At Symphony Hall.** two discs. MCA 2-4057.

J3.36   **Louis Armstrong. Plays W. C. Handy.** Columbia JCL 591.

J3.37   **Louis Armstrong. Satchmo: A Musical Autobiography.** four discs. MCA DX155.

J3.38*   **Louis Armstrong. Town Hall Concert, 1947.** two discs. RCA 731. 051/2. (French issue).
On October 6, 1946, Louis Armstrong recorded for Victor with a pick-up Hot Seven consisting of (among others) Vic Dickenson, Barney Bigard, and Zutty Singleton. Louis was back in his small group element, seeking improvisation, staccato, and legato devices. This was a step closer—or backwards—to New Orleans, influenced by the success of the revival music. The movie *New Orleans* aided his career and inspired several more studio recordings. He soon formed the "All Stars," a group that he would retain for over 20 years. His various concerts (such as at the Metropolitan Opera House in 1944; see item J1.19) helped to sway the decision to get Louis into the stimulating small group set-up. The May 1947 Town Hall concert has long been recognized as a classic. Jack Teagarden joins Armstrong for "Rockin' Chair," "Ain't Misbehavin'," "Pennies from Heaven," "St. James Infirmary," and others. This was followed by the November Symphony Hall concert in Boston, with virtually the same group, performing "Muskrat Ramble," "Royal Garden Blues," "How High the Moon," and so forth. The All Stars quickly became a vehicle for virtuoso jazz soloists, such as Teagarden's trombone, Hines's piano, Bigard's clarinet, and Catlett's drums. Combining musical sophistication, energy, and music drawn from the blues, the All Stars were undoubtedly one of the most important and influential groups of the forties and fifties. During these two decades, they performed about 300 nights a year, with few holidays, and with the same songs in 1967 as in 1947. Differing sidemen made for different solos at times, and since the repertoire did not change that much, studio recordings were reserved for special projects, such as the W. C. Handy salute. This virtuoso performance ranks with the very best of Armstrong. All the Handy blues are here—St. Louis, Yellow Dog, Aunt Hagor's, Memphis, Beale Street, etc. Armstrong gives virtually perfect readings on this occasion. Other salutes, such as to Fats Waller, were almost as good. The 1955 Crescendo Concert shows the All Stars almost a decade after their formation but with some new material added to their repertoire (e.g.,

"Perdido," "Don't Fence Me In," "Bucket's Got a Hole in It," etc.). Bigard at this point is about midway down his sliding career, but Louis carries him forward; Edmund Hall replaced him later in the year. Then, Louis made a four-album autobiographical set, re-recording new interpretations of most of his 1923-1934 successes, with arrangements by Bob Haggart and Sy Oliver. Armstrong introduces each selection with a few words commenting on the circumstances behind the original work. Also, there are a few cuts from previous All Star concerts. He reaches new heights with this set, proving immensely flexible when called upon to deal with the ensemble passages. These discs—recorded in great sound—do indeed capture his career's progress from Dixie, blues, stomps through the popular songs of Eubie Blake, Fats Waller, Harold Arlen, Hoagy Carmichael, and Jimmy McHugh.

J3.39   **Barney Bigard and Art Hodes. Bucket's Got a Hole in It.** Delmark DS 211.
      Bigard, discussed also in entry J4.132, was one of the great New Orleans clarinet players; Art Hodes was a stride pianist who has recorded for a variety of labels, both large and small, generally all featuring a clarinet player. This coupling shows that Bigard had lost none of his power and indeed had been spurred on to greater low register playing by the prodding piano and trombone of Georg Brunis (originally with the New Orleans Rhythm Kings). Standards reproduced here include "Tin Roof Blues," "Sweet Lorraine," and "Makin' Whoopee."

J3.40   **Albert Nicholas.** Delmark DL 207.

J3.41   **Albert Nicholas. With Art Hodes' All Star Stompers.** Delmark DL 209.
      Nicholas is firmly in the New Orleans mould as far as clarinet players go. He had performed with Jelly Roll Morton in the 1920s and with Luis Russell, Sidney Bechet, and James P. Johnson. Influenced by Jimmie Noone, he extended the round tones and group thought for absolutely rich solos within the band context. His earlier work, mainly with Harlem and New York bands, is described elsewhere under the band concerned. Since 1953, Nicholas has lived and recorded in Paris, but, in 1959, he returned to the United States and made the Delmark 207 album. By this time, he had been modified somewhat by the swing school of riffs, and he thus forms a bridge between New Orleans and "swing music." The quartet (with Art Hodes on piano) performs such items as "Rosetta," "Lover Come Back to Me," and "I'm Comin' Virginia"—all in the lyrical mode. The Stompers' album is a mixture of blues and Dixieland, again with the swing influence through Marty Grosz on rhythm guitar and Art Hodes on piano: "Lulu's Back in Town," "How Long Blues," "Creole Love Call," and "Runnin' Wild."

J3.42*   **Kid Ory. 1954.** Good Time Jazz L 12004.

J3.43   **Kid Ory. 1955.** Good Time Jazz L 12008.

J3.44   **Kid Ory. 1956.** Good Time Jazz L 12016.

J3.45   **Kid Ory. Favorites!** two discs. Good Time Jazz M 12041/2.

J3.46*   **Kid Ory. Tailgate!** Good Time Jazz L 12022.

J3.47   **Kid Ory. This Kid's the Greatest!** Good Time Jazz M 12045.

Kid Ory was the first recorded black artist in jazz. His Sunshine Orchestra recorded in 1921, but for a regional label. Thus, it got poor distribution. His major accomplishment was longevity: he created many good bands in New Orleans, introduced the new stars of jazz, and joined the Dixieland revival on several occasions, retiring to Hawaii until he died in 1974. Long before recordings came into existence, he led bands comprised of Johnny Dodds, Jimmie Noone, King Oliver, and Louis Armstrong. He was a *compère* of Buddy Bolden and Freddie Keppard. But it was not until 1919 that he left New Orleans for California and then for Chicago in 1925. For the next three years, he was trombonist for King Oliver, Jelly Roll Morton, and Louis Armstrong, and he can be heard on their records (listed with their own annotations).

He was musically inactive until 1944, when he made recordings under his own name. This comeback was a direct result of the Orson Welles radio series that revived Dixieland in the midst of war. These efforts are on the *Tailgate!* album, with trumpeter Mutt Carey, clarinetist Omer Simeon or Darnell Howard, and the great New Orleans drummer Minor Hall. Included also are tracks from 1945. Playing around the Los Angeles area in the following years, Ory again returned to the studio for the balance of the Good Time Jazz albums, from 1953 to 1956. This was his second most prolific period (the first being 1925-1928), and with Don Ewell, Ed Garland, Alvin Acorn, and others, he recorded virtually the entire Dixieland-New Orleans repertoire with few duplications ("High Society," "South," "Panama," "Careless Love," "Maryland, My Maryland," "1919 Rag," "Oh, Didn't He Ramble," "Bugle Call Rag," etc.). Hall's drumming makes this all a consistent corpus of great Dixieland music from the man who "invented" the tailgate trombone. Other great Ory records with co-leaders include Johnny Dodds (Epic LN 24269), Red Allen (Polydor 2682 006), and Jimmie Noone (Folklyric 9008).

J3.48   **Jabbo Smith. The Trumpet Ace of the Twenties.** two discs. Melodeon MLP 7326/7.

Jabbo Smith played trumpet in several good New York bands during the late 1920s. In 1929, he was asked by Brunswick to record some small unit numbers as competition to OKeh's Louis Armstrong. Within six months, 20 items were recorded (all are on this double album set), but then the project was dropped. Twelve other tunes here come from varying ensembles that Smith was in (but some of these are suspect). Influenced by Armstrong (as was every trumpeter from the 1920s), Smith, though, was not content to just emulate "the master." He had to exceed him. In a rare burst of thought and ideas, he may just have done so. The Rhythm Aces (the quartet that accompanied him) was a drummer-less unit. Unique for this period, the percussion was carried by piano, banjo, and bass. The major melodies were carried off by the trumpet and clarinet, in most cases, the latter coming from Omer Simeon. Simeon was at a high point in his career: he had just returned to Chicago from the Jelly Roll Morton band to join Earl Hines's new band (and was ostensibly a replacement for clarinetist Jimmie Noone). Simeon was highly influenced by the orchestral organization that Morton presented through his arranged music. Together with Jabbo Smith, they created small masterpieces in "Sleepy Time Blues," where Smith takes darting phrases and introduces scat vocal choruses, and in "Decatur Street Tutti," where much use is made of bent notes. Smith produced advanced jazz solos for the day: multi-noted attacks, melodic twists, and awkward intervals. He was definitely ahead of his time in these recordings, which perhaps explains why the public never bought them. But musicians did, and they learned. Smith could have fit into the bop period if it had been 1939 and not 1929. Other tunes—all of them, surprisingly, expressly written for the sessions—include "Jazz Battle" and "I Got the Stinger."

J3.49   **Clarence Williams. 1927/29. v.1/2.** two discs. Biograph 12006, 12038.

J3.50*   **Clarence Williams Blue Five. With Louis Armstrong and Sidney Bechet.** CBS 63092. (French issue).
Clarence Williams was an arranger and producer with OKeh Records. During his long recording history, he did work for and played with, among others, Louis Armstrong and Bessie Smith. The personnel for the groups under his own name were much like a house band, as he had direct access to all the performers under contract with OKeh. As a composer, he worked mainly in the blues idiom, and some of those works are available on these three discs: "Just Wait Till You See," "Kansas City Man Blues," "Wild Cat Blues," and others. This CBS record, with 16 selections, is a milestone in the history of jazz for at least two reasons. First, this is the recording debut for Louis Armstrong on *lead* cornet, and it revealed his aristocratic elegance and perfect sense of timing. The impact cannot be underestimated. Second, this is the recording debut of Sidney Bechet. Although he had done much playing since 1908, his travels to Europe (where he would eventually retire) precluded his presence in the studio until this date (1923). Credit must be given to Williams for bringing these two geniuses together; jazz would not see a similar pairing until twenty years later with Parker and Gillespie. Eva Taylor, Williams's wife, provided the vocals on the blues numbers. This is superb sound in view of the fact that some of these are acoustical recordings.
Williams's forte was in two areas: writing and arranging. He was able to make a small band sound much larger by scoring the trombone part to assist *both* the brass and the reeds, and by combining the low-register cornet with the saxophone (thus emulating a complete sax section). Everyone played all the breaks on a Clarence Williams record, and the musicians included virtually everyone who played in New York City at the time. Williams had no regular band, and relied on sidemen (usually from the Henderson band) such as Urbie Green, Don Redman, Tommy Ladnier, Coleman Hawkins and Buster Bailey. Coupled with the Blue Five and the bands were the washboard "good-time" ensembles, often with Williams's scat vocals, and the jug bands. From all of this resulted such items as "Pane in the Glass," "Shut Your Mouth," "Jingles," "Sister Kate," and "Midnight Stomp." These are all on the Biograph collections, and further prove his versatility by the unique combination of instruments, such as two clarinets plus rhythm, or a cornet and tuba duet.

DIXIELAND AND THE REVIVAL

Innovators

J3.51*   **Original Dixieland Jazz Band.** two discs. RCA 730.703/4. (French issue).

J3.52*   **Original Dixieland Jazz Band. London Recordings, 1919-1920.** World
Record Club SH 220 (British issue).

The ODJB—as it became known—made the first authentic jazz recordings in
New York City in 1917. Yet they were a white group. Some black groups and performers were approached before this time to record, but they did not want anyone
to steal their "hot" solo secrets by playing the records and then memorizing the
sequences. Thus, Bolden and Keppard were shut out before the 1920s. After that
time, it no longer made any difference. There was some musical integration later as
light-skinned blacks and Creoles passed as white bands. Thus, as here with the
ODJB, there were few blues, and those that were recorded were generally regarded
as inferior to other recordings because of the lack of feeling. The leader of the
ODJB was Nick LaRocca, who became an influence on Beiderbecke and others.
Yet the shining light of the group was simply the ensemble playing. This was never
equalled in Dixieland (it was not intended to in New Orleans music, as the front
line played in different patterns; that was one of the characteristics of New Orleans
music: unique lines by the soloists). Perfection existed with LaRocca (cornet),
Eddie Edwards (trombone), and the most creative Larry Shields (clarinet). Blending ragtime, dance music, and marches, the ODJB set the definitive pattern for jazz
for the next 20 years (until bop). From 1917, there is "Tiger Rag," "Lazy Daddy,"
"Sensation Rag," and "Livery Stable Blues"—all virtually ODJB compositions.
There are 29 recordings on the double French RCA set, and these include some 1920
tracks with a terrible saxophone added, and some later recordings from 1936 in
which the ODJB re-recorded their earlier hits. Needless to say, there is better sound
in this later work, and the close arrangements can be studied much more easily.
The seventeen 1919-1920 tracks from London, England, are particularly instructive,
for the sound is top-notch (in view of the recording equipment of the time) and new
titles are presented such as "Sundown," "Ostrich Walk," and "Satanic Blues."

Standards

J3.53*   **Bix Beiderbecke and the Chicago Cornets.** two discs. Milestone M
47019.

Bix's legend has grown with jazz, but too few have actually heard what this
remarkable musician did. These tracks from his earliest recordings exemplify his
gift for melodic improvisation. The Wolverines tracks are from 1924, as are the
items by Bix and His Rhythm Jugglers. The Gennett label's sound was certainly
not the best in the world, but with historical acoustic recordings that is something
the listener has to live with. Bix was only 20 when he made these recordings, and
several of his solos—most notably on "Oh! Baby," "Jazz Me Blues," "Riverboat
Shuffle," and "Toddlin' Blues"—show that he had already stepped out as an
individualist. His tone was crystal clear, his phrasing was on a legato basis (ensuring
a clean, flowing phrasing unusual for the time), and, perhaps most important of
all, he based his improvisation on the harmony rather than the melody of the tune.
Technically, he was not great (his range was limited), but he made up for all this
with a pure tone and an intense lyricism that were to be greatly influential on
succeeding cornet and trumpet players. Nineteen tracks here concern the early Bix;
the other nine feature two with Jimmy McPartland as lead, and a Muggsy Spanier

group–the Bucktown Five, again all from 1924. This is a superb set of classic jazz, especially, of course, the Bix items.

J3.54*   **Bob Crosby. Best.** two discs. MCA2- 4083.

J3.55   **Bob Crosby. Stomp Off, Let's Go!** Ace of Hearts AH 29 (British issue).
The orchestra was formed shortly after the 1934 break-up of the Ben Pollack group. It began as a cooperative in which all the musicians shared the proceeds; but it needed a front man, or star, to handle the announcements and make the group a name. Bob Crosby was available. The heyday of the group was 1937 through 1942, and it specialized in orchestrated Dixieland music. It was an exciting rhythmic band, devoted to the two-beat style of jazz and kicked along by New Orleans born-drummer Ray Bauduc. Yet, they were carried in the swing craze, primarily because it was a big band and because it offered a gutsier alternative to the soaring swing of the other white bands. The more important members of the group were able to keep going in different configurations after the 1943 dissolution.
Bauduc was strongly influenced by Baby Dodds and Zutty Singleton; Nappy Lamare was a superb guitarist and vocalist; Matty Matlock was a clarinet player of repute and an equally good arranger; Eddie Miller was a highly melodic tenor saxist, somewhat influenced by the Chicago brand of Dixie. These man stayed throughout the life of the band. Others included Bob Haggart (bass), Yank Lawson and Billy Butterfield (trumpets), and Irving Fazola (clarinet). The 32 selections here are mainly from the Orchestra, and feature the more enduring items, such as "South Rampart Street Parade," "Dogtown Blues," "What's New?," "Panama," and "I'm Free." Of particular interest are a few boogie woogie piano tunes that were orchestrated: Lewis's "Honky Tonk Train Blues," "Boogie Woogie Maxine," "Gin Mill Blues," "Little Rock Getaway," and "Yancey Special." Included also is "Summertime," the band's theme. This is a reminder that Crosby's band was also a commercial outfit that featured his vocals on many occasions, although this is not easily remembered today as there are no reissues of his "sweet" music.

J3.56*   **Bob Crosby's Bob Cats. v.1/2, 1937-1942.** two discs. Swaggie S1245 and S1288 (Australian issues).
Crosby's band-within-a-band was entitled the Bob Cats. It was usually an octet that rendered such typical Dixie performances as "Can't We Be Friends," "Tin Roof Blues," and "Mournin' Blues." Personnel varied depending on who was in the band, but the leading soloists have been Yank Lawson, Eddie Miller, Bob Zurke (piano), Irving Fazola, Matty Matlock, with a rock-steady rhythm by Bob Zurke, Jess Stacy, Bob Haggart, Nappy Lamare, and the drummer Ray Bauduc. Most had been born, raised, or instructed in New Orleans music, and Chicago jazzmen would join also. Early recordings, from 1935, were made under the pseudonym Mound City Blue Blowers. A number of solo features were also recorded, such as Eddie Miller on "Slow Mood," Bob Zurke on "Big Foot Stomp," and several novelty items, such as the unusual "Big Noise from Winnetka" performed by bassist Haggart and drummer Bauduc as a duo. The 32 selections here are firmly in the Dixieland mould for the most part, and many years later, Haggart and Lawson, along with some others who played for Bob Crosby, would form the World's Greatest Jazz Band, utilizing many of these arrangements.

J3.57*   **New Orleans Rhythm Kings.** two discs. Milestone M 47020.
The New Orleans Rhythm Kings was one of the earliest, most influential bands in jazz history. Their classic recordings from 1923 are collected here and offer some of the most inventive melodic improvisation of the whole classical jazz era. These recordings also include Jelly Roll Morton on six sides, examples of the first interracial collaboration in jazz history. In these versions, he alternates playing with harmony, unison, and often polyphony, yet can maintain his momentum to leave room for solo passages. This is to be noted on the classic "London Blues." The Kings were deep in the New Orleans tradition, mainly because of the inspired lead of Paul Mares, heavily influenced by King Oliver, the ensemble sense of Georg Brunis (on trombone), and the sterling performances by clarinetist Leon Rapollo. This excellent front line turned in some good performances, especially on "Milenberg Joys." Typical Gennet poor sound cannot defeat the impression of spirited ensemble playing and interplay. Good notes are by Max Harrison.

J3.58*   **Muggsy Spanier. The Great Sixteen.** RCA LPM 1295.
A hot cornetist modeled on Louis Armstrong, Spanier could certainly drive a band to its limits. In part these 16 tracks were greatly responsible for the 1940s Dixieland revival. They were recorded in New York in 1939, and the front line also consisted of Georg Brunis (trombone) and Rod Cless (clarinet). Joe Bushkin did most of the piano work. Traces of King Oliver could be found in the ensemble work, as well as in Spanier's performance, especially on "Big Butter and Egg Man" and "Dippermouth Blues." Spanier used the plunger-mute to good effect on "Relaxin' at Touro." Typical Dixie tunes included "I Wish That I Could Shimmy Like My Sister Kate," "At the Jazz Band Ball," "Livery Stable Blues," and "Dinah."

J3.59*   **Lu Watters. San Francisco Style, volumes 1/3.** three discs. Good Time
　　　　　Jazz 12001/3.
Featuring Bunk Johnson and the vocals of Clancy Hayes, along with Watters, these discs are the collected works of the finest West Coast traditional jazz revival group. They were the prototype of white Dixieland and were instrumental in creating the anti-bop feeling through a reversion to "roots" of New Orleans music. The 36 items embrace most of the repertoire of Dixieland.

J3.60   **The World's Greatest Jazz Band. Live at the Roosevelt Grill.** Atlantic
　　　　　SD 1570.
Most of the members of this nonet, put together and financed by a western millionaire, had previously performed with the Bob Crosby co-op of the 1930s. The present record is a direct extension of that co-op's "swing" version of Dixieland items. The rhythm unit, featuring Ralph Sutton, Bob Haggart and Gus Johnson, Jr., is augmented by the doubled front line of two trumpets (Yank Lawson and Billy Butterfield), two trombones (Vic Dickenson and Lou McGarity), and two reeds (Bob Wilber, clarinet and soprano sax, and Bud Freeman, tenor). The blend of Chicago style, Crosby "swing," and the added instrumentation succeeds quite well in a program of standards: "That's a Plenty," "Black and Blue," "Royal Garden Blues," and "Jazz Me Blues" (among others). The group was at its best before an eating and drinking audience. Not all the band members performed in each and every tune, but the arrangements were stylish and fresh, not warmed over, as many other groups in the 1970s were to be.

CHICAGO

Anthologies

J3.61   **Chicago in the 30's.** Tax m-8007 (Swedish issue).

J3.62   **Chicago Jazz.** Coral CP 38 (British issue).

J3.63* **Chicago Jazz, 1923-1929. v.1/2.** two discs. Biograph BLP 12005 and 12043.

J3.64* **Chicago Southside, 1926-1932. v.1/2.** two discs. Historical HLP 10 and 30.

J3.65   **Chicago Style Jazz.** Columbia CL 632.

J3.66* **Eddie Condon's World of Jazz.** two discs. Columbia KG 31564.

J3.67* **Jazz Odyssey: The Sound of Chicago.** three discs. Columbia C3L 32.
    There are different brands of "Chicago" jazz. One is the logical urban develop-
ment of the marching bands in New Orleans; another comes from the transitional
period between New Orleans and the New York scene. Yet a third is the simple jazz
played in Chicago, a mixture of all jazz influences at the time. Among the white
performers, Eddie Condon and his various groups did the most to create a distinctive sound, characterized by what is known as "Chicago shuffle," a pronounced beat
on the rhythm guitar of Condon and the rhythm section, along with the attempt by
the clarinet (in most cases, Pee Wee Russell) to take over the lead from the trumpet.
The Columbia salute to Condon complements his last book (*Eddie Condon's Scrapbook of Jazz*) and features 27 tracks of both issued and unissued selections that
reflect his brand of jazz, 1927-1954. Condon himself only appears on a few cuts.
Featured are: Henry Red Allen, Louis Armstrong, Sidney Bechet, Bud Freeman,
Miff Mole, Lee Wiley, Fats Waller, and Muggsy Spanier. The Coral compilation comes
from 1939-1940, with Eddie Condon, George Wettling, Jimmy McPartland, Max
Kaminsky, Pee Wee Russell, Joe Sullivan, et al., with tunes such as "Sugar,"
"Friar's Point Shuffle," "China Boy," "Sister Kate," etc. Notes by George Avakian
neatly summarize the characteristics of Chicago jazz: the impact of Friar's Society
(later the New Orleans Rhythm Kings), the Wolverines with Beiderbecke, and Austin High School, all performing with a powerful drive, tension between the rhythm
and the front line, solos, crescendos, diminuendos, and other devices. The Columbia single disc explores this phenomenon a bit further, with Condon, Miff Mole,
Bud Freeman and others through the 1927-1935 period. The second volume of the
Jazz Odyssey set (others covered Harlem and New Orleans) presents 48 tracks
culled from 1923 through 1940, showing some roots in King Oliver, Carroll Dicker-
son, Luis Russell, Rod McKenzie, Condon, some blues singers (Wallace, Tampa Red,
Lofton, Broonzy, Yancey), and leading through to the big bands of Hines, Eldridge,
and Horace Henderson. This set, complete with a lavish booklet containing pictures
and discographical information and comments on each track, shows the entire wide
range of musical influences going on at the time of the 17-year period. The Biograph,
Tax, and Historical reissues present minor bands that were performing in working

styles, such as J. C. Cobb's Grains of Corn, Jimmy Wade and his Dixielanders, Chicago Footwarmers, State Street Ramblers, Jimmy Blythe's Washboard Wizards, Tiny Parham, Clarence Jones, Sammy Stewart's Ten Knights of Syncopation, Lovie Austin's Blues Serenaders, and some masters from the thirties, such as Earl Hines and Richard M. Jones.

Innovators

J3.68*   **Eddie Condon. Best.** two discs. MCA2-4071.

J3.69   **Eddie Condon. Condon à la Carte.** Ace of Hearts AH178 (British issue).

J3.70   **Eddie Condon. Gershwin Program, 1941-1945.** Decca DL 9234.

J3.71*   **Eddie Condon. Town Hall Concerts, 1944/5.** two discs. Chiaroscuro CR 108 and 113.
    Condon played adequate rhythm guitar and banjo. His forte was in leadership and organization. He quickly became the leader of the "good time" New Orleans-based "Chicago jazz" school. In 1927, he co-led an outfit with Red McKenzie; in 1928, he headed for New York and studio work. Throughout the 1930s, Condon led several sessions, and then began creating the Chicago style for a series of recordings sponsored by the Commodore Music Shop in 1938, among which were "Strut Miss Lizzie," "Ballin' the Jack," "Georgia Grind" and "Pretty Doll" (these are on the Ace of Hearts release). Max Kaminsky and Pee Wee Russell were the outstanding performers, and were also involved with various Lee Wiley song book projects for Commodore. A long association with Decca began, and it included some very worthwhile Gershwin interpretations. The Decca material is highlighted by such as "Friars Point Shuffle," and "Someday Sweetheart." Over a period of years, Condon fashioned regular groups out of Bobby Hackett, Billy Butterfield, Pee Wee Russell, Yank Lawson, Ernie Caceres, and Lou McGarity. During the war, he participated extensively in V-Discs (recorded for the armed services) and helped in the revival of jazz on the "mouldy figs" side of the bop controversy by presenting regular Town Hall Concerts. Both Chiaroscuro reissues last nearly an hour apiece, and are gems of spontaneous relaxation. These concerts went out over the Blue Network, and were transcribed for the AFRS. Musicians included Sidney Bechet, Gene Krupa, Hot Lips Page, Ed Hall, and Jess Stacey, in addition to the regulars. CR 108 features Pee Wee Russell; CR 113 examines the role of the keyboard men. J. P. Johnson is featured on two original solos ("Just before Daybreak" and "Caprice Rag"), while Willie "The Lion" Smith performs exuberantly on some originals and standards. Earl Hines does "My Monday Date," and Cliff Jordan bangs out "There'll Be Some Changes Made." Hot Lips Page even sings and is especially good on "Uncle Sam's Blues."

J3.72*   **Bud Freeman. Chicagoans in New York.** Dawn Club DC 12009.
    Freeman was the leading tenor of the so-called Chicago's Austin High School gang. He was a prominent participant in the New Orleans style as adapted to "Chicago jazz." His achievements were a flamboyant but melodic tenor style, with exceptional phrases. For instance, his own composition "The Eel" (found on this

disc) displays a slithering technique, and it seems difficult to pin Freeman down, as he is slippery in going over the chords. In some sense, this pre-dates bop techniques. There are 18 tracks here—from 1935 (two, including "The Buzzard"), from 1939-1940 with his Summa Cum Laude orchestra (four, including "I've Found a New Baby" and "China Boy"), and the balance from July 1940, which included masterful reconstructions of "That Da-Da Strain" and "Muskrat Ramble." Some alternate takes are also here. Freeman's rare clarinet can be found on "Tillie's Down town Now." Accompanying musicians scattered among the recordings include Bunny Berigan, Claude Thornhill, Eddie Condon, Max Kaminsky, Pee Wee Russell, Dave Tough, and Jack Teagarden.

Standards

J3.73*   **Billy Banks and His Rhythmakers.** CBS 52732 (English issue).
The 16 tracks here, recorded in mid-1932, feature a wide range of New York musicians, such as Red Allen, Pee Wee Russell, Joe Sullivan, Eddie Condon, Pops Foster, and Zutty Singleton. Yet, the music is typified as Chicago jazz because the clarinet vies with the trumpet for the lead, and there is that "Chicago shuffle" set up by Condon's banjo and the guitar rhythm. Banks was an obscure figure who assembled the boys, and the recordings are slightly marred by his vocals on most of the tracks. However, it is superb jazz from the pre-swing era, with the individualistic Allen and Russell working together for a change. Typical tunes include "Oh, Peter," "Who's Sorry Now?," "I Would Do Anything For You," "Bugle Call Rag," "Yellow Dog Blues," and "Who Stole the Lock?."

J3.74   **Wingy Manone. v.1.** RCA LPV 563.
Manone was an Armstrong-influenced trumpet player, actually born in New Orleans. He had played with the New Orleans Rhythm Kings in 1934, and subsequently led small ensembles for the Bluebird label (1936-1941). Much of his work was in the safe middle registers, and this is the range of most of his solos. The group work was excellent, and all the 16 tracks here swing. In the group were, from time to time, Buster Bailey, Chu Berry, Georg Brunis, Matty Matlock, Eddie Miller, Nappy Lamare, Ray Bauduc, Mel Powell, Carmen Mastren and Joe Marsala. Typical standards included "Limehouse Blues," "Sweet Lorraine," "Boo-Hoo" and "Dallas Blues." On his last session (March 19, 1941), he recorded the prophetic "Stop the War (The Cats Are Killin' Themselves)," one of the few instances of topicality in jazz.

J3.75   **Pee Wee Russell.** Everest FS 233.

J3.76   **Pee Wee Russell. Memorial Album.** Prestige 7672.
Russell has been firmly thought of as being Eddie Condon's clarinet player, and indeed, in that role, he has performed on almost all of Condon's recordings from the Chicago school era. He was a flexible performer, playing almost any style. His trademark was the raspy clarinet that often sounded as if Pee Wee were twisting the licorice stick. After the war, he began to make records under his own name, and these two are perhaps the finest of the mainstream revival albums that he produced. The Everest is a reissue of a 1958 session for Counterpoint, featuring great

sympathetic accompaniment from Vic Dickenson, Ruby Braff, and Bud Freeman. Dickenson fits in particularly well, for both men have a sly sense of humor. The latter feeds Russell the patterns with a mute on "I Used to Love You" and "Oh, No!," and Russell responds admirably. With just rhythm, Russell excels on "Exactly Like You" and "If I Had You." The *Memorial* album is equally strong, with arrangements by Buck Clayton (trumpet) for "Wrap Your Troubles in Dreams," among others. Blues predominate with the standards in a classic mainstream album.

J3.77*   **Omer Simeon.** Ace of Hearts AH 97 (British issue).
Simeon was the New Orleans clarinet in Jelly Roll Morton's first orchestral records in 1926. His style—categorized as New Orleans *in* Chicago—was influenced by Jimmy Noone and Lorenzo Tio. Later, he would go on to play with other groups in Chicago (with Tiny Parham, King Oliver, and Earl Hines). The material on this disc comes largely from the Chicago of 1929, and features Simeon in a trio format ("Bean Ko Jack" and "Smoke House Blues"), with Reuben Reeves ("River Blues," "Parson Blues," plus two others), and with the Dixie Rhythm Kings, Alex Hill, and Harry Dial. On some of the tracks, Simeon is heard with alto sax. Many of the tunes are transitional jazz items, dealing with some hokum and some early swing.

NEW YORK AND HARLEM

Anthologies

J3.78*   **Big Bands Uptown, v.1: 1931-1943.** Decca DL 79242.

J3.79   **Harlem Jazz, 1921-1931.** Classic Jazz Masters CJM 1 (Swedish issue).

J3.80*   **A History of Jazz: The New York Scene, 1914-1945.** RBF RF 3.

J3.81   **Jazz from New York, 1928-1932.** Historical HLP 33.

J3.82*   **A Jazz Holiday.** two discs. MCA2-4018.

J3.83*   **Jazz Odyssey, v.3: The Sound of Harlem.** three discs. Columbia C3L 33.

J3.84   **New York Jazz, 1928-1933.** Historical HLP19.

J3.85*   **New York Scene in the 40's: From Be-Bop to Cool.** Columbia J-27
         (French issue).
The above listed eleven records give the general flavor and an indication of the diverse activity in the New York area. There are black sounds from Harlem (where many believed that jazz was really born); there are large bands and small combos; there are white bands, mainly recording units; there are diverse styles that led to be-bop and cool jazz. In fact, the entire spectrum of what is now jazz was found at one time or another in New York, and it might appear ludicrous to even list some anthologies. The RBF covers the widest time span, embracing 1914-1945 and presenting representative recordings of the Original Dixieland Jazz Band from

1917, Jim Europe's Society Orchestra in 1914 (the same group that developed in Europe out of the army after World War I, made a successful tour, and introduced Europeans to jazz), the Louisiana Sugar Babies, the Missourians, Mamie Smith from 1920, Henderson from 1925, Cab Calloway in 1934 (as well as Lunceford), a Miff Mole 1929 recording, Ellington in 1928, Thelonious Monk in 1944, and Gillespie in 1945. This is a very good survey, presenting as it does the first recording of important stylists and innovators. The two Historical albums continue by presenting rare and largely unknown (at least to us) bands that are collector's items, such as early Luis Russell (appearing as Lou and His Gingersnaps), Earl Jackson's Musical Champions, the Harlem Hot Chocolates, the Moonlight Revelers, and Connie's Inn Orchestra (really Fletcher Henderson).

The Decca set collates four tracks each from Don Redman, Claude Hopkins, Benny Carter, and Lucky Millinder. These bands quite regularly played in Harlem at the ballrooms or the Apollo theatre. There, they sharpened their tones by playing cutting sessions in which the audience would determine who won a performance battle. This is good, jumping swing music. Immediately preceding this activity, there were a large number of bands (as found on the Classic Jazz Masters set) such as Jimmie Johnson's Jazz Boys, the Metropolitan Dance Players, Marvin Smolev and his Syncopators, and the Harlem Hot Shots. These groups paved the way for later acceptance of the style.

The most comprehensive set here is the triple disc from Columbia, with lavish notes, discography, photographs, and a report on the various clubs and ballrooms in which the music was heard. The 48 tracks cover 1920-1942, and reveal the "sound of Harlem" through Mamie Smith, Eubie Blake, James P. Johnson, Fletcher Henderson, Ethel Waters, Louis Armstrong, Fats Waller, some blues singers, Cab Calloway, Chick Webb, Erskine Hawkins, Frankie Newton, Billie Holliday, Teddy Wilson, Jimmie Lunceford, and Cootie Williams. The MCA twofer has all-white jazz from the twenties and thirties, with Benny Goodman, Red Nichols, Joe Venuti, Eddie Lang, Jack Teagarden, and Adrian Rollini, among others. These small groups were largely freelancers who assembled in the studio to play jazz for a commercial market; as such, they were largely derivative, but interesting nonetheless. The French Columbia set is a very good anthology, showing the changes from be-bop music to cool jazz (the ultimate reaction) as it occurred in New York City, and featuring Cootie Williams, Dizzy Gillespie, Claude Thornhill, Gil Evans, Sarah Vaughan, and the Metronome All Stars.

J3.86*   **Thesaurus of Classic Jazz.** four discs. Columbia C4L 18.

This is a superb and useful compilation of New York "white" jazz of the 1920s. Characterized as "hot" dance bands, with stiff rhythm sections and competent (but not inspired) interpretations, New York jazz took hold of an audience and shaped people's impression of jazz for decades to come. At the other extreme, there was "Harlem" jazz, from the same geographic area, but composed of black bands that played in Harlem. They were more related to stride and barrelhouse music, the type that had infectious rhythm and that "swung" (Fletcher Henderson was in this group, and his arrangements, coupled with the Basie riffs from Kansas City, created the great swing bands of the 1930s). None of the Harlem groups are here. Miff Mole, a trombonist who furthered the development of that instrument away from the tailgate style of New Orleans, has a disc here under his own name. During the 1920s he was prolific, appearing on most records in this category. Here, in "I've Got a Feeling I'm Falling," he displays his rapid technique and good tone. He is his most assured self on "Davenport Blues." His accompanying clarinetist, Fud Livingston, takes a good solo on "Crazy Rhythm." Eddie Lang established the guitar as a solo instrument in the jazz band (more of his items can be found under his annotation). Here, he is mainly the rhythm guitarist in small groups, as on "Bugle Call Rag" or "Hot Heels." Adrian Rollini was an exceptionally fluent bass saxist who alternated between the bass rhythm section and solo passages. He is heard to great effect on "The New Twister," "My Gal Sal," and "Honolulu Blues." Frank Trumbauer played the C Melody sax. This instrument was pitched in that key and was easy to play along with a piano. In many hands, it can be boring to hear over and over again; not so with Trumbauer. He was a close personal and musical friend of Bix Beiderbecke (more can be found under Bix's annotation). He was an influence on Benny Carter and Lester Young, possessing a light touch that produced sweet phrases without being slick and cloying. He is heard at his best on the ballad "Singing the Blues."

Red Nichols and his Charleston Chasers are perhaps the epitome of white New York jazz. Many people believed that he was the kingpin of the jazz cornet. He did produce refined, melodic music of the hot dance type, but he is seen mainly as a popularizer. He leads, in this set, groups from a quintet (often called the Five Pennies) through to the 14-piece band configuration. "That's No Bargain" features a Lang solo, with a Jimmy Dorsey alto section. While Fud Livingston (clarinetist) was the composer of "Feelin' No Pain," it is Pee Wee Russell who takes the clarinet solo here. "Rose of Washington Square" has uptempo solos from Teagarden, Bud Freeman, and Pee Wee Russell, while "China Boy" features Teagarden, Goodman, and Joe Sullivan. The Dorsey brothers also appear on this set. Jimmy had an immense technical facility on alto saxophone, and indeed was cited as an influence on Charlie Parker, Johnny Hodges, and even Ornette Coleman!! Just listen to "Beebe" for his dazzling technique, or to "Delirium" for the emotional outburst. On clarinet, the instrument with which most people associate him, he appeared to be influenced by Jimmie Noone, as on "That's a Plenty" and "After You've Gone," complete with trills. Tommy Dorsey, at this time, was also playing trumpet as well as trombone, but his style on both these instruments was underdeveloped then. These 64 tracks come from the Columbia catalog, plus its subsidiaries and later acquisitions. There was certainly a lot of activity in New York, and other anthologies are annotated below (these come from the other recording companies). Enclosed is a hefty booklet with full discographical information, texts, and illustrations.

Innovators

J3.87*   **Bix Beiderbecke. Bix and Tram, 1927/8.** two discs. Swaggie 1242 and 1269 (Australian issue).

J3.88*   **Bix Beiderbecke. Legend.** RCA LPM 2323.

J3.89   **Bix Beiderbecke. Story, v.1/3.** three discs. Columbia CL844/6.
Beiderbecke was one of the big three cornetists in the 1920s, along with Armstrong and Miley. He was also the first jazz legend because of his early, tragic

death. His unique talent influenced Bing Crosby in his phrasing, as in "Mississippi Mud," which has a Crosby and Trumbauer vocal. An enigmatic composer, he was one of the first modernists. His four best-known works are "In a Mist" (the only one he recorded for Columbia on piano), "In the Dark," "Flashes," and "Candlelights." All the music is of a worrisome frame with tempo changes and deep figures, as if Bix really opened his mind through composition. Simply put, he had a *unique* talent for the period. The Columbia set is often marred by either terrible vocals or inept sidemen. (It has often been said, though, that Bix was not so good but that his sidemen were quite poor.) From the OKeh period are 31 selections on the Swaggie reissues, with accompaniment by Frankie Trumbauer, Eddie Lang, and Adrian Rollini. Selections include "Clarinet Marmalade," "Trumbology," "Riverboat Shuffle," "Three Blind Mice," "Sugar," "Japanese Sandman," "I'm Coming Virginia," and the best solo passage for Bix, "Singing the Blues." The RCA reissue comprises the best from the Jean Goldkette and Paul Whiteman bands, and includes exceptional melodic variations on "Clementine," "Dardanella," and "From Monday On."

J3.90*   **Jack Teagarden.** RCA LPV 528.

J3.91   **Jack Teagarden. Big T's Jazz.** Ace of Hearts AH 28 (British issue).

J3.92*   **Jack Teagarden. "J.T."** Ace of Hearts AH 168 (British issue).

J3.93*   **Jack Teagarden. King of the Blues Trombone.** three discs. Epic SN 6044.

J3.94   **Jack Teagarden. The Legendary.** two discs. Polydor 2682 034 (British issue).

Teagarden's trombone playing displayed a perfect technique. Glissandi and staccato runs were used without affectation, and they were not rushed or pushed to deliver a smooth flowing harmonic sense. His playing obviously was derived from his blues background in Texas. He recorded for many companies, mainly on the New York scene, but was never really part of any one band (except under his own name). The Epic set, arranged chronologically, collates 48 tracks from 1928-1940, mainly cut for the Columbia and Brunswick labels. His personal style and blues have often been imitated, but never duplicated. The bands here include Ben Pollack's, Benny Goodman's, and (in 1939) Teagarden's own big band, the one that made him bankrupt. Good happy fun is on such items as "Whoopee Stomp," "When You're Smiling," "Bugle Call Rag," "Dirty Dog," and "Diga Diga Doo." Some of the finer band swing pieces were with Goodman, such as "Dr. Heckle and Mr. Jibe" and "Texas Tea Party." Teagarden's vocals could never be duplicated: a bluesy, lazy voice that never pronounced any consonants—completely effortless.

Full discographical information and photographs are included in a posh booklet with the Epic set. The RCA single album covers 1928-1957, with Eddie Condon, Paul Whiteman, the Metronome All Stars, Louis Armstrong, and Bud Freeman. AH 168 examines the 1929-1931 era in more detail, with 12 tracks ("After You've Gone," "Beale St. Blues," "Sheik of Araby," etc.). Twelve more items appear on AH 28, from 1944, 1947, 1953, and 1955, such as his famous theme "I've Got a Right to Sing the Blues," "Aunt Hagar's Blues," and "I'm Gonna Stomp Mr. Henry

Lee." The Polydor set from 1960-1961 (reissued from Ranlette) was his single last great effort, along with Don Ewell and clarinetist Henry Cuesta, in a program of 25 Teagarden-associated standards. His blues-based singing and playing was also strongly influenced by Jimmy Harrison of Fletcher Henderson's New York band, and some of this comes out in the session with Bobby Hackett on EMI E052-81005 (J4.142).

Standards

J3.95   **California Ramblers. v.1/2.** two discs. Biograph BLP 12020/1.

J3.96   **Rare Vertical Jazz, 1926-1928.** Historical HLP 8.   ·

The New York "white" school of jazz of the 1920s was composed—to some extent—of Red Nichols, Phil Napoleon, Tommy and Jimmy Dorsey, Miff Mole, Joe Venuti, Adrian Rollini, and others. To a greater extent, they played a more sophisticated urbane style of Dixieland, and acknowledged Bix Beiderbecke and Frank Trumbauer (both white) as models. The California Ramblers was one of the most successful of such groups, but it encompassed many jazzmen who were under contract to other record companies. The 24 selections on the Biograph set show a concern for "hot" music, as on "Charleston," "Five Foot Two, Eyes of Blue," "Clap Hands, Here Comes Charlie," and "Everything Is Hotsy Totsy Now." The group was influential in creating a wider audience for jazz, particularly in New York City, where many black performers ended up after traveling from Chicago. The Historical album contains an additional six tracks, plus five others by various spin-off groups employing the same personnel.

Vertical recordings—hill and dale, it was called, because the stylus rode up and down, rather than from side to side—were never really popular. It was merely a device to sell one type of gramophone, but it fits into the long history of recording in that it represents the industry's constant attempt to kill itself through competing devices (e.g., cylinder versus disc; 33-1/3 rpm versus 45 rpm; albums versus long-playing records; tape versus disc; stereo versus mono; stereo versus quadrophonic, etc.). One outstanding feature was that longer recordings could be made, and all of the tunes here are about four minutes long (plus or minus a few seconds).

J3.96a   **Bill Dodge. Swinging '34, v.1/2.** two discs. Melodeon MLP 7328/9.

These recordings were originally on three 16-inch transcriptions made exclusively for radio broadcasts. They were vertical, inside-out tracking, at 33-1/3 rpm. Nobody knows who "Bill Dodge" was, and it probably was a pseudonym, a collective name for the group that consisted of, among others, Benny Goodman, Bunny Berigan, Mannie Klein, Art Rollini, and Gene Krupa. This is another sterling example of session men—or freelancers—assembling in the studio to cut solid numbers with a minimum of rehearsal time and other preparations. Head arrangements were the order of the day, and the 24 tracks are all models of good solos and ensemble work. Red McKenzie takes four vocals, and the tunes "Aintcha Glad," "Tappin' the Barrel," "Dr. Heckle and Mr. Jibe," "Honeysuckle Rose," "Riffin' · the Scotch," and "Love Me or Leave Me" clearly show the beginnings of the swing era, when most of Dixieland had been put away. These records were played constantly on the radio throughout the 1930s and had the effect of spreading the word.

J3.97   Joe Venuti and Eddie Lang. Hot Strings, 1927-1933. (Sounds of New York, v.2). RCA FPM 1-7016 (French issue).

J3.98*   Joe Venuti and Eddie Lang. Stringing the Blues. two discs. Columbia C2L 24.

Venuti was one of the first violin soloists, but he never did achieve the status of Eddie South or Stuff Smith. Perhaps this was because he was sophisticated and measured in his performances; his best work certainly was with good accompanists (such as Lang, who was also of Italian ancestry). Lang established the guitar as a solo instrument in jazz; formerly it was thought of as just rhythm or as a blues accompaniment. His single string work and chord patterns preceded Charlie Christian. Much of his best material was of the nature of guitar duos (hear the great collaborations with blues guitarist Lonnie Johnson [q.v.]). Lang also accompanied Bing Crosby and Hoagy Carmichael, among others (Hoagy can be found on the RCA set). When Venuti and Lang played together, they sounded like the necessary preliminary for Django Reinhardt and Stephane Grappelli. Both of these sets are a hodge podge of material. Venuti and Lang are not both on every track, but at least one of them is. Being part of the New York white jazz scene, they recorded for various companies as non-exclusive artists. Thus, other items can be found on *A Jazz Holiday* (J3.82), an MCA set from this period. Various configurations and names were employed.

The RCA set includes some material from Jean Goldkette's orchestra, as well as Hoagy Carmichael and four duos. The Columbia twofer presents 32 tracks from 1926-1933, plus an illustrative booklet with text, discographies, and sources. There are Lang guitar solos ("Church Street Sobbin' Blues") of importance; duos (the 1927 cuts "Goin' Places" and "Doin' Things"); accompaniment by King Oliver and Clarence Williams ("In the Bottle Blues"); guitar duos with Lonnie Johnson ("Guitar Blues"); and other selections including "A Handful of Riffs." The most common group appears to be the Joe Venuti Blue Four, but Tommy Dorsey crops up as well. Much New York hokum is provided by multi-instrumentalist Adrian Rollini who plays the goofus (a two-reeded sax), fountain pen, vibraphone, and piano. Humor lives in this jazz.

TERRITORY BANDS

J3.99   Byways of Jazz. Origin Jazz Library OJL 9.

J3.100   Jazz in St. Louis, 1924-1926. Parlophone PMC 7157 (British issue).

J3.101* Kansas City Jazz. Decca DL 8044.

J3.102   Rare Bands of the Twenties, v.1/8. Historical HLP 3,6,7,9,10,11,12,16.

J3.103* The Territory Bands, 1926-1931. v.1/2. two discs. Historical HLP 24/26.

J3.104* The Territory Bands, 1926-1929. Parlophone PMC 7082 (British issue).

J3.105   **The Territory Bands.** Classic Jazz Masters CJM 10 (Swedish issue).

J3.106   **The Territory Bands.** International Association of Jazz Record Collectors IAJRC 6.

J3.107*   **The Territory Bands.** Tax m8009 (Swedish issue).

The major recording companies were located in New York and Chicago, and to achieve any measure of fame throughout the United States, a band's records had to be issued on a major label that would ensure national distribution. Numerous large outfits, though, played everywhere in the United States, particularly in the South and Southwest, and they often recorded for smaller labels for localized fame. They also never ventured far from their area; thus, they became known in the jazz world as "territory" bands. The most famous territory outside of New York and Chicago was the "Southwest," centered in Kansas City (yes). There are rarely any anthologies of Kansas City music, as most of the major figures have had their own albums of reissues and thus can be found under their own names (e.g., Pete Johnson, Joe Turner, Mary Lou Williams, Count Basie, Bennie Moten, Andy Kirk, Hot Lips Page, Eddie Durham, etc.). These just-named people, though, are on the Decca album as a brief introduction to the whole Southwest scene.

The mammoth Historical series includes such unknowns as Robinson's Knights of Rest, Reuben Reeves' River Boys, J. C. Cobb's Grains of Corn, early Bennie Moten and other Kansas City groups, Blue Rhythm Orchestra, Nashville Jazzers, Kentucky Jazz Babies, Zach Whyte's Chocolate Beau Brummels (six cuts), Alphonse Trent's Orchestra (five cuts), Walter Page's Blue Devils, Sonny Clay's Plantation Orchestra, and so forth. Some individuals rose to fame, such as Moten and Page. Overall, the Swedish labels have superior sound and more tracks (sixteen apiece), so it is mostly a matter of whether to bother to import, and the quantity a collection would need. On these discs are Blanche Calloway, Jeter-Pillars, Bob Pope, Carolina Cotton Pickers, Original Yellow Jackets, Bobby Gordon, Original St. Louis Crackerjacks, Syd Valentine, etc.

Parlophone PMC 7082 concentrates largely on the South and Midwest, with performances from Troy Floyd, Roy Johnson, and J. Neale Montgomery. Similarly, the IAJRC disc presents more from the Midwest and from the West Coast, including Curtis Mosby, Hunter's Serenaders, Red Perkins, and Grant Moore. The Origin set is a radical departure for a blues and gospel reissue label. But much of the material appears to be blues-based, as, from the South, Carl Bunch and His Fuzzy Wuzzies or the Black Birds of Paradise. Other bands here include Eddie and Sugar Lou's Hotel Tyler Orchestra from the Southwest, and some interesting Midwest tracks from John Williams's Synco Jazzers and Dewey Jackson's Peacock Orchestra. Parlophone PMC 7157 returns us to the local bands of one city far from the major recording studios: St. Louis. Material here largely comes from Charlie Creath and Fate Marable. This cursory annotation has attempted mainly to list the diverse groups found on these 17 albums. Much research has yet to be done with the "territory bands," particularly in their apprenticeship role for future jazz greats. Personnel listings are often missing, so we really have no way of determining who played with whom during the 1920s. Their influence, though, is important in determining the impact of jazz diffused through wide geographic areas. Not *all* jazz came from only New Orleans, New York, Kansas City, or Chicago.

Mainstream Swing
and
Big Bands

MAINSTREAM SWING AND BIG BANDS

"If you have to ask [about swing]
you ain't got it."
—attributed at times to Louis Armstrong,
Fats Waller, etc.

INTRODUCTION

Swing music is basically four-beat jazz from the Southwest (Kansas City, Texas), in which the stress is applied equally to all four beats in the bar. Tension was derived from the rhythms produced by internal developments in big bands. Black musicians have been credited with creating swing by introducing the *riff* in a call and response pattern quite similar to that of gospel music. Bennie Moten began this in Kansas City, and Count Basie continued it. Henderson in New York emphasized the sectional performances of unison trumpets, trombones, and saxophones. Lunceford (and Basie) created additional rhythms by sometimes giving extra stress to the second and fourth beats of a measure, but it was up to the bandleader to determine how often and how much emphasis to give (this same afterbeat was heard in New Orleans music). Usually, emphasis was pronounced in the background when a soloist was outlining his ideas. Certainly, white bands made effective use of black swing. They blended New Orleans music with the riff concept, employed technically proficient musicians, and used the soloist in the European concert pattern of antagonist and protagonist. Thus, the stars of Roy Eldridge and Chu Berry began to rise—they were the best of the trumpet and saxophone soloists in swing bands. At the same time, the "star" system developed and national acclaim was being given to regional stars who toured. With this music fans both listened and danced; they collected discs and later would record radio broadcasts. These fans also created swing magazines such as *Downbeat* and *Metronome*, and they completed the takeover of black jazz. Certain bands became integrated by 1940, but this proved arduous while touring through the Deep South. Jazz criticism took shape during this period, although most writings were of the common "biopix" type.

Big bands, though, had developed before 1920. The black musician James Reece Europe led a widely acclaimed black band that performed for American soldiers overseas during World War I; they later toured Europe with the group, thereby introducing Europeans to jazz and big bands. But big bands never really flourished in the United States until the early 1930s, with the rise of instrumental competencies, section playing, and arrangers. Credit belongs to Fletcher Henderson, Don Redman, Edgar Sampson, and Benny Carter—all arrangers who promoted the concept of swing. They segregated the instruments into sections (all of the trumpets played together, all of the trombones played together, and so did the reeds). The saxophones were used to countervoice the brass to create tension, with soloists giving relief. Ellington, though, liked to mix the sections (such as the clarinet with muted trumpet and trombone on "Mood Indigo") for expressing tone colors. Thus, his band did not quite properly "swing." His influence extended instead to Claude Thornhill and Thornhill's arranger, Gil Evans, which in turn had impact on Miles Davis and Gerry Mulligan and the whole "cool" school—all more interested in tone poems and instrumental shadings rather than the beat.

Variations developed. At first, there were four saxophones (two tenors and two altos)—and in the Ellington band, there was also a baritone sax. By 1940, more bands added this latter instrument to give the group a stronger bottom, thereby permitting more advanced harmonies. Woody Herman conceived the "Four Brothers" sound of three tenor saxes and a baritone; later, five saxophones became the ideal. Also at first, there were three trumpets and two trombones for five voices, but as brass sounds predominated in power, this became four trumpets and three trombones (and even five trumpets and four trombones). Brass writing and arranging became so advanced that leads were split between two trumpeters to cover all the tiring high passage work. The format eventually stabilized at five saxophones (with some musicians doubling on flute, oboe, and cor anglais), four trumpets and three trombones. The rhythm section remained set at piano, bass, drums, and (often) guitar, as with Count Basie. Their main function was to play on the beat. Most bands (including jazz bands) had two singers—a woman and a man, the latter featured more extensively. Both sang ballads and novelty tunes. Count Basie, though, used the man (Jimmy Rushing) for the blues, while the woman (Helen Humes) sang the ballads. Early in the swing period, these vocalists were used mainly for dancing and change of pace numbers. Later, as the bands got a bigger sound, vocal choruses (Merry Macs, Bob Cats, Pied Pipers, etc.) were added to replace the band members who formerly had chanted in the background. Eventually, the singers would become stars on their own, and again, mainly the men succeeded (Sinatra, Haymes). On balance, though, it was mostly the instrumentals that the fans wanted to hear.

Literature

Besides the books and periodicals mentioned in the general literature survey of jazz, many specialized studies can be found through Gregor (45), Kennington (59), and Merriam (73). Dance's (22) book surveys the entire world of swing, and more volumes in his set are forthcoming. McCarthy's (66) work is a history of the origins, progress, and decline of 550 big bands in the United States and elsewhere; Simon's (109) book is similar but with more details on dance bands. Fernett (34) concentrates only on the black bands. Stewart (113) presents essays on the innovators of 1930s jazz, while Chilton (14) researches the life of Billie Holiday, which takes in other singers as well. Russell (96) examines the jazz style of Kansas City and the Southwest, tracing the evolution of swing and bop. Allen (1) details the life of Fletcher Henderson and the impact of swing bands. Shaw (108) presents a specialized study of 52nd Street in New York, during the heyday of swing and the newly developing bop music. An important jazz magazine in this area is *Jazz Journal* (10), which specialized in articles on swing or mainstream music.

ANTHOLOGIES

J4.1   **Carnegie Hall Jazz Concerts, October 1939.** Collector's Classics CC 18 (Danish issue).

J4.2*   **From Spirituals to Swing, 1938/39.** two discs. Vanguard VSD 47/48.
Armstrong and Benny Goodman in a number of settings, as well as Cab Calloway and Claude Hopkins. The *Spirituals to Swing* concert is the famous one created by John Hammond that lent authenticity to jazz and blues, or rather legitimatized the music by virtue of it having appeared at Carnegie Hall. The stellar collection of musicians here includes Count Basie, Benny Goodman, Lester Young, Buck Clayton, Sidney Bechet, Joe Turner (who electrified the audience with his blues shouting), Helen Humes, Big Bill Broonzy, Charlie Christian, James P. Johnson, Albert Ammons, etc. Hammond had the acetates for almost 20 years before they were released, and they clearly show the high state of the art that jazz had achieved by 1938 and 1939, in the heyday of swing and with the realization that the Depression was fading.

J4.3   **Esquire's All-American Hot Jazz.** RCA LPV 544.

J4.4   **The Panassié Sessions.** RCA LPV 542.
These two discs are prime examples of assembling jazz musicians for a special one-shot session. *Esquire* established a jazz poll in 1944, and over the next few years, RCA assembled the winners (or most of them) into the studios to make leaderless recordings, being billed variously as All Stars. One difficulty with these recordings is that many musicians were going through stylistic changes, for the era of bop and Charlie Parker was upon the world. Another more obvious factor was that certain musicians could not stand others. This made for a certain amount of tension, with the result that many ballads and some blues were given just average performances. However, on the uptempo selections, much good music was heard and would seldom be heard again. Musicians include Louis Armstrong, Don Byas, Harry Carney, Benny Carter, Buck Clayton, Vic Dickenson, Duke Ellington, Coleman Hawkins, Johnny Hodges, and Jack Teagarden. The Panassié work was assembled by French critic Hugues Panassié, who visited the United States in both 1938 and 1939. He chose his favorite performers (such as Sidney Bechet, Mezz Mezzrow, Tommy Ladnier, James P. Johnson, Frankie Newton, Pops Foster, and others) and wanted to recreate a New Orleans sound, for, as he mentioned, the last New Orleans sound record was in 1932, six years previously. In 1939, his approach was radically altered to include swing, and for these he got Frankie Newton and did "Rosetta," "Who?," and "The World Is Waiting for the Sunrise."

J4.5*   **Great Big Bands.** Music for Pleasure MFP 1085 (British issue).

J4.6   Item deleted.

J4.7   **Jazz in the Thirties.** two discs. World Records SHB 39 (British issue).

J4.8   **Swing Exercise.** Capitol T-11035.
A variety of contrasts are presented here from the Swing Era (1935-1945).

The first and last discs listed above show the influence and impact of the black bands of the time. MFP 1085 (all from 1933, at the start of the period) features the orchestras of Duke Ellington ("Sophisticated Lady"), Benny Carter ("Blue Lou"), and Fletcher Henderson ("Nagasaki") and clearly shows that they were light-years ahead of their time for the swing period. But they had no recognition, such as screaming fans and radio broadcasts. All three were superb arrangers. Henderson's band here had Red Allen and Coleman Hawkins, two of the greatest soloists in jazz history. The Capitol is from 1945, at the so-called end of the period, and it features Sid Catlett's band, the Al Casey group, and some spinoffs from the Ellington ensemble, being led by Rex Stewart and Sonny Greer. As a bonus, there is a Billie Holiday with Paul Whiteman from 1942. The other two discs show the white kings of swing in large and small performances: Gene Krupa, Bunny Berigan, Bud Freeman, Jack Teagarden, Benny Goodman, Joe Sullivan, Jess Stacy, Joe Venuti, Adrian Rollini, and others, from 1933 and 1935. Some exciting things happen as swing got underway, with such titles as "Jazz Me Blues," "Dr. Heckle and Mr. Jibe," "Sweet Lorraine," "Three Little Words," "Texas Tea Party," and "Satan's Holiday."

J4.9   **The Swing Collection: The Big Eighteen.** two discs. RCA DPS 2058 (British import).

In June and July 1958, seventeen performers from the swing bands (both black and white) assembled in New York City to record some of the classic melodies of that period. Personnel varied from session to session, but the most important included Billy Butterfield, Buck Clayton, Charlie Shavers, Rex Stewart, Vic Dickenson, Dickie Wells, Johnny Guarnieri, Peanuts Hucko, and Yank Lawson. Tunes included "Tuxedo Junction," "Easy Does It," "Liza," "Summit Ridge Drive," "Swingtime in the Rockies," and "Skyliner." This is excellent, stereo-recorded, music of the same drive and intensive rhythm as the swing period (but 20 years later), some with the original arrangements, some with Buck Clayton arrangements.

J4-10*   **Swing Street.** four discs. Epic SN 6042.

J4.11*   **The World of Swing.** two discs. Columbia KG 32945.

These six discs neatly illustrate what swing was all about. The Epic set concentrates on the smaller groups located in New York and performing often on 52nd Street; hence, the title. Included among its riches are a hot "You'se a Viper" by Stuff Smith and His Onyx Club Boys, "The Isle of Capri" by Wingy Manone, "Let's Have a Jubilee" by Louis Prima and His New Orleans Gang, the famous version of "Loch Lomond" sung by Maxine Sullivan, and the comic "Flat Foot Floogie" by Slim (Gaillard) and Slam (Stewart). *The World of Swing* was meant to accompany Stanley Dance's book of the same name. The 20 tracks, collected by Dance, have a definite bias and instructional value, illustrating several of the points that Dance makes and including most of the musicians who figure prominently in the book. Arranged chronologically, the records show the changes in band instrumentation, tempos, arrangements, and soloistic conceptions. Dance analyzes each track and clearly shows why the particular piece is of value. For example, Claude Hopkins's "Three Little Words" shows the lightness of his stride piano. Full discographical details are presented for such as Don Redman's "I Got Rhythm," Chick Webb's "Stompin' at the Savoy," Teddy Hill's "Passionette," Erskine Hawkins's "Swinging in Harlem," Fletcher Henderson's "Rose Room," John Kirby's "Effervescent Blues," and many others. The only problem with these sets is that all the material was derived from the Columbia and its subsidiary labels; hence, they are representative of but one company and the performers it contracted.

J4.12*   **Tribute to Fletcher Henderson.** Concert Hall SJS 1268 (French issue).
The idea behind this record is a simple one: it carries a tribute to Henderson played by the most famous members of his early orchestras, led by trumpeter Rex Stewart. The line-up is incredible in richness: Coleman Hawkins, Emmett Berry, Taft Jordan, Benny Morton, J. C. Higginbotham, Dickie Wells, Ben Webster, Buster Bailey, Red Richards, and others. The record opens with the famous "Honeysuckle Rose," and right on through nine selections to "King Porter Stomp," the band combines all the virtues of a small group of inspired soloists and complete relaxation with the dynamic drive and discipline of a large orchestra. The warm tones of Hawkins and Webster contrast with the imaginativeness of Stewart and the powerful drive of trombonist Higginbotham. Recorded in 1957, using the original Henderson scores, this is probably the greatest swing style big band record of the past three decades, according to noted jazz critic Albert McCarthy. Involvement is deep, the solos on a high plane, and the record just clearly swings.

INNOVATORS

J4.13*   **Count Basie. Best.** two discs. MCA2-4050.

J4.14*   **Count Basie. Swinging the Blues, 1937-39.** Swaggie S1275 (Australian issue).

J4.15   **Count Basie. Swinging at the Daisy Chain.** Coral CP75 (British issue).

J4.16   **Count Basie. You Can Depend on Basie.** Coral CP76 (British issue).

J4.17*   **Count Basie. One O'Clock Jump.** Columbia CL997.

J4.18*   **Count Basie. Super Chief.** two discs. Columbia G31224.

J4.19*   **Count Basie. With Lester Young.** two discs. Epic 66212 (French issue).
Basie's orchestra was one of the top three true jazz outfits of the 1930s. (The other two were Ellington and Lunceford.) Of the three, Basie was the epitome of swing. He was less polished, but he had the best rhythm sections, the best multifaceted soloists, and the best vocalists; he represented the spontaneity and drive of wild Kansas City (although he was a native of New Jersey). Serving an apprenticeship as pianist with Bennie Moten, he collected the remnants of that band to produce definitive swing by employing the recurring riff, the blues of four beats to the bar, and "head" (no written scores) arrangements for the band. The rhythm section was rock steady and driving, with Freddie Green on the best of all possible rhythm guitars, the pounding bass of Walter Page, the high hat percussion of Jo Jones (which preceded and influenced the boppers), and, of course, the sparse, lean piano style of Basie himself that fused the rhythm unit into a solid whole. Basie has been reckoned as the most perfect orchestra pianist. Influenced by Fats Waller

and Earl Hines, his economical playing produced short-phrased solos with the right hand, while the left hand played isolated notes or fed chords to the rhythm section. The soloists were completely outstanding. On tenors there were the directly opposite styles of Lester Young (lean, with perfect silent pauses taken as part of the music) and Herschel Evans (who was in the Hawkins broad-tone mood). On trumpet, there were the jamming style of Buck Clayton and the beautiful phrasing of Harry "Sweets" Edison. For trombones, Basie had Dicky Wells and Bennie Morton, both top-flight on the slide. His vocalists embraced Jimmy Rushing (a tenor blues singer), Billie Holiday, Helen Humes, and later, Joe Williams.

Basie's best period was undoubtedly 1936-1942, and for the bulk of this period, he made recordings with Decca. Taken in the order above, then, the MCA twofer has 24 items, including the epic "One O'Clock Jump" with its classic riff figures, "Jumpin' at the Woodside," "Every Tub," "Doggin' Around," "Topsy," "Blue and Sentimental," "Out the Window," and the quintet version, with Lester Young, of "Lady Be Good." The two Corals, although duplicating some titles, add some more Decca material. The Swaggie presents 8 orchestral tracks, including the full band version of "Lady Be Good." The other 8 tracks here are interesting blues performed by just Basie with his rhythm trio. For these, he made greater use of his left hand, as on "Boogie Woogie" or "The Dirty Dozens" and "The Fives." The double Epic reissue goes up to 1940, and it complements the Columbia twofer in presenting Jones-Smith, Inc., the early pre-Decca quintet of Basie and Lester Young. Here are the great early, small group versions of "Shoe Shine Boy," "Boogie Woogie" and "Lady Be Good." Also, the definitive version of "Lester Leaps In," from 1939, with the Kansas City Seven, which was drawn from Basie's Band.

The Epic set is more important than the Columbia as it draws on "Rock-a-Bye Basie," "Riff Interlude," "Clap Hands Here Comes Charlie," and "Blow Top." Dickie Wells here contributes the definitive "Dickie's Dream." The Columbia twofer is a hodge podge, with unissued masters, airchecks, different groups using Basie musicians (Mildred Bailey, Harry James, Glenn Hardman, and Teddy Wilson), but it is discographically sound and presents written testimony by former members of the band. The single Columbia was one of the first Basie reissues, and it concentrates on a less interesting period, 1942-1950. During this time, after 1939, the soloists in the Basie organization changed. Lester Young left, Herschel Evans died, and the government drafted quite a few for World War II. Buddy Tate, Illinois Jacquet, Vic Dickenson, and Don Byas were introduced, but they were not as good as the previous set of tenor saxophonists and trombonists. As the forties progressed, the arrangements became tighter and more written out instead of "head," the most notable done by Jimmy Mundy and Buster Harding. The band lost its spontaneity, more personnel changed, and it disbanded in the 1950s. (See J4.165 for the Basie band of the 1960s.)

J4.20*   **Benny Carter. 1933.** Prestige 7643.

J4.21*   **Benny Carter. 1940/1.** RCA 741.073 (French issue).

J4.22   **Benny Carter. Big Band Bounce, 1943/5.** Capitol T-11057.

J4.23   **Benny Carter. Melancholy Benny, 1939/40.** Tax m8004 (Swedish issue).

J4.24*   Benny Carter. Further Definitions. Impulse S12.
     Beyond a doubt, Carter is perhaps one of the greatest and most versatile musicians in all of jazz. He plays most brass and reed instruments plus piano, excelling on the alto sax. Along with Fletcher Henderson, Don Redman, Duke Ellington, and Sy Oliver, he is a superb arranger, especially for the sax section, He took over as arranger for Henderson's band in 1928, right after Don Redman left for McKinney's Cotton Pickers. After that, his career was peripatetic: the Chocolate Dandies, McKinney's, Coleman Hawkins, Fats Waller, Chick Webb. He had made countless recordings with all of these men, and the annotations are found under their names. In 1933, he did the arrangements for the marvelous Spike Hughes (q.v.) band. He also formed his first real group, performing beautifully arranged renditions of "Lonesome Nights" and "Devil's Holiday." Being highly influenced by Trumbauer, Carter projects a graceful alto that lends dignity to all situations. His was one of the two most influential altos of the pre-Parker period; Hodges's was the other. Basically, Carter made little use of vibrato, employing a legato phrasing and flawless technique to produce the feeling of what is known as "thematic improvisation": *knowing* (or at least giving the feeling of knowing) what is going to come next in the solo passage, as if the conception of the solo was already arranged.
     During the 1930s, Carter made many records in Europe, returning to America in 1938 to set up his own band. He made significant contributions to Lionel Hampton's small band, and then formed his own, doing such items as "Plymouth Rock," "Scandal in a Flat," "Lady, Be Good," and "Shuffleboy Shuffle" (all on the Tax disc). Moving to RCA, they did "All of Me" and "Cocktails for Two" (superbly arranged), "Sunday," and "Back Bay Boogie," both with good Carter solos. Band personnel varied, but included were Sidney De Paris, Benny Morton, Jonah Jones, Vic Dickenson, Eddie Barefield, and vocalist Maxine Sullivan ("What a Difference a Day Makes"). Carter's two years with Capitol were fraught with the tensions of bop musicians in the band, such as J. J. Johnson and Max Roach. But the materials— "I Can't Get Started," "Love For Sale," "Prelude to a Kiss," "I Surrender Dear"— were important statements in the history of a transitional period in jazz. Throughout all this period, he was also a successful composer, and in the mid-forties, he began to write scores for movies, and then television, as well as do session work for the Verve label (along with Oscar Peterson). He re-emerged in the jazz world with a 1961 effort for Impulse that reunited him with Coleman Hawkins plus two other saxes. A number of originals predominate in this excellent session, which features much successful scoring for saxophone.

J4.25*   Roy Eldridge. Little Jazz. CBS 80089 (French issue).

J4.26*   Roy Eldridge. Swing Along With Little Jazz. two discs. MCA Coral
          COPS 6855 (West German issue).
     Trumpeter Eldridge's influence has been profound throughout the jazz world. He stands midway in the tradition from Armstrong to Gillespie. The CBS reissue puts him in the band context with six enduring tracks from 1937, featuring some hot choruses on "Wabash Stomp," "Florida Stomp," and "Heckler's Hop." The other 10 cuts come from the Gene Krupa band of 1941-1942, which featured Eldridge on first trumpet and as a prominent soloist. The 23 tracks on the MCA twofer are derived from his own big band of the 1943-1946 period, which

featured at various times the De Paris Brothers, Ike Quebec, Yank Lawson, Ernie Caceres, Cecil Payne and Cozy Cole. Throughout, there is a high level of musicianship, drive, and intensity. Eldridge plays brilliantly in the high register, masters fast tempi with little effort, and phrases flexibly. It is obvious from listening to this set that Eldridge's expressionism took off from the Armstrong mould and led to the quaver beat style of Gillespie, assimilating the melodic flexibility and extensive phrasing of Benny Carter's alto sax. Selected, important titles include "Minor Jive," "Stardust," "I Can't Get Started" (the Berigan vehicle), "After You've Gone," "Body and Soul," "Twilight Time," "Embraceable You," and "I Surrender Dear."

J4.27*   **Duke Ellington. Complete, v.1-7.** (In progress, about 20 discs). two discs each set. CBS 67264, 68275, 88000, 88035, 88082, 88137, 88140.

J4.28*   **Duke Ellington. v. 1: The Beginning (1926/8).** Decca DL79224.

J4.29*   **Duke Ellington. v. 2: Hot in Harlem (1928/9).** Decca DL79241.

J4.30*   **Duke Ellington. v. 3: Rockin' in Rhythm (1929/31).** Decca DL79247.

J4.31*   **Duke Ellington. The Works of Duke. Integrale.** twenty discs. RCA DUKE 1/4 (French issue).

J4.32*   **Duke Ellington. In a Mellotone.** RCA LPM 1364.

J4.33*   **Duke Ellington. This is . . .** two discs. RCA VPM 6042.

J4.34   **Duke Ellington. Carnegie Hall, Dec. 11, 1943.** Saga PAN 6902 (British import).

J4.35   **Duke Ellington. The Golden Duke.** two discs. Prestige P 24029.

J4.36   **Duke Ellington. Blues Summit.** two discs. Verve V6-8822.

To attempt to summarize the total musical activities and influences of Duke Ellington in a mere few hundred words is absurd—yet, for the purposes of this book, it must be done. His career spanned more than 50 years of uninterrupted activity from before his first recordings in 1924 through to his death in 1974. During this time, he achieved immeasurable success in all phases of music. Indeed, every single jazz musician (as well as popular performer) owes an immense debt to Ellington. Many modern jazz performers cite Parker, Coleman, Ayler, other modernists, "and Ellington" as influences (whether they really mean it or not is another story, for every performer seems obliged to credit Ellington). By 1927, he was the most successful bandleader in New York City and a long-term resident at Harlem's Cotton Club, a prestigious operation that catered to whites only but presented black talent. Several recordings from the Club are available from small foreign companies, such as the Swedish Tax label. His best, overall, and most productive period was 1927 to 1941. In these 14 years, his band personnel remained virtually unchanged.

The economics of war disruption and post-war travel seriously reduced his band's ability, and diverse musicians came and went.

By 1950, Ellington was also playing piano trios, but at the start of the 1970s, his orchestra suddenly found tremendous popular acclaim in America again (no doubt influenced by the 1969 Medal of Freedom award presented to him). His overall accomplishments are classified below.

Pianist: This is largely dealt with later along with other pianists, but it should be noted that Ellington was a master in the *stride* school, being influenced by James P. Johnson and Willie "The Lion" Smith. Unfortunately, his richly orchestrated ensemble compositions make piano reductions very difficult. Only two pianists have ever had success performing his compositions: Earl Hines and the Duke himself. This is because both utilize all 88 keys with their immense reaches of hand. Yet, Ellington still needs rhythm accompaniment, while Hines can invest solos with a multiplicity of runs and complex configurations. In the role of pianist Ellington became the virtuoso entertainer—the "piano player" that was always introduced at concerts.

Composer: Ellington composed over 1,000 pieces, plus suites, film music, theatre, television work, and religious concerts. He wrote for the band as a whole, with featured soloists prominently displayed. Indeed, many works were dedicated to the soloists, such as "Concerto for Cootie." His main corpus concerned basic jazz: blues, stomps, and ballads. This resulted in a remarkable consistency over the years, as the personnel of his groups rarely changed. The outlines of each tune were ultimately the same, for his compositions were based on a sequence of solos within a structured framework.

Bandleader: Ellington was instrumental in encouraging his musicians to develop their resources, especially Bubber Miley and bassist Johnny Blanton, who both created a whole new band style that involved the trumpet and the bass. Billy Strayhorn became assimilated into the band as an alternate to Ellington in his compositional, arranging, and pianistic ability (e.g., "Take the 'A' Train").

Arranger: The arrangement of a piece ultimately determines the characteristics of a band's sound, despite what compositions are used. While Ellington's compositions and their arrangements go hand in hand, it is often apparent that such non-Ellington tunes as "Rose Room" become endowed with Ducal magic when subjected to his particular kind of arranging. In this respect, there are two main periods in Ellington's band. The first, 1924-1929, was dominated by Bubber Miley, the trumpeter responsible for the "jungle" sound with his muted growls. To showcase Miley, Ellington added tom-toms, cymbals, and wailing saxes. Truly it was jazz that had the aura of African roots by virtue of its mysteriousness, feeling of unease, novelty of sound, and percussion. After Miley left the band, the plunger mute was retained by Cootie Williams (his successor) and others, and Ellington turned to the band for inspiration. All his arrangements (and those of Billy Strayhorn, his alter ego) were to make use of the existing, available resources of a fairly stable band. He created new patterns from existing harmonies for rich sounds. One of these was the good use of the warm New Orleans clarinet of Barney Bigard; another was the extension of the mute to the trombone; a third was the texture of the resonating reed section from Harry Carney's baritone saxophone, which gave a "bottom" sound to the ensemble and which was so important to the early recordings; and last are a variety of inventions contributed by the various musicians (see below). Essentially, Ellington was interacting with the band,

utilizing their knowledge; coupling this with solos available in his own compositions, he induced a feeling of relaxation that is only achieved in a jam session (e.g.,
"Concerto for Cootie")—all this in spite of a written score.

The Musicians: Most of the Ellington band members were soloists and jazz
creators in their own right. He wrote tunes with specific people in mind, knowing
full well what potential they had to play and their limitations. Unfortunately, few
sounded so good outside the band, and the history of the orchestra shows many
musicians leaving, and then coming back "home" after a few years of mediocre
success (e.g., Cat Anderson, Shorty Baker, Louis Bellson, Lawrence Brown,
Johnny Hodges, Ray Nance, Juan Tizol, Ben Webster, Cootie Williams, et al.).
However, there was certainly some success when a "band within a band" was created
for Hodges, Stewart, Bigard, or Williams. From 1935-1942, Ellington made 125 sides
with sextets chosen from the orchestra. These discs were released under their own
names, but the tracks' importance should not be overlooked, as they served both as
a safety valve for frustrated soloists and as recordings of original versions before
adoption by the whole orchestra.

Because Ellington emphasized the creative solo, most records from former
band members sounded similar to Ducal material—it could not be avoided—and,
hence, a whole school of jazz musicians developed called "Ellingtonians." Baritone
saxist Harry Carney was the most consistent of all Ellingtonians. With his rhythm,
resonance, and deep textured playing (especially on "Perdido"), he virtually created
the rich ensemble sound of the band and this was from 1926 to 1974! Trumpeter
Bubber Miley was responsible for the "jungle" sound, employing a plunger mute for
growls. He was one of the big three trumpeters of the twenties (Beiderbecke and
Armstrong being the other two). His concept of total muted brass and inventive
melody had a great influence on Ellington, no less from the fact that Miley was
erratic in showing up for engagements and, thus, *all* the brass were forced to learn
the growl to substitute for him. His playing was effective on "Black and Tan
Fantasy," "Creole Love Call," "East St. Louis Toodle-oo," and "The Mooche."
Although bassist Jimmy Blanton was only with the band during 1939-1941 (he
died at age 21), he completely revolutionized the art of playing with pizzicato
melody and harmony, especially on "Concerto for Cootie."

Clarinetist Barney Bigard, influenced by Jimmy Noone, brought with him the
New Orleans manner of a warm and fluid blues-tinged style. He greatly developed
the clarinet in an orchestral context, as on "Tiger Rag" or "Rose Room." Altoist
Johnny Hodges was one of the big three, which also included Benny Carter and
Charlie Parker. He produced a balanced tone, melodic ballads, blues, and overall
singing lyric phrases, as on "The Mooche," "I Let a Song Go Out of My Heart,"
"In a Mellotone," and "Mood Indigo." Drummer Sonny Greer gave a flamboyant
but powerful swing to the unit. His cymbal work gave color to the "jungle" music.
"Tricky Sam" Nanton developed the "talking" trombone and gave organization
plus expression to the band ("Black and Tan Fantasy," "Saturday Night Function").
Juan Tizol developed the valve trombone, and contributed the compositions
"Caravan" and "Perdido." These were all of Ellington's basic musicians of the
1920s (except for Blanton).

The second crew, of replacements and additions, began with Cootie Williams
filling in for the ailing Miley. His growl was more technically competent, being
influenced by Armstrong and the blues. The swing and vitality are apparent on
"Ring Dem Bells," "Echoes of Harlem," and "Concerto for Cootie." Rex Stewart

moved from trumpet with Fletcher Henderson to cornet with Ellington, utilizing a
high register, uptempo solos, blue notes, and growls. He played his notes with the
valves half depressed, an overall unorthodox style best heard on "Margie" and
"Dusk." Tenorist Ben Webster owed a heavy debt to Benny Carter and Coleman
Hawkins, and he contributed swing, melody, and near-perfect tone to such items as
"Cotton Tail." Ray Nance replaced Cootie Williams, and his triple threat of cornet,
violin, and vocals produced warm and versatile versions of "Take the 'A' Train,"
"Solitude" and many other re-recorded Ellington classics. Trombonist Lawrence
Brown introduced legato, round tones, and idiomatic blues, while trumpeter
Shorty Baker added lyrical phrasing and tone to the ballads, along with a mute to
the blues. Billy Strayhorn was almost as good as Ellington himself in the fields of
composing, arranging, and piano work. His forte was lyricism. The 1950s saw relatively few additions, but two outstanding performers were tenorist Paul Gonsalves
(who replaced Ben Webster) and the technician Clark Terry.

    The Recordings: The Ellington orchestra made about 2,400 "official"
recordings in addition to sound tracks, transcriptions, unissued masters, private
recordings, etc., that have been circulated on the bootleg markets. It is very difficult to select records that would please everybody because of the immense time
span, stereo versus mono sound, different musicians, and different recording companies. For most of his life, Ellington was a non-exclusive contracted performer.
This meant that he could record for anybody, and if the contract made it difficult,
then he would use a pseudonym or let the band record under someone else's name.
Generally, his best work was for the major companies, and he peaked during the
1940-1942 period. After this time, he had different personnel, re-recorded his
standards, did various suites and related jazz works, and coupled with such other
performers as Ella Fitzgerald, Frank Sinatra, and Louis Armstrong. He also began
to develop more compositions evoking a mood that demanded much of his time,
and worked in the trio format.

    The French CBS reissues cover the essential period of 1925-1940, including
the middle thirties when he was largely recording ("Trombone Blues," "Jubilee
Stomp," "Harlem Twist") for that company and its since-acquired subsidiaries.
There are about 240 tracks plus liner notes of text, discographic information, and
illustrations. (Much material with Ivie Anderson as vocalist will be found annotated
in the *Contemporary Popular Music* volume of this set.) The period since 1947 is
at present being reissued on Columbia twofers. The Decca set presents 42 tracks
from 1926 through 1931, his "jungle" music period.

    The Works of Duke: Complete Edition, v.1- promises to be the most involved
series, reproducing the entire Ellington catalog (including significant alternate takes)
from Victor in the 1920s upwards, beginning with "If You Can't Hold the Man You
Love." The series is projected at over 20 discs, with 20 available as of mid-1978.
Alternative collections exist with the 20-track "This Is . . . " set, and the marvelous
16-track *In a Mellotone*, containing the core of Ellington's best period, 1940-1942
(" 'A' Train," "Portrait of Bert Williams," "Perdido," "Cotton Tail," "Sepia Panorama," etc.). An important live concert is represented on the British Saga discs, from
1943. Material included the then-current repertoire—"Ring Dem Bells," "Tea for
Two," "Jack the Bean"—and was a follow-up to the *Black, Brown, and Beige* suite
performed earlier in the year but never recorded completely at that time. The Prestige set includes 1946 Musicraft tracks that contained boppish attempts for a November Carnegie Hall concert, plus piano trios and quintets.

The next really significant recordings in a jazz context were the 1958-1959 sessions, originally issued as *Back to Back* and *Side by Side*, but here called *Blues Summit*. These were highly successful dates with Johnny Hodges, Harry Edison, Lawrence Brown, Ben Webster, Jo Jones, Ray Eldridge, and Billy Strayhorn. All the material was comprised of blues, either improvised or such standards as "Weary Blues," "Squeeze Me," "Beale St. Blues," "Loveless Love," and "St. Louis Blues." These 16 tracks (really a jam session) are a milestone of fluid expression and must serve as Ellington's "roots" albums. Perennial favorites scattered on all of the above discs include the titles already mentioned plus "Satin Doll," "Sophisticated Lady," "In a Sentimental Mood" (opening with Gershwin's chords from "Someone to Watch Over Me"), "C Jam Blues," "I Got It Bad and That Ain't Good," "Three Little Words," and "Don't Get Around Much Anymore."

All was not roses with Ellington. Three weaknesses stand out, none of which are directly related to mainstream jazz. First, apart from Ivie Anderson, Ellington made weak choices of vocalists. Second, his compositions are difficult to sing, and this has been compounded by diverse lyricists attempting to create poems after the fact of composition. And third, not all of his larger suites or regular orchestral compositions came off successfully (but this does not mean that they were also "poor"). See J5.56 and J5.57 for the acknowledged two best outings during the final decade of his life.

J4.37*   **Benny Goodman. v.5/6 (1935-1938): The Fletcher Henderson Arrangements, Parts One and Two.** two discs. RCA 741.044/059 (French issue).

Fletcher Henderson was of crucial importance to the swing bands; hence, this separate annotation of his arrangements for the premier band of the thirties. His ideas, simple in themselves, were at first difficult to execute. The arrangements were done to give more importance to the band at the expense of soloists. They were simple and relatively easy to perform, with thematic clarity and a light construction. Whenever soloists did engage in musical communication, they performed on either a simulated or a soft (bland) background. Some of the major components of Henderson's ideas were to create dialogs between instrumental sections, with contrasts from the different ensemble textures of reeds and brass; to employ riffs developed from the Kansas City scene; and to have a rhythm section with a powerful drummer (borrowed from Chick Webb). Henderson, who also wrote for Isham Jones and the Dorsey brothers, created 50 orchestrations that Goodman recorded. All have jazz interest, and certainly they are the most jazzy of Goodman's stylings. The 32 better ones are on these two French discs, and they include "Blue Room," "Down South Camp Meeting," "Bugle Call Rag," "King Porter Stomp," "Blue Skies," "When Buddha Smiles," "Christopher Columbus," "I Know That You Know," "Sugar Foot Stomp," "Big John's Special," "Get Happy," "Rosetta," "Stardust," "When It's Sleepy Time Down South," "Louise," and "It Had to Be You."

J4.38*   **Benny Goodman. Carnegie Hall Jazz Concert.** two discs. Columbia 02L 160.

This 1938 concert was the first presentation of jazz in Carnegie Hall—and in any other "classical" music auditorium. As an attempt to show the value of jazz to a largely non-jazz-oriented audience, its impact was immeasurable. A variety of configurations were tried—the orchestra, the trio, the quartet, the vocals. Virtually all selections were extended performances, the most notable being "Sing, Sing, Sing" with the "Christopher Columbus" interpolation and stunning solos by Krupa and Harry James. The climax of this long piece was the swing summary provided by Jess Stacy, who put down on the keyboard all that he knew about piano jazz at that time. Guests with the augmented Goodman band included Lester Young and Buck Clayton from the Basie band, and Johnny Hodges, Harry Carney, and Cootie Williams from the Ellington band. Bobby Hackett was a special trumpet soloist. This, of course, presented a racially integrated band—almost unknown in that day. Outstanding selections include also "Don't Be That Way," the riff closing of "One O'Clock Jump," Goodman's solo on "Blue Room," the trio performances, and Stacy's piano on the Henderson-arranged "Big John's Special."

J4.39*   **Fletcher Henderson. Complete, 1923-1936.** two discs. RCA Bluebird AXM2-5507.

J4.40*   **Fletcher Henderson. v.1/2, First Impressions [and] Swing's the Thing, 1924-1934.** two discs. MCA DL 9227/8.

J4.41*   **Fletcher Henderson. A Study in Frustration, 1923-1938.** four discs. Columbia C4L 19.

Henderson led the very first important big band in jazz history (at New York's Roseland Ballroom). He began a logical evolution from the then-current dance bands that were playing "hot" numbers as novelty items. He set the instrumentation at three trumpets, one trombone, and three saxes, which allowed for doubling. The strong rhythm section had his piano, a banjo, bass, and drums. He was an excellent, creative bandleader, writing scores and doing superb arrangements. Yet, he allowed sufficient scope and room for individuals. Thus, many musicians received their breakthroughs with his organization, such as Coleman Hawkins, Tommy Ladnier, Roy Eldridge, and Chu Berry. He fostered the development of arranger Don Redman. Occasionally, Henderson accompanied many "classic" blues singers on solo piano.

The Columbia set presents 64 titles in chronological order (plus an illustrated booklet with full discographical information). Important titles include "King Porter Stomp," "Copenhagen," "The Chant," "Shag It," "Wang Wang Blues," "Sweet and Hot," and "Sugar." Redman did the early arranging, producing sectional integrity and contrasting brass and sax passages. After Redman left, Henderson took over the arranging. By 1933, he had rediscovered the gospel call in the fashioning of a call-and-response pattern, which became the standard for the white swing bands of the late 1930s. The rhythm section became more tone-conscious when the banjo and tuba were dropped in favor of the guitar and string bass. By 1934, he had created the first swing band, resulting in "Can You Take It," and (from the MCA set) "Down South Camp Meeting," "Shanghai Shuffle," and "Wrappin' It Up." This arranging style found total expression with Benny Goodman. The element of swing (call and response) overshadowed the development of the melody, but it did free soloists from the ensemble passages. Thus, individuals rose to prominence in bands—so much so that many felt they could lead their own bands.

Consequently, swing proliferation and a watering down of the music came about, and it was killed during World War II as draft notices wiped out whole bands.

Henderson's last good band was in 1936 (recording for RCA), with Roy Eldridge, Chu Berry, and Buster Bailey. In 1939, he joined Goodman's outfit. Several years before, in dire financial circumstances, he had sold some arrangements to Goodman, and these created the white swing craze (hear the Henderson arrangements on Goodman's RCA French Black and White reissues). The *Frustration* Columbia offering refers to the fact that Henderson's records never allowed him to reach the big time, for others were alway‿ borrowing from him and leaving him behind. Certainly, his best work was "live," for, according to written accounts, his band was a stomping one that would play a tune for 5-10 minutes. Unfortunately, the long-playing disc was not perfected then, although there was a great "reunion" recorded in 1957 that featured longer versions (see item no. J4.12*).

J4.42*   **Woody Herman. At Carnegie Hall, March 25, 1946.** Verve 2317 031 (British issue).

J4.43*   **Woody Herman. Best.** two discs. MCA 2-4077.

J4.44   **Woody Herman. Early Autumn.** Capitol T-11034.

J4.45   **Woody Herman. Jukin', 1937/42.** Bandstand 7108.

J4.46*   **Woody Herman. The Thundering Herds.** three discs. Columbia C3L 25.
    Clarinetist Herman's music can be divided into three distinct periods. In 1936, he took over the Isham Jones group, a medium weight but highly stylish blues-oriented dance band. All the material then fit into the swing era's characteristics. Herman was the vocalist and lead clarinet player, and his band was called The Band That Plays the Blues. Their efforts were mainly for Decca (the Bandstand issue presents further Decca material from this pre-war period for a total of 36 tracks). Joe Bishop was the leading arranger and soloist (using the flugelhorn), especially on "Blues [parts one and two]." By 1942, there was every indication that Herman was moving away from the blues. He was firmly in control of his ensemble. His was the most exciting and exacting clarinet in the business; others may have "swung" more, but Herman was the super showman. Typical titles here include such dandies as "Woodchopper's Ball," "Yardbird Shuffle," "Hot Chestnuts," and "Get Your Boots-Laced, Papa [parts one and two]."
    Herman moved into his second period because of the draft. He lost most of his band and had to restructure it. He called the new group the First Herd, and it contained men who had great spirit and drew some inspiration from the bop idioms of Parker and Gillespie. This was one of the most exciting of the bop bands (next to Gillespie's), and its output can be found on the Columbia set. The First Herd lasted two years, until the end of 1946. Superb musicians here included tenorist Flip Phillips, arranger Neal Nefti, Shorty Rogers, Red Novro, and drummer Dave Tough. Head arrangements were employed, but group consensus was sought. Hits from this period included "Apple Honey," "Caledonia," "Summer Sequence," and "Blowin' Up a Storm." The ensemble dynamics accounted for the sound, as well as the entry of soloists at crucial climaxes. Also included in the Columbia set are most of the "band within a band" performances of the Woodchoppers, originally inspired by the Ellington small groups. In 1946, the First Herd delivered a definitive concert at Carnegie Hall, with specially written material; here, Herman previewed

Stravinsky's "Ebony Concerto" (but did not record it). Top solo honors were divided between Flip Phillips on "Sweet and Lovely," Red Novro on "The Man I Have," and trombonist Bill Harris on "Everywhere." The brass section's work was impeccable. Of the 22 selections played, 15 are on this set, which stretches for an hour.

Late in 1947, Herman put together the Second Herd, grouping more soloists who had been emulating Young or Parker. The Columbia set contains 8 tracks of this group, including the stunning and classic version of "Four Brothers." Herman had hired four saxists: Stan Getz, Zoot Sims, Serge Chaloff, and Herbie Steward (later replaced by Al Cohn). They swiftly became a team and Jimmy Giuffre, who was the band's arranger, wrote the "brothers' " motif. It and the instrumentation (three tenors and a baritone) were so successful that the impact remained with subsequent Herman bands. Alternate takes and a booklet come with this set. The Capitol reissue is derived from 1948-1950 recordings, a period notable for the lovely "Early Autumn," penned by Ralph Burns and touchingly played by Stan Getz. Many of the compositions here were by band members, including Sonny Berman's "Sonny Speaks," Al Cohn's "Music to Dance To," Burns's "Rhapsody in Wood," Shorty Rogers's "Lollypop," "Keeper of the Flame," and "More Moon." Red Rodney, a brilliant trumpeter who would go on to become a bop legend, was also a key element in this group. At the end of 1948, it too was disbanded, and Herman later assembled his Third Herd. Their beginnings can be found on the Capitol—a bit on the conservative side as it now cost money to maintain a large ensemble. For the next 20 years, Herman would pick up and cast off many bands, and while the music is certainly adequate, it was never up to the standards of the 1940s, nor of the 1970s, his third period (J4.170*).

J4.47*   **Spike Hughes. His All-American Orchestra.** Ace of Clubs ACL 1153 (British issue).

Hughes was a fairly successful British jazz composer and arranger of the early 1930s. He was heavily influenced by Duke Ellington, and when he visited the United States in 1933, he assembled most of the Benny Carter band and recorded 12 titles with them as arranger-director. This is an arranger's album, notable for unique, precedent-setting devices in the years before swing. First, there were many lush, romantic melodies and scoring, as on "Donegal Cradle Song," "Arabesque," "Nocturne," and "Pastoral," all written and arranged by Hughes. "Donegal" has a brilliant solo by Hawkins. Second, Hughes used two major tenor saxists (Hawkins and Berry) to devise a sound that Count Basie would later use. Third, he was superb in building climaxes by interweaving fragments of related melodies into the body of the tunes (as on "Bugle Call Rag"). Fourth, he had strong ensemble passage writing, as for "Firebird," that was later picked up by Sy Oliver when he arranged and scored for Lunceford. As the orchestrations were complex, much rehearsal time was needed ("Donegal" required 2½ hours). Two additional titles for contrast—"How Come You Do Me Like You Do" and "Sweet Sue, Just You"—were recorded as a jam, in which Hughes actually gets to play his bass. These were improvisations based on head arrangements, and they were probably needed to relieve the tensions of the sessions (most of the personnel had departed by this time).

J4.48*   **McKinney's Cotton Pickers. Complete Recordings, 1928-1933. v.1/5.** five discs. RCA 741.080/088/109; FPM 1-7007 and 7059 (French issues).

This strangely-named group was based in Detroit. After Fletcher Henderson, they were very much a favorite of the rare record purchasers. Three soloists of note were tenorist Prince Robinson, trombonist Claude Jones, and trumpeter John Newbitt. Don Redman left Henderson in 1928 and took over arranging for the MCP, utilizing the principles he had learned with Henderson: a blend of the ensemble passages; precision in timing and intonation; and introductions played by the saxophones. Many great tunes were fashioned: "Crying and Sighing," "Milenberg Joys," "It's Tight Like That," "Save It Pretty Mama," and "Some Sweet Day" (utilizing the brass on the verse segment). The 1929-1930 recordings were done in New York, with Rex Stewart from the Henderson outfit. Such tunes as "I Want a Little Girl" and "Laughing at Life" had a profound effect on the Dorsey brothers, who were in New York at this time. The Cotton Pickers' best overall period was in 1931 just as the Depression completed its spread. Titles included "Gee Baby Ain't I Good to You," "Okay Baby," and "You're Driving Me Crazy." By this time Sidney De Paris, Benny Carter, and James P. Johnson had joined the band.

J4.49   **Don Redman. 1932-1933.** Jazz Archives JA5.

J4.50*   **Don Redman. 1938-1940.** RCA 741.061 (French issue).

Redman's most effective work has always been as an arranger. He was the chief architect for Fletcher Henderson's band through 1927, and, thus, he had the opportunity to shape *all* of big band jazz. He was probably the first serious arranger in all of jazz. One aspect of his sound was *blending*, to achieve a "larger than life" sound from fewer instruments; another was the *climax* and the runs that led to it; a third was *timing*, or use of breaks effectively; and a fourth was the *ensemble sections*. By the time he left in 1928 to join McKinney's Cotton Pickers, the Henderson band, as well as others, had sections of trumpets, trombones, reeds, and rhythm. Redman continued his experiments with McKinney (see J4.48). His first band can be heard on MCA 79242 (*Big Bands Uptown*, v.1); the 1932 band introduces "Chant of the Weed," his masterpiece, with its eerie vibrato-less counterpoint scoring. Other tunes from 1938-1940 include "Milenberg Joys," "Shim-me-sha-wabble," "Jump Session" (with no vocal), "I Got Ya," "Sweet Leilani" and "About Rip Van Winkle." Throughout much of his career, Redman showed a heavy debt to Louis Armstrong, whom he first heard in 1924.

J4.51*   **Chick Webb. v.1/2.** two discs. MCA Decca DL 9222/3.

J4.52*   **Chick Webb. Stompin' at the Savoy.** Columbia CL 2639.

Chick Webb was a great jazz drummer and led his own band, which was one of the first swing bands, and set many trends. Arrangements were generally by Edgar Sampson, and soloists of note included trumpeter Taft Jordan and, of course, Ella Fitzgerald, who joined in 1934. Over his long career, Webb provided the house band in the Savoy Ballroom. Many "cutting" sessions ensued, where one band was pitted against another to see which could win over the audience of the night. Webb invariably won. The Decca set covers 1929 through 1939, showing

Webb's development from a New Orleans style to a swing style. It was Webb who inspired the band with his enthusiasm, despite his being in pain from a hunchback. Exceptional items included "Blue Lou," "Don't Be That Way," "Harlem Congo," "Liza," and two showcases for Ella Fitzgerald: "A-Tisket A-Tasket" and "Undecided." The Columbia set comes from a more restricted period: 1934-1935, and also includes a Taft Jordan group spinoff from the same period. All of the music on these three discs is exceptionally buoyant and created much towards the contribution of Harlem music.

STANDARDS

J4.53   **Louis Armstrong. Rare Items, 1935-1944.** MCA Decca DL 79225.
     Most critics seem to agree with the evidence that Louis Armstrong's trumpet was vastly superior to his mediocre orchestra. Thus, he has never had acclaim as a band leader, although his own playing has never been questioned. The 1935-1945 decade was a rough time in Armstrong's career. The Depression was on; he had constant trouble with his lip; he had management problems and personal problems; the material he recorded was trite; etc. After leaving OKeh, he recorded for Victor and then for Decca, in both cases utilizing the big band formats. Many selections were difficult to record, so several takes were needed. A re-evaluation of this period by Dan Morgenstern has led to the above reissue, containing some of Armstrong's best jazz over the troubled decade. Tracks include "Struttin' with Some Barbecue" (a 1938 remake), "Jubilee," "Skeleton in the Closet," "Ev'ntide," and "Swing That Music." Others deal with hokum and humor.

J4.54   **Willie Bryant/Jimmie Lunceford.** two discs. RCA Bluebird AXM2-5502.
     Bryant was originally a dancer who, like so many other personalities of the 1930s, fronted a band. His vocals were individualistic in that they were personal and conversational. The 22 tracks here are derived from the 1935-1936 period, and feature several important musicians, such as Teddy Wilson (who also did some of the arrangements along with Edgar Battle), Cozy Cole, Benny Carter, Ben Webster, Ram Ramirez, and Taft Jordan. There is some humorous swing here through "A Viper's Moan," "Rigamarolle," "Steak and Potatoes," and "Throwin' Stones at the Sun." The arrangements, unlike other swing or big band sounds, left lots of room for many individualistic solos. The 10 Lunceford sides are historically important for noting the shaping of the band. These were its formative years, right after Lunceford came off the Chickasaw Syncopators. Most of the tracks are from 1934, with arrangements from Eddie Wilcox, Sy Oliver, and Will Hudson. The originals include "In Dat Mornin'," "Sweet Rhythm," "White Heat," and "Jazzocracy," showing the beginnings of the brassy gloss that Lunceford would be famous for after moving to the newly founded Decca records.

J4.55*   **The Chocolate Dandies, 1928-1933.** Parlophone PMC 7038 (British issue).
     The Chocolate Dandies were a studio group of changing personnel, often racially mixed, and led by either Don Redman or Benny Carter, both sax players. Again, as was the case with the California Ramblers, this was an attempt to record outside of contracts held by various companies. The material here is from OKeh,

covering five years, and presenting such jazzmen as the Dorsey brothers, Teagarden, Lonnie Johnson, Rex Stewart, J. C. Higginbotham, Coleman Hawkins, Fats Waller, John Kirby, Max Kaminsky, Teddy Wilson, Chu Berry and Sid Catlett. Everything crackles with energy, and the arrangements by Carter and Redman (two of the very best jazz arrangers in recording history) are the main reason for their success. Good notes are by Brian Rust. The 16 selections include "Cherry," "Stardust," "Bugle Call Rag," and several Redman and Carter originals.

J4.56   **Duke Ellington. The Great Paris Concert.** two discs. Atlantic SA2-304.
This set is drawn from unissued material taped at the Olympia Theatre on three nights in February 1963. Other selections, not found here, were on Reprise label's *Duke Ellington's Greatest Hits.* Consequently, the flagwavers and audience appeasers are missing, allowing us to hear new and rarely performed material. The surprise here is *Suite Thursday* in four sections, a seventeen-minute epic written for the 1960 Monterey Jazz Festival and featuring Johnny Hodges. When the number was to be recorded by Columbia, Hodges was sick and did not play. Here he is both present and well. This is a well programmed set—side one showcases Hodges; side two presents Cootie Williams; side three, the other soloists in the Duke's band; and side four, the band as ensemble. This last side concludes with "Tone Parallel to Harlem," a 1950 NBC Symphony commission. Good and complete notes are by Stanley Dance.

J4.57   **Duke Ellington. New Orleans Suite.** Atlantic SD 1580.
This is ostensibly Ellington's "roots" album; maybe not his personal roots but at least the roots of jazz. It was also the last recording Johnny Hodges made, and the first recording the band made after his death, for he died mid-way through the sessions, on May 11, 1970. There are four portraits (the material done after Hodges died): for Louis Armstrong, Wellman Braud, Sidney Bechet, and Mahalia Jackson. Each is a finely sketched representation of the best characteristics, with Cootie Williams, emulating and extending Armstrong; bassist Joe Benjamin and Harry Carney on bass clarinet, for bassist Braud; a simulation of an organ background, for Jackson; and an emotion-laden Gonsalves salute to Bechet (this tune was intended for Hodges's long-forsaken soprano sax). The other items appear to be accurate reflections of the blues, Bourbon Street, the Delta land, marching bands, and the Creole aristocracy. This is a richly detailed record, perhaps one of the more successful of the Ellington "suites," particularly in view of the circumstances under which it was recorded.

J4.58*   **Benny Goodman. All Time Hits.** two discs. Columbia KG 31547.

J4.59   **Benny Goodman. Clarinet a la King.** Epic. EE 22025.

J4.60   **Benny Goodman. Complete, v.1-** (In progress, about 18 discs).
RCA Bluebird AXM 2-5505, 5515, 5532, and 5537.

J4.61*   **Benny Goodman. Thesaurus, June 6, 1935.** three discs. Sunbeam SB 101/3.

J4.62*   **Benny Goodman. This Is Benny Goodman, v.1/2.** four discs. RCA VPM 6040, 6063.

Goodman derived his style and technique from the trills of Jimmie Noone, with shades of register work from Johnny Dodds and Frank Teschemacher. He has been admired both as a soloist and as an influence on future clarinetists. He first began to play with Ben Pollack's group, a semi-Dixieland ensemble, and then he freelanced in New York City in the late twenties and early thirties. He slowly built up to being an accomplished and polished performer, and with good Henderson arrangements, he became the standard bearer of swing during the summer of 1935 (after the craze caught on at Los Angeles's Palomar Ballroom). In 1936, he created the trio with Krupa and Wilson (later, the quartet, with Hampton added), the first interracial group to give public appearances to a white audience. Many of the musicians in the Goodman organization went on to form their own big bands, such soloists as Gene Krupa, Teddy Wilson, Harry James, Lionel Hampton, and Bunny Berigan.

Overall, Goodman's band was not as good as the three leading black bands of Basie, Ellington, and Lunceford. Yet it was important for a number of reasons. Goodman brought swing and riffs to the masses, and in many respects, he changed *popular* music forever. His was a white band that made the breakthrough from black music to white music; hence, other big bands—both white and black—became successful as well. His best period was undoubtedly 1935-1939, during which he made the following discs (featured soloists are in parentheses after the title): "Sugar Foot Stomp" (James), "King Porter Stomp" (Berigan), "Sing, Sing, Sing" (Krupa), "And the Angels Sing" (Ziggy Elman), "Stompin' at the Savoy" (Art Rollini), "Bugle Call Rag" (James), plus "Japanese Sandman," "Blue Skies," "After You've Gone," etc.

The Bluebird reissue series has some alternate takes, plus good to excellent notes. Special mention must be made of two sets of Sunbeam records. SB128-132 is a five-volume set from the Congress Hotel (Chicago) in 1935, 1936; SB116-127 is a twelve-volume set from the Manhattan Room (New York) in 1937. Both album series are broadcast performances and shed much light on Goodman's work during the swing period. Of great historical interest is the *Thesaurus* release. On June 6, 1935, a fourteen-piece ensemble recorded 51 tunes in one take each. This was the Rhythm Makers Orchestra (actually Goodman's outfit of the day) performing for the NBC transcription service. Not only was it a momentous feat, but it gave the band a chance to work out the 37 tunes in their repertoire and to add 14 more. Goodman takes a hot solo on "Yes, We Have No Bananas," and three weeks later, Berigan would rerecord "King Porter Stomp," giving the Goodman orchestra its first big hit. These three records are an interesting and fascinating document of great historical value.

The Columbia and Epic material augments existing Goodman tunes, as they come from the same time period and extend into the Second World War. They feature different soloists. The two RCA VPM twofers are recommended as the 40 most listenable Goodman, and they form a core of selections so that one need not go any further except to purchase *all* of Goodman. Goodman has often been criticized for being too "cool" or removed from the music, and of often taking perfunctory solos. Occasionally, this does happen when a band plays night after night, but it should be remembered that Goodman was at his best when he was stimulated—as in the early New York days or with Charlie Christian. If pushed hard enough, Goodman makes a positive response and can solo better than anybody on clarinet—exchanging ideas, feeding motifs, and accepting themes.

J4.63   Lionel Hampton. Steppin' Out, v.1 (1942-1945). Decca DL 79244.
   After spending five years with Victor fashioning some of the greatest small group jazz in history, Hampton literally stepped out into the world of big band jazz on his own. His basic concept was to extend the small combo format by adding to it until he had the proportions of a big band; in essence, this meant that he would still front the band with his vibes being recorded up front. Despite the plagues of the draft, the shellac crisis, and the lack of recordings from 1942 to 1944, Hampton weathered all storms to produce credible swinging music in the same fashion as the earlier swing bands of the late thirties. It is just unfortunate that he did not do it five years earlier and thus make more of a name for himself. The tracks here, all 14 of them, come from 1942 and 1944-1945 and feature the Septet as well as the Orchestra. His two biggest successes are here ("Flying Home" and "Tempo's Boogie"), along with sterling performances by Cat Anderson, Earl Bostic, Al Sears, Milt Buckner, and Snooky Young.

J4.64*   Erskine Hawkins. v.1/3. (1938-1946). three discs. RCA
   730.708, 741.116, and FPM 1-7024 (French issue).
   Hawkins's group was one of the true swing units of the 1930s, falling just behind Count Basie. The orchestral arrangements of Sammy Lowe, Bill Johnson, and Avery Parrish gave the band its unique sound. Another reason for its consistency (and hence popularity) was the fact that the band had virtually kept every member from 1938 to 1942 (as did Basie's and Ellington's). This cohesion, coupled with the rigors of playing Harlem theaters and cutting sessions with Chick Webb, was responsible for its solid performances and, in retrospect, the exceptionally high caliber of playing. Unfortunately, Hawkins's outfit did not sell all that well on disc. Their biggest hit was "Tuxedo Junction," composed by Hawkins and tenorist Julian Dash; but it was successfully covered by Glenn Miller, and it is usually attributed to him and to his style of playing. Other original items here include "Gin Mill Special," "No Soap," "Norfolk Ferry," "Raid the Joint," "Rifftime," and "Baltimore Bounce" (among the 48 total selections).

J4.65*   Earl Hines. The Father Jumps. two discs. RCA AXM 2-5508.

J4.66   Earl Hines. Hines Rhythm 1933/38. Epic EE 22021.

J4.67   Earl Hines. 1929 Complete Recordings. RCA FPM 1-7023 (French issue).

J4.68*   Earl Hines. South Side Swing, 1934/5. Decca 79221.

J4.69*   Earl Hines. Once Upon a Time. Impulse AS 9108.
   Hines led a number of bands at different times. The 1929 ensemble was the beginning of his explorations beyond the small group context. Previous to this time, he had been with Louis Armstrong and was also developing a dramatic piano style. In effect, he had brought the piano out of the orchestra as "accomplished" solo instrument equal to the clarinet or to the trumpet, and his orchestra was built around this concept. On almost all of his records, there are strong piano openings

and breaks, as with the chorus of ragtime piano at the opening of "Maple Leaf Rag" (on the Decca set). In his work with Armstrong (q.v.), they were complementing and inspiring each other, as on "West Side Blues" and the duet on "Weatherbird." The full band was an innovative one, recording for many companies over a period of time. The Epic and Decca sets cover most of the thirties, and include excursions into "Darkness," "Cavernism," and "Honeysuckle Rose" (all on Epic), with Jimmy Mundy's strong tenor solos and balanced arrangements. The Armstrong-influenced trumpeter Walter Fuller handled the brass solos, while Darnell Howard and Omer Simeon (who had played with Morton) covered the reeds. Popular music and jazz standards of the day were stressed, such as "Copenhagen" or "Sweet Georgia Brown." "Angry" has two good Hines solos that epitomize the casual approach here.

The overall best band was in 1939-1942, when the RCA twofer was originally recorded. This was his Grand Terrace Club Band from the South Side of Chicago, where he had a 12-year tenure. By this time, Budd Johnson had replaced Mundy in the saxophone section and as arranger. He brought the Basie Kansas City riff, as in "XYZ" and "Riff Medley," as well as the Jummie Lunceford polish. Selections include "Boogie Woogie on St. Louis Blues," "Body and Soul," "Deep Forest," "Rosetta," and "Grand Terrace Shuffle." Billy Eckstine joined in 1940, and soon the band became a breeding ground for the early boppers. By 1946, Hines's band was deeply influenced by Gillespie and Parker—and Hines encouraged this. After the late forties, Hines spent 15 years in San Francisco with either a trio or a Dixieland lineup. In 1966, he made his best band recording of modern times. In essence, the Impulse album is Hines with the Duke Ellington band (substituting for the Duke on piano). Dynamic tension fills performances—which included "Black and Tan Fantasy," "Cottontail," "The Blues in My Flat"—played with spirit by Hodges, Pee Wee Russell, Elvin Jones, and others. The piano statement is more powerful here than Ellington may have scored it, but that is because Hines is a determined pianist.

J4.70*   **Andy Kirk and His 12 Clouds of Joy. March, 1936.** Mainstream MRL 399.

These recordings—18 tracks recorded throughout March 1936—show the effortless swing of this Kansas City band, particularly on "Lotta Sax Appeal," "Walkin' and Swingin'," and "Moten Swing." Solos are very pleasing, and the outstanding arrangements and scoring were done by Mary Lou Williams, the band's pianist. The period here is a full 10 months before the Basie band was to record its own style of Kansas swing. Kirk's band's main strength was in the ensemble passages. Beyond Dick Wilson's tenor sax, there were no exceptional soloists (Williams did very few single items), just merely good, solid players.

J4.71*   **Gene Krupa. Drummin' Man.** two discs. Columbia C2L 29.

J4.72   **Gene Krupa. The Essential Gene Krupa.** Verve V6-8571.

J4.73   **Gene Krupa. Sidekicks.** Columbia CL 641.

J4.74*   **Gene Krupa. Swingin' with Krupa.** RCA International INTS 1072 (British issue).

J4.75*   **Gene Krupa. That Drummer's Band.** Epic EE 22027.

J4.76   **Gene Krupa. Wirebrush Stomp, 1938-1941.** Bandstand 7117.
Krupa constantly played to the audience, for he was a showman. They wanted
noise and lengthy solos; he gave it to them. This meant that the entire band had to
be loud, and all subtlety was lost, all of which made him one of the best of the swing
drummers for the flagwaver pieces. Influenced by Chick Webb, Krupa drove the
Goodman band for many years before setting up his own organization. He was
instrumental in creating the rippling sounds of the Goodman trios and quartets.
His first studio-led group was in 1936, on the RCA reissue, and was comprised of
four titles: "Swing Is Here," "I Hope Gabriel Likes My Music," "I'm Gonna Clap
My Hands," and "Mutiny in the Parlour," accompanied by Eldridge, Goodman, Chu
Berry and Jess Stacy. These were instant swing classics, much sought after for years.
The balance of the album is largely Chicago-style jazz, recorded in 1950.
     In 1938, Krupa formed his first band. The double Columbia album covers
a ten-year period, and it is supplemented by the Columbia single album, the Epic,
and the Bandstand (all from this early period up through 1942). Classics include
Roy Eldridge on "Rockin' Chair," Anita O'Day on "Boogie Blues," and "Let Me Off
Uptown," the Krupa hit "Drummin' Man," a boppish "What's This" with a Dave
Lambert scat vocal, and "Disc Jockey Jump" from Gerry Mulligan. Then began
Krupa's long recording career for Verve records. Most of these are reinterpreta-
tions in different configurations (trio to big band) from the 1950s, and the better
efforts can be found on the Verve artist anthology cited.

J4.77*   **Jimmie Lunceford. v.1/4.** four discs. MCA Decca 79237/40.

J4.78   **Jimmie Lunceford. Lunceford Special.** Columbia CL 2715.
     Lunceford's band was the most highly disciplined in all of jazz. His major
contribution was showmanship of a high order, combined with definite solo spots
for such musicians as altoist Willie Smith and trombonist Trummy Young. He
brought trumpeter Sy Oliver into the band as an arranger, and Oliver later went on
to Tommy Dorsey's band, both recreating former Lunceford hits and doing new
material. Oliver's first effort was "Swinging Uptown" (1934), where he meshes a
sterling sax section with the trumpets. Cross-cutting from one section to another
reaches its heights in "Stomp It Off." "Slumming on Park Avenue" has more of the
same, but this time, each section tries to outdo the other for an astonishing series
of climaxes. Phrases were arranged in countless variations with interpolations
by the soloists. Contrasting ideas appear in the shortest passages, such as the eight-
bar introduction to "Annie Laurie," (Oliver's best arrangements were for such
traditional items). Every tune has something of note, and it would take too long to
catalog them here. Other arrangers employed by Lunceford were almost as good:
pianist Eddie Wilcox ("Sleepy Time Gal," "Miss Otis Regrets"); guitarist Eddie
Durham ("Harlem Shout"); altoist Willie Smith ("Rose Room"); and others, who,
being nearer the 1940s, preceded the Stan Kenton progressivism. Along with good
soloists, in addition to those mentioned, such as Teddy Buckner and Snooky Young,
the Lunceford organization produced flagwaver after flagwaver, perhaps summed up
best by the title on the 1933 Columbia set: *Flaming Reeds and Screaming Brass.*

J4.79   **Jay McShann. The Band That Jumps the Blues!** Black Lion 2460 201
           (British issue).

J4.80*   **Jay McShann. New York—1208 Miles (1941-1943).** MCA Decca DL
           79236.
           McShann's band has been characterized as a parallel development to Count
Basie's, but one with a little more assertiveness and punch. It was the band that
gave Charlie Parker his first start on records, as the second alto saxist, although his
solos are not prominent (he appears on 11 of the 14 tracks on the MCA set). The
band was a Kansas City outfit, utilizing the familiar riffs, and it was the last great
band to arrive on the jazz scene (1941). Walter Brown was the vocalist (as on "Hootie
Blues" and "Confessin' the Blues"), and most of the material was written by
McShann. The Black Lion reissue comes from the 1947-1949 period, with a somewhat reduced ensemble that sounded larger than it was because of improved recording techniques and skillful arrangements. This time, the vocalist was Jimmy Witherspoon, the great blues shouter (other McShann backings for Witherspoon can be
found under the latter's name in the **Blues** section of *Black Music*). Material here is
again largely by McShann, with as much concentration on the blues style as formerly.
McShann, since this time, has worked with a quartet or less. (See the subsection herein
on piano for his efforts of the previous decade.)

J4.81   **Glenn Miller. Concert.** RCA LPM 1193.
           Miller has—quite rightly—split the big band swing and jazz enthusiasts right
down the middle: was his a jazz band or a dance band? Perhaps his immense popularity mitigated against his acceptance by the jazz world. This disc rectifies the situation by presenting the Miller band in front of audiences (radio broadcast studios,
clubs, armed services camps) and blowing jazz tunes. Miller had arranged a tune for
the Ray Noble band, where he placed a single clarinet to play the melody with the
sax section. A tenor saxist in that area doubled the lead line an octave lower. This
sound, coupled with riffs and the brass employing hats for a wah-wah sound, produced a unique feeling that was tagged with Miller. The highly structured arrangements did not lend themselves to improvisation, the basis of jazz, but properly
utilized, they did give the "appearance" of improvisation. Miller had risen out of the
jazz session men who were responsible for so many small group backings of vocalists
from 1927-1935 (Dorsey brothers, Goodman, Teagarden, Mannie Klein, etc.). The
sterling items on this record include "One O'Clock Jump," featuring boogie woogie
piano by Chummy MacGregor, tenor sax from Tex Benecke, and many driving trumpet choruses from Clyde Hurley. "St. Louis Blues" employs the Miller pianissimo
ensemble playing before a rousing ride-out. "Tiger Rag" is the flagwaver, Miller giving space to the trombone section and to the drummer. Bobby Hackett plays the
trumpet on "April in Paris." "Dippermouth Blues" has Miller's trombone duplicating King Oliver's original cornet passage. Other tunes included "My Blue Heaven,"
"Georgia on My Mind," and "Jersey Bounce."

J4.82   **Benny Moten. v.1/5.** five discs. RCA 741.056/078/108, and FPM
           1-7004/7062 (French issue).

J4.83*   **Benny Moten. Kansas City Orchestra, 1923-1929.** Historical HLP 9.
           Moten was best known for his version of "South." And he was an inestimable

bandleader in a rather arid jazz area—Kansas City. His was the beginning of the Southwest influence on jazz. Note the date—1923—when the first four tunes on the Historical reissue were cut in St. Louis: "Elephant's Wobble," "Crawdad Blues," "Evil Mama Blues," and "Break O'Day Blues." This collection of blues riffs over a steady rhythm eventually became that of Count Basie's band in the early thirties. It is not difficult to see (or rather, hear) why this was perhaps the finest touring band of the twenties. As was the case with most groups in the twenties, the band is centered on the trumpet—either open or muted. It was not until Hawkins (through Henderson) or Young (through Basie) came along that emphasis shifted to the tenor saxophone. This album of fourteen cuts is an important document in recorded jazz history, and it should be treated with respect.

The more commercial recordings of RCA, extending to 1932, contain virtually all of Moten's Victor output. The 75-odd tracks here show the early influence of Jelly Roll Morton and the later influence of Fletcher Henderson. The 1920 band, when first formed, followed a path of social dances based on the ragtime of the day. Significant performers included Woody Walter (clarinet and glass), Leroy Berry (banjo), Thamon Hayes (trombone), and other riffing and rhythmic performers who were later to have their own bands—Eddie Durham, Harlan Leonard, Walter Page, and "Count" Bill Basie. Ensemble work was excellent on "Hot Water Blues" and "Slow Motion," while the soloists take over for "Rite Tite." All six discs here provide fascinating documentation on band style changes; in 1930, the band underwent another shift with "Jones Law Blues" and the arrival of Bill Basie's solo piano. Eventually Basie took over the band when Moten died.

J4.84   **Red Norvo.** Epic EE 22009.

Norvo is a swinging vibraphone and xylophone performer. His style is straightforward, with light, no vibrato or shadings, and good organization, and he can really be exciting. Since the late 1920s, he has been active in various groups of all sizes, playing all kinds of jazz. These 1933-1938 recordings have been classed as "chamber jazz," despite the presence of Chu Berry, Bunny Berigan and Teddy Wilson. Many of the 16 tracks are his own compositions ("Knockin' on Wood," "Hole in the Wall," "Dance of the Octopus"); the balance are current swing items. These are all good tight group performances in a variety of settings, from a quartet to a full band (with singer Mildred Bailey, his wife, on one track). Norvo has played with Goodman, Herman, and many small groups of the 1950s and 1960s. Although lacking the flamboyancy of Lionel Hampton, he does have the technical skill for clear consistency.

J4.85*   **Luis Russell. His Louisiana Swing Orchestra.** two discs. Columbia KG 32338.

This is wonderful in all regards except for the major point that recording dates are not given, and the minor point that the jacket print is very small and difficult to read. Full discographical information (other than dates) and sharp notes by Frank Driggs make this a welcome reissue indeed. The last time out was for 16 tracks on British Parlophone; here we have 32 as a full set. Russell was a pianist-orchestra leader, working with eight to ten other performers at the Saratoga Club in Harlem, 1929-1930 (where these performances come from). Most of his drive was achieved by Pops Foster's bass. Louis Metcalf played cornet, and the early sides (with a tuba brass bass) reflect New Orleans roots. With the advent of the string bass, the band hit its stride. Red Allen was introduced, and lifted "Song of Swanee" and "Saratoga Shout" to titles of pre-eminence in jazz. J. C. Higginbotham and Albert Nicholas take very good solos as well. But it was not until the later 1930 recordings that the ensemble came together through arrangements—something new and unique for New Orleans-inspired music. This is a good set from the OKeh and ARC records.

J4.86*   **Artie Shaw**. RCA LPV 582.
Artie Shaw usually suffers by comparison with Benny Goodman. He is nearly always categorized as being second and just a step behind. Take his Gramercy Five, for example (represented here by six selections plus an unissued take of "Misterioso"). This group-within-a-band came later than the Goodman quartets and quintets. Yet, as evidenced by "The Gentle Grifter" and "The Sad Sack," the music is just as good; it only pales after one hears Goodman. But their five are the best on this disc, with Roy Eldridge (trumpet), Dodo Marmarosa (piano), and Barney Kessel (guitar). All sixteen tracks come from 1944-1945, rather late as big bands go, and suffer somewhat by the manpower shortage caused by the War and the rush to the studios after the recording ban was lifted. What saved the Shaw band at this point was his arrangers' penchants for show tunes with developed melodies that they could use for shading and balance. RCA has selected here that material with Roy Eldridge as first trumpet. He was with the band at this stage for 11 months and contributed greatly to its success in "Lady Day," "A Foggy Day," "Soon," and others.

J4.87*   **Cootie Williams. The Boys from Harlem.** Tax m8005 (Swedish issue).

J4.88*   **Cootie Williams. The Rugcutters, 1937/40.** Tax m8011 (Swedish issue).

J4.89   **Cootie Williams. Original Hit Recordings, 1944.** Phoenix LP1.
Cootie Williams, who left Duke Ellington from 1940 through 1961, was perhaps the most successful of the Ducal soloists to break away and form his own group. Much of his work can be found on the Ellington discs (he replaced Bubber Miley in 1929) and as one of the Ellingtonians in the anthologies. His style, of course, was plunger trumpet and growl, along with the blues and swing. For the first year after leaving Ellington, he worked with the Benny Goodman Sextet (at the same time as Charlie Christian and Lionel Hampton). Then, he formed his first orchestra and his own sextet. Nineteen forty-four is the date for the Phoenix reissue, and its 16 tracks include much music in the then new jump style that was to evolve into r 'n' b and soul music. Pearl Bailey handled the vocals for the large band (e.g., "Tess's Torch Song," "Red Blues"), while boppers and jumpers such as Eddie "Cleanhead" Vinson, also a vocalist, Eddie "Lockjaw" Davis, and Bud Powell played in both the band and Sextet. Typical uptempo titles include "You Talk a Little Trash," "Floogie Boo," and "Honeysuckle Rose." His most rewarding group was The Rugcutters, from the late 1930s. The 32 tracks on the Swedish Tax reissues provide ample evidence of the hot jazz in New York. Drawing on the personnel of the Duke Ellington band, including Ivie Anderson for some of the vocals, Williams rips loose with "My Honey's Lovin' Arms" (lovely Anderson vocal here), "Black Beauty," "Watchin'," "Downtown Uproar," "Chasin' Chippies," and "Dry So Long," where he leads with Ellington's piano.

J4.90   Sam Wooding and His Chocolate Dandies. Biograph BLP 12025.
The personnel on this disc are not the Dandies led by either Don Redman or
Benny Carter, but rather the group that Sam Wooding took to Europe in 1925
as probably the first black touring jazz band (apart from Jim Europe's military band
in WWI). It was a whole show with a cast of 40, including 4 singers, an acrobatic
team, knee-drop dancers, other dancers, and a singing-dancing chorus of 10. They
recorded four sides for the German Vox label in Berlin (all are here, along with an
alternate take of "Albany Bound"). Later, they added a jazz version of "Tannhauser."
After being accorded rave reviews wherever they went, the usual ego tensions began,
and the band members left to go on their own apart from the whole show. The cities
of Hamburg, Copenhagen, Moscow, Leningrad, and the continents of Africa and
South America—they all fell under the influence of American jazz, and to many,
Wooding's group was their first live contact with such music. In 1929, 10 other titles
were recorded in Barcelona, with most of the band taking part in the vocals. Wooding returned to America just before WWII; but in the fifties, he started to tour again,
this time as a soloist or accompanist. The last track on this disc is from 1963 in
Paris—a piano trio version of "I Got Rhythm." His early influence was probably
incalculable for the audiences in Europe and elsewhere. Band members in the
twenties included such greats as Tommy Ladnier, Gene Sedric, and Doc Cheatham.
Not only is this disc good music, but it is also a significant historical document.

JAZZ COMBOS

Anthologies

J4.91*   The Bands Within the Bands. two discs. MCA Coral COPS 7360 D1/2
(West German issue).
This is a very interesting concept album. The time frame is 1938 through
1952. The 24 tracks illustrate the nature and evolving concepts of the smaller jam
bands formed within the structure of larger big band units. Such small groups provided great release from the arranged music that the musicians had to play night
after night. Some of the best jazz emanated from these people, such as Benny Goodman's Trios and Quartets and Sextets (unfortunately, not found on this set). From
the large MCA catalog come such as the Hampton small group cutting up "Chord-a-
re-bop" and "How High the Moon"; Artie Shaw's Gramercy Five doing "Shekomeko
Shuffle"; the Dorsey Clambake Seven tackling "Dirty Dozens" and "Trouble in
Mind"; the Woody Herman Woodchoppers cutting down "South," and the Bob
Crosby Bob Cats doing the same for "Palesteena." In addition to release of steam,
the groups often did intermission work during concert performances by their respective big bands.

J4.92*   The Greatest of the Small Bands. v.1-5. five discs. RCA 741.089,
741.106, 741.117, 741.103, FPM1-7014 (French issue). (In progress).

J4.93*   The Swinging Small Bands, v.1-3. three discs. MCA 510.071, 510.088,
510.111 (French issue). (In progress).
That small combos from the past (unless they happen to be with Benny Goodman) are not well served by American reissues from the major companies that own

the rights can be seen by noticing the place of issuance above. France is in the throes (and has been since 1970) of reissuing all kinds of American jazz, up to about 60 reissues a month! Small bands or groups achieved some popularity because big names or star soloists were fronting capable rhythm, and these sold well to jazz fans who favored one star over another. The economics of paying scale wages during the Depression, the War years, and afterwards, also favored such sessions because not much money was involved. RCA's first volume includes Red Norvo, with Harry Edison and Ben Webster from 1957, plus some filler from 1954. The late forties are in the second volume, with Coleman Hawkins, Mary Lou Williams, Lucky Thompson, Dizzy Gillespie, and Benny Carter. This is a bop album, from just after World War II. The third album goes back to the late thirties, with Hot Lips Page, Frankie Newton, Rex Stewart, and various Basie personnel. Volume 4 covers 1929 through 1945, with Red McKenzie and the Mound City Blue Blowers, Wingy Manone, Bud Freeman, and Jess Stacy. Volume 5 returns to the fifties, with Al Sears in an r 'n' b mood, and Red Allen. The MCA set is mostly from 1935-1944, with Stuff Smith, Hot Lips Page, John Kirby, Eddie Durham, Zutty Singleton, Mary Lou Williams, Sammy Price, Jabbo Smith, and Red Allen. Both sets are discographically untidy, although all tracks are identified as to source. The RCA has bilingual notes; the MCA is in French only. These important records document the "real" jazz.

J4.94   **Town Hall Jazz Concert, 1945.** two discs. Atlantic SD 2-310.
World War II was ending, and 52nd Street in New York was at the zenith of its exciting contribution to jazz. Leonard Feather had a hand in promoting this Town Hall concert, which would reveal to audiences at large the extent and scope of jazz music in small combos. It was a happy celebration by some of the greats, such as Teddy Wilson, Stuff Smith, Gene Krupa, Red Norvo, and Flip Phillips in various settings ranging from trios to medium-sized units. Some selections include "Indiana," "I Got Rhythm," "Where or When," "Sweet and Lovely," "Stardust," and "Perdido." Recording time is ample, almost two hours worth on two discs.

Innovators

J4.95*   **Benny Goodman. Small Groups.** RCA LPV 521.

J4.96*   **Benny Goodman. Trio and Quartet, v.1/2.** two discs. CBS 62853,
            63086 (French issue).
Goodman's trio and small groups were notable for quite a few innovations. They were the first "band-within-a-band" group, they were interracial (whites Goodman and Krupa playing with blacks Wilson and Hampton), and they were also a testing ground for bop when Charlie Christian joined to make it a sextet (these later discs are annotated under Christian)—and in so doing, actually prodded Goodman on to doing his best material. The trio (Wilson, Krupa and Goodman) performed either slow numbers ("Body and Soul" or "More Than You Know"—both with excellent Goodman solos) or fast numbers ("Tiger Rag" or "China Boy"), with few mid-tempo selections. Krupa is discreet, but Dave Tough is actually the best drummer, as heard through "Blues in My Flat" and "Blues in Your Flat." The tune "I Know That You Know" is the world-famous Jimmie Noone version, perhaps created here as Goodman was influenced by Noone and as Teddy Wilson's piano at

this period was in the Hines style with melodic solos. The CBS recordings are broadcasts, with good sound, of 1937-1938 items, including exceptionally long versions of "I Got Rhythm," "Dizzy Spells," and "Stompin' at the Savoy." The RCA is derived from the studio, 1936-1938, and of the 32 tracks heard here in total, only one is duplicated.

J4.97*   **Lionel Hampton. Complete, 1937-1941.** six discs. RCA AXM6-5536.
    Hampton brought the vibraphone to jazz, further expanding the horizons set by Norvo on the xylophone. He was at his best in the Goodman Quartets and other groups. At the same time, he was working with his own small groups and bands for RCA, shaping a superb unit into the swing idiom. In this period, he arranged for 23 sessions with some of the greatest jazz musicians around. These 96 items are arranged chronologically, and include such musicians as Ziggy Elman, Jess Stacy, Gene Krupa, Cootie Williams, Johnny Hodges, Buster Bailey, Sonny Greer, Rex Stewart, Lawrence Brown, Chu Berry, Harry James, Charlie Christian, and many others drawn from the Goodman, Basie, and Ellington bands from time to time. Hampton dominates by swinging on a loping vibe, punctuating a piano in vibe style, or hitting the drums from time to time. In all the history of jazz, this period produced an incredibly rich small group jazz that hung around the fringes of jazz. Perhaps the most interesting was the group with Dizzy Gillespie, Benny Carter, Coleman Hawkins, Chu Berry, Ben Webster, Charlie Christian, Milt Hinton, and others, performing "One Sweet Letter from You," "Hot Mallets," and "Early Session Hop."

J4.98*   **Coleman Hawkins. Body and Soul.** RCA Vintage LPV 501.

J4.99*   **Coleman Hawkins. Classic Tenors.** Flying Dutchman. FD 10146.

J4.100   **Coleman Hawkins. The Essential.** Verve V-8568.

J4.101*   **Coleman Hawkins. The Hawk in Holland.** GNP Crescendo GNP 9003.

J4.102   **Coleman Hawkins. The Hawk Flies.** two discs. Milestone M 47015.

J4.103   **Coleman Hawkins. The High and Mighty Hawk.** Master Jazz Recordings. MJR 8115.

J4.104   **Coleman Hawkins. Hollywood Stampede.** Capitol T-11030.

J4.105*   **Coleman Hawkins and Ben Webster. Blue Saxophones.** Verve 2304 169 (British issue).

J4.106*   **Coleman Hawkins and Lester Young.** Spotlite SPJ 119 (British issue).
    Coleman Hawkins had a career that spanned 47 recording years, from a 1922 date with Mamie Smith to his death in 1969. This period, of course, covers the whole of recorded jazz, and Hawkins was able to change with the times and the fashions, although he was not as innovative as later tenor saxists were to be. His major contribution was to bring the saxophone out of the orchestra—to give it a solo role with meaning far beyond section playing. The saxophone before Hawkins was an

ill-conceived instrument that apparently had little role to play in the formation of jazz. Hawkins did a number of things: he played in a two beat style, emphasizing the first and third notes rather than the usual four. He employed a constant chromatic *appoggiatura*. Thus, his style was based on a well-defined melodic system: few intervals, and the use of harmonic *appoggiatura* on the weak beats. This meant constant playing, as opposed to the lean lines of Lester Young, where even the silences counted as part of the music. Hawkins's style and romantic expression attracted many disciples and imitators, for it permits generally the playing of very acceptable things in almost any circumstances. Early in his career, he was influenced by Louis Armstrong, in 1924-1925, while with the Fletcher Henderson (q.v.) band, and he remained there until departing for Europe in 1934. There, he made many fine recordings, notably in Holland with a local hot dance orchestra, between 1935 and 1937.

Three originals on the GNP set include "Netcha's Dream," "A Strange Thought," and "Something Is Gonna Give Me Away." With Django Reinhardt (q.v.), on HMV CLP 1890, he made a number of exceptional tracks, including the lush "Stardust," "Honeysuckle Rose," and "Crazy Rhythm." Hawkins returned before the outbreak of war and created "Body and Soul" on October 11, 1939— one of the best-known and best-loved jazz classics of all time. This is on the RCA set, as well as 15 other tracks covering a 36-year period. Included are "One Hour," a formatic ballad with the Mound City Blue Blowers (largely the Condon gang); "St. Louis Shuffle," with Fletcher Henderson's orchestra; and material with Lionel Hampton, McKinney's Cotton Pickers, Red Allen, and Sonny Rollins (in addition to his own groups), truly a sampler album.

The 1940s were a good period for Hawkins. He led his own small groups, he jammed, he saw his influence spread wide and clear, he recorded often, he adapted his style to modern times. The Flying Dutchman set is from 1943. Four tracks here are just tenor sax plus rhythm and include two classics ("The Man I Love" and "Sweet Lorraine"), with Eddie Heywood, Oscar Pettiford, and Shelly Manne. There are four tracks by the septet here, and they clearly show the beginning of the bop influence on Hawkins. By 1945, Hawkins was into bop. On the Capitol album from that year are twelve tracks, mostly ballads such as "Talk of the Town" and "What Is There to Say?," but there are also bop pieces such as "Rifftide," based on "Lady Be Good." The sextet largely reappears again on the Spotlite reissue for "Mop Mop" and "Body and Soul."

Both the Flying Dutchman and Spotlite set offer some Lester Young quartet tracks as a point of comparison, but the hands-down winner of confrontation was the 1946 recording of the Jubilee All Stars, with Hawkins, Young, and Buck Clayton in the front line. The diametrically opposite styles still prevail despite each attempt to be boppish about "I Got Rhythm," "Lady Be Good," and "Sweet Georgia Brown"— all well-known tunes used by the bop movement for contrafacts. The Milestone two-fer contains some interesting pieces. Five tracks come from the end of 1946, when Hawkins had bop down pat, leading Fats Navarro, J. J. Johnson, Hank Jones, Milt Jackson, and Max Roach (a rather young crew) through such statements as "I Mean You" (by Monk) and two takes of "Bean and the Boys" (based on "Lover Come Back to Me"). Half of the set is taken up by a 1957 date that again included Jones and Johnson and ranks as one of Hawkins's finest sets in the 1950s, he being spurred on by the younger men in his septet (as on "Blue Lights" and "Chart"). The Verve offering collects together the 1947-1958 Norman Granz recordings, including the uniquely unaccompanied "Picasso," "The Walker" (based on "Stompin' at the Savoy"), "Hanid" (based on "Dinah"), and "Sunday"—the latter three with Roy Eldridge.

Blue Saxophones is a vital disc for its riches. Ben Webster (q.v.) was the number one disciple of Hawkins, and both are assisted here by the Oscar Peterson trio of 1957. Webster went deeper into the melody and breathier aspects of ballads, while Hawkins operated in the post-bop period with a certain aggression or forceful-ness. Selected titles include "It Never Entered My Mind," "Tangerine," and "La Rosita." The Master Jazz disc is a reissue from Stanley Dance's Felsted label of work recorded in 1958. It is one of Hawkins's best post-War efforts. Buck Clayton is featured in a quintet with rhythm furnished by Ray Brown and Hank Jones. The 11-minute long "Bird of Prey Blues" is the standout track, along with "My One and Only Love." This is a mainstream album all the way, full of moving statements and interplay among the musicians.

J4.107*   **Johnny Hodges. Back to Back/Side by Side.** two discs. Polydor 2682 005 (British issue).

J4.108   **Johnny Hodges. The Big Band Sound.** Polydor 2317 077 (British issue).

J4.109*   **Johnny Hodges. Hodge Podge.** Epic EE 22001.

J4.110   **Johnny Hodges. The Jeep Is Jumpin'.** two discs. Polydor 2683 056 (British issue).

J4.111   **Johnny Hodges. A Memory.** Master Jazz Recordings MJR 8107.

J4.112*   **Johnny Hodges. Things Ain't What They Used to Be.** RCA Vintage LPV 533.

Hodges was a great jazz soloist, performing on alto sax in the Duke Ellington band. He was one of the top three influential performers on the alto (the other two being Benny Carter and Charlie Parker). His projection of a warm, lyrical, often sensuous tone was a direct development from Sidney Bechet, an early mentor. His best solos and section work lay with the Ellington (q.v.) band; however, on his own he did reveal a certain freshness as he tried to get away from the Ellington mode (despite the presence of Ellington on some of these tracks).

The 16 tracks on the Epic disc cover 1938-1939. The septet here consists of Cootie Williams, Lawrence Brown, Harry Carney, Ellington, Sonny Greer, and either Billy Taylor of Jimmy Blanton on bass. As with most of the Ducal backings, the soloist (Hodges) played over a series of pre-constructed phrases. Most of the tracks are blues ("Jeep's Blues," "Empty Ballroom Blues," "Dream Blues," "Home-town Blues"), but there is a notable trio with only Hodges, Ellington, and Taylor doing "Finesse." The 1941 outing on RCA replaces Williams with Ray Nance and embraces more Ellington material, such as the original version of "Things Ain't What They Used to Be" and "Passion Flower."

The Master Jazz is a reissue from the French Vogue label, and it was recorded in 1950, again with Ellingtonians on tour in France. Noted French pianist Raymond Fol sits in for Ellington; others included Shorty Baker, Don Byas, Wendell Marshall, and Sonny Greer. The program is a mixture of Ducal standards ("Perdido,"

"Mood Indigo") and the blues associated with Hodges's tone. The British Polydor reissues are all derived from the American Verve catalog, and present him in a number of settings. Chronologically, *The Jeep Is Jumpin'* comes first, and represents Hodges's attempts at recording after he left the Ellington band. For the most part, he is ably supported by members of the Ellington band, so he is in familiar surroundings. Alter ego Billy Strayhorn sits in for the Duke at piano. The other musicians include Emmett Berry, Lawrence Brown, Ben Webster, Sonny Greer, Shorty Baker— and even John Coltrane. The 32 selections, from 1951-1956 again, include the blues and Ellington standards ("I Got It Bad and That Ain't Good," "Solitude," "Sophisticated Lady"). The big band album was recorded in 1956-1957, with Strayhorn again replacing Ellington in the piano chair. It is a looser version of Duke's current band, playing quite a few originals written by the members, such as Hodges, Cat Anderson, and Clark Terry. Many of the tunes are uptempo. As a co-leader with Ellington, Hodges worked long and hard on the 1959-1960 double disc *Back to Back/Side by Side.* The septet performs mainly blues, such as the traditional "Basin Street Blues" and "Beale Street Blues," "St. Louis Blues," "Loveless Love," and "Royal Garden Blues."

J4.113*   **Mel Powell. Out on a Limb.** Vanguard VRS 8528 (British issue).

J4.114*   **Mel Powell. Thingamagig.** Vanguard VRS 8528 (British issue).
     An assimilating pianist who can draw from many styles, Mel Powell presents an enigma. All of his work is tasteful, but it varies from context to context. The two discs here are his best works, one with a trio, the other with trios up through septets. He made solid contributions to the Benny Goodman ensemble from 1941 until induction into the armed services, then contributed to a Django Reinhardt (q.v.) session, and established four clear-thinking solos in 1945, reflecting a Teddy Wilson influence (these are on French CBS 62876). In 1954 and 1955, he recorded for Vanguard as part of that company's swing revival (John Hammond was working as their producer). The trio set has cornetist Ruby Braff and drummer Bobby Donaldson in a scintillating program that takes full advantage of Braff's lyricism and power ("Bouquet," penned by Powell). The inevitable chases and ballads appear here, as with the title track "Thingamagig" or "You're My Thrill." The other album was all done on the same day, with Braff, Donaldson, Peanuts Hucko, and Oscar Pettiford, among others, playing a supporting role to the pianist. Mainstream material embraces "Three Little Words," "You're Lucky to Me," "Liza," "Rosetta," and "Gone with the Wind"—a tastefully balanced program of diverse influences.

J4.115*   **Cy Touff and Richie Kamuca. Having a Ball.** World Pacific Jazz 1211.
     This is a collection of small band jazz items, combining good solo passages with arranging skills and some relaxed Basie-type blowing. Johnny Mandel did most of the arranging with musicians from the Herman "herd" of the time (1955). The eight tracks feature compatible and sympathetic performers, especially on "Keester Parade" and "Prez-ence." Touff (bass trumpet) and Kamuca (tenor sax), the latter formerly with Stan Kenton, are the prime soloists, both in the Lester Young style. Other musicians include Leroy Vinnegar's walking bass and Chuck Flores's drumming bombs. A nice, tight, little album that constantly rewards over many re-playings. As a very important note, this album is a special favorite with many jazz musicians.

J4.116   **Fats Waller. Complete Recordings, v.1-** (about 30 discs). RCA Bluebird AXM 2-5511- (In progress).

J4.117*   **Fats Waller. Ain't Misbehavin'.** RCA LPM 1246.
Fats Waller was greatly influenced by James J. Johnson, who decorated the
melody rather than improvised. Waller was a pianist, composer of some 360 items,
organist, vocalist, and a band leader who was trained in the classics. On Broadway,
he created *Keep Shufflin'* (1927) and *Hot Chocolates* (1930). In 1934, he began his
"comic" period with His Rhythm, while in 1942, at the close of his career, he performed solo at Carnegie Hall. His effortless style has been commented on many
times. It was polished and precise, with emphasis on the melody (he hated boogie
woogie), and he could seriously improvise from a little melody, such as on
"Smashing Thirds," "Valentine Stomp," or "Numb Fumblin'." He gave formal
organization by providing shapes to contrasts. In his group work, he preferred the
sextet or septet. Unfortunately, his band was always given trite material that was
funny and melodic, but they did the best they could through exaggeration and
talking. This, of course, gave many people the wrong impression about Waller's
total recorded output. Solos were handled by Waller, trumpeter Herman Autrey,
and saxist Eugene Sedric.
Despite the poor material, the band came through with classics such as
"Whose Honey Are You?," with a Waller introductory piano solo that summarizes
his style; "Got a Bran' New Suit," with some sharp stride piano; "Blue Because of
You," featuring good singing; and "Tain't Good," a Waller duo with Autrey. Waller
did all his recording under his own name with RCA; hence, the 25 or so discs here
contain around 400 items meant for the serious collector and libraries. They are
arranged in two sequences, in chronological order, with many alternate takes and
unissued items for comparison. Many of his alternates were completely different,
illustrating the type of material he had to deal with (except for his stride solos).
Combined with the separately available albums, the recorded legacy of Waller spans
his solo piano work (his best jazz efforts), his solo pipe organ (he was a master at
the organ, and indeed, it was his favorite instrument, as on "Soothin' Syrup
Stomp," "Lennox Avenue," and "St. Louis Blues"), his accompaniment to blues
singers for RCA such as Alberta Hunter (often playing the organ behind them),
and with Morris's Hot Babies, giving his best performances in a band not his own.
LPM 1246 is a sort-of "greatest hits" compilation. It is the popular Fats Waller and
includes "Honeysuckle Rose," "Ain't Misbehavin'," "Two Sleepy People," "I
Can't Give You Anything But Love," "Tea for Two," "I'm Gonna Sit Right Down
and Write Myself a Letter," "It's a Sin to Tell a Lie," plus five others.

J4.118   **Ben Webster. At Work in Europe.** two discs. Prestige P 24031.

J4.119*   **Ben Webster and Coleman Hawkins. Blue Saxophones.** Polydor 2304
169. (British issue).

J4.120*   **Ben Webster and Oscar Peterson. Soulville.** two discs. Polydor 2683
023 (British issue).

J4.121*   **Ben Webster and Art Tatum.** Pablo 2310 737.
Tenorist Webster was a direct disciple of Coleman Hawkins and was that

master's most successful pupil. However, Webster developed beyond Hawkins in that he took a certain melodic lyricism from altoist Benny Carter and merged the two styles into a breathy romanticism. Ballads and blues were his strong points. Playing off and on for Duke Ellington, Webster developed as a soloist of some note; after leaving Ellington he pursued a single career, usually performing with a piano trio. All of his records are characterized by consistency and a high level of fluency. Virtually any of his performances are recommended; consequently, we chose one of his last works, from 1969, recorded in Copenhagen and in Holland. The trios lay down the basic rhythm, propelled on one disc by bassist Niels-Henning Orsted Pedersen. There are just four selections here, but all are extended modern works, as Horace Silver's "The Preacher," Monk's "Straight, No Chaser," and Nat Adderley's "Work Song." The Dutch compilation includes six Ellington numbers: "Prelude to a Kiss," "Rockin' in Rhythm," "In a Sentimental Mood," and "I Got It Bad" (among others).

When he performed with equal giants, Webster was keenly whetted by the competition. His best work from the past has been with the three co-leaders indicated above, all for the Verve label. From 1956, he performed with Tatum (one of a series Tatum did with mainstream artists) in a reflective session of classics: "Night and Day," "Where or When," "All the Things You Are," and other musical ballads. The sessions with the Peterson trio cover 1953-1959 and embrace all of Peterson's different trios from the 1950s. Of particular interest are "Sunday," "When Your Lover Has Gone," and "The Touch of Your Lips." With Hawkins, it is master versus pupil as the two try to outdo each other. Webster is more breathy than normal, and Hawkins is more aggressive. Most of the tracks are ballads and Latin-inspired rhythms.

J4.122*   **Teddy Wilson. All-Stars.** two discs. Columbia G 31617.

J4.123*   **Teddy Wilson and Lester Young. Prez and Teddy.** two discs. Polydor 2683 025 (British issue).

Teddy Wilson was a superb accompanist, utilizing both hands equally at the keyboard in sympathetic arrangements behind various singers and musicians. His work with Benny Goodman created masterpieces of the trio and quartet genre. Recording with various pick-up groups in the 1930s for John Hammond-produced Columbia sessions, Wilson assembled and organized many small swing ensemble classics. The 32 tracks here show him accompanying Ella Fitzgerald on "All My Life," Helen Ward on "Here's Love in Your Eyes," and Billie Holiday on "Guess Who?," "He Ain't Got Rhythm," and "Mean to Me." The groups were drawn from the Basie organization (Clayton, Young, Green, Page, Jones), the Ellingtonians (Hodges, Carney, Webster, et al.), the Goodman band, and freelancers.

This is a good collection of the small outfits from the swing era. The twofer from Polydor was originally on American Verve and comes from a couple of 1956 sessions. Wilson nicely controls the aging Young, who turned in his greatest post-War performance of long, lean lines. All the 12 tunes are long, extended versions of classics: "Love Me or Leave Me," "Louise," "All of Me," and "Taking a Chance on Love."

J4.124*   **Lester Young. The Aladdin Sessions.** two discs. Blue Note. BNLA 456-H2.

J4.125*   **Lester Young. The Alternative Lester.** Tax m8000 (Swedish issue).

J4.126*   **Lester Young. Prez: The Complete Recordings.** two discs. Savoy SJL 2202.

J4.127*   **Lester Young. Jammin' with Lester.** Jazz Archives JA 18.

    Lester Young's tenor sax has inspired many. His vibrato-less sound, long, lean lines, and soft tones are a descendant of Trumbauer and are completely opposite to Coleman Hawkins, the other major tenor saxophonist in jazz history. At the time, it was apparently felt that listeners had to be either a "Bean" fan or a "Prez" fan, often to the exclusion of the other. There have been some interesting reissues allowing listeners to compare and contrast the styles, such as *Classic Tenors* (Flying Dutchman FD 10146, recorded in 1943) or the untitled Spotlite SPJ 119 (British issue). Basically, Young played the jazz phrase in an unhurried manner for the sake of the phrase and for its pure melodic value, without any reference to any systems. By a fluency of notes and by occasionally playing behind the beat, he achieved his objectives. Much of his early work (before the end of World War II) is regarded as his best. Unfortunately, he was seldom heard in small group context except for the 1936 Jones-Smith, Inc., sessions or with the 1938 Kansas City Six. Most of the time he was with Count Basie's big band or with Teddy Wilson. And *all* of the groups just mentioned utilized Basie performers; thus, the bulk of Young's work will be found annotated under Basie (q.v.).

    The Tax issue presents several alternative takes from the 1936-1939 period, giving further documentation to existing performances of such classics as "Shoe Shine Boy," "Pagin' the Devil," "Lester Leaps In," and "Dickie's Dream" (three alternative takes here) in the program of 16 tracks. Buck Clayton and Dickie Wells were his best accompanists. At this time, he strongly influenced Billie Holiday. His legato style had a very relaxing mood, especially whenever he used the metal clarinet to produce an ethereal, distanced sound. The Jazz Archives set presents the full sound track of the film short *Jammin' the Blues*, which won an Oscar nomination as best short feature of the year—"Midnight Symphony," "On the Sunny Side of the Street," and the title track—*plus* three other tunes filmed and recorded but not released. All the tunes are here, and the 1944 group is exceptional in its placement: Harry Edison, Dickie Wells, Illinois Jacquet, Marlowe Morris, a young Barney Kessel, Red Callendar, Sid Catlett, and Jo Jones. This was a superb jazz film, in both the music and the presentation.

    In 1940, Young left Basie to record on his own, joining Basie again in 1943 and until his induction into the army. During this period, he recorded with a mixture of groups for both Aladdin and Savoy. Current reissues of two discs from each source also include a number of sessions from after the war through 1949. Thus, there is the chance to compare styles. Young was miserable in the army, and this helped to contribute to his alcoholism, as well as forever changing his style to reflect tragedy, melancholia, and loneliness (not to mention bitterness). The Savoys include a number of separate sessions, some with Count Basie or his crew (such as "Tush" and "Circus in Rhythm" by the big band, or "Blue Lester" and "Indiana"—two takes apiece—by the Basie rhythm section); others were led by Johnny Guarnieri ("These Foolish Things," "Exercise in Swing") or Junior Mance. The number of alternates here clearly show the vast stylistic differences and changes that can go on in musical approaches. In some cases, the tune changes dramatically depending on

Young's mood and precision. The Aladdin offerings have pre-inductive Basie accompaniment as well as post-War material. Young emphasized with the boppers and produced musical circles around the basic tune (in line with bop thought about inventiveness and harmonics). Dodo Marmarosa, as well as Vic Dickenson, are here, and selections include "DB Blues," a swinging classic and best seller.

By 1950, the bop orientation was complete, as both the Savoys and Aladdins attest. After this period, Young played for Norman Granz, and his style once again became melodic and congenial. Usually he played with a piano trio.

J4.128   Item omitted.

Standards

J4.129*   **Buster Bailey. All About Memphis.** Master Jazz Recording MJR 8125.

J4.130   **Buster Bailey. Complete Recordings, 1934-1940.** Rarities 17.
Clarinetist Bailey was an academically trained musician who played with W. C. Handy in the Memphis area. From 1924 through 1937, he was with Fletcher Henderson, and he often backed many female blues singers (from the "classic" period). In jazz history, he was the first *non*-New Orleanian to have a jazz influence and power in the clarinet. Noone, Bigard, Nicholas, Bechet, Dodds—all were from the Crescent City. Rarities 17 presents an interesting assortment of groups in which Bailey was a prominent sideman, or leader in some cases. Some of the most powerful names in jazz are here: Red Allen, Frankie Newton, Charlie Shavers, Pete Brown, et al. The 17 selections include "Call of the Delta" and "Shanghai Shuffle," both from 1934, "Afternoon in Africa" and "Dizzy Debutante" from 1937, and "Planter's Punch" and "Sloe Jam Fizz" from 1938. From 1938 through 1947, he worked with the John Kirby Sextet, and then moved into semi-retirement. In 1959, he was persuaded by Stanley Dance to lead a group for the Felsted label (reissued on the Master Jazz label). The seven, long, extended works are all reminiscent of Memphis, and five were especially created for the session by Bailey, clearly showing his love and feel for the blues (the other two are Handy's "Beale Street Blues" and "Memphis Blues"). These stereo recordings allow us to hear Bailey's engaging clarinet tone, his lower register work, and the exceptionally mellow character of the tune constructions. Other members here include Red Richards, Vic Dickenson, Gene Ramey, and Herman Autrey.

J4.131*   **"Chu" Berry and His Stompy Stevedores.** Epic EE 22007.
Berry, although he was not as imaginative as other tenor saxists, was still perhaps the greatest tenor of the swing era simply because he *swung*, especially at medium or fast tempi. By extension, he is rather poor on slow numbers. In the past, his style has been called "jaunty" and "urgent," and he employed variable phrasing. He was also one of the first exponents of the higher register of the tenor saxophone. Eight of the selections here come from 1937, with a small group that included Hot Lips Page, Buster Bailey, and Cozy Cole. "Back Home Again in Indiana" and "Limehouse Blues" both have the variable phrasing of Berry. Before this, he was with Fletcher Henderson, and after this period, he moved onto Cab Calloway in time for Cab's last big band, recording terrific solos on "Lonesome Nights" and "I Don't

Stand a Ghost of a Chance with You" (both found here, along with six other Cab Calloway tracks). He died at age 31, leaving much speculation as to what swing would have been like in the 1940s had he lived. Throughout his life, he was a gifted follower of Coleman Hawkins.

J4.132*   **Barney Bigard/Albert Nicholas.** RCA LPV 566.

J4.133*   **The Duke's Men.** Epic EE 22005.

J4.134*   **Johnny Hodges/Rex Stewart. Things Ain't What They Used to Be.** RCA LPV 533.
　　　　　These three discs represent a good cross section of the small combo units that grew out of the Ellington band. The bands featured several soloists who led them, often with Ellington himself in the piano chair. Throughout, Ellington's personality still dominates, and more than one critic has suggested that these were Ducal combos with a front man. (Exposure of the soloist let off any steam or aggravation that may have accumulated in the larger group.) Bigard and Nicholas were New Orleans clarinetists who both studied under Lorenzo Tio, Jr., the teacher who also instructed Jimmie Noone, Johnny Dodds, and Omer Simeon. Only one of the personnel on the Nicholas sides ever played with Ellington; the purpose of the disc was to reissue the eight sides by Bigard, aligning Nicholas both for comparison and to fill out the album. The Bigard tracks come from 1940, and include Nance, Webster, Tizol, Blanton, Greer, and Ellington. Most of them are also on the Epic anthology, but from 1936. Bigard made extensive use of the low tone to create mellow stylings. The Hodges selections, from 1941, include a slow tempo "Things Ain't What They Used to Be," while Stewart's high register work concentrated on faster selections, such as "Subtle Slough" or "Rexatious" (the latter on the Epic label). The other major soloist was Cootie Williams with his group, The Rugcutters. Williams was a master of the "growl" trumpet style, and he soon became the featured plunger player with Ellington. His feel for the blues was phenomenal, and the three selections on the Epic disc show his power and aggressiveness, especially in "Echoes of Harlem" from 1938.

J4.135   **Ruby Braff. Ruby Braff Special.** Vanguard VRS 8504 (British issue).

J4.136   **Ruby Braff and Ellis Larkins. The Grand Reunion.** Chiaroscuro CR 117.
　　　　　Braff plays both trumpet and cornet, although lately it has been solely the latter. He achieved some small measure of fame in the early 1950s, playing a swing era style of trumpet loosely modelled on Louis Armstrong (and he was partly responsible for the resurgence of interest in swing musicians at this time). He is a technician, employing fast runs that can be melodic bursts or rococo decorations, bright tones, and often a ballad style for the slower numbers. Unfortunately, he has not been well recorded for 20 years, peaking around 1955. The Vanguard reissue (employing the original serial number) consists of a sextet with Basie rhythm (Page and Jones) and Vic Dickenson on trombone. All the techniques alluded to above are evident in such swinging numbers as "Linger Awhile," "I Don't Stand a Ghost of a Chance with You," and even Lil Green's "Romance in the Dark." This was 1955; in 1972, he was reunited with Ellis Larkins, pianist, in a series of

piano-cornet duets. These fine miniatures included "Fine and Dandy," "Skylark," Ray Noble's "The Very Thought of You," "Ain't Misbehavin'," and other standards of a high caliber. Both are able to sustain rich harmonies and interest through the set. In the mid-1970s, Braff embarked on highly successful tours and records with guitarist George Barnes and bass-drums rhythm.

J4.137*   **Vic Dickenson. Essential.** two discs. Vanguard VSD 99/100.
During the thirties, trombonist Dickenson worked with the big bands such as Count Basie's. In the 1940s, he worked with small groups and continued to do so through the 1970s. Over this period of time, his swing phrasing underwent a metamorphosis to a very personal style, with much reliance on such gimmicks as twisting the melody, surprise entrances, growls, double-accenting, and other idiosyncratic devices. Humor is his strong point, as with Louis Armstrong, the Saints and Sinners, the World's Greatest Jazz Band, and other such groups. And on this set, there are "Keeping Out of Mischief Now" and "Jeepers Creepers." Another tune associated with him is "In a Sentimental Mood" (composed by Duke Ellington, but not recorded here: see Sidney Bechet's 1958 Brussells concert). This twofer is equally important in that it was responsible for the revival of swing music in the early fifties. The 12 extended selections are solidly performed by Ruby Braff, Edmond Hall, Sir Charles Thompson (piano), and Jo Jones, among others.

J4.138   **Roy Eldridge. The Nifty Cat.** Master Jazz Recordings MJR 8110.

J4.139*   **Roy Eldridge and Dizzy Gillespie. Trumpet Kings.** two discs. Polydor 2683.022 (British issue).
Eldridge is perhaps the most influential trumpeter in jazz since Louis Armstrong. He had a strong effect on Dizzy Gillespie. His fiery and mercurial runs showed good range and swing. Unfortunately, there is a dearth of records under his name (a problem in this book since the approach is by record, not by name). Briefly, Eldridge can be found on Fletcher Henderson records, such as "Stealin' Apples"; with Gene Krupa; and then as a member of various groups assembled by Norman Granz for the Verve company. Eldridge has mentioned that Rex Stewart and Red Nichols were two of his earliest mentors, and he assimilated their methods. His tone and style of piling climax upon climax stood him in good stead with the big bands; his flexibility and melodic invention were drawn together by the 1950s and his return from Europe. He could play from a whisper to a scream without losing any of the impact of the mood being established.
The set with Gillespie perfectly illustrates this. Here, he is surrounded by his ace pupil and the Oscar Peterson trio of 1954-1955. One disc contains two series of ballad medleys, where Eldridge gains the uppermost hand over the competitive horn of Gillespie. There are only four items on the other disc, but again they provide good contrast and competition, as on the Eldridge-associated tune "I Can't Get Started," "Limehouse Blues," "Blue Moon," and "I've Found a New Baby." A more recent venture, featuring all Eldridge-composed materials, has accompaniment by Budd Johnson, Bennie Morton, and rhythm. The six tunes are all extended, and there are unusually good solos from all, with Eldridge weaving around the melody line.

J4.140*   **Bobby Hackett. The Hackett Horn.** Epic EE 22003.

J4.141   **Bobby Hackett and Vic Dickenson. This Is My Bag.** World Records
ST 1080 (British issue).

J4.142*   **Bobby Hackett and Jack Teagarden. Jazz Ultimate.** EMI E052-81005
(Danish issue).

Hackett, because of his glamorous looks, was dubbed as another Bix
Beiderbecke. Yet his prime lyrical influence has always been Louis Armstrong:
melodic variations and relaxing music. In the big bands, he played with Benny Goodman to recreate some Beiderbecke solos for the 1938 Carnegie Hall concert. He also
performed with the Glenn Miller band, but mostly on guitar. Occasional trumpet
solos produced minor gems of clarity, such as on "String of Pearls." Later, he was
both to accompany many singers (such as Tony Bennett), excelling on the trumpet
obbligatos, and to be lead soloist with recording bands such as those of Jackie
Gleason (for that dreamy mood music). Under his own name, he made a series of
Columbia recordings with pick-up units from 1938 to 1940. Outstanding solos
include his work on "Embraceable You" and "I Don't Stand a Ghost of a Chance
with You."

All of his work was with the cornet, and supporting musicians cover the range
of personnel available from the swing bands of the time. Hackett has shown a strong
affinity for trombonists. Perhaps his best-ever jazz record was the 1957 Capitol
session with Teagarden, Ernie Caceres, Peanuts Hucko, and rhythm. Among the
ballads, he gives a sensitive reading of "'S Wonderful"; he is at his most aggressive
with "55th and Broadway," a tough out-and-out blues. By the end of the 1960s,
he formed a liaison with Vic Dickenson, also a first-rate trombonist, and this quintet played together for about six years, making numerous recordings in a variety of
settings. The material on this disc covers all of jazz from "Sweet Georgia Brown"
through "St. Louis Blues," "Sister Kate," and "Blue Turning Grey Over You."

J4.143   **Edmond Hall. Swing Session.** Ace of Hearts AHC 180 (British issue).

Hall represents an almost perfect blend of New Orleans, or traditional, clarinet style (through his upbringing and the Albert clarinet system), with elements of
swing performance based on Benny Goodman. He worked with Claude Hopkins, 1930-
1935, and then created many sessions for the balance of the thirties. He was at his
best and most creative during the 1940s. His attack made him stand out in any group
setting, and his broad tone was clearly developed in the small combo units. The
above disc, from 1943-1944, presents him at his height, in settings with a large
group that included Emmett Berry, Vic Dickenson, Eddie Heywood, plus rhythm,
and with a rhythm trio led by Teddy Wilson. During this time, he was playing constantly throughout the New York area. These original Commodore tracks show him
"up" for the sessions, having just come from club engagements late at night. This
is definitely in the swing idiom, as with "Coquette," where he weaves background figures in the group passages, or even the lyrical melodies in his solo work
on "Where or When" and "It Had to Be You." Later in life, he made sterling recordings with Vic Dickenson (see item J4.137) and became one of the Louis Armstrong
All Stars.

J4.144   **The Jazz Giants.** Sackville 3002 (Canadian issue).
If anything, this 1967 disc shows that the greats from the swing era of thirty years before could still hack it. Personnel include Wild Bill Davison (cornet), Buzzy Drootin (drums), Herb Hall (clarinet), Claude Hopkins (piano), Benny Morton (trombone), and Arvell Shaw (bass). The music on this record is more than just another swing variation of Dixieland. It is an authentic recording of jazz played by some of the elder statesmen of the idiom. Collectively and singly, their music carries the stamp of creativity and experience. Traditional items include "Black and Blue," "I Found a New Baby," "I Surrender Dear," "Yesterdays," and so forth (nine substantially longish pieces). The band just gets up and plays. It was assembled for a one-shot night club engagement and recorded in a studio. Thus, it may be thought of as a studio group. But the interactions are profound in yet another document of solid, mainstream jazz.

J4.145   **John Kirby. Boss of the Bass.** two discs. Columbia CG 33557.
This sextet, led by bassist John Kirby, was billed as the "biggest little band in the land." The material has been commented on as chamber jazz because it did not seem to swing much (the same charges had been leveled at Ray Norvo); however, the six members, through the clever arrangements of trumpeter Charlie Shavers, emulated the big band sounds as Clarence Williams did earlier in the 1920s and as Maynard Ferguson was to do in the early 1960s. Kirby's group began in 1937, and diverse personnel over the years included Frankie Newton (trumpet), Russell Procope (alto saxophone solos), Pete Brown (tenor sax), and Buster Bailey (clarinet).

J4.146*   **Artie Shaw. His Gramercy Five.** RCA LPM 1241.
The small combo unit within the band was an interesting development from the swing period. Frustrated musicians who had to play riffs and regimented ensemble passages could let out their steam in the studio on these blowing sessions. One of the best was the Shaw group, and it certainly is of more interest to jazz listeners than the Shaw big band. "Summit Ridge Drive" from 1940 featured some precise noodling from Shaw, inspired trumpet from Billy Butterfield, and good solos from Johnny Guarnieri on piano. Other titles here include "Cross Your Heart," "My Blue Heaven," and "Smoke Gets In Your Eyes." From 1945, with Roy Eldridge, Dodo Marmarosa, and Barney Kessel, they recorded "The Gentle Grifter" and "The Sad Sack," along with a few others. Also here are some tracks from a 1949 session, so this set covers a decade in the history of Artie Shaw. All the selections are clean, relaxed, good jazz, as it ought to be.

J4.147   **Stuff Smith. Black Violin.** MPS 15147 (West German issue).

J4.147a.   **Stuff Smith. 1935.** Collector's 12-12 (British issue).

J4.148*   **Stuff Smith and Stephane Grappelli. Stuff and Steff.** Barclay
920067 (French issue).
Smith was one of the first to perform on the amplified violin. With this power, he became positively violent—an unorthodox surging manner, but with an apparent facile technique. His best records have been his last (he died in 1967). With Grappelli (in 1965), he concentrated on ballads, such as "S'posin'," "How High the Moon," and "This Can't Be Love." Good contrast comes through with the more relaxed

Grappelli. Smith's last record is entirely derived from the swing era, featuring a German tenor sax quartet in tunes such as "Cherokee," "Yesterdays," "Sweet Lorraine," "One O'Clock Jump," and "What Is This Thing Called Love?"

J4.149   Rex Stewart. Rendezvous with Rex. Master Jazz Records MJR 8123.
     Stewart here leads two separate groups of seven musicians, forming an octet. These were initially recorded in January 1958 for Stanley Dance's Felsted label. Stewart, like many Ellingtonians and the Duke himself, has since died, but his happy, exuberant cornet and occasional vocals (as on "My Kind of Gal," heard here) live today in this reissue. Many of the musicians here have been mainstays in jazz for years, but, sadly, are unknown except for live performances. Hayward Henry went on to accompany Earl Hines; Willie "the Lion" Smith, of course, was a recognized genius in his own right. The six tunes—all extended pieces—are evidence of Stewart's playing with Fletcher Henderson and Duke Ellington. The small band ensemble puts verve and zest into the Stewart originals. This album was the beginning of his comeback, and he later went on to do good work for Prestige and other assorted labels. Other material can be found on Epic LN24203 and diverse RCA reissues, all with members of the Ellington band.

J4.150*   Billy Strayhorn. Cue for Saxophone. Master Jazz Recording MJR 8116.
     In 1939, Strayhorn joined Ellington as an arranger and composer. This became one of the greatest partnerships of jazz, and Strayhorn was often referred to as Duke's alter ego. His pianistic style greatly resembled Ellington's, and his compositions have often been confused with Ellington's. He wrote the band's theme "Take the 'A' Train," the great "Chelsea Bridge," and "Johnny Come Lately" (for Johnny Hodges). The seven tracks here come from a 1959 Felsted recording, produced by Stanley Dance. Without taking anything away from Strayhorn, the disc perfectly creates the feeling of Ducal assimilation, as if Strayhorn were putting down themes in the same nonchalant manner. Musicians came from the Ellington band, and included Johnny Hodges, Russell Procope, Quentin Jackson, and Harold Baker. The septet largely improvises, with a minimum amount of writing involved. Two of the numbers were originals from Strayhorn and Hodges: "Cue's Blue Now," a slow blues of 10 minutes in which the two reeds and two horns take engaging solos, and "Watch Your Cue," a short dance for Hodges. Traditional classics included Don Redman's "Cherry," "Rose Room," and "You Brought a New Kind of Love to Me." This is good listening music in the mainstream area.

J4.151   The Sunset All Stars. Jammin' at Sunset, v.1/2. two discs. Black Lion
     132/137.
     The Sunset label (operating on the West Coast from 1944 to 1946) produced minor gems of jazz documentation, in the style of Savoy, Dial, Blue Note, and others. (Jazz owes a great deal to the pioneering works of the small, independent companies.) By assembling a small group of modernists, Eddie Laguna (owner and producer of the label) was able to arrive at some very interesting music in the determination of "whither jazz?" after the bop revolution. These musicicians explored new ways and means, new manners of expression, and so forth. They were not tied down by the crass commercialism of the major companies who only wanted to sell records. Personnel for these trios, quartets, quintets, and other sized combos included Howard McGhee (trumpet) who played with Charlie Parker, Charlie Ventura (tenor

sax), Nick Fatool (drums), the budding André Previn, Willie Smith (probably the most underrated alto sax player in jazz history), Lucky Thompson (tenor saxophone), Red Callendar (bass), Harry "Sweets" Edison (trumpet), Les Paul (guitar), Dodo Marmarosa (piano), Vic Dickenson (trombone), and Emmett Berry (trumpet).

Throughout this time, there were great periods of unsettlement. Many bop performers were in swing bands and felt frustrated, yet had no security to go out on their own. Many performers were returning from the War, and band positions were to be keenly fought for. The general economic uncertainty did not help ease the pain of War, and the restrictions of wartime endeavors had not been lifted (such as the running battles between radio stations, the AFM, and either BMI or ASCAP). Immediate musical reactions were to create more punchy, sullen music, such as in "I Found a New Baby," or "Tea for Two." Other straight material that was toughened up by growls and double-timing included "All the Things You Are," "Get Happy," and "My Blue Heaven." Sunset was one of the first of the independents to document this material so early in the 1940s, and it fills a decided gap.

J4.152*   **Buddy Tate. Jumpin' On the West Coast!** Black Lion BLP 172.

J4.153   **Buddy Tate. Unbroken.** BASF 20740.

J4.154   **Buddy Tate. Swinging Like Tate.** Master Jazz Recordings MJR 8127.

Tate replaced tenorist Herschel Evans in the Basie band, and stayed from 1939 until the end of the forties. During the 1950s, he got caught up in the swing revival and in the small group "mainstream" resurgence. He became the leading tenor saxist of this time. All of this was predicted by the 1947 Supreme recordings (reissued by Black Lion), crafted in Los Angeles with a small group from the Basie band. There are highly reliable recordings of better swing from the 1940s. The 12 tunes here include "Blue and Sentimental" and "Ballin' from Day to Day," plus originals from Tate, such as "Tate's a Jumpin'," "Vine Street Breakdown," and a few alternate takes. Jimmy Witherspoon has a few vocals on some blues. The Master Jazz is a reissue from Felsted, recorded in 1958. Half of the disc features Tate's regular Celebrity Club Orchestra, an octet with Tate on occasional clarinet. On this instrument, he seems to follow the Young lean lines, while his tenor is in the Hawkins full sound. The second half finds him with former Basie performers, such as Buck Clayton, Dickie Wells, and Jo Jones, with material by Tate and Clayton, similar to Kansas City jams. The BASF album is a modern version (1972) of the Celebrity Club Orchestra cut down to a septet. Together with original contributions by the band, there are such standards as "Tuxedo Junction," "Body and Soul," "Undecided," and "Airmail Special." Tate and his bands are virtually the only ones left from the swing era who are still creating and composing new music in this genre.

J4.155*   **Art Tatum. Group Masterpieces.** eight discs. Pablo 2625.706.

Tatum performing with other musicians was a lesser individual. He was more subdued, but fulfilled his role as an accompanist and soloist more than adequately. His position in jazz history came about because of his solo work; however, the mainstream material with others still has compelling features. There are 60 performances here—all extended versions, originally recorded for Granz's Clef label. One of two best sets is the two-disc work with altoist Benny Carter and drummer Louis Bellson. Here, in "Blues in C," are four marvelous opening choruses in an eight-minute performance. Other tracks include "My Blue Heaven," "A Foggy Day," " 'S Wonderful," and "Undecided." The other important set is with Ben Webster, emphasizing the counterpoint of fast piano and slow tenor, as on "Night and Day" or "My Ideal." The largest group features Hampton, Edison, Rich, and Kessel in such older standards as "September Song" and "Deep Purple," plus the nominal blues outing "Verve Blues." The trio reduction with Hampton and Rich provides "Perdido" and "How High the Moon." The session with Buddy De Franco, Red Callendar, and Bill Douglas delves into "Lover Man" and "A Foggy Day," while the outing with Roy Eldridge produces "You Took Advantage of Me" and "Night and Day." A session with Jo Jones turned in remarkable versions of "Love for Sale" and "Blue Lou."

J4.156*   **Dickie Wells. In Paris, 1937.** Prestige PR 7593.
Wells was one of the finest swing trombonists in the world, and his best work was recorded early in his career. He appeared with Spike Hughes (reissued on Ace of Clubs ACL 1153), the Count Basie band (see items J4.13-19), and with several small groups when he toured Europe. In July 1937, he recorded his greatest small group work, all for the Swing label that was started by French jazz fans Charles Delaunay and Hugues Panassié. On July 7 he teamed with Django Reinhardt, Bill Coleman, and members of the Teddy Hill band then touring Europe. Some of Wells's greatest work is here among the six tracks of standards: "I Got Rhythm," and "Between the Devil and the Deep Blue Sea" stand out. Coleman puts in a long solo on this latter, and Reinhardt stands out in the rhythm section, with some imaginative and tasty solos in that same number and on "Japanese Sandman." The July 12 session omits Reinhardt (replaced by Roger Chaput), and the focus shifts naturally to Wells again. The important tracks (from among the six recorded) are the two solos by Wells on "Lady Be Good" and "Dickie Wells Blues," accompanied loosely by a rhythm trio.

JAM SESSIONS

J4.157*   **Buck Clayton. 1953-1955.** two discs. CBS 88031 (French issue).

J4.158*   **Buck Clayton. Essential.** two discs. Vanguard VSD 103/4.

J4.159   Item deleted.

J4.160   Item deleted.

J4.161*   **Buck Clayton and Buddy Tate. Kansas City Nights.** two discs. Prestige
           P 24040.
Clayton rose to prominence as a trumpeter with Basie, obtaining his first solo role in 1936. Until the 1950s, he recorded as accompanist for many others, such as Billie Holiday, Lester Young (the Kansas City Six recordings), and Jazz at the Philharmonic jams. Throughout this period, and on into his solo career, Clayton reveals a heavy debt to Armstrong, while at the same time being a master of both melody and the mute. His effective, delicate playing had great consistency, so much so that it is difficult to recommend any recordings since they are really *all* great. Those cited

above come from three distinct sessions, spanning an eight-year period of fluent inventiveness. The two-disc CBS set is derived from monster jams that Clayton took charge of, each selection running to more than 15 minutes or so; they were largely produced by John Hammond (who also arranged for the similar swing Vanguards). From 1953 to 1955, with assorted musicians from the Basie fold (Urbie Green, Freddie Green, Walter Page, Jo Jones, the latter three being the Basie rhythm unit), they recorded "The Hucklebuck," "Robbin's Nest," "Christopher Columbus," "Undecided," "Blue and Sentimental," and so forth, with long lines and changes for Clayton to switch mutes. On VSD 103/4, he is joined by Ruby Braff as well as by other Basie players, including Vic Dickenson and Buddy Tate. With the latter, Clayton recorded more sides in 1960 and 1961, with the Sir Charles Thompson piano trio as rhythm accompaniment. Tate is on tenor for the earlier date, but on clarinet for 1961. Good swinging tracks include many originals by either Tate or Clayton, and the general feeling is that the band assembled and just began to play. Hammond is again involved, contributing the liner notes.

J4.162   **Jam Session in Swingville.** two discs. Prestige P 24051.
    "Jams" really came of age for records when tapes and long-playing albums were developed. The constriction of the three-minute record was over, and jams could be recorded at leisure, either from a remote on the radio or concert, or from overdubbing in the studio (as with Miles Davis). The two discs here come from 1961, and feature two groups, one being led by Coleman Hawkins, the other by Pee Wee Russell. The accompanying musicians were "picked up" for the session and include the assortment of Joe Newman (trumpet), J. C. Higginbotham (trombone), Claude Hopkins (piano), Tiny Grimes (guitar), Vic Dickenson (trombone), Buddy Tate (reeds), and J. C. Heard (drums), among others. Most of the selections are long (between 7 and 11 minutes) and the individuals solo at will (but in turn). It was simply a matter of letting the tapes run while the musicians performed. The late Ralph Gleason contributes good notes on the history of the jam session and its impact on nightclubs. One key element in this set was the pairing of Hawkins (a hard-driving combo man) with a Dixie-flavored group, and a Dixie-flavored Pee Wee Russell with a swing group. The results are interesting, and of a high caliber, proving that a jam is a jam, no matter what the background of the individuals. Good key phrases and a sense of timing must be augmented by a good rhythm section.

J4.163*   **Session at Midnight: Los Angeles.** Capitol E 052-81006 (Danish issue).

J4.164*   **Session at Riverside: New York.** Capitol E 052-81004 (Danish issue).
    These two discs continue the tradition of the jam session. They both come from the 1950s, and each features a dozen top-notch jazz giants blowing away in an informal surrounding. The Los Angeles session was in 1955, and by that time, many jazz performers had found regular work in films (and soon television): Benny Carter, Willie Smith, Plas Johnson, and Harry "Sweets" Edison. All of these musicians had received their early training in the swing era; thus, it was relatively easy to do "head" arrangements in which the musicians would agree on a tune, arrange the order of solo and ensemble choruses, and then work out the section figures or riffs. The rest was improvisation and interweaving: "Moten Swing," "Sweet Georgia Brown," "Stompin' at the Savoy." Biographical information about the musicians is included here, as well as the order of solos. The next year (1956), the effort was repeated with

a group of musicians on the East Coast centered in New York: Coleman Hawkins, Charlie Shavers, Billy Butterfield, Peanuts Hucko, and eight others. The same successful technique was employed, and again the notes provide biographies and order of solos for such items as "I Want to Be Happy," "Undecided" and "Out of Nowhere." Each disc contains six tunes, including the title selection as a catch-all, strung-out-late-at-night-blues item. For this type of music in the 1950s, these discs stood out as an oasis in mainstream jazz, with the added importance that it was a major record company that produced the efforts.

MODERN BIG BANDS

J4.165*   **Count Basie. The Atomic Mr. Basie.** Roulette SRCP 3000 (British issue).

J4.166*   **Count Basie. Echoes of an Era: Kansas City Suite/Easin' It.** two discs. Roulette RE124.
During the quarter century since 1950, the Basie band had suffered many personnel changes and increasingly tightened its arrangements, thereby losing its swinging unpolished sound. Also, in the public's eye, Basie's band was looked upon as an accompanying group that backed up vocalists such as Frank Sinatra, Ella Fitzgerald, Sarah Vaughan, Tony Bennett, Billy Eckstine, Sammy Davis, Bing Crosby, Tom Jones, et al. The total music was not unlike any other big band of the times, and any proficient musician could play the scores. But then Basie got three top composer-arrangers, and in the early 1960s, recorded his best post-War efforts. The *Atomic* album was looked after by Neal Hefti, and it includes "The Kid from Red Bank" (a stride tempo piece of contrast with the band), "Flight of the Foo Birds" (which featured brilliant Eddie "Lockjaw" Davis tenor excursions), and the dramatic, original version of "Lil' Darlin' " (all texture, with basic saxophones, muted brass, and diverse obbligatos). *Kansas City Suite* was written and arranged by none other than Benny Carter. There is little to relate the 10 items to each other; the suite is merely an umbrella name. But the quality of the scoring is superb for the recreation of the atmosphere and color of Kansas City. Ensemble passages prevail, with individual standouts according to the selection: Thad Jones, Joe Newman, Al Grey, Frank Wess, and Freddie Greene. Frank Foster, in addition to being a sax player in the band, created a heavy blues vein with his compositions-arrangements for *Easin' It*. He displays the entire brass section, including trumpets and trombones. The obvious standout is "Brotherly Shore," an arrangement for three tenors and a chase.

J4.167   **Maynard Ferguson. Echoes of an Era: A Message from Newport/ Newport Suite.** two discs. Roulette RE 116.

J4.168*   **Maynard Ferguson. M. F. Horn.** Columbia C 30466.

J4.169*   **Maynard Ferguson. Screamin' Blues.** Mainstream MRL 316.
Ferguson developed his screech trumpet while in the Stan Kenton band. Basically, this is an emphasis on the high notes, leading to an aggressiveness rarely seen in big band trumpeters. Essentially, he is a superb band organizer, like Woody Herman, able to assemble a crew of musicians, inject them with verve and enthusiasm,

rehearse them thoroughly, and provide inspired arrangements. Some early notables who passed through his band included the late Bobby Timmons, the late Bill Chase, Don Ellis, Don Sebesky, Joe Farrell, Willie Maiden, and Jaki Byard.

The Roulette offering is from 1958 and 1959. Ferguson was *not* at Newport with these groups; thus the titles are misleading. Both sets employed 13 musicians, including those named above, but efficient scoring and proper placement made the group sound bigger than it was. The long "Frame for the Blues," created by Slide Hampton, is a case in point, as it builds layers of sound upon coarse textures. Three trumpet chases highlight "Three More Foxes." The Mainstream set highlights arrangements by Sebesky and Maiden, and features 28 (!) musicians for a powerhouse swing attack on the blues. Richard Davis (bass) and Mel Lewis (drums) kick the band through such pop items as "Night Train," "Every Day I Have the Blues," "What'd I Say," and "I've Got a Woman." This is the type of material that Ferguson loves, and it is very difficult to contain him. His career peaked, and it was a decade before he arrived back on the big band scene. This time for Columbia he assembled a British band, with stunning, modern arrangements by Keith Mansfield, Adrian Drover (especially "MacArthur Park"), and Kenny Wheeler. By this time, he had developed a technically perfect screech horn built to his specifications, and began to produce an album a year through the 1970s. Along with Buddy Rich and Woody Herman, Ferguson was responsible for the resurgence of the brash big band.

J4.170* **Woody Herman. Giant Step.** Fantasy 9432.

Herman's 18 pieces (five trumpets, five reeds, three trombones, and rhythm) here play some of the best melodies that modern jazz has to offer. There is less pop here than on *The Raven Speaks* (Fantasy 9416), an earlier work from this, his third, period. Worked over by four arrangers, material includes Chick Corea's "La Fiesta"; a dance from Eddie Harris's *Freedom Jazz Suite*; Coltrane's "Giant Steps"; and Thad Jones's "A Child Is Born." As Herman stated in the *New York Times* in July 1973, "It's the youth audience I want to cultivate. Their tastes aren't frozen in 1945. They have the time, flexibility, interest and energy to really groove on all kinds of music." His is a major touring band, like those of Kenton, Ferguson, Rich, and Basie. The loud sound, not as prominent as Kenton's, emphasizes a rocking brass. This is a good record for supporters of jazz-rock, richly detailed and innovative. It is conclusive demonstration that Herman has the innate ability to fashion a solid band from a handful of youngsters.

J4.171* **Thad Jones—Mel Lewis Orchestra. Consummation.** Blue Note BST 84346.

J4.177* **Thad Jones. Monday Night.** Solid State 18048.

Jones, one of the famous Jones brothers (Hank and Elvin are the others), is a trumpeter and former arranger for Count Basie. He also scores and composes. Lewis is a drummer who worked with Gillespie and Kenton. Together, they formed a rehearsal band in 1965 in order to get a creative studio recording, without necessarily having to have a band on the payroll week after week. Over the years, they have become the best and most influential of all the big bands of the previous decade. They stressed technique and unusual intervals, incorporating section work and color of instrumentation. Musicians who have passed through their band include Richard Davis (bass) and Jon Faddis (trumpet).

J4.173*   **Stan Kenton. The Kenton Era.** four discs. Creative World St. 1030.
These 47 tracks present the making of a band through the early years (1940-1954) of "progressive jazz." Side one opens with Kenton speaking of the development of his music, with excerpts running in the background. Side eight is similar and is called "epilogue." The discs are supplemented by a huge 44-page illustrated booklet, with the names of tracks, changing personnel, philosophies of music, and lots of black and white photographs. This is jazz in a serious vein, not everybody's bag, but the listener should play sides two through seven (essentially a reissue of Capitol W569, with material from unissued takes, radio broadcasts, and concerts). The year 1941 introduces the Jimmie Lunceford influence, and brings on the "Artistry in Rhythm" theme. The early days had Dick Coles on trombone, and material included "Two Moods," "Etude for Saxophones," and "Arkansas Traveller." By 1949, Pete Rugolo was doing composing and arranging; Stan Getz and Art Pepper were in the band, and from this period came the near classics "Opus A Dollar Three Eighty," "I'll Remember April," and "Russian Lullaby." By 1946, Kai Winding and Shelly Manne were members. The music became more complex, more other-worldly, with different rhythms and experimentation on themes of standards, modern jazz, and the 1950 addition of strings and Maynard Ferguson. The years 1947-1948 were the period of "progressivism." After that, much time was spent elaborating or justifying.

J4.174   **Buddy Rich. Take It Away.** World Pacific Jazz 20126.
Swing drummer Rich has had a big band off and on since after World War II, but the best group that he had (in terms of discipline and material) was surely the 1966 aggregation, one of the first bands besides Kenton's to feature a considerable number of young, brash musicians. Kenton, Rich, and later Ferguson, were to lead the way to a big band revival through constantly touring and offering clinics wherever they went. The Rich band has been characterized as energetic, with great drive coming from the drummer, although the comment has been made that there is too much emphasis on the drumming solos. This 1966 date was recorded at Las Vegas, and among the material are arrangements by some of the finest craftsmen in the business: Bill Holman, the late Oliver Nelson, Phil Wilson, and Bill Reddie, the latter orchestrating a collage from *West Side Story* and some of the infamous Rich drumming solos. Two good examples of the advanced arranging that Rich employed are on "The Rotten Kid" and "New Blues."

Bop, Cool, Modern

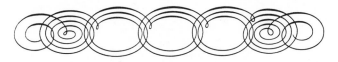

BOP, COOL, MODERN

"We never get credit for
what we're doing. But we're going
to create something that they can't steal
because they can't play it."
—Thelonious Monk

INTRODUCTION

The term "bebop" came about when Leonard Feather confused the *title* of a 1944 tune by Gillespie and Pettiford with a term for its *style*. Basically (and simply), bop was nothing more than harmonic exploration. Yet, the reasons for the violent reactions to it were several. The prime reason was that the 1942-1944 wartime recording ban meant that the music of that period was not released until after 1944, and bop came as quite a shock to new listeners who never heard the transitional documents that could have been available had recording continued. The second reason was, as Monk indicated above, that very few whites could play the music and many began to denigrate it. Third, the New Orleans revival was beginning, and this was latched onto a firm foundation during the changes.

Bop Characteristics

Historically, bop came from the Southwest, as did swing. The Kansas City nightclub audiences had become used to the Basie riffs and his "head" arrangements. These arrangements, plus spontaneous improvisations where available, gave a great deal of freedom to the soloist; and the constant space in each song at each club gave him a chance to stretch out and change his "cadenza" each night. When the Kansas City bands ended up in New York, they began to sit in at diverse Harlem nightclubs after their night's work was done. The two most famous cabarets were Minton's Playhouse and Monroe's Uptown House. It was here, at 3:00 a.m. or later in the morning, that those performers who were *used* to improvisation and head arrangements would jam with the small house band (or even after the house band went home). Ultimately, in their explorations of harmonies, the musicians would come to play only for themselves. The listeners (if any) were secondary. These instrumentalists used *contrafacts* and *chord variations* to scare off the people with little talent. Thus, bop is a musician's music, started in the experimentation of informal jam sessions. The only documentation we have of this period is through Jerry Newman's homemade paper discs and paper tapes—much of this music was *not* on radio, nor was it recorded commercially. Thus, there was no concession to public taste, as this was small group music meant for listening. Some of its greatest impact was on Europeans, especially those caught up in the emerging philosophies of surrealism and existentialism.

As with any musical trend, there were transitions through the music of Roy Eldridge, Lester Young (his use of space and linear modes), Jimmy Blanton (who used the bass violin as more than just a rhythm instrument), and Jo Jones. By 1940, the small group performances used the flatted fifth as an interval; this is a blue note that was employed by such diverse performers as Thelonious Monk, Kenny Clarke, Charlie Christian, Dizzy Gillespie, and, of course, Charlie Parker. Parker advanced the music the most. His harmonic sophistication and rhythmic complexity presented such a wealth of ideas that nobody else could really keep up, except perhaps Gillespie (but certainly *not* Miles Davis, who later established himself in the "cool" reaction to bop). Bop, like all modern jazz, cannot really be codified by its style, but it does exhibit characteristics that recur in almost all performances. Its style precluded decorative notes, as the music was highly concentrated—even thought of as a shorthand account of musical ideas, where the silences counted as much as the notes themselves. Many of the tunes were standards of the day that had been inverted or had been stripped of their melodies. The musicians played nervous phrases and fragmented melodies, or weaved their way around the melody without even playing it (excluding the obvious, which the listener would have to fill in for himself). And it was obvious that this was bitter, frustrated black music.

Cool Characteristics

Reaction to bop created the obvious retrogressive step of audiences supporting traditional or New Orleans music, a simple form that could be understood. But another reaction was the erroneously titled "cool" jazz, which was simply "arranged" jazz fostered by Miles Davis in 1949 because he could not come to grips with bop. This music was calm, smooth, and relaxed; it was also emotionless and, to some extent, classically derived. And it was appreciated by fans who had come through the tumultuous forties with its war, changes in lifestyles, economic failures, urban migrations, and what appeared to be a severe shift in musical emphasis, not only in jazz, but in all forms of popular music: jump blues (later, r 'n' b), honky tonk—western swing—bluegrass in country music, and the song stylist. John Lewis, later to form the Modern Jazz Quartet (which operated in the cool mode), did arrangements involving contrapuntal techniques and the fugue. Gerry Mulligan did arrangements for Davis, and later Mulligan would use a pianoless quartet. Gil Evans did arrangements for Davis, and Evans heavily influenced Davis right through the 1960s. Evans had previously done arranging for Claude Thornhill, and both had been strongly affected by Ellington's use of diverse instruments to create tone coloration. But at the time of "cool," it was mainly melodic improvisation and gentle tones that counted, and practitioners included arranger-pianist Tadd Dameron, pianist Lennie Tristano (and his disciples Lee Konitz and Warne Marsh), Lester Young (through his use of silence), Stan Getz, and Milt Jackson.

In the 1950s, this music ultimately became known as "West Coast jazz," and it was strongly influenced by the classics of serious music. Notables here included Shorty Rogers, Shelly Manne, Jimmy Giuffre, Chico Hamilton, Bob Brookmeyer, Quincy Jones, and Gerry Mulligan. In retrospect, it appears as if the music was just meant for white technicians, because those were the people who played it the most.

"Hard bop" was a mid-fifties development that extended and revitalized bop after the cool period, and like bop, it was essentially New York-based. Charlie Parker had died; his disciples were taking over on their own. Extensions to the music meant at least three things: black playing, in which the 32-bar song structure was redistributed (Jelly Roll Morton did this thirty years before!); polymetric structures; and funky blues, in which slow or medium blues were played hard on the beat with emotion (this was derived from r 'n' b and introduced to jazz by Horace Silver, pianist for Art Blakey's Jazz Messengers). Art Blakey defined the style through his drumming and his musical dialog with the front line's sax and trumpet. The Brown-Roach Quintet and Sonny Rollins were equally influential as the leaders of the second generation boppers. Others included Donald Byrd, Lee Morgan, Elvin Jones, Barney Kessel, Freddie Hubbard, Miles Davis (when he found his level of development), and John Coltrane.

Modern Characteristics

Much of the 1950s and 1960s, though, was spent on *free jazz* in a search for new ways of expression. This music was atonal and featured the complete disintegration of meter (which resulted in tension), the collapse of the beat (now referred to as the "pulse"), and the lack of symmetry. It was influenced by other cultures, such as India (which has 108 beats in its rhythmic cycle), Africa, Japan, Arabia, and other parts of Asia. There were few rules for playing modern jazz except that orgiastic intensity must be reached, and that whatever cyclical pattern is established and whatever rambling the instruments do, they must meet again on the *first* beat as relief from tension.

One of the first to work in the modern jazz vein was Lennie Tristano, who influenced Lee Konitz in the formless jazz field as early as 1949. "Modal" jazz was worked on by Miles Davis and John Coltrane beginning in 1958. This was a scalar improvisation based on scales and modes rather than on chords. Davis's work was later extended by Coltrane, Elvin Jones, and McCoy Tyner.

Charles Mingus and others who had also toured Europe fell under the spell of classical, traditional European influences, and used such themes in their orchestrated works. Albert Ayler took the opposite route with his use of primitive motifs, going back to black field hollers of slavery days, plus other styles borrowed from novelties and country music. The r 'n' b style of honking horns gave a background to Ornette Coleman, Archie Shepp, and Pharoah Sanders (all of whom worked for an r 'n' b band at one time or another).

By the 1970s modern jazz had begun to reflect everything that previously had been discovered in its exploratory period. There were four main developments. One was the characteristic use of free, *collective* improvisations of the group plus the free *solo* improvisations of a single performer (usually a piano or saxophone) or occasionally a *duo*. Another was the use of not only more classical influences but also more traditional jazz roots. A third was the move to more melodic and wide-ranging compositions, all of them lyrically pleasing. And the fourth was the Davis influence of rock beats, electronics, and keyboards with setups involving wah-wah pedals, varitones, feedback units, multividers, echoplex, phase shifters, ring modulators, synthesizers, and so forth. In 1970, Davis also introduced the notion of mass editing recorded tapes to create a "produced" music. The more successful performers working in all four of these developments include the pianists Cecil Tayler, Herbie Hancock, Keith Jarrett, Chick Corea, Joe Zawinul, and McCoy Tyner. And the best music here can be found on European labels such as ECM, Freedom, and SteepleChase.

Literature

Besides the books and periodicals mentioned in the general literature survey of jazz, there are many specialized studies which can be located through Gregor (45), Kennington (59), and Merriam (73), with a general close-off year of 1969. Unfortunately, not much has been written about modern jazz beyond biographical pieces. Some attempts at musical analysis are being made in books such as Cole (18) on Miles Davis, or one of several biographies of John Coltrane. Russell (96) presents the basic elements of Charlie Parker's rise through bop. Gitler (41) also covers the 1940s, while Goldenberg (43) does the same with the 1950s. Williams (125) works expertly with the 1957-1969 period.

The important jazz periodicals here are *Coda* (4) and *Downbeat* (7), the former for its lengthy interviews, and the latter for its transcriptions of music.

BOP

Anthologies

J5.1*   **The Anatomy of Improvisation.** World Record Club F 526 (British issue).

J5.2*   **The Be-Bop Era.** RCA LPV 519.

J5.3   **Six Faces of Jazz.** Ember CJS 826 (British issue).

J5.4   **Strictly Be-Bop.** Capitol MT 11059.

J5.5*   **Supersax Plays Bird.** Capitol ST 11177.

Anthologized materials of the bop period are difficult to find, for so many recordings were made of just a few persons that the tracks have come out under their own names (and hence are not on collective anthologies). *The Book of Jazz*, by Leonard Feather, has several transcriptions of improvised solos, and the originals are featured in the World Record Club offering, covering 1949 through 1956. Basically, it is a wide-ranging album, with contributions by Dizzy Gillespie ("Jessica's Day"), Charlie Parker ("Bloomdido"), Bud Powell ("Hallucinations") and others. The RCA collection features Coleman Hawkins, Illinois Jacquet, Lucky Thompson, Kenny Clarke, Charlie Ventura, Dizzy Gillespie, and even Count Basie, with such typically bop titles as "Mutton Leg," "Ooop-Bop Sh-Bam," "Ha," "Ow!," and "Jump Did-Le Ba." In essence, this is a good collection, but the materials are second generation, and to some extent, commercial renditions.

The true producer of bop music in the 1940s was the small, independent record producer (Dial, Savoy, etc.). One of these was the Continental label, which has reissued recordings on the Ember disc. Once again, there are Dizzy Gillespie,

Charlie Parker, Buck Clayton, Coleman Hawkins, Trummy Young, Don Byas, and others. Of note is the vocal by Rubberlegs Williams on "That's the Blues," an hysterical performance made possible by his consumption (mistakenly) of Parker's benzedrine mixture. The Capitol set is derived from 1949-1950 recordings, with Tadd Dameron, Babs Gonzales, and Dizzy Gillespie and their groups (including Fats Navarro, Dexter Gordon, Cecil Payne, Sonny Rollins, and J. J. Johnson). While some of these recordings are complicated in a high harmonic order, they are still commercial issuances. The Supersax album was a reasonably good attempt at analyzing Parker's harmonic structures and scoring for trumpets, trombones, and reeds: "Hot House," "Night in Tunisia," and "Lady Be Good."

J5.6*   **The Greatest Jazz Concert Ever**. two discs. Prestige PR 24024.
    Re-released in time to celebrate its twentieth anniversary, this epic bop concert was performed May 15, 1953, at Massey Hall, Toronto, Canada. The best of the boppers were present: Dizzy Gillespie (trumpet), Charlie Parker (alto sax), Bud Powell (piano), Max Roach (drums), and Charles Mingus (bass). The latter was responsible for taping the sets, although he dubbed-in the bass parts later because the original was inaudible. This was a temperamental group, its members known to clash among themselves. But the evidence on this twofer points out their joint geniuses. Words cannot adequately describe the impact. For instance, on "A Night in Tunisia," the first solo by Parker seems to indicate the precarious hold that he had on the meter. This creates tension in the listener, who is kept on the edge of his seat. The New Jazz Society of Toronto took a poll to form their favorite quintet, and the winners were invited for this performance. Unfortunately, it was held on the same night as the Marciano-Walcott fight, so that only 600 people showed in a place that seats 2,832. Other problems seemed to create bop tensions: Parker left his Selmer alto at home so he had to make do with a local *plastic* one; Powell was playing his first concert since his shock therapy began, and he was drunk all the time he was on stage; Gillespie kept checking the fight via radio during the others' solos, and his wanderings increased the antagonism in his then-present feud with Parker; Powell had never played with Gillespie before but had for six years with Parker, while Parker and Gillespie had not been together for three years.
    That the concert was able to come off at all is a minor miracle, and that it was a definitive statement of bop can only be reckoned as incredible. This was the first and last time the group played together. Parker died two years later, Powell left for France, and Gillespie formed a series of big bands. All the items here are well-known as bop anthems: "Perdido," "Salt Peanuts" (where Parker plays so fast to tempt Gillespie), "All the Things You Are" (in which Powell and Parker get into an interplay and both appear lost until the final stanza), "Wee" (with a breakneck Parker solo and superb choruses by Powell and Roach), and "Hot House." But the value of the concert is that the boppers were allowed further extensions of ideas through the longer time available. Also, they could take more risks and try out new ideas. The first part of the concert was simply a Powell trio, and of the ten selections, four are tunes *not* from the concert (they act as a filler for this 12-inch disc, as the trio originally appeared on a 10-inch disc twenty years earlier). Tunes include "Cherokee" and "I've Got You Under My Skin," in which Powell takes a Tatum-esque approach to the music by being excessively ornamental. Taken together, this set is a significant, historical, essential, and basic document.

J5.7   **Café Society**. Onyx ORI 210.
There were two good jazz clubs in New York in the 1940s—Café Society Downtown (basement, seating 210) and the Café Society Uptown (two stories, seating 350). They operated for a decade, but closed in 1950 as a result of the "Red" scare. The historical notes (and a wealth of them, no less) are by Dan Morgenstern, and include details about the rest of the New York club scene. The 1944-1946 material here comes from an important transitional period for jazz (betwixt swing and bop). Four groups are presented, with four tracks each. All of these three-minute miniatures are originals, and no standards are heard. These are the bands that played in the two nightclubs and were caught by Continental records, one of the many, many small independents that proliferated in the war years and through various recording bans. J. C. Heard often led house bands, and he has with him here Budd Johnson in a sextet configuration. Edmond Hall, on clarinet, presents the most robust band here, nicely augmented by a young Ellis Larkins. Mary Lou Williams heads an all-girl group that is so-so, and the schmaltz continues with Maxine Sullivan singing ahead of violins. Variable sound, but it is a nice document.

Innovators

J5.8*   **Art Blakey. Moanin'**. Blue Note BST 84003.

J5.9*   **Art Blakey. A Night at Birdland, v.1/2**. two discs. Blue Note BST 81521/2.
Art Blakey was among the first to translate Charlie Parker's music to percussion. Since the late forties he has led several editions of a Parker-inspired combo called the Jazz Messengers. Each group has been different in its qualities insofar as solo expression is concerned. The basic philosophy was quite simple: the front line horns were given all the time and space they needed for their solos to explore further bop expressions; and, the relationship of the horns to the drums drastically strengthened when Blakey's drumming was put on an equal footing with the soloists. He could attack furiously as a soloist or remain in the background with the persistent swing of his renowned rim shots. In either case, he was clearly present. The quintet found its greatest expression with the 1954 edition (recorded live at Birdland). Included were Clifford Brown, Lou Donaldson, Horace Silver and Curly Russell. By now, the piano and bass had minor roles, being consigned to the business of rhythm, while the horn man and drummer engaged in a dialog. Thus, Blakey assumed the bandleader position from the drummer's spot, directing the action by sending out signals from the drums much as a marching band would. In many cases, these might simply have been background beats or complex cross-accents. In total, his music was characterized by aggressiveness, clashes with the frustrated rhythm section for tension, and restless solos among the four-bar exchanges.
Blakey's dramatic approach was ceaseless energy. He had to sell his idea of bop drumming. He developed a steady cymbal beat that was augmented by dancing patterns on the bass and snare drums. This continuous flow of percussion varied with the piece being played and was, of course, subject to much syncopation from the high-hat. In essence, then, he competed with the soloist for the audience's attention. This is clearly detailed on the live set, where his polyrhythmic approach

produced cross-accents that largely contributed to but often overpowered the soloist. This set contains the classic version of "A Night in Tunisia," which became Blakey's theme. The ten selections all capture the spirit of bop. Included is an alternate version of "Quicksilver." While Silver's piano never really played a strong role in the Blakeyan bop concept, he did serve as the group's arranger and main composer. The front liners here were all Blue Note solo artists, and Blakey has to stretch his devices to keep them all in line. Despite this tension (or because of?), Brown produces some of his best music, particularly in "Once in a While," where he switches back and forth from long phrases to 32nd notes in attempts to break the mold. The second album has blues and ballads, including a Parker theme, "Now's the Time," one of the "Hucklebuck" musical variations. The *Moanin'* album was a commercial success. With Benny Golson originals and Bobby Timmons's impressive title selection, Lee Morgan led a highly simplified brand of the Blakey polyrhythms. Perhaps this was why it was successful. "Blues March" and "Moanin' " became successes, and Lee Morgan developed other lyrical themes on other records.

J5.10*   **Charlie Christian. v.1/2.** two discs. CBS 52538 (British issue) and CBS 62581 (French issue).

J5.11*   **Charlie Christian. At Minton's.** Everest 219.

J5.12*   **Charlie Christian. Together with Lester Young, 1940.** Jazz Archives JA6.

J5.13*   **Charlie Christian. With Benny Goodman's Sextet, 1939/41.** Jazz Archives JA 23.

There were three greats of the jazz guitar: Lang, Reinhardt, and Christian. The amplified guitar of Christian took the blues and rhythm of the other two and produced a style that was halfway between swing and bop. The basics were *blues* (such as "Blues in B"), the *swing riffs* (producing the tension of "Flying Home," "Honeysuckle Rose," or "Stompin' at the Savoy"), and *harmonics.* This latter led to a number of devices that preceded bop, as found in "Till Tom Special," "I've Found a New Baby," or "Seven Come Eleven." One was the transition from Lester Young to Charlie Parker in accenting the off-beats of 4/4, as in "Airmail Special" or "Blues in B." Another was the displacement of notes, as in "Breakfast Feud" or "Shivers." A third lay in the long runs of eighth notes that subdivided the beat, as Gillespie and Kenny Clarke were to do.

Christian's style could then be characterized as a mixture of single notes in both fragmented phrases and advanced harmonics, making use of augmented and diminished chords. His best recordings were with the Benny Goodman Sextet, 1939-1941, which at various times included Count Basie, Fletcher Henderson, Lionel Hampton (q.v.; Christian recorded for Hampton's group also), Johnny Guarnieri, Cootie Williams, Dave Tough, etc. In fact, such was his influence that he dominated the group at all times. His overall best performance was undoubtedly when he played with Lester Young. The Jazz Archives set presents five tracks of semi-improvisation, never released before, with Christian, Goodman, and Young, plus Basie rhythm and Buck Clayton. There are superb renditions of "Wholly Cats," which involves splitting notes, "Charlie's Dream," and "Lester's Dream."

The 1941 jam at Minton's Club is historically significant. Christian was at his zenith, and while he has no really new ideas here above what was described already on disc, none of his studio items match his playing style here. At the same time, Gillespie, playing here, is sharpening his ideas from Roy Eldridge, and the listener can clearly hear the changes on "Stardust I" or "Kerouac." Kenny Clarke and Thelonious Monk complete the rhythm, and this could be considered the first bop rhythm section. Changes and transitional elements abound on the track "Swing to Bop" (from "Topsy"), which is really a condensed history of jazz as riff after riff from the swing age are laid down until the complex phrases are reached. Every notable electric jazz guitarist has been influenced by Christian, especially Barney Kessel.

J5.14*   **Tadd Dameron. Strictly Bebop.** Capitol M 11059.
        Dameron had a great career in the 1940s as an arranger and composer for several bands, beginning with Harlan Leonard and creating the classics "Dameron Stomp" and "Rock and Ride." He worked with Gillespie, Lunceford, Eckstine, Sarah Vaughan, Fats Navarro, Jimmy Dorsey, Ted Heath, and John Coltrane. His was basically a swing background, but he came to grips with bop music. His scores included astonishing interludes of calm between the choruses (these were little ensemble variations on the melody), and occasionally he would put in a theme quite different from the sequence that the soloists would then improvise on. This led to complicated arrangements that were also logical. Fats Navarro was probably the best interpreter of Dameron. This 1949 group on Capitol (together since 1947) displays integrity in both orchestrations and solo work. The various personnel included Kai Winding, Dexter Gordon, Sahib Shihab, Cecil Payne, Kenny Clarke, and Miles Davis, with Dameron on piano. Selections include "John's Delight" and "Sid's Delight," as well as "Focus." "Casbah," enhanced by Rae Pearl's wordless vocal, was based on "Out of Nowhere."

J5.15*   **Miles Davis.** two discs. United Artists UAS 9952.

J5.16*   **Miles Davis.** two discs. Prestige PR 24001.

J5.17   **Miles Davis. Collector's Items.** two discs. Prestige P 24022.

J5.18   **Miles Davis. Dig.** two discs. Prestige P 24053.

J5.19   **Miles Davis. 'Round about Midnight.** Columbia PC 8649.

J5.20   **Miles Davis. Tallest Trees.** two discs. Prestige PR 24012.

J5.21*   **Miles Davis. Workin' and Steamin'.** Prestige PR 24034.
        All of these discs show Davis in his *hard* bop years, 1951-1956. The United Artists twofer contains all of Davis under his own name, from three Blue Note sessions. With a sextet and quartet, in May 1952, he recorded "Dear Old Stockholm" and "Woody 'n' You" (among others). In April 1953, the group was more aggressive, as Art Blakey and his rim shots replaced Kenny Clarke. Here are two takes of Bud Powell's "Tempus Fugit." J. J. Johnson's trombone added bite to the date. The March 1954 quartet (with Horace Silver, Percy Heath, and Art Blakey) was a miniature Jazz Messenger session. Innovations included "It Never Entered My

Mind" (on which Davis has a mute near the mike) and the resounding "Well, You Needn't."

The five twofers—ten discs—present virtually all of Davis's Prestige recordings, 1951-1956. The earlier period had "Blue Room" (1951) with Sonny Rollins; 1953 was prolific, with "Walkin' " (one of Davis's best solos) including J. J. Johnson and Lucky Thompson. This was recorded just a month after the Blue Note session; hence, Silver, Blakey, and Heath were along. On other material, Davis was assisted by Al Cohn and Zoot Sims, while there are four tracks (including two takes of the renowned "Serpent's Tooth") that offer Charlie Parker in his only recordings in *support* of Davis, who had begun his disc career as Bird's sideman but was now a leader in his own right. "Blue 'n' Boogie" and a dual *tenor* sax version of " 'Round about Midnight" (Rollins and Parker) are also included. Nineteen fifty-four was a tremendous year for Davis, with the Blue Note sessions, and a series of Prestige recordings with Rollins, Silver, Heath, and Clarke that included Parker's "Oleo," "Airegin," "Doxy" (based on "Ja-Da") and two takes of "But Not For Me."

The highlight of the year, though, was Christmas Eve. Davis had Milt Jackson, Thelonius Monk, Heath, and Clarke. Davis and Monk were at odds throughout the session, so there was much tension (which produced good music). Davis excels on the two takes of Jackson's "Bags' Groove," and on "Bemsha Swing." On "The Man I Love," after Jackson's good solo, the group goes into two different tempos simultaneously as Monk fools around with halving the time. An impatient Davis is flustered, and angrily toots his horn to bring Monk's solo to a swift close. Of particular interest here is the scalar work "Swing Spring," which foreshadowed Davis's future directions. Through 1955-1956, Davis tried to get out of his Prestige contract by speeding up the delivery of his albums. He took his working group—now with pianist Red Garland, saxist John Coltrane, bassist Paul Chambers, and drummer Philly Joe Jones—into the studio many times, re-recording some of his earlier works.

These albums (originally called *Cookin'*, *Relaxin'*, *Workin'*, and *Steamin'*) stand as a landmark in recorded jazz for their tight consistency. Throughout, Garland is an orthodox bop pianist, Chambers constructs some of his first *free* bass lines, Jones produces percussive cross-rhythms, while Davis and Coltrane (beginning to develop his "sheets of sound") trade solos. Here are two versions of " 'Round about Midnight," "Dear Old Stockholm," "Four," "Oleo," "Airegin," and "Tuneup." This was the group that Davis took to Columbia for his first recording there, and that disc neatly fits into this survey. Later, Davis would develop in alternate directions. At the moment, though, he was a hard worker, fighting exhaustion and drugs to produce the occasional gem of a solo. But he had to work at it. Davis is not in the stream of Armstrong—Eldridge—Gillespie—Brown; they were far more fluid performers than he was at this time. Only by constantly playing and *slowly* shaping his style could Davis succeed. His role now and in the future was as a leader and bossman, whipping his accompanists into satisfactory musicians in their own rights.

J5.22*   **Dizzy Gillespie. In the Beginning.** two discs. Prestige P 24030.

These are Diz's first recordings as a leader and come from Musicraft 78 rpms of 1945 and 1946. Every bopper knew and memorized these sextet performances: "Blue 'n' Boogie," "Groovin' High," "Dizzy Atmosphere," "Salt Peanuts," and so forth. Foils included Dexter Gordon, Charlie Parker, Al Haig, Sonny Stitt, and vocals by Sarah Vaughan in her golden period. The Gillespie Big Band performs on eight tracks, and amazingly, the entire band sounded like Diz in unison. An incredible, representative track here is "Things to Come." This set is rounded out by three selections from the Prestige catalog of 1950. Here Diz reverts to the sextet mould and gives an impressive performance of the remarkably cool "Thinking of You."

J5.23*   **Howard McGhee. Trumpet at Tempo.** Spotlite SPJ131 (British issue).
    McGhee was one of the leading bop trumpeters of the 1940s, just under Gillespie in importance. He was a direct link between swing and bop, a transitional figure who once performed with the 1943 Andy Kirk band. At that time, Fats Navarro was with the group (McGhee was a heavy influence) and so was Mary Lou Williams, who developed current bop themes through her arrangements. Kirk's outfit was an important unit in the breakthrough to bop. For Dial records, McGhee was an important sideman who contributed greatly to Charlie Parker sessions. This collection of 19 tracks from Hollywood and New York (1946-1947) runs for almost an hour and features some of Dial's leading performers. Dodo Marmarosa plays excellent piano on "Dialated Pupils," "Midnight at Minton's," "Up in Dodo's Room," and "High Wind in Hollywood." Milt Jackson romantically swings and bops his way through half of the album, while James Moody, Hank Jones, and Ray Brown also make their contributions.
    McGhee had a number of substantial credits. He was extremely dependable, always showing up on time, and this made him a top session man and nightclub act. He was an excellent composer of originals (and not just changes, solos, and breaks). His bravura trumpet was a direct inheritance from and a logical extension of Armstrong and Eldridge—a sort of "advanced swing" or "hot bop." The former was heard best on the ballads, with mainstream legato and vibrato. Gillespie and Navarro, on the other hand, transformed the trumpet in bop by matching the sax changes of Charlie Parker. McGhee's clean, swing articulation made him fluent in the upper register, thereby making it possible for extensive use of augmented and whole tone scales modeled after Debussy. His sure embouchure and secure fingering allowed him a bop tone of stop chords, clusters, blues, and alternating fast-slow tempos— all of which had a dramatic influence on the young Navarro. Throughout most of the selections here, McGhee constantly demonstrated his prowess on triple tonguing and staccato phrasing, leading to good climaxes in his structures. With his technical ability, it was no wonder that he was a demanding composer.

J5.24*   **Thelonious Monk. Complete Genius.** two discs. Blue Note BNLA 579-H2.

J5.25*   **Thelonious Monk. Monk's Mood.** Prestige 7159.
    Pianist-composer Monk had definite roots in stride music and was a forerunner of bop. As one critic put it, he was "of bop, but not in it." And this was true of most of his recorded output, which, after 1955, seemed to get cliché-ridden as he was subjected to the whims of producers. It was not so much the tune that mattered as the technical aspects such as timing, meter, spacing, and accenting. The Blue Note set embraces 1947-1952. These were his first chances to record as a leader, from trio through sextet, for 24 tracks. Diverse personnel includes Art Blakey, Sahib Shihab, Milt Jackson, Max Roach, Lou Donaldson, Al McKibbon, et al. All of Monk's music was fresh in conception. He believed in the logical development of theme and the harmonic potential of ideas (which counted more than the orchestration, for *what* is said is more important than the *how*). There was, thus, a

certain amount of difficulty in putting together these abstract compositions, and
it was equally difficult for the front line to improvise over Monk's economical chords
for he was not feeding them anything (unlike Blakey or Roach). At any rate, the
material is unique and interesting, for Monk had been composing long before he got
a chance to record. These are original renditions of "Mysterioso," " 'Round about
Midnight," "Epistrophy," "Ruby My Dear," "Straight, No Chaser," "Monk's Mood,"
and "Well, You Needn't." Taken as a group they appear to have no inessentials,
but a great deal of motive development and rhythmic invention.

Between 1952 and 1954, Monk recorded for Prestige, and his trio here plays
ten selections. Percy Heath (bass) and either Blakey or Roach (drums) provide input
for Monk's idiosyncratic harmonic ideas, and while Monk projects no sensational
techniques, he does advance the thematic variations of such standards as "Sweet and
Lovely" or "These Foolish Things" (both humorous items). Of some originals,
"Blue Monk" is his best-known blues composition, and it gets another definitive
presentation. "Little Rootie Tootie" is based on the ubiquitous train themes. Monk
has made invaluable contributions to jazz for almost 40 years, beginning with the
boppers at Minton's, through Davis and Coltrane, and back again with the revival
of bop.

J5.26*   **Fats Navarro. Prime Source.** two discs. Blue Note BNLA 507-H2.

J5.27*   **Fats Navarro. Savoy Sessions: Fat Girl.** two discs. Savoy SJL 2216.
The amazing thing about trumpeter Navarro's records is that his work contains
not a single flaw. His execution was faultless, which is more than anyone can say about
all of the recordings of Armstrong, Eldridge, Gillespie, and Davis. Of course, in Armstrong's case, it was mostly a technical problem of growing up (both he *and* the
trumpet, for his period was just barely the dawn of jazz). That Navarro should be
this way is all the more remarkable, since he died when he was only 26! His style is
clearly derived from the swing trumpet, perhaps less flamboyant than Gillespie
but influenced by the latter in some respects. His vibrato-free tone came from Armstrong's broad tone. The Savoy tracks cover the material done at age 23 (1946-
1947), and include "Boppin' Riff," "Stealin' Trash," "Everything's Cool," and
the fast drive of "Dr. Jazz." Accompanying musicians include Kenny Dorham, Sonny
Stitt, Bud Powell, and Al Haig. Over the next two years, several Blue Note recordings were made, with Sonny Rollins, Powell, Milt Jackson, Howard McGhee, Tadd
Dameron (who did much of the composing and arranging), and Kenny Clarke.
Navarro exhibited all of the characteristics that most trumpeters aspired to. He had
complete control of a vast range of notes, flawless articulation and accuracy, melodic
flexibility and speed, and a large, warm, consistently immaculate tone. Staccato
notes are employed in the Savoy "Hollerin' and Screamin'," and again with "Ice
Freezes Red," where he quickly reached the high notes in his solo and then
attempted to resolve the tension on his own terms. This recurring feature appears
many times in the Blue Notes as well, with the effortless cruise and swing of notes
on "The Chase," which makes it all sound so simple. Other Dameron items included
"The Squirrel," "Our Delight," "Dameronia," and the very relaxing "Boperation."

J5.28*   **Charlie Parker. First Recordings!** Onyx ORI 221.

J5.29*   **Charlie Parker. On Dial.** six discs. Spotlite 101/6 (British issue).

J5.30*   **Charlie Parker. Bird: The Savoy Recordings.** three discs. Savoy
          SJL 2201, 1107.

If there are any performers in the jazz world who should be called *unique*,
then Armstrong, Coleman, and Parker are the leading candidates. To sum up his
career, Parker was raised in Kansas City, where he heard many saxophone "cutting
contests" (in which each musician tried to out-do the others). Eventually, these
contests evolved into music for musicians' ears only. Kansas City was the home of
the "band blues" and of the riff employed in swing music. Watching others perform
(and getting booed off the stage at one point), Parker began to teach himself to
play alto saxophone through long hours of perseverance. He practiced the blues
chord sequence in every key for additional facility. He practiced his fingering for
complete control over extremely fast tempos. His influences here were Lester
Young and Charlie Christian (later, he admired Varèse and Hindemith).

Going through the basics over and over, Parker employed double-timing,
half-timing, various chord progressions, and so forth to produce new compositions.
Thus, he developed what is described by the term *contrafacts*, which is the original
harmony plus a new melody on chord progressions. About one-quarter of his output
were contrafacts. From "I Got Rhythm" (the most famous chord progression
sequence used in bop music) came "Dexterity," "Anthropology," "Oleo," "Salt
Peanuts," "Red Cross," and "Moose the Mooche"; from "Indiana" came "Donna
Lee"; from "Lullaby in Rhythm" came "Crazeology"; from "Rosetta" came
"Yardbird Suite"; from "Honeysuckle Rose" came "Scrapple from the Apple";
from "All the Things You Are" came "Bird of Paradise"; from "Embraceable
You" came "Quasimodo" and "Meandering"; from "How High the Moon" came
"Ornithology"; and from "Perdido" came "Klactoveedsedstene." One added
advantage was that listeners originally did not know the modes, and they appeared
to be hearing new compositions that were relatively difficult to duplicate unless the
technique was known. After spending 4½ years with McShann (meanwhile playing
at Minton's and Monroe's Uptown House in New York), Parker joined the bands
of Earl Hines and, later, Billy Eckstine.

The Onyx disc is a hodge podge of radio transcriptions from 1940, Jerry
Newman's 1942 wire tapes, and various 78 rpms from 1945. None of the material
appeared originally under Parker's name. With the Jay McShann band, Parker
recorded the 1940 tracks six months before his first commercial outing (see the
McShann big band entry, J4.79). Of note from the Newman tapes is a 2:45 fragment of an extended "Cherokee" solo. Here, Parker hit upon the idea of playing
the upper extension of the chords as a melody line. This statement became the
basic document of "Koko" and bop music. The commercial releases were recorded
under Clyde Hart's name, with Don Byas, Dizzy Gillespie, and singer Rubberlegs
Williams.

Then began what is commonly referred to as "Parker's decade," 1945-1955,
when he recorded mainly for Dial, Savoy, and Clef-Verve (see J5.69-70
for the latter). His best years were 1947-1948, and these are ably documented here with a number of alternate takes. The Dials are in chronological order;
the Savoys are too, but the alternates are mixed. All the performances are mainly
by the Quintet, which was composed of Dizzy Gillespie, Miles Davis (later), Max
Roach, Duke Jordan, Al Haig, and Bud Powell. Of the thirty-plus master selections
and many alternates on the Savoys, at least six are based on "I Got Rhythm"
("Thriving from a Riff"), nine are twelve-bar blues ("Now's the Time"), and seven

are derived from such popular standards as "Honeysuckle Rose," "Embraceable You," and "Indiana." Thus, it can be immediately seen that Parker's work was mainly in technique (he was a superb technician and fantastic improvisor), for he did not bother to stray beyond the familiar 12- or 32-bar patterns, nor did he bother with unfamiliar basic chord sequences. There is nothing strange about this, and in retrospect, Parker's main impact was in freeing music from harmonic structures, to pave the way for "free form" music.

He was little interested in the exploration of harmony. He simply employed superb linear compositions based mainly on existing harmonies, such as the previously mentioned "Koko" from "Cherokee." Some original blues, such as "Billie's Bounce" were fashioned, but generally the blues themes seem to be common material anyway. On both the Savoy and Dial recordings, the alternate takes are exceptionally valuable for comparison purposes. They are better arranged on the Dial reissues as they are programmed chronologically. His solos were generally of two types. First, they were in fast tempos. Here was improvisation that was quickly developed under pressure. His phrasing had to be elastic, and thus a certain amount of tension was created as when long linear phrases topped each other or when shorter phrases were constantly reiterated in different ways. Second, his medium tempos were much more relaxed being carried forward by the rhythmic momentum.

Overall, Parker was notable for five innovations. First, there was the obvious emotion and intensity of his playing—a passionate attack that was almost bursting at the seams, suggesting raw primitive powers in his blues orientation. Second, the Lestorian flow of notes that floated across the beat, across the bar line and "phrase line," and across the chorus breaks. Third, the incredible complexity in the rhythmic superimpositions led to dense harmonic structures. Fourth, Parker often produced complex *initial* theme statements before the solo passages, and these set the tone and ideas for the improvisations that were to follow, especially for the other four members of the quintet. And fifth, he *retained* the melodic worth of the composition (whereas modern jazz musicians usually discard the melody). Melodies were used as launching pads to set up a chord progression, a tempo, and a mood. These melodies were paraphrased, and improvisations were created around the melody. Parker could construct a solo from one simple motif, altering it rhythmically and melodically to fit the changing harmonies underneath.

In performing all these musical acrobatics, he was surrounded by and was an influence on Max Roach (twenty years old by the time of "Koko" and already developing the cymbal beats and timing), Bud Powell (who echoed Parker by transcribing his ideas for the piano), and Miles Davis (in a negative sense, as his disjointed trumpet passages were not at home with bop, he being weak on the trickier themes; one consequence of this was Davis's reaction and development of "cool" scales and modes). Other *immediate* disciples included Dizzy Gillespie, Kenny Clarke, Fats Navarro, Kenny Dorham, Sonny Stitt, Dexter Gordon, Red Rodney— *plus* every single musician now active in post-bop jazz!

J5.31*   **Bud Powell. Amazing, v.1/5.** five discs. Blue Note 81503/4, 81571, 81598, 84009.

J5.32   **Bud Powell. Trio.** Roost LP2224.

Powell's darting right hand almost completed the transition of the piano out of the rhythm section and into the main jazz elements. As Parker did, Powell took immense risks in his playing, and deft execution was required. The Hines trumpet style of his emphasized right hand provided the treble impetus, yet on the balance, his overall conception of solos was weak. The trio format was very important to his style: the bass provided harmony and the drums, the meter. All of these contrasts were needed as support to his definitive fast tempos or blues. His attack was tireless, and full of emotion. On this matter, he influenced *all* pianists to follow, for he had perfectly distilled the essence of jazz piano. The Roost recording on 12 tracks comes from 1947, with four additional titles recorded in 1953. Here, on "Bud's Bubble" he emphasizes rhythmic complexities, while on "Somebody Loves Me" (made popular by George Shearing) he provides solid chording. His exact timing comes through on "I'll Remember April," needing both concentration and precision. The lighthearted "I Should Care" illustrates his uncommon variations, perhaps coming from his early mentor Art Tatum and giving the listener insight into his facility for attacking at extremely fast tempos. At the same time, Powell had an incredible storehouse of ideas that he offhandedly tossed out as throwaways. His innovations became the standard by which to judge jazz piano procedures.

The Blue Note albums, largely from 1949-1953, clearly show how his attacking lines were based on chordal substructures. By transposing Parker to the keyboard, Powell revealed his own virtuosity in asymmetrical phrasing (as on "Un Poco Loco," heard here in three versions). There are no accents like Earl Hines. At the same time, Powell could delve into ballads, and here he reveals touches of Teddy Wilson (as on "It Could Happen to You"). The material on the Blue Notes is about equally split between the trio format and the combo. Fats Navarro and Sonny Rollins combine on "Dance of the Infidels" to produce a two-bar phrase with a hesitation accent occurring just in front of the third beat of the second bar; Rollins makes a two-bar riff out of "52nd Street Theme." Other tracks include "Night in Tunisia," "Wail," a sterling Rollins horn on "Bouncing with Bud," "Ornithology," and "Parisian Thoroughfare." Many alternate takes are included in this five-disc set; thus, it is possible to hear changes within the same tune, either as single-note lines or as moody harmonic inventions. Powell was with bop from the beginning, playing at Minton's, joining the boppers, stinting with Parker, and reaching a climax at the 1953 Jazz Concert at Toronto's Massey Hall (see item J5.6).

J5.33*   **Max Roach-Clifford Brown Quintet. In Concert.** GNP S 18.

In 1954, Clifford Brown joined Max Roach, and for two years (until Brown's tragic death), the two co-led a quintet that was at the forefront of modern jazz. This disc is perhaps the best representative example of their work. It was recorded in the early days (1954) of the group, when they had not yet settled down but were proficient enough to recognize each performer's limitations while taking advantage of solo space. The eight tracks come from two separate concerts. Bud Powell's atmospheric "Parisian Thoroughfare" and the long workout of Duke Jordan's "Jordu" get their early definitive versions here. Brown excels over and over, producing an exceptional rendition of "Tenderly" that has proven to be the standard that has never been matched. Brown was a trumpeter in the style of Gillespie and Navarro, thus, a direct descendant of Armstrong, through Roy Eldridge. Roach is a brilliant drummer, who has in no small measure contributed to the success of percussive movements in jazz. His main challenge was to get jazz away from 4/4 time, and in that, he succeeded.

J5.34   **Horace Silver. Blowin' the Blues Away.** Blue Note BST 84017.

J5.35*   **Horace Silver. Finger Poppin'.** Blue Note BST 84008.

J5.36*   **Horace Silver. With the Jazz Messengers.** Blue Note BST 81518.
Silver began his career with Stan Getz in 1950 as a Bud Powell-influenced pianist. His early style did not change much, being largely a combination of extended single note phrases in the right hand and chording in the left. But, as on the BST 81518 disc (recorded in 1954-1955), he did play behind the beat, and his short phrases did produce the variety needed in hard bop. This disc was the earliest to be made by the Jazz Messengers, even though it is issued under Silver's name. Adapting the Parker quintet format, Blakey virtually created the term "hard bop," a style characterized by a dedication to the beat and to aggressiveness, trading off the drummer and the soloist. Following Parker's lead, the Jazz Messengers played mainly blues. With the Blakey policy of demoting the piano, Silver was always in a quandary. He was the best composer and arranger of the group, producing such classics as "The Preacher" and "Doodlin'," and thereby he found a way out. In so doing, he created and influenced a whole new style in jazz: *funk.* By playing his short phrases as loud as he could, with repetitive blues lines and sustained notes behind the beat, he produced the anticipated syncopated note that leads to "finger popping." That particular disc is rewarding, as one critic said, for its velocity, as on the fast blues "Cookin' at the Continental." An additional track, "Melancholy Mood" (from the *Blowin'* album), further extends the hard funky sound.

Standards

J5.37   **Gene Ammons and Dodo Marmarosa. Jug and Dodo.** two discs.
Prestige PR 24021.
Both "Jug" Ammons and Marmarosa have been under-represented and under-valued as jazzmen. Most of what Ammons, son of the boogie pianist Albert Ammons, has recorded with his tenor sax has been derivative and banal, fitting more into a second-generation soul-funk mood. He believed that "jazz is fun" and teamed with Sonny Stitt to produce early r 'n' b music (his blues playing was strongly influenced by Charlie Parker). Marmarosa came to prominence during the bop period and quickly dropped out of sight. He was the pianist for Shaw's Gramercy Five recordings, but in 1945 he appeared with Parker and Gillespie for a series of epic recordings on the Savoy label. He had a hard touch, with compelling bass figures and a flowing, melodic treble line. He ably supported Lester Young on the 1945 Aladdin "These Foolish Things." He also accompanied Parker on most of the Dial recordings. All of these gave him a following and tremendous influence; the only difficulty is that most of his work is chordal with no solos. Thus, it was up to Bud Powell to effect the definitive "bop" piano statements.
Dodo resurfaced in 1961 with a hard-to-find album. In 1962, with Ammons, he recorded this twofer, which has lain in the can for so long that it should be a criminal offense for it to happen again. Half of the album is just Dodo with Sam Jones (bass) and Marshall Thompson (drums); the other half adds Ammons. In a word, brilliant: that is all that can be said of this set. The Ammons addition includes such standards as "Georgia," "For You," "Where or When," and "Falling in Love

with Love" (in two completely different takes), where Ammons develops a high spirited breathy tone similar to Ben Webster's. The piano trios are more boppish and even reveal Marmarosa's classical training: "Just Friends," "Yardbird Suite" (two takes), and "I Remember You" stand out. Quite rightly, the material should have been recorded and issued about 1950; it is unnerving to find the unissued session as an oasis twelve years later.

J5.38*   **Clifford Brown. The Beginning and the End.** Columbia KC 32284.

J5.39   **Clifford Brown. Immortal.** two discs. Mercury SMCL 20090/1 (British issue).

J5.40*   **Clifford Brown. In Paris.** two discs. Prestige PR 24020.
Trumpeter Brown had the good fortune to arrive on the scene when jazz was beginning to sag from the "cool" period. He was an exceptionally melodic performer, phrasing in tight, lightly-tongued note clusters. Thus, he was able to provide good accents in double-timing and to employ a relatively pure vibrato-less tone. He was best associated with Max Roach (entry J5.73) in the Roach-Brown Quintet and made relatively few recordings under his own name. In 1953, he toured Europe with Lionel Hampton. The Paris recordings were all done in that year, with members of the band plus some French musicians, and range from the large scoring of "Brownskins" (with 18 musicians) to some quartets of slow tempo ballads, such as "Come Rain or Come Shine," "I Can Dream Can't I?," and "It Might As Well Be Spring." The 19 selections display a wide variety of styles and approaches. On his return, Brown joined Art Blakey (q.v.) and then did his most recording with Roach on the West Coast. Included were Harold Land on tenor and Richie Powell on piano.
The better efforts of the 1954-1956 period are collated on the double Mercury set. This cross-section includes four worthwhile tracks of Brown with a small string section ("Willow Weep for Me," "Laura," "Stardust," and "Embraceable You"). A variety of other settings includes accompaniments for Dinah Washington vocals on "I've Got You under My Skin" and "Lover Come Back to Me" and for Sarah Vaughan on "September Song" and "It's Crazy." Some jam sessions include interesting duels with Maynard Ferguson and Clark Terry. The balance is a good representation of Quintet items, such as "Cherokee," "Dahoud," an excellently constructed "Joy Spring" full of climaxes, the impressive "Jordu," plus one item with Sonny Rollins ("Flossie Lou"). The Columbia set includes two throw-away tracks with an early r 'n' b ensemble. The balance of 30 minutes comes from Philadelphia on June 25, 1956, just hours before he died on the Turnpike. Some great jazz was performed here, including a meteoric solo on "Donna Lee" and the series of slashing choruses on "Nights in Tunisia." Like the tragic Fats Navarro, Brownie was considered an heir apparent in the line from Armstrong–Eldridge–Gillespie. But he died too soon for the full expression of his ideas.

J5.41   **Don Byas. Le Grand Don Byas.** Master Jazz Recordings MJR 103.

J5.42*   **Don Byas. Midnight at Minton's.** Onyx ORI 208.
Byas developed his tenor sax style in the Coleman Hawkins mode. He played with several bands throughout the swing period, such as Andy Kirk's and Count Basie's. His melodic innovations and mental alertness made him cross over to bop

music, and after the war, he played with Dizzy Gillespie. The Minton set (from 1941) is very revealing, documenting the transition between traditional jazz and bop. All the tempos are comfortable and fit in with Byas's ballad style. Helen Humes produces two vocals, "Stardust" and "Exactly Like You"; the rhythm section included Monk and Clarke. The six items here also include the tenor sax test piece "Body and Soul," and Byas puts his stamp on it. In 1946, he left for Europe with Don Redman's band and took up permanent residence in Paris. His greatest impact was on the style of ballad playing in Europe, and because he lived in Europe for 25 years, he was a continuing source of inspiration for continental tenorists. The Master Jazz reissue comes from the Vogue catalog in France, recorded in 1952-1955. French accompaniments clearly show a deference to Byas, and they are just what are needed to show off the leader. His ballad style shines best on Harry Warren's "Remember My Forgotten Man" and on "Them There Eyes."

J5.43   **Donald Byrd. The Cat Walk.** Blue Note BST 84075.
The difficulty in conceptions with Byrd is that he has consistently been one step behind Miles Davis in interpretation but has never contributed anything to extend the medium of delivery that Davis used. For instance, his reaction to Davis's modes was the 1958 *Fuego* (Blue Note BST 84026) album of modes. The *Jazz Lab* album (Columbia CL 998) was derived from Davis's 1949 Capitol sessions. Thus, there was some substance to his being a direct imitator of Davis through his tendency to re-arrange stock phrases. He was a slow developer who hit his peak in 1961 (at the time of this recording), and then he declined. During his recording years he was exceptionally popular—in fact, he appeared on more than 50 albums during his first two years of recording activity. This album stands out as something of a masterpiece, lifted above Byrd's usual but casual output. Pepper Adams and Philly Joe Jones made good accompanists. There is varied material here by Byrd, Duke Pearson, and Neal Hefti. The general tone, though, is of a Tadd Dameron influence, as on the several duets (e.g., Byrd and Jones on the title selection). Byrd makes a very effective use of the mute here, and the sidemen make good contributions, especially Adams's baritone sax.

J5.44   **Serge Chaloff. Blue Serge.** Capitol T-11032.
Often called the first bop baritone saxist, Serge Chaloff quickly absorbed the Parker influence. This collection from 1956 illustrates his techniques with love ballads. Melodic paraphrases are uppermost in his tender searchings, as revealed in "Thanks for the Memory," "All the Things You Are," and "Stairway to the Stars." What makes this album unique is the wide variety of material in which he skirts around the melody in a deliberate expression. This is one of the bop characteristics and, of course, not everything need be played fast. At the time he played in these quartet performances, Chaloff had contracted spinal paralysis, and perhaps he knew that he did not have long to live. Phrasing—so important in jazz—is impeccable.

J5.45   **Kenny Clarke. Klook's Clique.** Savoy MG 12042.
Clarke was the prototype bop drummer. He adapted his style to Parker's and Gillespie's as early as 1940, and he contributed much to the after hours clubs in New York, as he was a resident drummer at quite a few of them. In 1956, he gave up the frenetic rush he was in and settled in Paris, emerging in America via the occasional record and the Clarke-Boland Big Band (with Francey Boland and

European performers). This Savoy recording comes from 1949 and 1956 sessions. The nine titles include Kenny Dorham, Milt Jackson, and Lucky Thompson in a group that is driven without the loud explicitness of modern drummers. Clarke here accompanies the soloist as a section man, in such relaxed and swinging music as "Conglomerations," "Wild Man," and "You Go to My Head." On many selections, Jackson is contrasted and played off against Thompson. This is an easy bop record to listen to.

J5.46   **Sonny Criss. Up, Up, and Away**. Prestige PR 7530.
Altoist Criss was strongly influenced by Parker when the latter turned up to perform on the West Coast. He built on Parker's ideas with a surprisingly high technical expertise and emotional power. The material on this disc is wide-ranging, including a fast tempo "Scrapple from the Apple" with wild choruses. Pianist Cedar Walton and guitarist Tal Farlow are good sounding boards in the six selections. Criss stands out as an assimilator of styles (Parker, Carter, and Hodges—all altoists) who produces warm, improvised ballads such as "Willow Weep for Me" and "Paris Blues."

J5.47   **Kenny Dorham. Whistle Stop**. Blue Note BST 84063.
Trumpeter Dorham was influenced by Navarro, but he based his improvisational style on thematic material, with a rhythmic phrasing and some fragmentation. His compositional skills have always been important, as with "Philly Twist" (a fast blues, after Charlie Parker), the free form "Sunset," and the slow blues "Buffalo." This typical bop quintet nicely complemented each other for the seven selections: Hank Mobley (tenor), Kenny Drew (piano), Paul Chambers (bass), and Philly Joe Jones (drums). But Dorham is the obvious star with his polished tone, trills, and inflections scattered among the seven titles from 1961.

J5.48   **Billy Eckstine. Mr. "B."** Ember EMB 3338 (British issue).

J5.49*   **Billy Eckstine. Together**. Spotlite 100 (British issue).
Bandleader and vocalist Eckstine was a key developer of bop talent. In his band, he nurtured the trumpets of Miles Davis, Fats Navarro, and Kenny Dorham; the saxes of Sonny Stitt, Dexter Gordon, Gene Ammons, and Lucky Thompson; and he employed the pianist-arranger-leader Tadd Dameron. This reissue, with the first nine tracks from 1944, is laden with swing riffs and bop figures. "I'll Wait and Pray" features the singing of Sarah Vaughan. "Opus X" has a nice statement by Dizzy Gillespie. "Blowin' the Blues Away" has a tenor battle between Gordon and Ammons. The title "Good Jelly Blues" is important here, for the opening phrase was used by the boppers for the introduction to the "All the Things You Are" changes. Together with the Earl Hines band, this group was a breeding ground for early bop. Later, Eckstine was to pursue a solo singing career, and an annotation for this may be found in *Contemporary Popular Music*.
The *Together* album is derived from a series of airchecks from 1945 and presents the raucous side of the band rarely heard on disc. Soloists included Shorty McConnell and Budd Johnson, in addition to many of the boppers named above. Vocals were handled by either Lena Horne or Sarah Vaughan. Tracks include "Blue 'n' Boogie," "Airmail Special," "Don't Blame Me," and "Without a Song."

J5.50 **The Giants of Jazz.** two discs. Atlantic SD2-905.
Recorded at the Victoria Theatre, London, England, in front of an audience, the musicians on this set (in a vein similar to traditional Dixie revivals, mainstream swing, and ragtime) show that they still "have it" from the days of be-bop. The personnel include: Art Blakey (drums), Dizzy Gillespie (trumpet), Al McKibbon (bass), Thelonious Monk (piano), Sonny Stitt (tenor and alto sax), and Kai Winding (trombone). Throughout 1971 and 1972, George Wein took this crew on a world-wide tour that ignited flames everywhere, and the London performance was the best of all. The tunes, largely from the bop period, are firstrate, as are their interpretations in very good stereo sound. Diz is best represented, and, in fact, this is largely his album, with "Night in Tunisia," "Woody 'n' You," "Tour de Force," and "Blue 'n' Boogie." Monk was certainly in a cooperative mood during this period and turns in stunning leadership on his own "Blue Monk" and " 'Round about Midnight." Other featured soloists include Stitt and Blakey (rim shots). This record had the impact of revitalizing bop when it was found that not all music was (in Armstrong's term) of the "Chinee" type, at least in comparison to modern, post-1970 styles.

J5.51 **Dizzy Gillespie. Big Band Sound.** Polydor 2317 080 (British issue).

J5.52 **Dizzy Gillespie. Essential.** Verve V6-8566.

J5.53* **Dizzy Gillespie. The Greatest.** RCA LPM 2398.

J5.54* **Dizzy Gillespie. Groovin' High.** Savoy MG 12020.
Trumpeter Dizzy Gillespie was very heavily influenced by Charlie Parker. He played on Dial and Savoy recordings with Parker, and together they wrought a whole new musical experience. His main contribution to bop music was the concept of *orchestration*. He was a talented band leader, and took a few State Department tours in the mid-fifties. Unfortunately, he could not afford a big band beyond his last one of 1956-1958. *Groovin' High* presents the basic bebop statements, such as "Things to Come," "Emanon," the title tune, "Dizzy Atmosphere," "All the Things You Are," "Salt Peanuts," "Hot House," and perhaps his finest trumpet work on "Oop-Bop-Sh-Bam." These tracks were laid down in 1945-1946, with Parker and other sidemen from the swing era. Thus, there was the inevitable musical tension for half the disc, and Gillespie relied on the good arrangements to get them through. For the balance of the disc, he was supported nicely by Al Haig, Sonny Stitt, and Milk Jackson.
The RCA compilation collects his first big band material from 1946-1950 and features his scat singing and warm ballad playing. "Cubano Be Cubano Bop" is the George Russell composition; the exciting "Manteca" features some of the first uses of bongos; "Anthropology" showcases Gillespie's solos in a sextet. Moving on to his next big band period, 1954-1957, there is the Polydor set from the Verve catalog. Here are selections from two studio bands plus three tracks from the second regular band. The richness of musicians is difficult to comprehend: Quincy Jones, Ernie Royal, Hank Mobley, J. J. Johnson, Lucky Thompson, Charlie Persip, Taft Jordan, Gigi Gryce, Budd Johnson, Sahib Shihab, Wynton Kelly, Lee Morgan, Al Grey, and Benny Golson performing minor classics such as "I Remember Clifford," "Begin the Beguine," "Joogie Boogie," and "Hob Nail Special." The *Essential* set

presents diverse outings from the small group to the big band. From all three of the latter come "The Champ," "Jessica's Day," and "Birks Works." From a sextet with Getz and Peterson, Diz recreates "Sometimes I'm Happy," (see also Eldridge in this section) and a nifty line-up with Rollins and Stitt together brought forth "I Know That You Know."

J5.55* **Dexter Gordon. Long Tall Dexter.** two discs. Savoy SJL 2211.

J5.56* **Dexter Gordon. Doin' All Right.** Blue Note BST 84077.

J5.57 **Dexter Gordon. Go!** Blue Note BST 84112.

J5.58 **Dexter Gordon. Our Man in Paris.** Blue Note BST 84146.
   Gordon was a prime disciple of Lester Young. He was a terrific bopper (known as "Vice-Prez") from the 1940s, influencing Stan Getz and other shapers and extenders of the Lestorian mode, but he quietly declined in the 1950s. The Savoy offering collates three sessions from the bop period, including the classic "Dexter Digs In," and "Dexter Rides Again," accompanied by Max Roach and Bud Powell. Other musicians here included Fats Navarro, Tadd Dameron, and Art Blakey. There is also a 16-minute jam ("After Hours Bop"). In 1961, he surged back with some brilliant Blue Note albums. For example, 84077 is full of emotional intensity, featuring the interplay of Gordon, Freddie Hubbard, and the Horace Parlan Trio. From this and other Blue Note albums, it is quite easy to see Gordon's influence on John Coltrane. The ballad "You've Changed" and the medium-paced blues "Society Red" reveal Gordon's expansive tone and timing with regard to dynamics and melody. The long playing album was a decided factor in Gordon's recordings, for now he could spend more time developing the slower ballads. Number 84112 was a very compatible outing featuring ballads such as "Where Are You" and "Guess I'll Hang My Tears Out to Dry." Gordon moved to Europe in 1962 and remained there until his death. Number 84146 has Bud Powell and Kenny Clarke in a program of such bop remakes as "Scrapple from the Apple" and "Night in Tunisia."

J5.59 **Wardell Gray. Central Avenue.** two discs. Prestige PR 24062.
   Gray died young, at age 34, in 1955. He was of the same time period as Charlie Parker, yet he worked within a synthesis of Parker and Young. His consistent tone and actual, swinging solos made him a good musician to have around at the various jam sessions. One of the discs here comes from a Los Angeles club in 1950, and it features a number of 10-minute jams such as "Move" and "Scrapple from the Apple," both with Sonny Criss, Clark Terry, and Dexter Gordon. Other material from this same time included work with Art Farmer and Hampton Hawes. The second disc is a superb combination of Gray and the Al Haig trio, and it includes "Easy Living," "The Man I Love," and "Twisted," the latter containing the important solo for Annie Ross to fashion her bop-scat singing both for herself and for Lambert, Hendricks, and Ross. Indeed, Ross borrowed quite a few of Gray's solos for vocal transformations ("Farmer's Market," "Jackie," etc.). Through such items as "Sweet Lorraine," "Man I Love," and "Lover Man"—all delivered in a swing-bop style—it is easy to see how Gray made such an impact on the Benny Goodman bop band and sextet of the late 1940s. Apart from the jams, the other 20 tracks were

initially released on diverse 78 and 45 rpm discs (there are three previously unissued takes here).

J5.60   **Bobby Hutcherson. Dialogue.** Blue Note BST 84198.

J5.61   **Bobby Hutcherson. Happenings.** Blue Note BST 84231.
    Vibraharpist Hutcherson clearly derives his style from the leaders Hampton and Milt Jackson. These two discs, reflecting bop from the 1950s, also show that, unlike Hampton and Jackson, Hutcherson can be an extremely good accompanist to other jazz musicians (such as Dolphy and Jackie McLean: see their annotations). *Dialogue* features Andrew Hill (grossly underrated), Freddie Hubbard, and Sam Rivers. *Happenings* has Herbie Hancock. On both discs several lines of development are being performed at the same time, furthering the scope of rhythm and tone color. "Aquarian Moon," in 4/4, is a good, fast improvisation, while "Bouquet," in 3/4, is slow. The effects are clear.

J5.62   **Milt Jackson.** Blue Note BST 81509.
    Vibraharpist Jackson made his best contributions to the Modern Jazz Quartet; much of the material issued under his own name is decidedly inferior in scope and development. His Blue Note recordings have long been regarded as his best work, and these come from 1948-1952. Half of this album is the Modern Jazz Quartet before they called themselves by that name. Assisting performers include Thelonious Monk, Art Blakey, John Lewis, and Lou Donaldson. The music is mainly a cross between bop and cool, and only Jackson could pull that off because of his contributions to the jazz of the vibraphone. He emphasized the *vibrato* and the melody, making the instrument a solo one within a precise framework. Contrast predominates on this disc, such as Jackson's fluidity on "Mysterioso" and Monk's explicit ragged time.

J5.63*   **J. J. Johnson. Boneology.** Savoy MG 12106.

J5.64*   **J. J. Johnson. The Eminent, v.1/2.** two discs. Blue Note BST 81505/6.
    Charlie Parker's efforts for the jazz saxophone meant that any changes going on in bop music had to consider the element of speed to produce legato bop lines. This meant that early trombone techniques had to be discarded; J. J. Johnson developed new techniques, with no slurs or deviations as in the "gatemouth" style. In doing so, Johnson became a pacemaker for bop saxophonists and the leading trombone performer in bop music (matched only by Kai Winding, but never exceeded). The Savoy recordings (from 1946 and 1949) show immense changes in three years as Johnson perfected his style, increasing his speed and purifying his tone. This disc included Cecil Payne, Bud Powell, Max Roach, and Sonny Rollins in twelve performances that included "Don't Blame Me" and the tonal "Mud Bebop." Very impressive here is Payne, who contributed alto solos to four tracks. He was influenced by Carter, Parker, and Pete Brown, but later he was to tackle the *baritone* sax. The Blue Note sessions are collated from 1953 through 1955, with a total of 20 tracks. The various musicians included Clifford Brown, Jimmy and Percy Heath, Hank Mobley, John Lewis, Kenny Clarke, Charles Mingus, and Wynton Kelly. Here there are high standards of writing, as in "Time After Time" and "Capri," plus some tunes by Lewis. Johnson provides good sustained notes for the ballads

"Lover Man" and "It's You or No One," as well as near-perfect articulation and timing for "Coffee Pot" and "Turnpike." The speed on "Get Happy" (along with the timing) is difficult to believe.

J5.65   Elvin Jones. Puttin' It Together. Blue Note BST 84282.
Jones's best records have always been with other performers, as on the Sonny Rollins Vanguard set or with John Coltrane. Often, he had been characterized as being difficult to work with for other soloists; consequently, his work is not as well developed as it could have been. He re-introduced decorative drumming, along with precision and variations to percussive instruments. In doing so, however, he had to reduce the cymbal beat, a component of hard bop.

J5.66*   Jackie McLean. Bluesnik. Blue Note BST 84067.
Altoist McLean was, of course, influenced by the basic principles of Parker's playing. This record was made in 1961, when McLean was at the peak of his powers. It is a masterful, thorough investigation of the blues lines through melody and the free use of rhythm. The startling aspect here is the question of why it was never done before, as bop was at that time almost 20 years old. It was simply a matter of the right people at the right time; certainly, McLean could not handle the charts until he was more experienced. Kenny Drew, the pianist, composed the best pieces here, such as "Cool Green" and "Drew's Blues." The tonal power and emotionalism of the blues are craftily explored by McLean and his trumpeter, Freddie Hubbard (also at or near his peak). This austere collection emphasizes long, lean lines and offbeat notes, in much the manner of Lester Young. For example, the title piece itself is a series of fast-paced solos that developed from an opening riff, and like all blues, great liberties are taken with chords, bent notes, and aspects of phrasing.

J5.67   Hot Lips Page. After Hours in Harlem. Onyx ORI 207.

J5.68*   Hot Lips Page. Trumpet Battle at Minton's. Xanadu 107.
Page was a heavily influenced disciple of Armstrong, whose major specialty was the blues. His material, recorded for a large number of companies, is scattered over quite a few labels and anthologies. The largest corpus is on RCA 730.675 (from France), being some eight RCA recordings from 1938. As an accompanist, he was superb—perhaps even better than Armstrong, the latter characteristically liking to show off. The present discs are from the Jerry Newman New York location discs and were recorded in 1940-1941 as the transition from swing to bop was being made. After playing in various swing bands, Page liked to let loose with several cutting sessions including Roy Eldridge, Dizzy Gillespie, Red Allen, and Joe Guy (largely heard here in the latter disc). Accompanying musicians who always seemed to be at Minton's included Charlie Christian, Kenny Clarke, and Thelonious Monk. This trio (until Christian died) laid down some of the basic tenets of bop, and Page liked to join them. Besides being a vehicle for Page's ideas (based on Eldridge in the swing tradition), snatches of the bop to come can be found on "Rhythm-a-Ning," with excellent Monk piano on "Sweet Lorraine" and "My Melancholy Baby." Throughout, blues riffs abound, yet Page seems at home with the pre-bop element. All the tracks are long, including originals based on improvisation, such as "Forty One," which contains some decent solos by pianist Clyde Hart. On Onyx ORI 207, Page is with various groups, mostly unknown, but Tiny Grimes (guitar), Monk, Joe Guy (trumpet),

and Herbie Fields (tenor) can be identified. The four 1940 tracks were relaxed cuts from Newman's home. On all of them ("I'm in the Mood for Love," "Dinah," "Tea for Two"), Fields is a wildman who knew no restraint, like Coleman two decades later. The five 1941 tracks are from Minton's and are less predictable, as with the nine-minute fast blues "Konk." The sound here is a little distant.

J5.69*   **Charlie Parker.** Verve VC 3509.

J5.70   **Charlie Parker. The Definitive Parker, v.1/8.** eight discs. Polydor 2356 059/082/083/087/088/091/095/096 (British issue).
        Under contract by 1948 to Norman Granz's Clef label, Parker was in serious physical decline. Most of his creativity was masked by both the illnesses he suffered and the arrangements Granz had laid on. These recordings are *not* Parker at his best; but certainly they are bona fide jazz performances that stand heads above any similar undertakings, and they gave confidence to Parker through their respectability. Granz presents Parker in as many different configurations as possible, all with a commercial bent. VC 3509 is a compilation of all of these styles, while the 8-album set covers all the Parker titles under his name. Generally, they can be characterized as lightweight, with slow tempos for the most part. There were a fair number of good blues ("Blues for Alice" and "Back Home Blues," from 1951), mood themes where he ignored the background ("Just Friends" and "La Cucuracha"), and some 1952 and 1953 sessions with Max Roach ("Cosmic Rays" and "Now's the Time"). Different settings included Latin American beats, strings (where Parker definitely feels inhibited), vocal sessions with Dave Lambert and others, and even a reed setting of flute, oboe, and bassoon. The first seven albums are in chronological order, 1948-1954; the eighth picks up additional tracks from the same time period (including "Love for Sale," "I Love Paris," and the "Afro-Cuban Jazz Suite"). Standards throughout are: "April in Paris" and "Summertime" (1949), "Leap Frog" and "Dancing in the Dark" (1950), "Why Do I Love You?" and "Lover" (1951), "I Can't Get Started" and "La Paloma" (1952), and "I've Got You under My Skin" (1954).

J5.71*   **Charlie Parker. v1/3.** three discs. Everest 214, 232, and 254.

J5.72   **Charlie Parker. Broadcast Performances, v.1/2 (1948/49).** two discs. ESP BIRD 1/2.
        The "Royal Roost" was the first of the Broadway jazz palaces that killed 52nd Street. As innovations, it introduced the $0.75 cover charge (the first to do so in New York), a milk bar for minors, a long bar for adults, and bleachers for those who didn't want to pay the cover. For the musicians, it had decent dressing rooms and a well-lit stage. These albums were originally recorded there. They are of excellent technical quality, being transcriptions from the Boris Ross archives. With a recording ban effective in 1948-1949, these give us glimpses of Parker between records. And, of course, they allow for extended playing and great solo work (nobody could steal solos off the air; just from repeated listening to records, for not everyone could afford a recorder). One suddenly notices that it has been 35 years since the bop changes started.
        Parker's sessions are happy ones. As a reward for his health kick, he was booked into the RR with his then-quintet of Davis, Dameron, Roach, and Russell—his best

quintet ever (the second, after Diz split). The two tracks from September are the onimous "52nd Street Theme" and "Koko." The January 1949 quintet is a little draggy, with only pianist Al Haig shining. Still, it is interesting to hear Parker on this New Year's Day presentation. The three Everest discs are from "Royal Roost" radio broadcasts—September 4, 1948, through February 1949—and also from the "Café Society" of May 1950. All performances are further demonstration of Parker's range and of his willingness to take chances.

J5.73   **Max Roach. Percussion Bitter Sweet.** Impulse AS8.

Along with Art Blakey, Max Roach succeeded in transposing Charlie Parker's music to drums. After being in and out with the Parker quintet over 1946-1948, he acquired technical excellence in every aspect of the drum and its equipment. He partnered Clifford Brown for three years until the latter's death, and he then formed other groups, beginning to compose in 1959. His best and most influential record was created in 1960-1961. He regrouped his septet to include wife Abbey Lincoln for dramatic vocals, Eric Dolphy on alto, and Booker Little on trumpet. The fates continued to haunt Roach, for while the disc is superb, he again lost his front line, for within a short time both Little and Dolphy died. All aspects of drumming are explored here, as well as band-leading from the percussion area, similar to Blakey's (except, in this case, Roach also composed). Choosing a variety of tempos and meters, he left it up to the soloists to decide on harmony and rhythm. Forcefulness and a range of tones by the soloists are hence made against either bare lines or an attack by Roach, as on "Garvey's Ghost."

J5.74   **Red Rodney. Bird Lives!** Muse MR 5034.

J5.75*   **Red Rodney. The Red Arrow.** Onyx ORI 204.

After playing sweet, swinging trumpet with Gene Krupa, Claude Thornhill, and Woody Herman, Rodney came over to the bop style of Gillespie and Navarro. His fuller tone and smoother phrasing led to certain innovations in melodic bop, and for a time (1949-1951) he was with Charlie Parker's quintet. This Onyx album, recorded in 1957 and previously only available on the rare Signal label, features the tenor horn of Ira Sullivan, a leading Chicago jazz performer at the time, plus a rewarding rhythm trio of Tommy Flanagan, Oscar Pettiford, and Philly Joe Jones or Elvin Jones on drums. During the late 1950s, the disciples were in action. The cool period was over, but Clifford Brown, Charlie Parker, and others were dead. The second generation came along for a period of stagnation—the return to hard bop— while waiting for the second coming of Miles Davis's modes, John Coltrane's "sheets of sound," plus Ornette Coleman's free jazz. Thus, *Red Arrow* stands out as a beacon of high-powered phrasing from the mid-fifties period, featuring three standards ("Star Eyes," "You Better Go Now," and "Stella by Starlight") and three originals for the date. The standards are romantic and melodic, keeping in mind Rodney's attitude toward trumpet playing. The originals are largely blues with some Latin tinges.

Rodney dropped out of jazz after disappointing sales on this album, and ended up in Las Vegas and Los Angeles doing session and band work. In 1973, he was persuaded to get his chops together and come out with a jazz album. Rather than develop on themes implied on 1957's *Arrow*, Rodney harkened back to the bop period with "I'll Remember April," "Donna Lee," " 'Round about Midnight," and "52nd Street Theme." No real new ideas, but he felt more comfortable with restatements and produced enjoyable listening.

J5.76*   **Sonny Rollins.** two discs. Blue Note BNLA 401-H.

J5.77*   **Sonny Rollins. Freedom Suite Plus.** two discs. Milestone M47007.

J5.78   **Sonny Rollins. Plus Four.** Prestige 7821.

J5.79*   **Sonny Rollins. Saxophone Colossus.** Prestige 7326.
Rollins was in debt to Parker and Young for his manner of presentation, but he developed his own high sense of anticipation, of knowing what must come next in the music. By shaping the music as an organic whole, he could begin on thematic advancement and improvisation. This meant reconciling all the possible melodies and phrases within a music and deciding on the best chords to use. Once that was done, the solo advanced just that chord(s). "Blue Seven" (on the *Colossus* album) is perhaps the greatest piece of recorded jazz improvisation, yet it simply comes from a common blues pattern. A logical extension is the "blowing session," a bop term for the swing era's jam session.
The Blue Note set was a very successful "blowing" of improvised styles. Assisting Rollins were J. J. Johnson, Horace Silver, Monk, Blakey, and Paul Chambers. Although all of the material bears repeated listening for the unusual responses and relationships among the musicians, attention should be paid to the classic, exacting duel on "Mysterioso" between Silver and Monk and to the interrelationship of Monk and Rollins on "Reflections." The two Prestige sets, with five items each, were made in 1956. *Plus Four*, in March, was recorded with the Roach-Brown Quartet. Actually, it was the Quartet's date, but they needed Rollins's name for contractual reasons. Special items included "Valse Hot," in 3/4 time, a chord sequence adoption of the better melodies in "Somewhere Over the Rainbow." Aided and inspired by this disc, Rollins moved onto the *Colossus* album. (Roach was free to perform because Brown had just died.) This was Rollins's first record showing growth outside the sextet or quintet format, and he derived much inspiration from Roach's drum feeding. Many of the items, especially "Moritat," were successful recordings of standard materials, and the conventional format meant a period of consolidation.
Rollins only did one set for Riverside as a leader. These items here on Milestone are from that label's discs 241, 243, and 258, originally recorded in 1957 and 1958, with Oscar Pettiford, Max Roach, and Percy Heath. Most of the sixteen tunes are standards, but there is an alternate take of "Till There Was You." Notable occurrences include a feeling of detachment and mind numbing in "Shadow Waltz" and a brilliant "Freedom Suite," with only Pettiford and Roach for a whole side of controlled but skilled tension over things anticipated but never arriving.

J5.80*   **Sonny Stitt. Genesis.** two discs. Prestige P 24044.

J5.81   **Sonny Stitt. Stitt's Bits.** Prestige P 7585.
Stitt's work has always borne a close relationship to Charlie Parker's, so much so that Stitt switched over to *tenor* saxophone to avoid direct comparisons. Actually, Stitt and Parker had developed their similar alto techniques quite independently of

each other, but somebody had to be first with the breaks, and the nod went to Parker. Consequently, Stitt has always lived in Bird's shadow. This double album comes from 1949-1951, the period when Stitt was trying to break away from the Parker mould. The 32 tracks were previously available on a number of Prestige albums (7024, 7077, 7133). All are small group efforts, with varying personnel, but including Bud Powell, Art Blakey, Max Roach, Gene Ammons, Junior Mance, and J. J. Johnson. The track "Imagination" shows the fluid nature of his alto; "P.S. I Love You" shows innovative use of the difficult baritone saxophone, with no loss of strength or expression. The single album is from 1950 and features uptempo work with the Gene Ammons Septet. These albums highlight an important period in Stitt's development, albeit a transitional one that is important for admirers of the genre.

COOL

Innovators

J5.82*   **Miles Davis. Birth of the Cool.** Capitol M 11026.

J5.83*   **Miles Davis. Miles Ahead.** Columbia PC 9633.

J5.84   **Miles Davis. Porgy and Bess.** Columbia PC 8085.

J5.85*   **Miles Davis. Sketches of Spain.** Columbia PC 8271.
   Davis began the so-called "cool" reaction to bop in 1948 by performing in public for two weeks with his Tuba Band (that is, the group had a tuba). His nonet was used for the maximum colors and arrangement possibilities developed by Claude Thornhill. This was the smallest number of musicians that could be used for these arrangements of bop themes. Gil Evans did the arranging charts, as he had with Thornhill, and one of the results is that the middle register is lacking. This was the first time that such principles of bop as harmonies and complex melodic lines were applied to a group larger than a quintet. The French horn (played on this 1950 studio recreation by Gunther Schuller) gave dissonance for blending; the tuba was first of all a melodic instrument and was *not* used for bass effect. Kai Winding was on trombone, Lee Konitz on alto sax, Gerry Mulligan on baritone, Max Roach for drums, and John Lewis and Al Haig split the pianistic styles. These instruments were played at the extremes of their ranges (spanning 3½ octaves), lending tension and edginess to the proceedings. Much was, surprisingly, borrowed from Ellington: treating instruments individually, blending sounds, and producing fresh situations.
   Double-timing was borrowed from bop, but other devices were left alone (such as harmonic density and linear tenseness). This *arranged* music had an air of detachment about it, and it was also the beginning of modal music, with voice groupings unique in their explorations of tone colors. Yet Davis's ensemble never went beyond this stage, and Davis himself had to wait eight years for the modal technique to develop and be explored. Titles mean little here—"Boplicity," "Deception," "Budo"— as each miniature stands on its own as an attempt to develop or explore themes.

Lewis and Mulligan did some scoring. The impact on the jazz scene was tremendous for its time, fostering a whole "West Coast" cool school of detachment. Lewis went on to form the Modern Jazz Quartet, basing some contrapuntal ideas on those of Evans; Mulligan got together with trumpeter Chet Baker for a unique piano-less quartet; Kai Winding promoted trombone duos with J. J. Johnson; Lee Konitz became the archetype of cool with his Tristano leanings and Parker influences; Gunther Schuller developed "Third Stream" music; and Gil Evans, who had arranged Parker material for Thornhill, would go on to develop more expressions based on tone quality.

In fact, Evans and Davis did come together before the decade was out. There is a strong Ellington influence evident on these three Columbia discs, where the soloist (Davis) is placed against the orchestra. Added instrumentation included French horn, oboe, harp and bassoon. *Miles Ahead* was a logical extension of the Capitol album. Ten selections are played by a 19-piece orchestra (brass and reeds). Evans's architecture was the first systematic advance over Ellington's work (aided by Thornhill). Whereas Ellington composed with a particular soloist in mind (one with techniques to exploit), Evans began with the music, analyzing all chords, and specific instruments were chosen to determine the best possible notes. Mathematical calculations were made for effects of instruments on one another, as well as for the overall rationale for each chord in the first place. Upon examination, it was found that some combinations were new to all orchestral jazz. The Suite on the *Ahead* album (Delibes's "Maids of Cadiz") was entirely recomposed and orchestrated by Evans into one piece, with Davis on flugelhorn. The Gershwin score provided highlights—such as "Summertime," where there are variations in texture on just one riff presented and the preaching role of Davis on "Prayer." *Sketches of Spain*, besides the brilliant "Adagio" from Rodrigo, shows Davis again in a religious role, this time as a hondo singer in a Spanish procession ("Saeta"). It was not too big a step from chords to modes.

J5.86*   **Lennie Tristano. Crosscurrents.** Capitol T 11060.

J5.87*   **Lennie Tristano. Line Up.** Atlantic 1224.

J5.88*   **Lennie Tristano. The New Tristano.** Atlantic 1357.

Blind pianist Tristano created his own musical expression: improvisation that relied on linear invention played in a cool, introspective manner. This was in direct contrast to the bop music of the 1940s, which stressed harmony and rhythm. Yet, the two streams developed at the same time. The Capitol recording contains seven of his repertoire, recorded in 1949, after he had been working on his personal style for some time. Many musicians were influenced by his methods of composition and improvisation, Miles Davis and Lee Konitz, to name two. While his single line and single note style were his own, the rough technical expertise and chording came from Earl Hines and Teddy Wilson. The Capitol material was of two types. First was the Tristano method, with an airy feeling from long lines contributed by Lee Konitz, especially on "Crosscurrent" and "Sax of a Kind." This material has never really been equalled by others. Second were free form exercises, as on "Intuition" and "Digression." Free form means playing without a fixed chord progression, without a time signature, and without a specified tempo. This was never again attempted until latter Coleman and the primitivism school.

Since 1949, Tristano only made two other records, both for Atlantic. *Line Up* is from 1955, and the nine titles clearly show an influence on both Bill Evans and early George Shearing. Most selections are recorded from the Confucius Restaurant in New York, with Konitz and Gene Ramey. There are also two piano solos. All show a restlessness produced by the alternation of tense and relaxed lines that are moving very quickly, as on "Line Up" and "East 32nd Street." These unpredictable pulsing accents are very difficult to grasp, and certainly they avoid clichés. Tristano used multiple recordings to overdub himself on several pianos. This was a direct ancestor of Bill Evans's *Conversations with Myself*, yet many critics rejected them for lack of purity.

The 1962 solo piano set is really melodic invention of a high order, showing some rhythmic intensity, harmonic variety, and use of formal structures. The walking bass in the left hand contrasted with the single notes and chorded figures of the right hand, sometimes playing in different time signatures at once. Certainly, it is an adventuresome album, complete with tempo shifts that no accompanists could ever follow. Improvisation reached a high spot with this illustrious album. Tristano employed contrafacts, much as Parker did. For instance, "Becoming" is based on "What Is This Thing Called Love?," "Deliberation" is based on "Indiana," and "Scene and Variations" is derived from "Melancholy Baby." Tristano has spent much of his life in seclusion, and, although he was influential on other musicians, he appears to have no influence on audience and critics, for he rarely performs and never records anymore.

Standards

J5.89   **Stan Getz. Echoes of an Era: The Best of Stan Getz.** two discs. Roulette RE 119.

J5.89a*   **Stan Getz. Focus.** Verve V6-8412.

J5.89b*   **Stan Getz. Greatest Hits.** Prestige PR 7337.

J5.89c   **Stan Getz. Jazz Samba.** Verve V6-8432.
Tenorist Getz is probably the best-known jazz soloist in the relaxed pop music field. He established his reputation with the Woody Herman band (being one of the Four Brothers in the saxophone section) and then applied Lestorian principles to meld and shape his ballads by modifying the Hawkins breathing. The Prestige set covers 1949-1950, and it presents 12 miniatures (including "There's a Small Hotel," "What's New," "Too Marvelous for Words," and "I've Got You under My Skin"). At this time, he had just left Herman. He took a free, almost casual approach to the standards and created new chord sequences on others (e.g., "When Your Lover Has Gone," "Zing, Went the Strings of My Heart"). He translated ideas into action, as on "Crazy Chords" (a 12-bar blues with a key change introduced at the end of each chord). His quartet was comprised of Al Haig, Percy Heath, and Gene Ramey. Together, all four were fairly introspective (given their collective natures). The Roulette reissue continues the quartet or quintet through to 1951 (originally recorded for Roost). The pianists here are either Al Haig or Horace Silver. Getz has had much luck and satisfaction from his piano players. Standards are again

emphasized, such as "Gone with the Wind," "The Song Is You" (empathic lyricism), and "Yesterdays," but there are also some Getz originals plus two of Gigi Gryce's compositions (the first of his ever to be recorded).

In 1961, Getz returned from four years in Europe, and was musically fresh to begin recording once more. *His* favorite album (*Focus*) was fashioned by Eddie Sauter, who composed and arranged some scoring for strings, leaving odd musical holes here and there. It was Getz's job to fill the holes and to weave around the plucked or bowed strings. Exceptionally lyrical in conception and performance is "Her," dedicated to Getz's mother, who had died shortly before. The frivolous "I'm Late, I'm Late" is quick-paced, being urged on by the darting Getz and the drumming of Roy Haynes. Six months later, Getz recorded with Charlie Byrd to create *bossa nova*, a blending of jazz techniques and samba rhythms. Both were familiar with the samba patterns. "Desafinado" was the hit, and it is deliberately off-key; "Samba Triste" is more Byrd, a mournful mood; "Samba de Una Nota So"—a one-note samba, and the lushness of "Baja" (a Latin American folk melody also in a Walt Disney film). This record was influential in creating a resurgence of uptempo Latin music in the United States, thus giving employment to many jazz musicians. Getz's technical proficiency makes the elegance all seem easy. Certainly there are *no* clichés.

J5.90*   **Jimmy Giuffre. Clarinet.** Atlantic 1238.

Giuffre was one of the few clarinetists in the post-bop period. The limitation factors for this reed instrument made it unpopular for performing the bop and cool idioms, where the saxophone and trumpet reigned supreme. Giuffre worked mainly in the low register. On this album, recorded in 1956, he explores the coloration in eight different settings. No two titles have the same instrumentation. There are different improvisations and scorings, as well as other compositional devices to push to dark tonal qualities. "Solow" is the obvious solo work; "Deep Purple" explores clarinet and celeste; "Sheepherder" is a multi-colored pastorale with three clarinets (alto, bass and regular); "My Funny Valentine" gets a contrapuntal workout; and "Down Home" is blues with a full band.

J5.91   **Chico Hamilton.** World Pacific Jazz 1209.

Hamilton played with Mulligan in the piano-less quartet. Although tending towards "smart" jazz in the West Coast mode (this issue had a cello added for tonal color), Hamilton does add depth and color through his persistent drumming. Buddy Colette (on alto and tenor) plus Jim Hall on fluent guitar provide the necessary tone on such adventuresome items as "Free Form" and "My Funny Valentine" (the latter emphasizing the cello). All five long, extended tracks were recorded at the Strollers Club in 1955.

J5.92*   **Lee Konitz. Ezz-thetic.** Prestige PR 7827.

J5.93   **Lee Konitz. Konitz Collates.** Prestige PR 7250.

Konitz's sax work was heavily influenced by Lennie Tristano and, indeed, extended Tristano's cool or free form ideas with a relentless attack on the music that was pure improvisation. Twelve tracks are on Prestige 7250 (from 1949 and 1950). His alto is accompanied by Tristano, Shelly Manne, and Warne Marsh (tenor)– all of them founders of the West Coast mode. Konitz was hampered at this time because every other alto player was imitating Parker. He had to find new directions, and he did so with cool music, the so-called reaction to bop. Everybody here projects a feeling of mobility, and they certainly complement each other, so much so that this must be the definitive recording by the leaders of the "cool" school. Tristano's impact was in projecting a linear invention of statements that were complete in themselves, not reprises or choruses. Thus, the chord progressions were really fairly orthodox: it was the method that was unique. Included here are versions of "Marshmallow" (borrowed from "Cherokee"), "Fishin' Around" (from "I Never Knew"), a tense "Tautology" (from "Idaho"), and others. This disc is important for Tristano's contributions. The other Prestige disc was recorded with Miles Davis and features the soft "Hi Beck."

J5.94   **Gerry Mulligan**. two discs. Prestige PR 24016.

J5.95*   **Gerry Mulligan**. Vogue LAE 12050 (French issue).

J5.96   **Gerry Mulligan. Sextet**. Mercury MG 36056.

J5.97*   **Gerry Mulligan. Tentette: Walking Shoes**. Capitol T 11029.
    Mulligan's best work appears to be his earliest. He has changed little over the years. His hefty baritone sax style still appears to have naiveté plus wit. He experimented with having no piano in the quartet and two horns up front. The 1953 groups with Chet Baker produced the best version of such a line-up. This Vogue reissue emphasizes such standards as "Tea for Two," "Frenesi," and "Love Me or Leave Me." Baker's trumpet was easily heard over the drummer's brushes and the exposed bassist's notes. More can be heard on the Prestige set, particularly new compositions such as "Walkin' Shoes," and "Bernie's Theme." The eight tracks with the Tentette clearly show Mulligan's arranging skills. Also from 1953, this is the piano-less quartet augmented by brass, and Mulligan and Baker take most of the solo space. Except for Vernon Duke's "Taking a Chance on Love," all the material was composed by Mulligan. Paring the group down to a sextet (the piano-less quartet plus Bob Brookmeyer's valve trombone and Zoot Sims's tenor sax), Mulligan worked on the 1955 Mercury album, again with standards and recreations of previously recorded originals.

J5.98   **Art Pepper. Gettin' Together**. Contemporary S 7573.
    Altoist Pepper is firmly in the West Coast school and came up through the ranks with Stan Kenton. His performances are characterized by a lyrical expression, some inventiveness with rhythms, and an ability to create inner tensions when dealing with melodies. These seven tracks, from 1960, are performed with pianist Wynton Kelly and the superb bass accompanist Paul Chambers (both having been part of the Miles Davis rhythm team; hence, they are very active participants on this recording). Pepper's creativity is at once noticeable in his handling of ballads. He is very, very good, especially on "Softly, As in the Morning Sunrise" or "Why Are We Afraid?," because he transforms these songs by redistributing the phrases and creating new melodies. In other titles, such as "Bijou the Poodle" or "Rhythm-a-ning," Pepper uses space in his rests, in much the same manner as Parker, Young, and Monk. Illustrating these two techniques is the emotional "Diane" track.

MODERN

Anthologies

J5.99   **Energy Essentials.** three discs. Impulse ASD 9228-3.

J5.100   **Impulsively.** Impulse AS 9266.

J5.101*   **Jazz Years; 25th Anniversary.** two discs. Atlantic SD2-316.

J5.102   **No Energy Crisis.** Impulse AS 9267.

J5.103   **The Progressives.** two discs. Columbia KG 31574.

J5.104*   **Twenty-Five Years of Prestige.** two discs. Prestige P 24046.
    The above eleven discs were intended as "samplers" by the recording companies involved: introductions to their catalogs. At the same time, though, they present reasonably good quality through the compilation of popular and successful items. Most of the material here comes from the 1960s and 1970s. The series on Impulse presents some new and unreleased alternate takes, in addition to commercially available material. Included are representative samplings of John Coltrane, Pharoah Sanders, Ornette Coleman, Sonny Rollins, Archie Shepp, Albert Ayler, Charlie Mingus, Freddie Hubbard, Eric Dolphy, Max Roach—all in the *Energy Essentials* package. Moving to the 1970s, the other discs collate Gato Barbieri, Keith Jarrett, Michael White, John Klemmer, Dewey Redman, Marion Brown, Sun Ra, and Sam Rivers. Atlantic contains a wider chronological survey, with items by Lennie Tristano, Ray Charles, Jimmy Giuffre, Milt Jackson, the Modern Jazz Quartet, Art Blakey, Charlie Mingus, Joe Newman, Charles Lloyd, Roland Kirk, and Yusef Lateef.
    The Progressives is modern, electric music from John McLaughlin, the Mahavishnu Orchestra, Bill Evans, Ornette Coleman, Albert Dailey, Keith Jarrett, Weather Report, Soft Machine, Mingus, Don Ellis, and even Maynard Ferguson. Some of the Prestige items are rare and unissued materials, with the best notes of all the records here. Included are Lennie Tristano, Lee Konitz, Stan Getz, Fats Navarro, Miles Davis, Thelonious Monk, Sonny Rollins, Eric Dolphy, Gene Ammons, and Dexter Gordon (among others).

Innovators

J5.105*   **Anthony Braxton. For Alto.** two discs. Delmark DS 420/1.
    Nothing Braxton has done in the 1970s would surpass this double set of solo saxophone music. At the time, it was unique, and Braxton has gone through many changes and variations since (with *Circle*, and in duos or trios with other performers). These sensitive recordings—with all the apparent time in the world—illuminate the approach of the black jazz musician, who,getting deeper into every possible note and squeal, becomes very involved with the music. Each of the eight long pieces here is dedicated to various people as mood pieces. Contrasts are presented by the obnoxious squeals to John Cage, and the soft, classical-like sustained notes to Ann and Peter

Allen. Technically, the set was well-recorded. Braxton has since categorized his ideas, explanations, and variations into the "book" of his scores. He no longer gives titles to the pieces, but rather lets the title be the same as his page-indexing notation system, so that he can refer back to older ideas that he has since explored.

J5.106   **Ornette Coleman. At the Golden Circle, v.1/2.** two discs. Blue Note BST 84224/5.

J5.107   **Ornette Coleman. Best.** Atlantic SD 1558.

J5.108*   **Ornette Coleman. Change of the Century.** Atlantic 1327.

J5.109*   **Ornette Coleman. Free Jazz.** Atlantic 1364.

J5.110*   **Ornette Coleman. Ornette!** Atlantic 1378.

J5.111   **Ornette Coleman. Ornette on Tenor.** Atlantic 1394.

J5.112*   **Ornette Coleman. The Shape of Jazz to Come.** Atlantic 1317.

J5.113*   **Ornette Coleman. This Is Our Music.** Atlantic 1353.
      Altoist Coleman has said of his music: "My melodic approach is based on phrasing, and my phrasing is an extension of how I hear the intervals and pitch of the tune I play. There is no end to pitch. You can play flat in tune and sharp in tune." Gunther Schuller has described it thus: "Little motifs are attached from every conceivable angle, tried sequentially in numerous ways until they yield a motific springboard for a new and continuing idea which will in turn be developed similarly, only to yield yet another link in the chain of musical thought, and so on until the entire statement has been made." The difficulty with Coleman's music is that, to the average listener, there is no real connection with previous jazz music. It is difficult to listen to as there is no harmonic base. On the other hand, both of these points are in favor of a new audience that enjoyed thematic material and suspended rhythmic figures.
      Coleman's melodic lines are sketchy and to some extent they are implied (much as Miles Davis's music was). The offbeat dissonance, while it has *no dependence* on blues or the popular music standards, is in fact blues-based and strongly rhythmic through powerful ebb and flow. The techniques that Coleman uses include an expressive series of statements based upon the range extremes of his instrument, such as high for the harmonics and low (which is unusual for an alto). He deliberately plays out of tune to arrive at additional tone colors; he purposely splits his notes for fragmentation. The rhythmic and melodic stress of his improvisations comes by his replacement of repetitive chord progressions with a minute examination of these through sound colors of honks, smears, glisses, growls, squeaks and noise. In this very real sense, he extended the alto beyond Charlie Parker. Within the group he stressed a large dynamic range that relied greatly on the interactions between group members in their transfer of musical ideas, especially between the drummer and the soloist. This interplay helped to break down the barriers between the rhythm section and the soloists, allowing for the development of such

people as Tony Williams. Drumming became important, and it was created by
Billy Higgins and Ed Blackwell, the two drummers used extensively by Coleman.
The Blue Note discs are the ones that lifted Coleman from obscurity in 1956.
Previous to this, he had been a horn man for various r 'n' b groups like so many
performers (Ammons, Ayler, and Coltrane, for example). This rock-steady background of "dirty" tones from the sax for crowd-pleasing effects led him to create
basically simple tunes, often suggestive of blues and all with a regularly recurring
rhythmic pattern. These performances were the beginning of free jazz—the rhythmic
ideas of "European Echoes," the mood themes of "Snow Flakes and Sunshine,"
the expressiveness of his alto during "Morning Song," and the short thematic fragments of "Faces and Places" or "Dee Dee."

But, undoubtedly, his best music is on the Atlantic issues. *The Shape of Jazz
to Come* was an amazingly prophetic album. With the basic group of Don Cherry
(trumpet), Charlie Haden (bass), and Billy Higgins (drums), this album of six tracks
is his first positive, thematic statement of the new era in jazz. First, there was a
series of implied rejections: no harmonic progressions (based on repeated chorded
sequences); no equal tuning (a European "classical" principle); no thematic phrases
of 4 or 8 bars (no predictability of melodic patterns); no chordal restrictions on
improvisations (which means that when the soloist caught the *next* chord as it came
up in the accompaniment, it was a pure coincidence and then becomes a thing of
beauty, as a Gestalt or two ships passing in the night). Thus, the moody "Peace" is
contrasted with the tonalities of "Congeniality." "Eventually" features expressive
alto voicings. "Lovely Woman" is very similar to a typical New Orleans funeral
march with its polyphony of brass band shadings. Listening to this disc, it
becomes obvious that bassist Haden created an independent bass in a quartet setting,
while at the *very same time* he synthesized the harmony and rhythm. He had to,
because everyone else was soloing.

The 1959 *Change of the Century* album is also important. By now the group
was closely knit, concentrating on themes and rhythms, such as the Charlie Parker
influences on the calypso of "Una Muy Bonita," where Don Cherry has a mute solo
indicative of the strong alto-trumpet fusion of improvisation. On the fast tempos,
Coleman is agile, even nervous. He has a lot to fragment and thus explore. *This Is
Our Music*—at once a fierce claim on black jazz—again shows that Cherry was the
ideal partner for Coleman. Ed Blackwell replaced Higgins on this 1960 date, and
all seven tracks clearly show the instrumental controls over slurs, sustaining notes,
and distortions. Growls are emphasized by Coleman, who by now had developed
"held" tones, in which both notes of the octave are played at once (involving the
embouchure and the octave key). Thus, logical solos can be found on "Blues
Connotations."

Ornette!, from the following year, introduces the marvelous bassist Scott
La Faro, who continued in the Haden tradition. All four tracks enlarge the repertoire of devices, and new effects include variable volume levels and more fragmented phrasing. By now, the listener is acutely aware that the accompanists must
listen to the soloist and improvise their line to fit with him because there are no
chord sequences to remember. This is a thinking man's jazz, for the increased
responsibilities of "collective improvisation" come from the increased freedom of
having options, and it must be done wisely. *Ornette on Tenor* is interesting because,
through its five tracks, Coleman uses a tenor saxophone because of its "soul"
expressiveness. Despite his occasional dominance and because of the full tone,

Coleman's fluidity is severely restricted, and even more reliance is placed on the other members (as Davis did a few years later).

Free Jazz, from 1960, is one of the most remarkable jazz records yet released (a fuller description is given below of the release of an alternate take). *Two* quartets, one per stereo channel, improvise for almost 40 minutes (with a quick fade-out and fade-in at the break of side one—two). Free form music and collective improvisation reach the heights here. Freddie Hubbard (trumpet), Eric Dolphy (bass clarinet), Haden and Higgins are lined up against the regular quartet (Coleman, Cherry, La Faro, Blackwell). Coleman made the decisions as to which performers could solo and who would give the accompaniment (in conjunction with the musicians), and he linked the solos with pre-charted interludes. Thus, the polyphonic lines were made by having the solos supplemented by relevant comments produced by the rest of the quartets. To control all of the action, Coleman's own solos were *not* predetermined but were to be reactions to what he heard. The *Best* collection, featuring such tunes as "Embraceable You," "C & D," "Ramblin'," "Lonely Woman," and "Blues Connotation," is a well-thought-out anthology of Coleman's works for Atlantic. It clearly shows his influences upon Albert Ayler, Anthony Braxton, Don Cherry, Sun Ra, and Cecil Taylor.

J5.114   **John Coltrane. Art of . . .** two discs. Atlantic SD2-313.

J5.115*   **John Coltrane. Africa Brass.** Impulse AS 6.

J5.116*   **John Coltrane. Ascension.** Impulse AS 95.

J5.117*   **John Coltrane. Cosmic Music.** Impulse AS 9148.

J5.118   **John Coltrane. Impressions.** Impulse AS 42.

J5.119   **John Coltrane. Interstellar Space.** Impulse AS 9277.

J5.120*   **John Coltrane. Live at the Village Vanguard.** Impulse AS 10.

J5.121*   **John Coltrane. A Love Supreme.** Impulse AS 77.

Coltrane was one of the greatest innovators and performers in jazz history (and beyond that, in blues and soul). He has been influential on just about every modernist since 1960, but his prime pupils have been McCoy Tyner, Elvin Jones, Pharoah Sanders, and many other former sidemen. By extension, almost all saxophone players have come under his style by the very means of these "pupils'" emulation. In turn, Coltrane was deeply affected by the blues. He began in Eddie Vinson's band and played the blues with Dizzy Gillespie and Johnny Hodges. From there, he moved to rhythm 'n' blues to be assured of nightly employment, working with Earl Bostic's combo. Coming under the influence and spell of tenorist Dexter Gordon, saxist Sonny Rollins, the architectural beauty of pianist Thelonious Monk, and the cosmic nature of Sun Ra, Coltrane progressed into Miles Davis's band. And then began the first of his five stages of development.

He began to pioneer in building *modal* harmonies onto one-chord riffs. This was the *sheets of sound* concept that was always uncomfortable but always improvisational. It was a "permutative approach to harmonic extensions which involved every note in every possible extension of every chord" (Palmer). It was a tireless progression grouped in series of five and seven notes; "Giant Steps" is a good example (on the Atlantic twofer), with its very demanding chord progressions, and "Kind of Blue" has a scalar structure that is similar. Much of Coltrane's early work with Davis can be found on the Prestige twofer PR 24001 (the 1955/57 Davis quintet).

Coltrane's second stage was *meditation through music*, where harmony is sacrificed. He did this best with drummer Elvin Jones because Jones introduced polyrhythmic drumming (6/8). In this version of music, new chords are extrapolated from a series of modes. Coltrane used the soprano saxophone as an Asian sound, the beginning of his "Near East" exploration into emotional sounds related to pitch and the time of day (as ragas in India are). "My Favorite Things," from the Atlantic twofer, nicely illustrates this type of music.

A third development occurred in 1961 with "Chasin' the Trane" (*Live at the Village Vanguard*, Impulse album). By this time, Coltrane had been able to produce a manipulation of harmonics related to the construction of the saxophone, which showed complete mastery of the instrument. The harmonics of the sax are such that secondary tones are slightly out of tune, the reason that the sax has never been acceptable as a "classical" music instrument: it has no pure tone. At this time, Coltrane's mastery impressed and influenced Sanders, Archie Shepp, and Albert Ayler.

In a complete switch, Coltrane embarked on a fourth level, African primitive rhythms. This was a search for roots, and it preceded much of his blues searching by at least a decade. In fact, Coltrane was the first jazzman to begin searching for African roots. The *Africa Brass* album is the result. The 14-man orchestra was arranged by Eric Dolphy, a grossly underrated performer. The result is sheer beauty. Basically, the stress was on rhythmic bass lines plus percussion and the piano of McCoy Tyner. Two bassists were employed, as well as the polyrhythms of Elvin Jones. Pygmy falsetto whoops were played by the brass section, whoops closely related to the Swiss yodel and to the blues field holler. Roots at last? Listen to the Art Ensemble of Chicago.

The combination of meditation, mastery of the instrument's harmonies, and primitive rhythms all converged to produce the *cosmic energy* stage, the fifth of Coltrane's career. This can be summed up by noting his manipulations of harmonies with African polyrhythms and Near Eastern structures. To his saxophone, which by now was an organic extension of himself, Coltrane added multiple drummers and many percussionists. The pieces and tunes grew longer, becoming suites. Tape recorders were turned on and left to run for hours at a time, while the musicians just played and played. The inevitable result was that many albums were more than an hour long and still did not contain all the ideas of the work involved. This explains why there is still so much unissued Coltrane material that appears at regular intervals from the head offices of Impulse Records and Atlantic.

The use of so many drummers and weird percussion vastly changed the face of "soul" music and much modern jazz of the 1970s. There is virtually a straight line from this type of music right back to Coltrane and Miles Davis. The tragic early death of Coltrane, however, meant that his works are incomplete, for all indications pointed to even further advances had he lived. Turning to the balance of the records listed above, *Impressions* comes from the early sixties and features the modal "India," the title selection, and the beautifully dreamy "After the Rain." *A Love Supreme* is in four movements, based entirely on a permutated four-note motif, and it is from this disc that "All Praise to God," comes. *Ascension* (more influential than listened to) is the definitive big band, avant-garde Coltrane, with Archie Shepp, Pharoah Sanders, Marion Brown, Freddie Hubbard, and Dewey Johnson. It was his most adventuresome work, being based on the epic Coleman album *Free Jazz*. Its ritualism led the way for *Cosmic Music*. This 1966 band had several drummers and two performances. The *Interstellar Space* album featured four duets with drummer Rashied Ali.

Except for his early Atlantic and Davis work, it is pointless to "anthologize" Coltrane in a greatest hits type of album (as Impulse has done). There are so many connecting passages within each temporal area in which he worked that each album or period must be taken as a whole.

J5.122*   **Miles Davis. Essential.** three discs. CBS 66310 (French issue).

This three-disc set provides a reasonably good overview of Davis's achievements in jazz, lacking only the 1948 and 1950 cool nonet (but later recast onto a larger scale by Evans, such as "Summertime" from *Porgy and Bess*, and "Concerto de Aranjuez" from *Sketches of Spain*, both found here) and the hard bop Prestige groups (but including the 1956 band that made its first Columbia recordings with the same personnel and instrumentation). Included here are "All Blues" (from *Kind of Blue*), "Springsville" and "Maids of Cadiz" (from *Miles Ahead*), a version of "My Funny Valentine" from his *Lincoln Centre* album, a track from *Bitches Brew*, and other selections. Davis went through many changes, and his albums are described elsewhere, in other subgroupings (see index).

This, however, is a good place for a brief assessment, first of Davis himself. Despite his lyricism and his sound architectural construction (making effective use of space—where to pause, where to rest—borrowed from Lester Young), in the 1950s he lacked both range and instrumental techniques. He rarely sounded happy in the bop format: he used no vibrato, emphasizing naked, clean lines. By the mid-sixties, Davis had finally mastered the use of the entire range of the trumpet. He was able to produce a variety of sounds and explore all dynamics. Another related aspect of Davis's groups was the exceptionally high quality of musicians in his organization. The talent that he introduced and fostered reads like a "who's who" of modern jazz: John Coltrane, Sonny Rollins, Philly Joe Jones, Jackie McLean, Bill Evans, and Paul Chambers from the 1950s; Hancock, Carter, Williams, McLaughlin, Zawinul, Corea, Jarrett, and Shorter from the 1960s. During this latter period, Davis surrounded himself with young musicians of talent and let their ideas affect the music. Davis became the "bossman" who picked up and literally created jazz greats from derivative followers. He has taken the management principles of delegating and fostering leadership to the point where some of his sidemen had overtaken him. The 1960s group were far more flexible than the earlier groups, and their styles were more relaxed. Of them all, Wayne Shorter was probably most influential on Davis. From him, Davis learned how to manipulate written themes. Shorter also helped to free harmonies more than anyone else. But, coupled with Williams's impact in directing a band's motions, Davis had a price to pay: he lost his flair and aggressiveness.

Over the years Davis has been a reasonably good commercial success in jazz without compromising his talent. His innovations have acted in a catalytic manner (although they affected Davis too when they later came back to him): the late 1940s West Coast development; the modal scales of the late 1950s; the rebirth of

Ellington through Gil Evans's work with Davis; the leadership given to musicians in the band; and the jazz-rock of the late 1960s. Davis has had a direct influence on such rock groups as Cream; Soft Machine; Mahavishnu Orchestra; Blood, Sweat and Tears; Gentle Giant; and all of European progressive rock (Focus, Kraftwerk, etc.).

J5.123*   **Jazz Composers' Orchestra.** two discs. JCOA 1001/2.
    The Jazz Composers' Orchestral Association was organized in 1964 as a self-help musicians' cooperative in New York, quite similar to the AACM in Chicago. Not only did they create recordings, but they also acted as a distribution agent (under New Music Distribution) for smaller, similarly-minded companies and groups. The driving forces were Carla Bley (pianist and composer) and Michael Mantler (arranger and composer). They both believed that the improviser-soloist should be placed into the context of a formal but flexible and fluid gathering, with comparable material. In this outing, their first and one of their best records, the JCOA included such soloists as Don Cherry, Charlie Haden, Larry Coryell, Pharoah Sanders, Steve Lacy, and Cecil Taylor. Others more involved with the JCOA included Richard Davis, Ron Carter, and Gato Barbieri. The time is 1968 and, essentially, the music was scored in the European pattern. The titles were "Communications, Nos. 8, 9, 10, 11." These were harmonies (slow-moving and convoluted) impressed with long-held chords and details of richness. Occasional complex patterns were contrasted with the subtle shading of the musicians' phrasing. "No. 10" is obviously the best drawn work in the issue, although Cecil Taylor dominates "No. 11." The instruments move about quite a lot, but they are subjected to the overall framework under which each title operates (Mantler's and Bley's conceptions).

J5.124*   **Charles Mingus. Better Git It in Your Soul.** two discs. Columbia G30628.

J5.125*   **Charles Mingus. Blues and Roots.** Atlantic 1305.

J5.126*   **Charles Mingus. The Candid Recordings.** Barnaby KZ 31034.

J5.127*   **Charles Mingus. The Great Concert.** three discs. Prestige 34001.

J5.128*   **Charles Mingus. Pithecanthropus Erectus.** Atlantic 1237.

J5.129   **Charles Mingus. Presents the Charles Mingus Quartet.** Barnaby Z 30561.
    Mingus, with roots in Parker, Ellington, and Tatum, is one of the most complex of jazz personalities. He has been or tried everything—bassist, composer, arranger, big band, small group—and often has been dissatisfied with the results. He has developed many fine jazzmen, including pianist Jaki Byard, tenorist Booker Ervin, altoist Charles McPherson, and drummer Danny Richmond. One reason for this development was his Ellingtonian conception of jazz as being composed and orchestrated, with all the diverse elements (and personalities) integrated. He began as a bop bassist, assisting Parker's group, as when he played the Massey Hall concert. He began to consolidate many influences, such as traditional Dixieland, blues, gospel, swing and early bop—as on the 1956 *Pithecanthropus Erectus* album. The theme

here was the complete history of man's evolution from barbaric savage to destructive modernism. Using unusual forms such as duets, grunts, harmony, squeals, and chaos, he gave it structure. It is a collection of basic solos and improvisation, with cacophony in the C Section near the end. Although not well appreciated at the time, much of the roots of modern jazz are here, and this is now the disc that modernists keep listening and referring to. There were no outright freedoms for the soloists, who included Jackie McLean (tenor) and Mal Waldron (piano). The quintet (which had two saxophones) were charged with creating "building up" and "tearing down" periods throughout the five choruses of 80 bars length. Throughout, there are little snatches of the roots mentioned above.

The next step in Mingus's refashioning of jazz was for a large ensemble to cover *Blues and Roots*. With Booker Ervin and Jackie McLean, he fashioned a neat balance of solo freedom and group organization, especially in the tensions of "Moanin' " and "Cryin' Blues." Included are humor in "My Jelly Roll Soul" and an early version of "Better Git It in Your Soul," co-titled here as "Wednesday Night Prayer Meeting." The cusp period of 1958-1961 was the most fertile for Mingus. He fashioned two records for Columbia (retitled when reissued as a twofer). These large groups featured altoist John Handy, Booker Ervin, and pianist Horace Parlan, as well as drummer Danny Richmond who evolved into Mingus's best sympathetic drummer. About this time, Mingus also developed into a highly virtuosic bassist who could give direction and impetus to his performers. These Columbia discs emphasize his great compositional skills, and more than other Mingus records, these recreate Ellington, who had always been a major influence. There are two direct Ducal items—"Mood Indigo" and "Things Ain't What They Used to Be"—as well as snatches here and there, plus the salute, "Open Letter to Duke." Frenetic activity is the key here, all of it detailed if one carefully listens to the set over and over. Often, it appears difficult to comprehend because of the shifting textural undercurrents and above-board patterns. Apparently, the ensemble work, by alternating with defined solo space, creates the illusion of innovative mobility.

The two *Candid* recordings, from 1960, are largely by the performing quartet of Ted Curson (trumpet), Eric Dolphy, and Richmond. By this time, and with this small group, Ornette Coleman's influence had attracted Mingus. Despite the cohesion of a year together, there were still two separate groups here—the fluidity of Curson and Dolphy versus the intuition and virtuosity of Richmond and Mingus. The five titles include "Stormy Weather" and the absurd "All the Things You Could Be by Now If Sigmund Freud's Wife Was Your Mother." "Folk Form, No. 1" is superbly introduced by Mingus, with a statement by Dolphy and a good interplay with Curson. Here the drums are playing the melody. "What Love" features Dolphy on the bass clarinet, a warm sinuous tone, after Mingus opens with a solo. Dolphy begins to weave in and out of the bass strings, setting up a call-and-response pattern leading to a lovers' quarrel. Three other tracks include worthwhile large ensemble experimentations with pairing off of soloists.

The *Great Concert* was in Paris in 1964, with a sextet that included Dolphy, Clifford Jordan, and Byard. This album has won a half dozen prizes, both inside and outside of France, and rightly so. A challenge was the illness of trumpeter Johnny Coles, so that all arrangements had to be reworked hours before the concert. Dolphy added flute to his repertoire. A good many tributes and much soul-searching are here: "Goodbye Pork Pie Hat" covers 30 minutes, and relates to Lester Young; "Parkeriana," almost as long; "Sophisticated Lady" for Ellington, with sharp pizzicato by Mingus. Other selections were also reworkings of the existing repertoire, such as "Meditations on Integration" and "Fables of Faubus," both half an hour, and concerned with racial strife (the latter is also on the Columbia set). Since this time, Mingus has created enjoyable works but made no major, new statements.

J5.130* **Sun Ra. Heliocentric Worlds of Sun Ra, v.1/2.** two discs. ESP 1014 and 1017.

J5.131 **Sun Ra. Magic City.** Impulse AS 9243.

Sun Ra (né Sonny Blount) must be the most recorded jazz artist, covered from the early Delmark reissues through ESP and original Impulse recordings, plus over 200 separate albums on his own Saturn and Transition labels (some of which have been reissued on Impulse, such as *Magic City*). The Saturns are extremely difficult to find because they are pressed in limited quantities for Ra's orchestral members, their families, and friends. His early work was relatively conservative, and showed the influences working on him, especially arranged music by Fletcher Henderson (with whom he worked in 1946-1947). By 1965, he had fully synthesized all of these diverse directions.

His work is very complex and can only be analyzed in terms of each individual piece. Several techniques run through most items. He believed in a tight ensemble orchestra and thought of it as an "organization" (they all eat, work, and live together, as in a commune). He tried to find a middle ground between controlling the orchestra and letting individual expression continue. Coherence, to him, rested on the precepts of a swing band from the 1930s (this was Henderson's influence): wind instruments and percussion. Tension, a bop attribute, developed between the thematic material and the solo work, aided by the contrasted techniques of long sustained notes against short, disconnected phrases and the high register playing against the low register. He let the melody develop only in the solos, not in the ensemble work. This balance (in favor of the soloist, as he has a rich melody to play) created some instrumental color through the textures. Borrowing from Coleman (or at least developing at the same time, if independent of what Coleman was doing), Sun Ra encouraged his musicians to react to each other in order to shape the music. This has all been termed "restless collective improvisation" on a large scale— beyond the normal quartet or quintet configuration.

Yet, he kept himself flexible by contradicting musical progress with his violently dissonant piano work, and by avoiding melodic development except through solo passages. "House of Beauty" illustrates many of the above points through its long melodic lines and use of counterpoint, while "The Cosmos" brings the listener an unaccompanied bass introduction followed by various percussive solo works. "Heavenly Things" is a flute solo. "Heliocentric" finds the sections being led by a bass clarinet and a bass trombone for interesting color textures. "Outer Nothingness" sums up his vast and complex techniques, using long sustained notes superimposed one on top of the other (*but in isolation*), the extremes of register work (both high and low), and short phrases of disconnection.

J5.132* **Cecil Taylor. Air.** Barnaby Z30562.

J5.133* **Cecil Taylor. Conquistador.** Blue Note BST 84260.

J5.134*   **Cecil Taylor. D Trad That's What.** Freedom FLP 40106 (British issue).

J5.135*   **Cecil Taylor. Unit Structures.** Blue Note BST 84237.

Cecil Taylor is one of the masters of the jazz movement, as influential as Louis Armstrong and Charlie Parker. His difficulty was as a pianist attempting harmonic breakthroughs. As the piano is basically a percussive instrument, it is very difficult to simulate the tone and harmonies of a trumpet or saxophone. Basically, what Taylor did was to simulate free linear movement by deflecting the listener's attention from the stabbing harmonic left hand figures by a dazzling display of rhetorical decoration in the treble. He thus is a logical extension of Waller, Tatum, Hines, and Ellington, and he follows in the tradition of pianist-composer-leader. Although classically trained at the New England Conservatory of Music, he has since regretted classical inculcation and feels that it has hampered his development. By 1955, he had gotten a group together, and he made his first disc for Contemporary in 1958 (*Looking Ahead*).

The *Air* date featured Archie Shepp on his first recording session (1960). The Freedom album comes from a 1962 engagement at the Café Montmartre in Copenhagen. *Unit Structures* features the brilliant "Enter, Evening." *Conquistador* (1966) is a fantastic piece of involvement that begins with the basic idea being expounded by Taylor, the rest of the group extending it logically with their own instruments (e.g., Jimmy Lyons on tenor and Bill Dixon on trumpet); then the piano follows in a chase that overcomes the group. Up to this time, the action was totally unlike a piano's role in a jazz group. Taylor's best work is always his latest record, but these four show his development from 1960 to 1966 and remain important and influential works for both other jazz musicians and listeners. Lately, Taylor has been involved with the Jazz Composers' Orchestral Association and with recording for his own company. Quite frequently he is unemployed and, to add to the misery, in 1974, all of his latest recording's pressings were lost and destroyed through a freakish accident. Taylor's overall style is that of a perfect marriage between bop and stride techniques. His ceaseless flow of musical ideas produces rich harmonies and good texture.

Standards

J5.136   **Art Ensemble of Chicago. Bap-tizum.** Atlantic SD 1639.

J5.137   **Art Ensemble of Chicago. Phase One.** Prestige PR 10064.

J5.138*   **Art Ensemble of Chicago. With Fontella Bass.** Prestige PR 10049.

Having been described as "the most significant and creative new group since the original Coleman and Coltrane quartets," the Art Ensemble should be something to behold (and listen to). The group is mostly ex-AACM Chicago black jazz musicians who were more or less resident in Europe since 1969, centered in Paris. Much of their earlier work—very exploratory—is available on the Delmark and Nessa labels. Basically, Lester Bowie blows brass, Roscoe Mitchell and Joseph Jarman are on reeds, Malachi Favors employs strings, and Don Moye (with everybody else) is on percussive noise and confusion. They have recorded about a dozen albums in Europe, 1969-1971, for various labels, and the two Prestige items

are reissues from the French-based America label. Fontella Bass is a former r 'n' b
singer (for example, her hit, "Rescue Me") now into free form jazz. She contributes jive talk to PR 10049's two selections (one side apiece). PR 10064 comes
from Paris in 1971, and it, too, has two selections. "Lebert Aaly" is dedicated to
Albert Ayler. Using "Ohnedavath" (also on the Atlantic disc) is an interesting way
to compare two versions, because modern jazz is never done the same way twice,
even more so than standards or swing jazz. And unless one goes to a concert, there
is little likelihood of anyone hearing it again (except by means of a record).

With a receptive audience, the live gig is even better than the studio rendition.
Thus it is that the Atlantic set is the best of the three, for the group seems to be
more "with it" on this occasion. At least, there appears to be an unlimited expansion
to this complete, unedited set from the 1972 Ann Arbor concert. Even so, with
music of this kind, it is difficult to evaluate whether it is performed correctly or not.
Bad notes, miscues, and so forth can be part of the act—a parody or satire. Fluffs
can be integral to the ideas of the group. The music is raw, unadulterated primitivism (like the primal scream) that goes to the womb. It takes over two hours to set
up the equipment and to get the group decorated with showy face and body paint.
As a show, it is heavily emotional and resembles nothing more than incoherent babies
throwing a tantrum. In some selections, as "Immm" where there is a gospel chant, the
action quickly turns to noises that suggest on-stage puking. Squeals and honks
abound. Certain of their fans feel that Charlie Parker was a "mouldy fygge."

J5.139*   **Albert Ayler. v.1/2.** two discs. Shandar SR 10.000/4 (French issue).

J5.140*   **Albert Ayler. Ghosts.** Debut DEB 144 (Danish issue).

J5.141   **Albert Ayler. Spirits Rejoice.** ESP 1020.

J5.142   **Albert Ayler. Spiritual Unity.** ESP 1002.
        Tenorist Ayler follows a direct line through Young, Rollins, and Coleman. His
work as a leader of "primitivism" predated much of the AACM and Art Ensemble
of Chicago and such others as Archie Shepp and Pharoah Sanders. Most of his ideas
were acquired from simple rhythm 'n' blues jump bands in which he performed when
he first began as a professional. The emphasis in these groups has always been on
rhythm, and the more basic this was, the better the conception. Briefly, Ayler
developed a logical fragmentation built on rather short themes that recurred from
time to time in a cycle. This was primitivism, incorporating a short attention span,
basic riffs, pre-natal memories, etc. Unfortunately, it also meant that he ran out of
material, and he recorded many of the same titles over and over, albeit with new
techniques and other decorations. To push his message across, Ayler employed the
squawk of the upper register with gross speed. This constant stream of notes led
to a blurred articulation if the listener let himself go.
        Spiritual Unity, with Gary Peacock on a melodic bass (someone has to carry
the melody) and Sonny Murray on drums, produced the modern jazz classic
"Irony," which used technician-like approaches to create raw primitive feelings.
The theme of "Spirits" is given four times, each followed by extensive solos (certain titles and their material keep recurring in his music). The 1964 Debut album
was recorded in Sweden, and in addition to Ayler's trio, there is now a fourth
dimension in the person of Don Cherry. This might be the best of Ayler's

recordings, because he used Cherry's trumpet for ideas, reflections, and various call-and-response patterns. With the above *Spiritual Unity* album, there are *four* versions of "Ghosts"; all are different but equally good. The *Spirits Rejoice* title selection emphasizes the pre-blues and pre-jazz nature of Ayler. On this track, the dominant theme is a bugle call, and the five tracks here are by a sextet, as are the Shandar issues. Ayler reacts with his audiences, for it is to them that he projects a harsh, disturbing music. The French discs come from Nuits de la Fondation Maeght at St. Paul de Vence in 1970, a year before Ayler died. These are some of his rare "live" efforts and must form a summary of his life's work. The eight tracks are all long, mostly re-recordings of titles already mentioned. Several idiomatic expressions include the title "Music Is the Healing Force of the Universe." Throughout, it is evident that separate phrases here are not as important as the sum of the work (and even its impact after it is over). This is Ayler's controlled logic.

J5.143*   **Gary Burton. Alone at Last.** Atlantic SD 1598.

J5.144*   **Gary Burton. A Genuine Tong Funeral.** RCA LSP 3988.

J5.145   **Gary Burton. New Quartet.** ECM 1030ST.

J5.146   **Gary Burton and Chick Corea. Crystal Silence.** ECM 1024 ST.
        Burton is clearly the most technician-minded vibraphonist that jazz has yet produced. Playing with four or more mallets at lightning speed, and employing vibrato, he can sound like an entire orchestra. His early output was inconsistent and, as is the case with many young musicians, must be thought of as a trying out period (at the consumer's expense). In the 1970s, he finally evolved his style: a vibraphone equivalent to Bill Evans's. The earliest antecedent to this was the Tong album, made with his quartet of the day including Larry Coryell, Steve Swallow, plus the Jazz Composers' Orchestral Association, in 1968. Carla Bley composed and controlled the project, which highlighted Burton with Gato Barbieri and Steve Lacy. Pianist Bley tried for a textural balance in the ensemble work and in the solo passages.
        From the 1971 Montreux Festival (plus a studio follow-up), Burton showed his orchestral playing on Atlantic through solo passages from contemporary composers and friends, such as Steve Swallow's "Green Mountains" and Keith Jarrett's "Moonchild." He overdubbed the studio efforts with piano and organ, and here produces a far better conception than his earlier *The Time Machine* (RCA LSP 3642), which came too soon after Evans's *Conversations with Myself* overdubbing effort.
        The atonal, contrapuntal music comes alive with the "new" quartet on ECM that included Michael Goodrick on guitar. Here Burton definitely is pop-oriented, reflecting the changes wrought in the music by Miles Davis and his pianists. In fact, most of the music here was composed by pianists, and one can only wonder if Burton will one day switch completely to piano. It is an overcrowded field; there are too few vibe players. Obviously, the next step in this development was the duet album with Corea, recorded in Oslo. The compositions are all by Swallow or Corea (plus a marvelous "Feelings and Things" by Michael Gibbs); the impressions are distinctly romantic, in the "pretty music" influence of Corea and Jarrett.

J5.147   **Don Cherry. Complete Communion.** Blue Note BST 84226.

J5.148   **Don Cherry. Symphony for Improvisers.** Blue Note BST 84247.
Trumpeter Cherry worked with Ornette Coleman from 1958 and appears on
the first eight Coleman discs. He was one of the few musicians at the time who
could understand Coleman. Cherry has been influenced collectively by Coleman,
James Clay (on sax), and of course, Fats Navarro. Despite a thin and watery tone,
he employs logic for an architectural development of solos. The first album (*Communion*) features the quartet of Gato Barbieri, Ed Blackwell, and bassist Henry
Grimes. The latter promoted discipline and organizational skill, so much so that the
bass and percussion were on the front line with the melody. There are only two
tracks here, the title selection and "Elephantasy." Each is four movements (and one
elpee side apiece). Along with the requisite tempo changes, Cherry's group employed
both improvised and written notes in a random sequence. The *Symphony* album
extends his compression of music. Here, there are but two movements; Pharoah
Sanders has replaced Barbieri (and adds the color of the piccolo). Grimes's arco bass
playing is superb, and the solos are meshed with the collectivity, because the texture, color, and density are changing all the time.

J5.149*   **Circle. Paris Concert.** two discs. ECM 1018/9 ST.
This is an important album for its content. The Circle group lasted for about
a year (1971) and comprised David Holland (bass), Chick Corea (piano), Anthony
Braxton (reeds and percussion), and Barry Altschul (percussion). This is collective
improvisation, with four soloists and little ensemble work, except in the aptly named
"Duet," where they pair off for 10 minutes of duos. This double album was recorded
on February 21, 1971, for French radio, and it lasts some 95 minutes. "Nefertiti"
is the Wayne Shorter composition; the ringer is "No Greater Love," by the dance
band leader Isham Jones. The rest of the material comes from within the band.
The only heavily fragmented work is on side three: "Toy Room—Q & A," from a
score by Holland. Corea interprets his music in terms of images and in communi-
cating those images. Admittedly, this is music that is difficult to listen to at one
sitting, or even just the one time. It needs to be played over and over for the images
it creates. At the same time, it is also music that creates a certain amount of unease,
as on Braxton's "73° Kelvin (Variation 3)." The problem lies in recognizing modern
jazz for what it is. There is so much material, and so much of it is inferior, that a
listener may simply not have the time to constantly listen to and evaluate the music.

J5.150*   **Ornette Coleman. Twins.** Atlantic SD 1588.
All five tracks are unreleased items from the 1959-1961 period. "Joy of a
Toy" is a comic diversion at the end of the disc—a four-and-a-half minute masterpiece of parody on jazz, with Coleman's cajoling solo and Don Cherry's improvised
phrases. "First Take" is a shorter version of the *Free Jazz* (Atlantic 1364) album,
one of the most influential records of the past 15 years. For seventeen minutes of
presumably the first take of this item, Coleman experiments with a double quartet—
that is, with Coleman, Cherry, Scott La Faro, and Billy Higgins on the left channel,
and Eric Dolphy (bass clarinet), Freddie Hubbard, Charlie Haden, and Ed Blackwell on the right. The idea is to catch the interweaving patterns. A brief ensemble
block-building sets the tone for the soloists, who are atonal and free to involve
themselves with any other member of any of the two quartets. This is certainly one

time when we should get all the takes released, because it can never run the same way twice. Thus, after sorting each other out, there are clear solos by Dolphy, Hubbard, Coleman, and Cherry, the leading antagonists, plus bass and drum duels. Nobody wins, nobody loses. The ten minute "Check Up" is from the period of *Ornette!* (Atlantic 1378) and it embraces a certain "border" quality (Coleman is from Texas) suggestive of Mexico. But it stands out for La Faro's counterpoint behind Coleman's solos. Openings are important, for without them the tunes have little to go on—so they must be crafted skillfully. "Little Symphony" has an unexpected stop and start theme; "Monk and the Nun" opens like Monk's piano.

J5.151*   **Miles Davis. Kind of Blue.** Columbia PC 8163.

J5.152*   **Miles Davis. Milestones.** Columbia PC 9428.

J5.153*   **Miles Davis. My Funny Valentine.** Columbia PC 9106.
      Davis began to break away from the three main structures of jazz: the twelve bar blues (also adopted by bop), the 32-bar standard popular song, and the theme-solo-theme development. Beginning with *Kind of Blue*, Davis employed *scales*, not chords, for his improvisations. The bare simplicity of the scale would virtually force any soloist to work in a melodic rather than a harmonic sense. Scales limit chord structures; thus, while there are fewer chords, almost infinite possibilities exist as to what to do with these chords. A benefit, too, is the acknowledgment that band sidemen can be given credit for composition, since, too often, the leader who actually does most of the soloing takes the compositional credits. But here, Davis was actually demanding that his band compose—or else. For instance, on the Spanish-tinged "Flamenco Sketches," each soloist was given five scales, and he was to play on each scale in turn *until* (and only when) he wanted to move to the next one. Davis's conception was to emphasize much freer use of the rhythm section (this, too, foreshadowed jazz-rock), with the bass player giving the *pulse* (not necessarily the beat) and the drummer creating color and tension. The best drummer for moving the percussion unit to the front line was Tony Williams, one of the youngest and most brilliant jazz-rock drummers. By using modal harmonies, free chords, and scales, Davis made the melodies most sketchy and much was implied on the part of the listener, who had to fill in the gaps—the most perfect use of Lestorian spaces yet devised.
      Beyond a doubt, the Davis band here were a *group* adventure with all members being equal. Davis himself reduced his solo times, so much so that in later times, he was a leader, contributing slight passages to key or guide another soloist. *Kind of Blue* was recorded in 1958, with Adderley, Coltrane, Evans, and Chambers. The only weakness was a wooden Adderley, who remained fixed in the blues patterns; but, as many critics state, he was good for relief. "So What" is based on the Dorian mode, transposed a semi-tone. "All Blues" has good wearing solos by Davis, whose lyrical playing around the notes works from *within* the scale, while the contrasted Coltrane developed his "sheets of sound" by working *from* the scale. Much the same line-up is on *Milestones*, which uses all modes. *My Funny Valentine* is derived from a concert at New York's Philharmonic Hall. The conception is scalar and modal, but the group has now four excellent soloists—pianist Herbie Hancock, bassist Ron Carter, and drummer Williams. Actually, this should really be credited under Williams's name, since he (not Davis) dictates the changes

in moods and tempos by his fast and precise drumming. (Davis certainly was a good bossman for developing talent.) All of these albums show the heavy Gil Evans influence, derived from his arrangements of the three Davis "cool" albums.

J5.154   **Eric Dolphy. Copenhagen Concert.** two discs. Prestige P 24027.

J5.155*   **Eric Dolphy. Out to Lunch.** Blue Note BST 84163.
This first set contains material formerly available as Prestige 7304 and 7366, recorded in Copenhagen in 1961, three years before Dolphy's death. The more concert material by multi-reedist Dolphy that is available, the better, for he was at his best with an audience. His personal music worked best with just a small group accompanying him, or as a solo. He was most emotional on the bass clarinet, and here he has a virtuoso seven-minute solo on Billie Holiday's "God Bless the Child," with a series of arpeggios based on a theme in the song. But his flute was equally as good, as in Randy Weston's "Hi Fly," where the arabesques are accompanied by only Charles Israel's bass for almost a quarter of an hour. This set, of all the Dolphy compilations available, is perhaps the one that completely illustrates Dolphy's essentials—retention of harmonic structure within fragmentation.
For a superb studio session, the *Lunch* album is the best of Dolphy's efforts. Here there is free tempo improvising, with no regular meters and no recurring chord structures. At this stage in his development, he was mastering the art of composition, which to him existed solely as melodies. Even in an accompanying role to another soloist, he remained virtually independent of the soloist's line. His strong, resonant tone showed superior control over double-timing, as "Straight Up and Down." The group on this date included trumpeter Freddie Hubbard, vibraharpist Bobby Hutcherson, bassist Richard Davis, and drummer Tony Williams, the latter fitting in particularly well on "Gazzelloni."

J5.156*   **Charlie Haden. Liberation Suite.** Impulse AS 9183.
Assisted by Don Cherry, Carla Bley, and Dewey Redman, plus others from the Jazz Composers' Orchestral Association (JCOA), bassist Haden led and helped to fashion certain political music related to events of the time (1969) or in recent history. Carla Bley was responsible for composing and arranging the dark and moving music, such as those on the Spanish Civil War, Ché Guevara, and the Chicago Convention of 1968. Different soloists in the band have their moments, such as Roswell Rudd on trombone. This record is difficult to obtain from distributors even today. The political nature of the titles (but not of the music) led the industry to suppress the album. Perhaps if Ms. Bley had just used kiddie phrases. . . .

J5.157   **David Holland. Conference of the Birds.** ECM 1027ST.
An engaging record, made in 1972 and dedicated to the concept of declaring freedom both in song and through communication, as would birds do when they gather. English bassist and composer David Holland is responsible for the program of six varied and melodic originals, including "Q & A," a fresh interpretation of a tune recorded the year before with the Circle group. The compositions, as is the case with much of modern jazz, serve merely as launching pads for the virtuosity of expression of tenorist Sam Rivers and altoist Anthony Braxton, both

accomplished musicians on their respective instruments (plus other reeds). The exploration of lyricism—very easy to hear and relax to—is a change of pace from some of the more radical and novel discs. True sympathetic interplay, including the melodic introduction and conclusion of "Four Winds," even leads to some hummable quotations.

J5.158*   **Pharoah Sanders. Best.** two discs. Impulse AS 9229-2.

J5.159   **Pharoah Sanders. Thembi.** Impulse AS 9206.
Sanders—quite early in his development—began an investigation of tone colors and the multiple expression inherent in all instruments (including more percussion). In doing so, he wanted to lay out all their capabilities (at least, their discovered capabilities) through what he called "phrase permutation." The important thing to note about the twofer collection is the sentence in the liner notes, "selections chosen by Pharoah Sanders." No one else could make the choice, for there was much material to choose from: every two months or so, it would appear that he had a new album out. He was constantly in the studio (to the detriment of his live performances). He blended Oriental themes and western free jazz to combine with polyphonous percussion. His tenor sax (later a soprano) wailed on typical long pieces based upon a motif theme until the original idea was exhausted by repetition. But by then, he would have fresh ones. To this extent, he lacked the discipline of John Coltrane and the circular pattern of Albert Ayler. As the sound and tone color were being emphasized to the detriment of other considerations, there appeared to be a certain sameness about the material.
The 1966 "Upper Egypt," with a Sanders vocal, is as undulating as the Nile. The three long tracks from 1969 show his Coleman derivation (Leon Thomas is the vocalist here). The basic pattern, illustrated in "The Creator Has a Master Plan," is to dissolve into chaos halfway through and then employ echoes to reconcile the fragments. When it begins to look like Sanders is losing all control, it comes together again as a coda or reprise ("as in the beginning").
On the two selections from 1970, Sanders has shifted to soprano, and has also brought in trumpeter Woody Shaw, altoist Gary Barth, and violinist Michael White. And as the years progress into the seventies, all the sidemen eventually end up playing percussive instruments when not blowing or otherwise not kept busy. It is this overtextured sound that has propelled Sanders to the front of "new black jazz."

J5.160   **Archie Shepp. New York Contemporary Five, v.1/2.** two discs. Sonet
SLP 36 and 51 (Danish issues).
Archie Shepp is somewhat of an enigma in black jazz. He has obvious roots in small band swing, yet he was a leader of the New York school of hard bop (which perhaps shows how close bop and swing were). He was a logical extension of such Harlem tenor saxophonists as Eddie "Lockjaw" Davis and Illinois Jacquet, yet he became a leader of the "Black Nationalist" group in jazz. His earlier work, such as these discs recorded in 1963, is usually considered his best because of his coherent style. (Later, he was to go to extremes.) Here, he shows the rich influence of Monk, using the full range of his instrument plus a varied tone to create attacks of short phrase stylings. Unlike Monk, though, Shepp needed time to build his solos for

maximum impact. The New York Contemporary Five was organized by altoist John Tchicai and derives its strength from good ensemble work and solos. With two saxes, the cornet of Don Cherry, plus rhythm, these discs were made at the Montmartre Jazzhus in Copenhagen. Much Monk material is here, as well as the long "Cisum" with extended solo work by Shepp.

J5.161*   **Wayne Shorter. Speak No Evil.** Blue Note BST 84194.

J5.162   **Wayne Shorter. Super Nova.** Blue Note BST 84332.
    Tenorist Shorter has made strong contributions to the recordings of Miles Davis and Weather Report. He was strongly influenced by Coltrane and Rollins, and in turn, he served as a catalyst to Art Blakey in his later Jazz Messenger recordings (Shorter served with Blakey in 1959). These two discs are a logical extension of the hard bop Jazz Messenger formula, coupled with the lyricism of Miles Davis. Compositions here are attributed to Shorter, although throughout the readings, the presence of Coltrane and Rollins can easily be heard. The group is composed of Freddie Hubbard (trumpet), Herbie Hancock (piano), Ron Carter (bass), and Elvin Jones (drums): one of the finest supporting quartets around. The firm rhythms of "Witch Hunt," "Fee-Fi-Fo-Fum," and "Dance Cadaverous" show the typical asymmetric designs being worked on and worked out. With sudden twists, solos, humor and moods, this is a quick-changing disc, revealing startling points of music, such as the rhythm section working against each other from time to time to produce just the right amount of tension and release.

J5.163   **Miroslav Vitous. Mountain in the Clouds.** Atlantic SD 1622.

J5.164   **Joe Zawinul.** Atlantic SD 1579.
    These two albums are direct predecessors to Weather Report. Vitous's effort was originally released in 1970 as Embryo SD524 (*Infinitive Search*) and is here newly mixed, with an additional track, "Cerecka," from that session (there is less echo and more separation than on the original). Most performers on the set came out of the Miles Davis groups, and they can be heard on both albums. Included are John McLaughlin, Joe Henderson, Herbie Hancock, and Jack DeJohnette. Vitous is a good bassist, with fresh ideas and consistency in playing (no embellishments). "When Face Gets Pale" is a Hancock showpiece; "I Will Tell Him on You" is eleven minutes of furious pacing; while "Freedom Jazz Suite" (by Eddie Harris) is a spontaneous reworking of themes for breaking loose. And that they do, as this whole album is a mixture of free and structured chords.
    Europeans have never seemed to do well in America, yet here are Vitous and Zawinul laying down some impressionistic tone poems in an Erik Satie manner. The European approach, based on folk and classic themes, is highly surrealistic and nowhere near primitivism. Subtitled "Music for two electric pianos, flute, trumpet, soprano saxophone, two contrabasses and percussion," this second album is a series of tone poems in the Austrian and Czech traditions. "Double Image" is the prototype for Weather Report (with Wayne Shorter, Vitous, and Zawinul) and is supposedly a concert piece of what man thinks he is, as opposed to what he really is. Hancock's echoplex piano certainly gets a workout. Much of the rest of the album is autobiographical. "In a Silent Way" documents Zawinul's early life as a shepherd

boy in Austria (and this tune was a prior success for Davis), "His Last Journey" is a setting for his grandfather's funeral, and "Arrival in New York" is first impressions in the New World. Good cerebral music, and certainly both discs are worth listening to.

J5.165   **Randy Weston. African Cookbook.** Atlantic SD 1609.
Although pianist Weston is influenced by Monk, he does turn a more melodic phrase. In addition, he is a prolific composer, as with the "Hi Fly" and "Where" pieces. Along with Booker Ervin, he is best in a group context, as on this disc.

Third Stream

J5.166   **Brandeis University, 1957 Festival of the Arts Jazz Concert.** Columbia WL 127.

J5.167   **Teo Macero and Bob Prince. What's New?** Columbia CL 842.

J5.168   **Music for Brass.** Columbia CL 941.

J5.169   **Outstanding Jazz Compositions of the 20th Century.** two discs. Columbia C2S 831.

J5.170   **Gunther Schuller. Jazz Abstractions.** Atlantic 1365.
The late 1950s and early 1960s saw the flowering and virtual death of "Third Stream" music, mainly fostered, composed and performed by white musicians. It was Schuller, the most powerful leader in this field, who gave it both the name and respectability. Third Stream is mainly a blend of classical and jazz music that exposed the cross-fertilization of various ideas and idioms. The belief behind this music was that jazz was actually the result of historical accident and appeared to be merely a *chance* synthesis of simple European and West African music. Schuller and others now wanted—at this time—a more complex fusion between the latest advances of both jazz and classical music, employing modal jazz concepts and atonal European classicism.
The above six records represent the best of the creative flowering. The Brandeis concert was largely performed by a jazz band, playing some large band compositions (a few were remote from jazz) by George Russell, Charlie Mingus, Jimmy Giuffre, Milton Babbitt, Harvey Shapero, and Gunther Schuller. The latter, even though he employs synthesis, comes closest to the balanced fusion of classical music and jazz. But then, he had the clearest conception of what the music is supposed to mean. Perhaps the most successful of the genre is *What's New?*, recorded in 1955-1956 with Art Farmer, John LaPorta, Phil Woods, Mal Waldron, and others. Here, Macero has tried to synthesize the latest symphonic music from Europe with the identity of jazz. More particularly, the "Sounds of May" track employs multi-recording techniques with many dubbing devices, differing tape speeds, and so forth. Again, though, because Prince has a better conception of what he is doing, he is the more cohesive performer—more so than the other jazzmen.
Gunther Schuller founded the Jazz and Classical Music Society in 1956, and they sponsored the *Music for Brass* album, recorded that same year. All of side one

is taken up by his composition "Symphony for Brass and Percussion," in which tonal purity is stressed. But again, different conceptions of the synthesis are made by each composer. Other titles include J. J. Johnson's "Poem for Brass," John Lewis's "Three Little Feelings," and Jimmy Giuffre's "Pharoah." The only constraint in this album is that no strings or woodwinds were to be employed; they were thought to give too much sentimentality. The double Columbia set (C2S 831) contains works by Schuller, Giuffre, Russell, Babbitt, and even Duke Ellington's "Idiom '59," which is by far the best work here (and is also the one closest to the jazz mainstream). Schuller tried a different tack with the Ornette Coleman quartet on the Atlantic offering. He tries to synthesize jazz and serialism for a coherent motive advancement, but with fragmented instrumental representation. He does achieve this, but needs Coleman's guiding genius to perfect the idiom. The restraining jazz modes *demand* sympathetic musicians, and this is the key to Coleman's own jazz. The four tracks here feature Eric Dolphy, Scott La Faro, Bill Evans, Jim Hall, and Coleman.

J5.171   **Carla Bley and Paul Haines. Escalator over the Hill.** three discs. Jazz Composers' Orchestral Association JCOA 3-EOTH.

It would be extremely foolhardy to attempt an explanation of what goes on during the time it takes to play this set, which is the nearest thing to jazz-rock-opera (if it could be called that). The performers were assembled by composer-musician Carla Bley, and they play the words of poet Paul Haines. It took two-and-one-half years to record this epic. The featured musicians and singers include Jack Bruce, John McLaughlin, Linda Ronstadt, Don Cherry, Gato Barbieri, Charlie Haden, Viva the superstar, and many others. Bley has been composing for twenty years, and her credentials are impeccable. Much of her work was for ex-husband Paul Bley and Gary Burton. She calls her work a "chronotransduction," and it is pretty difficult to understand. The story line here centers on a hotel and a couple of expatriates named Jack and Ginger, who are always at loose ends. The interactions of society and them forms the basis of the story. By skillful use of over-dubbing, vocals, and extended solos, Bley makes it all mesh, and it is one of the few modern jazz works that can be played over and over again, with the feeling of *satisfaction* afterwards. Not too many records can give that: there is always the demand for more, or even for less. Only *Jesus Christ Superstar* is similarly handled in the rock idiom. The illustrated libretto completes the package. A good set that combines humor with theatre of the absurd.

J5.172   **David Brubeck. Adventures in Time.** two discs. Columbia G30625.

Just as there are many jazzmen and composers who are (or have been) underrated, Dave Brubeck has been one of the few to be *overrated*. A cocktail lounge pianist at best, entirely derivative from the Shearing and early bop school, Brubeck is notable for three things: selling a lot of records, having altoist Paul Desmond in his quartet, and exploring time signatures in the pre-Ellis period. The 22 tracks on this "greatest" hits album are mainly vehicles for this latter expression. He claims that they are experiments, and while some succeed, others do not. Those that do include "Take Five" (featuring Paul Desmond) in 5/4 time, "It's a Raggy Waltz" (mixed timings), and "Waltz Limp," in a basic 3/4, but with variances as the programmatic ballerina loses a shoe (!). This compendium dates from the early 1960s; thus, it has a number of re-recordings of his earlier works, and even some concert hall versions. Only one tune is in 4/4 straight ahead jazz. Others are in 7/4, 9/8, 10/4, 6/4, etc. A worthwhile set for time experiments in Third Stream and white jazz music.

J5.173   **Don Ellis. Electric Bath.** Columbia CS 9585.

Don Ellis formed a mini-reaction to the blending of colors by Claude Thornhill and Gil Evans. He redrafted the sectional scoring in the "swing" manner, which had not been done before, nor was it ever adapted to bop. A good clean cut with the past was previously emphasized; Ellis was just going back to the big band roots. Thus, he leads a big band that has a forceful "swing" attack with basic riffs. Coloration has been added, not by blending, but by odd time signatures (where 7/4 becomes 2 + 3 + 2, 2 + 2 + 3, and 3 + 2 + 2), unusual instrumentation, and reinforcement by electronic amplification. His straight ahead drive revitalized the big bands of the 1960s.

J5.174   **Gil Evans. Out of the Cool.** Impulse S 4.

Evans is a successful arranger and composer who had done sterling work for Miles Davis in the 1950s (see also under the Davis annotation, item number J5.82-85). This 1960 album is the most successful and standard of all of his own ensemble playing. He devised rich orchestral textures within which solos can be made; however, the improvisations and the scoring are complementary. With proper placement of microphones and fourteen members, the group was able to recreate a "larger than life" sound. "La Nevada" is perhaps the greatest piece, with a stunning solo by trumpeter Johnny Coles; this is closely followed by "Bilbao" and the important bass solo by Ron Carter. On "Where Flamingos Fly," Evans provides flesh for the bones. His devices allowed him to reshape cool jazz from the introspective outlook to a fully clad statement. Later, Evans would develop blues themes.

J5.175*   **George Russell. Jazz Workshop.** RCA LSC 2534.

J5.176*   **George Russell. New York, New York/Jazz in the Space Age.** two discs. MCA 2-4017.

George Russell produced an entirely new concept in jazz scoring and writing, influencing probably hundreds of arrangers who are now appearing on the musical scene. This is a long-term influence, but Russell, having been discouraged more than once, is still living in Norway—away from American influences and life. He developed the "Lydian concept of tonal organization" in the late 1950s, a theory of music that systematized a new set of relationships among the traditional harmonic resources of the jazz band. Thus it was as different as serialism or twelve-tone. He wrote thematic material of quiet intensity, mainly for the soloist as an individual piece, but one also consistent with other individual pieces. This subtle but strong music was of a varied character, as exemplified by the stylings of pianist Bill Evans in the MCA twofer set. Several contrasting moods are expressed, but in surprisingly unified short pieces that do not exhaust harmonic possibilities. There is still much room here for improvisation.

J5.177   **Phil Woods. Rights of Swing.** Candid Barnaby KZ 31036.

Woods is an altoist influenced by Parker; indeed, he went so far as to marry Parker's widow. However, his approach comes near to perfecting the smoothness of

Benny Carter. He is a consistent performer, always phrasing over the best with his functional tone and giving opulent improvisations (again, from Carter). Like Davis and Armstrong, he is a strong architect concerned with dynamics. This led naturally to a medium-sized ensemble group performing a suite loosely based on Stravinskian ideas. This 1961 effort, his first large-scale composition, was conducted by Quincy Jones. The architectural development, the variety of moods and colors, and clarity of lines and voicings are ably represented by the group, which comprised Curtis Fuller, Sahib Shihab, Tommy Flanagan, and Osie Johnson from the octet. The six parts of the composition relate to ballet music as performed by jazz musicians. Transitional cyclic elements are emphasized in a structural whole, employing ballad, waltz, and various colorful themes. Throughout, there are the odd allusions to the Stravinsky work. Good program notes by Woods are included in the liner annotation.

Diverse Themes

DIVERSE THEMES

INTRODUCTION

There are many, many recordings in jazz music that simply do not fit into the above five sections, by reason of specialization or nature of issuance. We have selected three areas for annotation, but there are others. The four instruments that have shaped jazz include the piano, the guitar, the trumpet, and the saxophone. To many fans, the latter two *are* jazz and shaped the idiom; thus, many are to be found scattered in the rest of the chapter, and the materials cited in this section are "introductory" anthologies or educational. The piano and the guitar are important for being both solo and rhythm instruments and for their adaptability to other forms of music beyond the jazz idiom.

It is ironic that there are so few real jazz vocals, but then that would be imitative, as the jazz instrumental was originally a recreation of the melismatic human voice. (At any rate, Billie Holiday probably was the first and only singer of jazz of any consequence.) Pop jazz has created "pretty" music (as it is sometimes called by jazz fans), some of it in the jazz-rock fusion, other in the melodically-inclined style of Chick Corea, Keith Jarrett, or similar pianists.

INSTRUMENTALS

Specific Instrument Anthologies

J6.1*   **The Bass**. three discs. Impulse ASY 9284-3.

J6.2*   **The Drum**. three discs. Impulse ASY 9272-3.
In dealing with the character of rhythm accompaniment in jazz, it is difficult to isolate individual performances because there are other, more compelling soloists in the front line. The Impulse label, despite certain omissions because they had no legal access to the titles, does do a masterful job in compiling good representative examples of styles and contributions. The emphasis, of course, is on the Impulse catalog, which means 1957+ material (either new or in reinterpretive form by "giants" in their later years). *The Bass* presents 18 bassists, from Jimmy Blanton in 1939 through to Stanley Clarke in the mid-1970s. Unfortunately, it was not arranged in chronological order. There are, of course, substantial notes and discographies. One of the highlights here is the basic duo of drummer Elvin Jones and bassist Richard Davis in "Summertime."

The Drum set is decidedly weaker. It contains examples from 26 drummers, all of them in the modern style, but it does *not* contain such important performers as Art Blakey, Max Roach, Kenny Clarke, Philly Joe Jones, Jo Jones, Dannie Richmond, Buddy Rich, Baby Dodds, Louis Bellson, and other innovators of the 1930-1960 period. But it is handy to have a compilation that can be used for educational purposes, subject to the constraints of presenting a limited number of the really great personnel.

J6.3   **Battle of the Tenor Saxes.** International Association of Jazz Record Collectors IAJRC 15.

J6.4   **The Jazz Giants: Reeds.** Trip TLP 5518.

J6.5*   **The Saxophone: A Critical Guide to the Major Trends in the Development of the Contemporary Saxophone Tradition.** three discs. Impulse ASH 9253-3.

J6.6   Item omitted.

J6.7   **Saxophones.** Mercury SMWL 21026 (British issue).

J6.8*   **The Tenor Sax: The Commodore Years.** four discs. Atlantic SD2-306/7.

The saxophone became the king of the jazz instruments largely through the efforts of Coleman Hawkins, the first performer to become a star by performing as a soloist. Its tone and range, plus the harmonic distortion through the reed (as classicists call it, an "impure" tone), made it an instrument that one could play and study for years, with different styles and explorations. The material listed above is all relatively late, the earliest being 1938 with Lester Young and the Kansas City Six on the Atlantic set. These were some of the first combo instrumentations to feature the sax; previously, there had been many discs with other reeds, such as the clarinet or trumpet, and piano as lead instrument.

The Atlantic set comes from Commodore recordings done by Milt Gabler, and in different configurations there are Lester Young, Chu Berry, Ben Webster, Frank Wess, and Coleman Hawkins, generally with the equivalent of an elpee each (and stretching through to 1954 with Wess). The IAJRC set has 14 tracks (1945-1951) exploring the possibility that the saxophone's rise was a post-War development, but ignoring the impact of Coleman Hawkins. Be that as it may, the album attempts to line up those who followed the Hawkins school of the big sound (a firm but breathy tone), such as Ben Webster, Gene Ammons, Paul Gonsalves, Ike Quebec, and Illinois Jacquet. Side two turns the matter over to Lester Young for light, jumpy playing, along with his disciples Dexter Gordon, Allen Eager, Wardell Gray, James Moody, and Warne Marsh. An instructive disc, this is well worth listening to for the sake of comparison and contrast in styles. Also noteworthy is the British Mercury reissue (from the Keynote catalog of 1943-1946) featuring Lester Young, Coleman Hawkins, Willie Smith, Budd Johnson, Don Byas, and Flip Phillips.

The Trip anthology comes from the Emarcy catalog, and extends the time period through to 1953, with many of the same performers reappearing from the IAJRC and Mercury records. The Impulse offering does a good job for the post-1960 period, with two borrowings from other companies' catalogs for a Lester Young and a Charlie Parker selection (they had died before Impulse was founded). Thus, with recent Hawkins recordings such as a 1961 "Body and Soul" (again arranged by Benny Carter), the three giants of the saxophone (Hawkins, Young, and Parker) are represented. All others derive strength from them. The material here all has been available before on many Impulse discs, but the collection hangs together nicely by itself, with good notes by Robert Palmer. Through the above records, the history of the saxophone in jazz can be adequately traced with representative samplings of soprano, alto, tenor, and baritone saxophones.

J6.9   **Classic Jazz Piano Styles.** RCA LPV 543.

J6.10*   **History of Jazz Piano.** three discs. RCA FXM 3-7143 (French issue).

J6.11   **Hot Pianos, 1926-1940.** Historical HLP 29.

J6.12*   **A Jazz Piano Anthology.** two discs. Columbia KG 32355.

J6.13   **The Jazz Piano.** RCA LSP 3499.

J6.14   **Kansas City Piano, 1936-1941.** Decca DL 79226.

J6.15*   **Kings and Queens of Ivory, v.1: 1935-1940.** MCA 510.090 (French issue). (In progress).

J6.16   **Master Jazz Piano, v.1/3.** three discs. Master Jazz Recordings MJR 8105, 8108, and 8117.
The different piano stylings are much the same as a mini-history of jazz. A number of categories have been established, although they are loosely named, and most will be found in their own sections within this book. "Ragtime" was one root, as developed by Scott Joplin, with leading exponents Eubie Blake and Jelly Roll Morton. The latter transformed the style into "stride," which was greatly exemplified by James P. Johnson and Fats Waller. At the same time, there developed "barrelhouse," a rough and ready form that assimilated the syncopation of ragtime with the bent notes of the blues. Exponents include Speckled Red, Roosevelt Sykes, and Robert Shaw. Coupled with stride piano, the barrelhouse style soon evolved into "boogie woogie," with leaders such as Pinetop Smith, Cripple Clarence Lofton, and the more jazz-oriented Meade Lux Lewis, Albert Ammons, and Pete Johnson. Boogie woogie led naturally into the "jump blues" piano of Sunnyland Slim, with gospel flavorings added by Ray Charles and blues by Otis Spann. This style is now known as "Chicago" style. Bud Powell transformed bop into piano with his music.
    The Columbia double set is the widest ranging of the list above. It was compiled by Henri Renaud and originally released in France. Covering Eubie Blake, Fats Waller, James P. Johnson, Jimmy Yancey, Joe Sullivan, Jess Stacey, Art Tatum, Teddy Wilson, Albert Ammons, Count Basie, Mary Lou Williams, Duke Ellington, Bud Powell, Bill Evans, and Cecil Taylor, it cannot be faulted except on two counts: there are few blues, and there is no Jelly Roll Morton. Both are probably due to the restraints of the company, for Columbia and its subsidiaries did not record *everybody* of importance, and certainly not every track here is a gem. But every style is covered. The *Hot Pianos* offering covers some material by Fats Waller, Cow Cow Davenport, Jelly Roll Morton, and Montana Taylor, playing uptempo music, and nicely supplementing the weaknesses of the Columbia set. The Decca set, and most of the MCA imports, document the very important regional style of Southwestern piano, and the leading exponents from that area: Count Basie, Jay McShann, Mary Lou Williams, and Pete Johnson. Others on the MCA set include Meade Lux Lewis,

Cleo Brown, Willie "The Lion" Smith, and Clarence Profit. The RCA Vintage material brings together several different styles, such as the boogie woogie of Albert Ammons and Pete Johnson, the stomps and boogies of Jimmy Yancey, the rags and stride of Morton and Waller, and the sophistication of Earl Hines, who is in a category of his own.

The French RCA set presents forty titles done by 24 pianists, arranged nicely in chronological order and with superb notes. This picks up some of the slack of the Columbia reissue, and along with the MCA material, represents good value for the comprehensive overview, spread among some six-plus discs. Included are three Jelly Roll Morton outings ("Seattle Hunch," "Freakish"), Meade Lux Lewis ("Honky Tonk Train Blues"), Fats Waller, Duke Ellington solos ("Solitude"), a couple of Errol Garners, and Phineas Newborn, Albert Ammons, latter-day Count Basie, Willie "The Lion" Smith, James P. Johnson, and Clarence Williams.

Bringing it all together is the RCA LSP 3499 set, being the proceedings of a live piano workshop in Pittsburgh in 1965. Subtitled "a musical exchange," the set features various pianists on solos (Mary Lou Williams, Billy Taylor, Duke Ellington, and Earl Hines). There is a perfectly marvelous duet between Earl Hines and Duke Ellington, all improvised, and called, naturally, "House of Lords." A tribute to Hines in "Rosetta" brings on everybody for a monster jam. The Master Jazz anthologies present piano solos that were freshly recorded in the 1970s, allowing some band leaders to record their pianistic impressions (Jay McShann, Claude Hopkins, Teddy Wilson, and others). Styles are divided between standards and blues, with most of the blues being original compositions.

Piano

Innovators

J6.17   **Duke Ellington. The Golden Duke.** two discs. Prestige P24029.

J6.17a*   **Duke Ellington. Piano Reflections.** Capitol M11058.

J6.18*   **Duke Ellington. Money Jungle.** United Artists UAS5632.

J6.19   **Duke Ellington. The Pianist.** Fantasy 9462.

J6.20   **Duke Ellington. Duke's Big Four.** Pablo 2310 703.
     Ellington began to record in the piano trio format during the late 1940s. He was a master in the *stride* school, being influenced by James P. Johnson and Willie "The Lion" Smith. Piano reductions of his rich orchestrations are exceedingly difficult to handle, and any performance demands some rhythm or proper use of all 88 keys (as with Earl Hines's solos). His immense reach can cover the keyboard, but Ellington had the habit of involving all his sidemen (whether a full band or just rhythm), constantly feeding chords to all who played with him. One-half of the Prestige set concerns reissues from the Mercer and Riverside catalogs of 1950. The piano duos here with Strayhorn feature Wendell Marshall on bass, while the remaining four tracks have an empathetic trio augmented by Strayhorn on celeste and Oscar Pettiford on cello. At this time, Ellington was beginning experiments with the trio format.

He discarded this series of rich tonal ideas for the standard piano trio on the 1953 *Piano Reflections*. These 14 tracks have five standards and new compositions, mostly blues and further experiments with feeding chords to his rhythmic sidemen. It was nine years to the next major trio outing, this time the 1962 United Artists collaboration with Max Roach and Charles Mingus, both heavily influenced by Ellington. The program emphasized rich textures and rhythmic figures, including marvelous stride piano through "Caravan" and the delicate "Fleurette Africaine." The Fantasy issue from 1966 and 1970 presents ten trios with fresh Ellington ideas and compositions, while the Pablo disc comes from December 1973 and reverts to standards and blues, such as "Prelude to a Kiss," "Love You Madly," and "Cotton Tail." Guitarist Joe Pass was added to the rhythm of Louis Bellson and Ray Brown. The Fantasy set reveals Ellington's ability to completely switch moods from piece to piece. The Pablo effort (one of his last) presents orchestral sounds, especially with the addition of Pass.

J6.21*   **Earl Hines. A Monday Date, 1928.** Milestone 2012.

J6.22   **Earl Hines. Another Monday Date.** two discs. Prestige P24043.

J6.23*   **Earl Hines. At Home.** Delmark 212.

J6.24   **Earl Hines. Hines '65.** Master Jazz Recordings. MJR 8109.

J6.25*   **Earl Hines. Quintessential Continued.** Chiaroscuro CR 120.

J6.26*   **Earl Hines. Quintessential Recording Sessions.** Chiaroscuro CR 101.

J6.27*   **Earl Hines. Spontaneous Explorations.** Contact LP2.
          Earl Hines has to be considered the best and greatest overall jazz pianist. He influenced every pianist (save his earlier contemporaries, such as Morton), including those who assimilated some of his greatest techniques (such as arpeggios)—Art Tatum and Oscar Peterson. He logically extended the piano beyond ragtime, stride, and blues, bringing it out of the orchestra on a par with the solo work of such people as Jimmie Noone (q.v.) and Louis Armstrong (q.v.). One of his main approaches has been characterized as "trumpet style," in that he takes a positive stand and plays the piano as if it were a trumpet (which was the first instrument he learned to play). His stretch is to thirteen keys, and independent fingers can play any notes within that scope. He had a sense of form, beauty, and structure in all of his writings and interpretations. His power was often surprising, as on the Contact album, recorded in the 1960s, where he projects "Undecided" to a full-scale climax and gives similar treatment to "Fatha's Blues."
          Hines's first solo recordings had tremendous impact on the jazz world. These are on the Milestone set and include the influential "Blues in Chords" (also known as "Cautious Blues") and "Monday Date." Chiaroscuro CR 101 presents his important 1923 QRS piano rolls *plus* his 1970 reinterpretation of these fifty-year-old works. Some of this music Hines had not heard for decades, and he had to carefully restudy his earlier approaches. The Prestige twofer combines two mid-fifties albums made for Fantasy while both that company and Hines were in San Francisco. With Eddie Duran assisting on guitar, the piano trio moves through the first album here

with Fats Waller material, such as "Ain't Misbehavin'," "Jitterbug Waltz," "Black and Blue," and "Honeysuckle Rose." Other tunes are those associated with Fats, such as "Two Sleepy People" or "I Can't Give You Anything But Love." The second disc is solo piano, and this was only Hines's second attempt in thirty years to produce a solo effort. With one exception, the twelve selections here are all originals, and include "Deep Forest," "Straight to Love," and "My Monday Date." Much has been written about Hines's important "trumpet style" piano work. His right hand played octaves (thumb and little finger) with the middle fingers playing harmonic trills; his left hand began explorations beyond stride piano with agility—into off-time, double-time, and other dissonances—and without losing the beat. No other pianist took such risks.

The Delmark set is the most gorgeously recorded example of complex runs and subharmonies, for Hines was recorded alone, at home, with a brand new Steinway grand. On this occasion, the producer and engineer turned on the tapes and went outside. Complete privacy and familiarity with surroundings produced intimate sympathetic material. The other discs cited also represent the height of Hines's inventiveness.

J6.28   **James P. Johnson.** Blue Note BLP 7011.

J6.29*   **James P. Johnson.** MCA 510.085 (French issue).

J6.30*   **James P. Johnson. Father of the Stride Piano.** Columbia CL 1780.

J6.31   **James P. Johnson. The Original James P. Johnson.** Folkways FJ 2850.
Johnson was a great influence on Duke Ellington and Fats Waller, among other stride pianists. He virtually founded the stride school, which emphasized a strong left hand and melodic decoration. Technique was important, not improvisation. Johnson, in addition to fashioning the Harlem piano style, was also a major composer who mastered the variations needed to sustain the drive in the music. Heavily influenced by Luckeyth Roberts, Johnson created many piano rolls before his first recordings in 1921. His major activity was in the musical theatre, where he wrote "Runnin' Wild," "The Charleston," "Old Fashioned Love," "If I Could Be with You One Hour Tonight," and "A Porter's Love Song." He did make some solos (on the Columbia set), and he did accompany many of the classic blues singers, such as Bessie Smith. The Depression hit him hard, as theatres closed, and he turned to composing semi-classical works that have never been recorded (many can no longer be found).

In 1939, John Hammond recorded him with a small group (Red Allen, Gene Sedric, J. C. Higginbotham) in the Fats Waller mode. There is, of course, much irony in this. "Hungry Blues" and "Memories of You" are among the ten titles here. In 1943, Johnson made his best solos ever (for Blue Note), including "Caprice Rag," "Mule Walk," and "Backwater Blues." This was followed by MCA recordings in 1944, where he recreated his entire repertoire (mostly mentioned above from the shows) plus Fats Waller melodies ("Honeysuckle Rose," "Ain't Misbehavin'," etc.). Also, from 1943-1945, he recorded for Moe Asch's Disc label (reissued on the Folkways), and this included a virtuoso "Liza," a Spanish-tinged "The Dream" (after Morton), Joplin's "Euphonic Sounds," and "Snowy Morning Blues."

J6.32*   **Thelonious Monk. Pure Monk.** two discs. Milestone 47004.

Monk is one of the finest composer-pianists of all time, and here are reissued all of the studio solos that he did for Riverside between 1953 and 1959. These had previously been available on six or seven widely scattered discs and are here collated for the first time. And the set reveals some interesting facets of his development over the seven-year period. Despite certain critics' notions, Monk is really at his best in solo piano work, and this has been proved once again by the acclaim given him on his 1972 tour of England, where he did a lot of work utilizing only the piano (and made two Black Lion recordings as well, so that the documentation is available). Some claim that he lacks emotion—hear the economical lyricism from block-chordings of a jagged run and crashing fist-like fingers (or thumbs) on the keyboard of Irving Berlin's "All Alone" and "Remember." His best efforts have been within the blues mould, and here is the best recording ever (notwithstanding Abbey Lincoln's Candid track) of his own "Blue Monk." The two takes here of the blues piece "Functional" are very dissimilar, showing his awareness of the moods he can easily flit to in a moment. And, of course, his stride style is a laugh in itself, as he half-times and double-times himself.

J6.33*   **Jelly Roll Morton. 1923/1924.** two discs. Milestone M 47018.

Ferdinand "Jelly Roll" Morton, self-proclaimed inventor of jazz, was just as good as he claimed: a brilliant pianist, masterful composer, and pace-setting band leader. His great and exceedingly rare early solo and small group recordings (including all of the 1923-1924 classic Gennett piano solos) make up this definitive collection. The small groups later evolved into the Red Hot Peppers, but here they are deeply into hokum, and must be seen only as examples of this type of musical production. These recordings were taken from small labels, such as Rialto and Autograph, plus a few from Paramount.

The value of the 19 solos is that they bear repeated and sustained listening. By this time in his life, Morton had firmed up his impressions of what jazz should be. Thus, automatically, these recordings—"King Porter Stomp," "New Orleans Joy," "Grandpa's Spells," "Wolverine Blues," "Froggie Moore," "Shreveport Stomp," "The Pearls"—assume the status of definitive editions. At the piano, Morton always tried to *think* in an orchestral sense, so that listening to re-recordings of these works with his Red Hot Peppers reveals little difference except for the additional instruments. Max Harrison has said that the fact that "Morton could record such a large group of compositions in so short a time indicates how hard he had already worked on his music, and that they embody such a personal and consistent view of jazz suggests that he knew all along what he wanted to do." Good notes are by Morton-influenced pianist Bob Greene.

J6.34*   **Luckeyth Roberts/Willie "The Lion" Smith. Harlem Piano.** Good Time. Jazz S 10035.

Roberts became the head of the Harlem school of music and "taught" and influenced James P. Johnson and Duke Ellington. His massive hands could stretch a fourteenth on the keyboard, and he played tenths as easily as octaves. His tremolo was excellent, he could drum on one note with two or three fingers in either hand, and he retained this drumming style in his breaks. He never recorded until 1946 (for Circle Records) at the age of 53; the tracks here are from 1958. The six tunes—his own compositions—span his whole performing history.

"Nothin' " is a dance line; "Spanish Fandango" explores that country's influence on jazz; while "Railroad Blues" is his blues piece. "Complainin' " has a rugged bass line with effective dynamics. "Inner Space" is a waltz with inverted thirds and sixths, while "Outer Space" is a set of variations on his "Exclusively with You" theme.

Smith, explored later in this section, was an inventive composer. These 1958 recordings show this in the five tracks of his material, all melodic and relaxing. James P. Johnson once described this music: "New York developed the orchestral piano—full, round, big widespread chords and tenths—a heavy bass moving against the right hand." Sound harmonies and effective chords created the expansive sweep of the orchestrated piano.

J6.35*   **Art Tatum. God Is in the House.** Onyx ORI 205.

J6.36*   **Art Tatum. Masterpieces.** two discs. MCA 2-4019.

J6.37   **Art Tatum. Piano Solos.** Jazz Panorama LP 15.

J6.38*   **Art Tatum. Piano Starts Here.** Columbia CS 9655.

J6.39*   **Art Tatum. Solo Masterpieces.** thirteen discs. Pablo 2625.703.

J6.40   **Art Tatum. Solo Piano.** Capitol T 11028.

Tatum was the most gifted technician of all jazz. His pianistic style was orchestrated Jelly Roll Morton (and it took an ensemble to put across Jelly's ideas). His accomplishments even impressed the classicist Horowitz. In addition to technique, Tatum brought with him the greatest harmonic sense in all of jazz. He was an imaginative and infallible improviser, relying on great rhythmic freedom and his virtuosic sense. In his creative left hand work, he was influenced by Fats Waller. Through striding, he could find four different chords to the bar and then try to substitute chords and harmonize subtleties. His right hand lived with arpeggios of 16th note runs at fast tempos or with Waller-type choruses. He was at home with boogie woogie, but did not employ the device too much. He was too busy with other devices—so many, in fact, that he was often accused of just coasting through facile playing (an accusation now being made against Oscar Peterson, Tatum's successor).

Some of these devices had an immense influence on bop musicians, as the Onyx release from the Jerry Newman tapes so vividly illustrates. Tatum loved after hours clubs for the competition and stimulus they offered, and Newman recorded him (in 1940-1941) in his (Newman's) apartment, at Reuben's, the Gee Haw Stables, and Monroe's Uptown House. The 15 tracks of this Grammy Award winner include both solos and trios, some with Frankie Newton for "Lady Be Good" and the important "Sweet Georgia Brown" (handled with mutes). The tricks of his trade included allusions to other tunes, pure Tatumesque inventions of his own devising; a multitude of rests, rushes, and tempo changes; improbable configurations and impetuous chording (now carried on not by Peterson, but by Hines, who began with the improbable in the late 1920s); and a true genius at architectural construction. In this latter case, Tatum would use well-known ballads and standards—where the melody is obvious—to make a structure that he would take apart and reassemble. Rudy Koopmans said of this device that "he is always breaking up beautiful lines into amazing acrobatics, breaking up these acrobatics into a tender note, breaking up a tender note into a violent rhythmic approach." Later in life, the decorations became essential, as Tatum would never state the obvious melody but play around it, as Hines does today. "Architecture" was perhaps his biggest gift to bop.

When Tatum was in a group he simplified his playing lines, diluting them by a factor equal to the number of his accompanists. The MCA twofer offers some trios from the 1940-1945 period, such as "Moonglow" and "I Got Rhythm." (Tiny Grimes was the unique 4-string guitarist who could follow Tatum.) Other material here, from Tatum's middle period, includes the stride bass of "Get Happy," the compact "Begin the Beguine," the fragmented "Elegy," and the incredible "St. Louis Blues," which was the first jazz item to ever present a mini-history of jazz, from its roots in ragtime through stride, boogie woogie, and neo-bop triplets. Joe Turner, the blues shouter, is along for some blues items.

All of Tatum's first recordings from 1933 are found on the Columbia set: "Sophisticated Lady," "Tiger Rag," "Tea for Two," and "St. Louis Blues." The nine other tracks are from a 1949 Gene Norman Just Jazz concert in Los Angeles. This was a chance to hear new interpretations of his older works. "Tatum Pole Boogie" has his octave-jumping bass patterns; "I Know That You Know" is played initially at a fast pace, but then Tatum halves the time, and then doubles it again in a wry humorous twist. The Jazz Panorama presents more of his 1930s solos, particularly 1935 and 1939 (the lyrical "Indiana" and the acknowledgment to Hines in "Rosetta"). Some 16 of the 17 titles made for Capitol in 1949 are reissued on T 11028. Here are the masterful tone poems of "Dancing in the Dark" and "Willow Weep for Me," along with the fragmented "Blues Skies," where Tatum is searching for the melody. "I Cover the Waterfront" is a fresh reading. On some tunes, such as "Aunt Hagar's Blues," the three-minute restriction is in order, but for some other titles, it forces Tatum to condense his ideas.

The best has been saved for the last. On three sessions in 1953-1954, Tatum recorded 121 (!) titles for Norman Granz and Clef Records. Most were issued at the time, but now Granz's Pablo label has put out all of them—many 6-7 minutes each. From "After You've Gone" to "You Took Advantage of Me," this is an extremely rich collection—so rich that it is virtually impossible to listen to more than one side at a time in order to absorb the musical ideas. All the material consists of well-known ballads—"Blues in My Heart," "Makin' Whoopee," "Man I Love," "Louise," "Embraceable You," "Tenderly," "Yesterdays," "September Song," "Stardust," "Where or When," "All the Things You Are," etc., etc.—and features free introductions with the usual shift in tempos. At this time in his life, Tatum was at his architectural peak, merely stating the melody and doing everything with decoration and oblique techniques. He would "suspend the beat in his left hand without relaxing the tempo (implied by the right hand), and introduce subtle rhythmic interplay between the hands." This 13-disc set has a lavish booklet of pictures, discographic data, and a Benny Green musical biography.

J6.40a*   **Fats Waller. Piano Solos, 1929-1941.** two discs. RCA AXM2-5518.
Waller's stomping style has been commented on earlier in this book (see entry J4.16-17). Directly influenced by James P. Johnson (an influence on scores of later pianists, including Duke Ellington), Waller was a gifted, sensitive performer and composer. His material veered between the pop world ("Honeysuckle Rose," "Ain't Misbehavin'," "I've Got a Feeling I'm Falling") and the jazz world of rent

parties ("Handful of Keys," "Numb Fumbling," "Valentine Stomp," "African Ripples," "Viper's Drag"). His melody decorations (rather than line improvisations) are best in these latter jazz titles, simply because they have little melody, and Waller relied on an emotional handling of his introspection. This led to well-organized compositions full of contrasting textures and phrases. On balance, Waller's growth as a jazz pianist was decidedly hampered by the commercial pressures of recording inane titles with his small group. As the organ was Waller's first love, there just simply was not enough time for him to develop his piano. Consequently, he continued to rely on decoration, and his technique deteriorated after 1934. This double album, a nice-looking package with excellent liner notes, contains 33 tracks.

J6.41*   **Teddy Wilson. The Teddy Wilson Piano Solos.** CBS 62876 (French issue).

J6.42   **Teddy Wilson. With Billie in Mind.** Chiaroscuro CR 111.
    Wilson was set in his piano style early on in his career, and he has gone through no changes in the forty years since. His best group work was with Billie Holiday, a series of pick-up groups, and the Goodman Trio and Quartet. Wilson is a perfectionist and technician. He swings, he has a variety of chords to offer, and he plays with both hands—so much so that he can either provide good sympathetic accompaniment or stand on his own as an accomplished soloist. The two discs here are from among his best solo work. The 11 tracks on the French record were recorded in 1935-1937, and contain standards such as "Liza," "Rosetta," "Don't Blame Me," and two takes of "Between the Devil and the Deep Blue Sea." Thirty-five years later, Wilson recorded the solo piano salute to Billie Holiday, a wide-ranging selection of 14 items associated with the great Lady Day when she was recording with Wilson in the 1930s. These miniatures, while evocative of Billie, are still in the Wilson mould. It is difficult (sound quality apart) to tell the differences between these two discs. The tribute has "Easy to Love," "Body and Soul," "Them There Eyes," and "Why Was I Born?"

Standards

J6.43   **Joe Albany. Birdtown Birds.** SteepleChase SCS 1003 (Danish issue).
    Pianist Albany was a legend who, by translating Parker to the piano in strict accordance with Parker's solos, has influenced more pianists in bop than any other performer. Yet, he was rarely recorded himself and was largely overshadowed by Powell. Bud Powell injected quite a bit of himself into the bop translations, and perhaps it was for this reason that Powell recorded while Albany did not. This current album, recorded at the Montmartre Café in 1973 in Copenhagen, features a great deal of polyrhythmic and turbulent music throughout the 50 minutes. Bop interpretations include "Willow Weep for Me," "Night and Day," and "C. C. Rider," plus material composed by Parker, Monk, and Gillespie.

J6.44   **Paul Bley. The Closer.** ESP 1021.
    Pianist Bley creates deliberate fragmentations in a concentrated variety of dialogs with his accompanists (in this case Steve Swallow, bass, and Barry Altshul, drums), such as on "Cartoon" with his drummer. Other varieties include Ornette

Coleman's "Crossroads," which seems ripe with ideas, the gay "Figfoot," the rustic "Ida," and the tense "Start." Moods are creative because of Bley's subtle free improvisation that, despite his dislike for conventions (and hence, his lack of assertiveness), are still disciplined through organic, thematic motives. The manner of presentation is equally important to the variety; thus, when he is selective, he only uses a restricted part of the keyboard, and this part changes, of course, from idea—or song—to idea. The ten selections on this disc perfectly illustrate his unique contributions to integrity in jazz.

J6.45   **Dollar Brand. African Sketchbook.** Enja 2026 (German issue).

J6.46   **Dollar Brand. Anatomy of a South African Village.** Freedom FLP 40107 (British issue).

J6.47   **Dollar Brand. Sangoma.** Sackville 3006 (Canadian issue).
        South African pianist Brand was born the son of a Basuto tribesman, and both Africa and America are intertwined in his music. Since 1962, he has performed extensively in Europe. His Western influences have obviously been Duke Ellington and Thelonious Monk, but his African ones also contain traces of modern racial-torn South Africa; at times, it can be a very violent music. At the same time, despite obvious primitive rhythms of a percussive nature, the music is very melodic. It is a ceaseless energy, with Brand filling all the holes that others would make. He constantly plays to achieve his lyricism, never stopping in case he runs out of ideas. This goes against the Monk dictum of economy and even against devices employed by that other ceaseless wanderer, Art Tatum, who would never hesitate to use stop-time or tempo changes if they suited his mood or the music.
        The title selection of the British issue (originally recorded in 1965 at the world-famous Montmartre in Copenhagen) is a tone poem written in five parts for an orchestra: "Spring Morning," "To Work," "Mamma," "Portrait of a Bushman," and "Which Way?" This version is a piano trio reduction and forms the "compleat" Brand. Themes and devices include the Monkish stabbing explorations and rhythmic left and right hand patterns that alternate with melancholic tenderness. On the other discs, "Tintiyana" is an outright gospel-blues. Several items relate to Monk, such as "Light Blue," and " 'Round about Midnight," and there is a salute to "Fats, Duke and the Monk" in a six-part tone that includes "Honeysuckle Rose," "Single Petal of a Rose," and "Think of One." Other suites include "Ancient Africa," in three parts, and "The Aloe and the Wild Rose," also in three parts. If any music is to be called compassionate, then surely Dollar Brand's deserves to be.

J6.48   **Nat "King" Cole. Trio Days.** Capitol T-11033.
        Mainly known as a good popular singer, Cole started out in the business as a jazz pianist with his own trio, which also contained guitar (Oscar Moore) and bass. Moving over to Capitol from Decca, Cole continued the trio format, and this collection of 12 three-minute miniatures shows a heavy debt to Earl Hines. The trio was very compact and consistent, for these tracks were recorded over a five year period, 1944-1949. His crisp professionalism was no doubt due to his tidy and methodical mind, with the proper balance maintained between right and left hands. Some significant selections here include "Body and Soul," "What Is This Thing Called Love?," and "Smoke Gets in Your Eyes."

J6.49*   **Don Ewell. Free 'n' Easy.** Good Time Jazz S10046.

J6.50*   **Don Ewell. Man Here Plays Fine Piano!** Good Time Jazz S 10043.

J6.51   **Don Ewell. Music to Listen to Don Ewell By.** Good Time Jazz
          L 12021.

J6.52   **Don Ewell. Jazz on a Sunday Afternoon.** Fat Cat's Jazz FCJ 109.

J6.53*   **Don Ewell. A Jazz Portrait of the Artist.** Chiaroscuro CR 106.
          Ewell is one of the most proficient, efficient, and eclectic pianists in jazz
history. He has been able to assimilate all jazz piano styles, embracing what he
needs for any particular tune of the moment. He has been called the greatest white
stride pianist; he has played successful ragtime; he has performed with Bunk Johnson and other "strict" New Orleans performers (including a marvelous series with
Kid Ory [q.v.]); he has led numerous classic jazz sessions with Jack Teagarden and
his own quartets; he emotes with the blues. His overall style is pure and clean, with
overtones of logical innovations. In the mid-fifties, he made a series of recordings
for Good Time Jazz with Darnell Howard (clarinet), Pops Foster (bass), and Minor
Hall (drums). Apart from some originals such as "Delmar Drag" and "Frisco Rider,"
all the material comprises the tried and true standards, including some definitive
performances. Included are "You're Driving Me Crazy," "I Want a Little Girl,"
"Everybody Loves My Baby," items by Fats Waller, Jelly Roll Morton, Don Redman, and Harry Warren.
          Similar material was recorded for L 12021, although here Pops Foster is out,
and Ewell also records piano solos. The piano trios are definitely in the Morton
mould, but the solos are eclectic and difficult to pin down. Ewell's later work
has largely been in the solo idiom, a damn difficult performance to constantly pull
off. The Fat Cat's album includes his improvised "CCNY Rioter Blues," a very
moving statement. Throughout, sometimes sounding like an orchestra, he plays
tributes to Morton, Johnson, Waller and Hines. In addition, he assimilates the styles
of Willie "The Lion" Smith and Cripple Clarence Lofton, especially on "Migrant
Worker Blues" on the Chiaroscuro album. In a word, Don Ewell is Versatile.

J6.54*   **Bill Evans. Conversations with Myself.** Verve 68526.

J6.55*   **Bill Evans. The Village Vanguard Sessions.** two discs. Milestone
          47002.
          Bill Evans, noted as a superb solo pianist, is accompanied here by Paul Motian
(drums) and Scott La Faro (bass). This introspective session was previously available on two Riverside albums that had a tremendous impact when initially released.
All the material here (13 selections) by this empathetic group was done live at their
last engagement together. La Faro is outstanding on the bass, and it was tragic that
he died in an accident just 10 days later. One track—"Porgy"—was never released
before, and all the selections are in correct chronological order as they were recorded
at the Village Vanguard in 1961.

Evans's intellectual approach to jazz makes him more a craftsman and a technician rather than an emotive personality. His strength lies in introspection, and for this reason, it is difficult to select his "best" records. He had consistently high standards, but on the Verve set, he developed a very personal harmonic language based on *how* the notes are played. Here he plays *three* pianos through overdubbing. There is much textual richness here (particularly on "Blue Mark," which must be a classic version), but the lean lines preclude ornamentation. Remember that he had to keep his mind on all three sessions, and he needed much detailed musical thinking, so much so that he had to react to his own various musical personalities. Other fascinating selections include " 'Round about Midnight," an unusual "Hey There," and a dramatic "Stella by Starlight."

J6.56*   **Al Haig. Jazz Will O' the Wisp.** Everest FS 293.

J6.57   **Al Haig. Prezervation.** Prestige PR 7156.
Haig was the bop pianist with Parker and Getz; in fact, he was their favorite piano player, for he exhibited all the grace and charm of Teddy Wilson, while producing neat bop-oriented phrases. In many ways, he was just as important as Bud Powell, but not as exciting. All his variations were balanced, calm, short. His cogent, harmonic extensions are notable. The Prestige disc, a reissue from 1949-1950, features him in collaboration with Stan Getz and Kai Winding on some tracks. At this time, Getz was stylistically inclined away from the melody, and he produced some elastic phrasing for a series of ballads, such as "Stardust," "Stars Fell on Alabama," and "Stairway to the Stars." The quintet becomes a trio with the brass out, and Haig is on his own. This is better realized with the 1954 Everest material. The thirteen tracks here reveal a strong sense of swing for the ballads, such as "All God's Chillun Got Rhythm" (played fast), "Body and Soul," and "Royal Garden Blues." Haig does a beautiful Teddy Wilson-type performance on three solo tracks: "April in Paris," "My Old Flame," and "Don't Blame Me."

J6.58   **Hampton Hawes. Trio, v.1.** Contemporary C 3505.
Hawes has the ability to produce a literal keyboard transcription of Charlie Parker's music, especially with the blues (excessively, in some cases, even to inserting blue phrases into ballads, such as "All the Things You Are"). This record exhibits an extraordinary amount of cohesion, as the group had played together for some time: Red Mitchell on bass and Chuck Thompson on drums (1955). The ten selections include the fast action on "I Got Rhythm," the out-of-tempo version of "So in Love," and the original "Hamp's Blues."

J6.59   **Earl Hines. Hines Comes in Handy.** Audiophile APS 112.

J6.60   **Earl Hines. Hines Does Hoagy.** Audiophile APS 113.

J6.61*   **Earl Hines. Hines Plays Ellington, v.1/4.** four discs. Master Jazz Recordings MJR 8132, 28126.

J6.62   **Earl Hines. Hines Plays George Gershwin.** two discs. Classic Jazz CJ 31.

J6.63*   **Earl Hines. My Tribute to Louis.** Audiophile APS 111.

It made much sense to have Hines do integral recordings of composers' works. He could view the material as a whole, select a program, and then comment on the tunes by virtue of his improvisational skill. His usual plan was to doodle on the piano to work out complex chord changes, and then record the piece in one take, averaging 4 to 10 minutes for each. On all of these discs, Hines has a decorative style and introspective quality. His approach, though, is not the same for each composer. For instance, on the Handy set, besides the commonly known "St. Louis Blues" and "Beale Street Blues," there are also beautiful gems such as the rarely heard "Blues for Madeleine," in which Hines does a stunning run of triplets and double phrasing. This is perhaps the easiest of the Hines albums cited above to listen to and understand, for blues are relatively simple, and Hines is not his usual ornate self here (actually, he doesn't prefer the blues).

With all the other records, one must listen to actually believe what one is hearing. The pyrotechnical runs, inventiveness of ideas, time changes, and so forth are incredible. All of the material was recorded after 1970 (after Hines turned 65), and most of it is standard. The Carmichael album features a rather impossible "Stardust" that no one can perform, and this goes on for 10 minutes. The tribute to Armstrong was made just after Louis died, and presents tunes *associated* with Armstrong that Hines could have played back in the twenties, had Hines been a member of Armstrong's groups before 1928. The Gershwin set was recorded in Italy, and it is his first full foray into the world of musicals. All the standard Gershwins are here, and other material may be forthcoming about Rodgers and Hart, Cole Porter, etc.

The best overall set is the Duke Ellington four-disc set. This is from one pianist to another, recorded over a number of years, but with one disc done just a few months before Duke died. Hines spent much time scoring the music, but as Ellington wrote for specific people playing specific instruments, it was very difficult to transpose into a piano mode, whether for Ellington's style or for Hines's style. In all senses of the word, it was a great accomplishment; these may be the finest records of Hines's career. The depth of playing relates to concentration and the complexities of the arrangement, some of it almost completely unknown. (The discs cited above have been set off from the other solo Hines piano material because they represent integrative approaches.)

J6.64*   **Keith Jarrett. Solo Concerts: Bremen and Lausanne.** three discs. ECM 1035/7 ST.

Jarrett's lyrical improvisations are usually titleless. The seven pieces on ECM 1035/7 are simply named for the place and date. But, of course, the music is all different, all recorded in an evolutionary manner (on March 20 and July 12, 1973), and nothing appears to be repeated. Of many jazz pianists, Jarrett is an expert at the so-called "varying jazz piano styles," assimilating existing varieties and synthesizing them in his output. Different moods are detected, based on the fragments that drift by almost as throwaways. Both static notes and ostinato figures are high on his list of variations, characterizing the music as lyrical romanticism. Despite a touch of gospel and rhythm 'n' blues (giving particular pieces a harsh and jagged appearance), the rich melodies are enhanced by his sense of timing. Many people feel comfortable with Jarrett's solo outings because he is not searching for the "lost" chord or a new phrase. Thus, every chord and progression sounds strangely familiar and sure.

J6.65   Duke Jordan. Savoy MG 12149.

J6.66   Duke Jordan. Flight to Denmark. SteepleChase Records SCS 1011 (Danish issue).
Jordan was the superb piano accompanist to Charlie Parker. He was strongly influenced by Duke Ellington and Teddy Wilson but then translated their styles to bop music. On the Savoy disc, he is accompanied by Art Blakey and Percy Heath in a trio format. In "Flight to Jordan" and "Forecast," he presented a short sequence of diverse melodic details plus cogent introductions. As a composer, he favors strong rhythms and lyricism. On this Savoy disc is a perfectly marvelous "Summertime," an unaccompanied solo. The SteepleChase album is his first feature recording in over a decade (he has often played an accompanying role). That he had to go to Denmark to do it tells of the situation in the United States. Ed Thigpen is the knowledgeable drummer. This is an extremely lyrical album, featuring some originals and some standards, such as "Here's That Rainy Day," "Green Dolphin Street," and "How Deep Is the Ocean?" All of the selections are extended versions and the total timings are well over 50 minutes.

J6.67*   Jay McShann. McShann's Piano. Capitol C062-80813 (French issue).

J6.68   Jay McShann. The Man from Muskogee. Sackville 3005 (Canada).
McShann's piano is somewhat reminiscent of Count Basie's. They were both performing in the Kansas City area, and both employed riffs in their big bands of the 1940s. McShann has been with a trio or quartet for quite some time now. The 1966 Capitol session finds him in uptempo numbers (the liner notes push the record as being "brilliant rhythm 'n' blues"). Much of the material comprises McShann originals, such as "Dexter Blues," "Vine Street Boogie," "Confessin' the Blues," and "The Man from Muskogee." The Sackville recording, from 1972, shows what McShann can do when he has the options of choosing his own material. The material is wide-ranging, and there are few blues, as McShann would now rather play other forms of music. The group includes long-time drummer Paul Gunther, and Claude Williams, a violinist from McShann's hometown of Muskogee, Oklahoma. Titles include "After You've Gone," Charlie Parker's "Yardbird Suite," Rod McKuen's "I'll Catch the Sun," Ellington's "Things Ain't What They Used to Be," Basie's "Jumping at the Woodside," an uptempo soul version of Ray Charles's "Mary Ann," and a marvelously warm "These Foolish Things." Besides contributing a tune, Williams's violin adds great color to the proceedings, bringing to mind Eddie South and Stuff Smith.

J6.69*   Oscar Peterson. Exclusively for My Friends, v.1/6. six discs. 19-20668, 206696, 206701, 206718 (German issue); Polydor 2384 007 (British issue); MPS 20693(v.6).

J6.70   Oscar Peterson. Jazz History, v.6. two discs. Polydor 2632.006 (British issue).

J6.71*   **Oscar Peterson. Live from Chicago.** Verve V6-8420.

J6.72*   **Oscar Peterson. Night Train.** Verve V6-8538.

J6.73   **Oscar Peterson. Stratford Shakespearean Festival, 1956.** Verve MGV-8024.

Peterson has always been an exceptionally prolific pianist. He served in the house band put together by Norman Granz for Verve-Clef records, for the JATP touring series, and for many vocalists, such as Ella Fitzgerald, Anita O'Day, and Fred Astaire. In addition, since 1951, he has had a trio. Overall, his style is an extension of Art Tatum (q.v.) runs, with embellishments and ornamental notes coupled with a powerful drive. This leads to excitement and precision, except on the solo ballads. As an accompanist, Peterson has good sympathy with soloists and really shines on the "show songs," such as those from Broadway. Sometimes, he can be too perfunctory and just coast, but this same criticism was leveled at Tatum. The first trio had Ray Brown on bass and Herb Ellis on rhythm, and this was the most hectic time for Peterson, as he tried to create a name and style for himself.

Over the five years of their association, the most comprehensively creative album was their last, live from the Canadian Shakespeare Festival. The powerful styles of all three meshed nicely on "52nd Street Theme," a real group effort that jelled. Other selections featured one or the other musicians—such as Peterson's treatment of "Love You Madly." By 1959, Ed Thigpen (drummer) replaced Ellis, and the Peterson trio became a conventional trio. However, his style refined in view of the percussion and became more lyrical and simple. Such was the cohesiveness of "The Trio" that it became known by that name, or else as the "Ray Brown Trio" or "Ed Thigpen Trio" (depending on the tune of the moment). All play better when confronted with an audience, and the 1960 Chicago date proves this with inspired performances of "Chicago," "Sometimes I'm Happy," and "Whisper Not."

Power and relaxation immediately come to mind with the *Night Train* album from 1962. Standards here include "C Jam Blues," "Georgia on My Mind," "Bags' Groove," "Moten Swing," further Ellington pieces, and Peterson's own moving "Hymn to Freedom." This is the best single disc by this particular trio, with techniques emphasizing timing, tempos, and sympathetic—or empathetic—reactions. The double Polydor "History" offers 16 tracks of all phases of Peterson's Verve career, including "Tenderly," "Extended Blues," and "Reunion Blues." The MPS sessions are dramatically different from his previous work. Since 1961, Peterson has been an annual house guest of engineer Hans-Georg Brunner-Schwer. With a small live audience, Peterson performed *Exclusively for My Friends* on a superb piano with superb recording equipment. Most of the time, the sidemen were Sam Jones and Bobby Durham, the next rhythm section that Peterson acquired. Volume one (*Action*) emphasizes the superior recording equipment by closely tracking Brown's rich bass. This is a transition period for Peterson in which he acquires a warmer tone, logic, and a deeper sensitivity to dynamics. Slow tempi are emphasized in "Like Someone to Love," "Easy Walker," and "Tin Tin Deo." Volume two (*Girl Talk*) shows the piano gaining dominance in the trio format with the departure of Brown and Thigpen. Volume three (*The Way I Really Play*) is the best of the set, with a varied program including waltzes ("Gravy Waltz"), blues with double-timing and cross-rhythms, and standards ("Satin Doll").

Volume four (*My Favorite Instrument*) is Peterson's best record ever, one of
the greatest solo piano performances in history and comparable only to Earl Hines's
works. Every jazz style is covered, including Tatumesque runs in "Someone to
Watch Over Me," stride in Monk's "Lulu's Back in Town," stomp in "Perdido,"
ballads in "Little Girl Blue," and raw energy in "Bye Bye Blackbird." Every track is
a masterpiece. Volumes five (*Mellow Mood*) and six (*Travellin' On*) feature Peterson's most energetic and frenetic playing, especially on "In a Mellotone," "Green
Dolphin Street," the climax on "Sometimes I'm Happy," the introspection of
"Emily," (also recorded by Bill Evans), the Latin qualities of "Quiet Nights"
or "Nica's Dream," and Benny Carter's "When Lights Are Low."

J6.74*   **Willie "The Lion" Smith. Memoirs.** two discs. RCA LSP 6016.

J6.75   **Willie "The Lion" Smith. Memorial.** two discs. Vogue VJD 501/1-2
         (French issue).

J6.76*   **Willie "The Lion" Smith and Don Ewell. Grand Piano Duets.** Sack-
         ville 2004 (Canadian issue).
         "The Lion" was a master of the stride piano as found in New York City. His
earliest recordings were with small groups, but some of his early piano solo efforts
were deemed unsatisfactory because the stride heyday was over, and the producers
had control of the material. Thus, while in France in 1949-1950, he was at last able
to record the material to which he had the greatest affinity (including his own
compositions such as "Portrait of the Duke," "Cuttin' Out," "Relaxin'," "Con-
trary Motions," and "Late Hours"). Standards, with Buck Clayton and Claude Luter
(the French clarinetist), include "Darktown Strutter's Ball," "Nagasaki," "Ain't
Misbehavin'," and "Stormy Weather." Stomping solos included "Charleston" and
"Carolina Shout." His harmonic patterns and rubato come forth again on the
double RCA set, which involves talking, singing, and playing. He recalled the histor-
ic pre-World War I days to the Harlem nightclubs of the 1930s. Here are almost
two hours of a priceless documentary of life on the seamy side. Along the way,
he comments on vaudeville, Eubie Blake, James P. Johnson, Fats Waller, Louis
Armstrong, Duke Ellington (who proclaimed "The Lion" as a heavy influence on
himself), and the Ziegfeld Follies. Musical tributes are included, such as "Blue
Skies," "Nagasaki," "Chevy Chase," "Memories of You," plus a generous taste of
his own compositions, in which there are pleasant blends of ragtime and stride piano.
The duet set with Ewell, the greatest living white pianist in the stride school, reveals
further innovations. There are not too many duet or trio recordings available, except
for the boogie woogie recordings, yet this was a common form in bands and in rent
parties. "Everybody Loves My Baby," and "Keepin' Out of Mischief Now" are but
two highlights out of many.

J6.77   **Jess Stacy. Piano Solos.** Swaggie S1248 (Australian issue).
         Stacy has largely been unappreciated in jazz. Swing and a crisp touch are his
hallmarks, with a few shadings of James P. Johnson. He is certainly one of the
better swing pianists. His best known solo occurs in the 1938 Benny Goodman
Carnegie Hall concert, near the end of "Sing, Sing, Sing," in which he attempts to
summarize all of the many, long, and varied solos that had preceded him in this
lengthy number. The Swaggie label has collated a great deal of material spanning

21 years, including his first trio outing, "Barrelhouse" and "The World Is Waiting for the Sunrise," both masterpieces of the swing idiom. At the same time, he recorded "In the Dark Flashes," two introspective pieces written by Bix Beiderbecke. The balance of the album comes from 1951 and 1956 sessions (the latter a private tape). The eight 1951 tracks are a definite highlight, with George Van Eps on guitar and Nick Fatool on drums. Note "Fascinating Rhythm" and "Back Home Again in Indiana."

J6.78   **McCoy Tyner. Sahara.** Milestone M9039.

J6.79   **McCoy Tyner. Time for Tyner.** Blue Note BST 84307.
Tyner came to prominence while spending six years as John Coltrane's pianist. He quickly became a major force in improvisational piano, as Coltrane would only feed him a set of changes, and Tyner had to be fleet of mind. He solved this problem by experimenting with modes that, in turn, influenced many other pianists. Leaving Coltrane in 1965 to strike out on his own, Tyner further developed his idea of clusters of sound that related to both clarity and privacy. His chord patterns are very introspective, much like Bill Evans's in this respect, and his exceptional sense of form allows him to build his own structures for any tune. In many respects, he is better off as a soloist, but he lacks the momentum for sustained drives. Drummer Mouzon and bassist Calvin Hill make strong contributions here, particularly on *Sahara.*

J6.80   **Mal Waldron. Impressions.** Prestige PR 7824.
Pianist Waldron, who worked with Billie Holiday during the last three years of her life, was strongly influenced by Powell in the bop idiom. This disc is one of his best efforts, but it does come from his earlier recording career. Much of his later work has simply been a variation of this disc, but he was instrumental in showing the way for such pianists as Keith Jarrett and Chick Corea. His style (with no real devices) is simply to project a series of rhythmic clusters onto each other, with no gaps for breathing or otherwise pausing. The trio here, dealing with an original Waldron suite that is mainly circular in content and without melody, is completely filled with the tension that comes with layering and no relief. Not a relaxing record.

J6.81   **Mary Lou Williams. Zoning.** Mary Records M 103.
Mary Lou Williams played piano for the Andy Kirk band (see entry J4.70) and also handled many of the arrangements. She was solidly in the Kansas City mould, contributing many uptempo tunes; yet, she was also advanced for her time and stayed in the forefront of jazz music. During the 1930s, she actually employed many bop themes in her work (except they were not called "bop" at that time), and later, she even composed bop music, such as "In the Land of Oh-Bla-Da" for Dizzy Gillespie and a reworking of the "Blue Skies" theme for Ellington, calling it "Trumpet No End." Over the years, she has been a good steady composer of mood and thematic suites. Of course, she is the most well-known woman in jazz. Of late, she has turned to religion and has composed many masses and religiously inspired jazz works. She has also been employing a restless style in her piano wanderings (for her earlier works, see the anthologies *Kansas City Jazz* [MCA Decca DL 8044] and *Kings and Queens of Ivory*, volume 1 [MCA 510.090]). But, being religiously inspired, she now seeks interpretation in her playing. All the music here is ceaseless

and active, in a probing sense. Different rhythm accompaniment (drums and/or bass and/or congas and/or another piano) accentuate the tension of her new lifestyle. Inspiration is the keynote, and perhaps it is significant that the first selection is entitled "Intermission."

Boogie Woogie

J6.82*   **Boogie Woogie Man.** RCA 730.561 (French issue).

J6.83*   **Boogie Woogie Trio.** Storyville 670.184 (Danish issue).

J6.84*   **Library of Congress Sessions.** Jazz Piano JP 5003 (Danish issue).
      The crowning achievements of the boogie woogie period were the series of trio performances by Albert Ammons, Pete Johnson, and Meade Lux Lewis; the impact and power of these fast-moving giants were enormous. The Jazz Piano issue comes from performances given at the Library of Congress, while the Storyville issue is derived from the Sherman Hotel in 1939. These were all broadcast over NBC, and the 15 selections here show the powerhouse style of cascading notes that thundered forth from the pianos (was there really any need for the radio's carrier wave?). Typical performances include "Pinetop Blues," a salute to Pinetop Smith (who created the term "boogie woogie"), "St. Louis Blues," "Shout for Joy," and "Boogie Woogie Prayer." The RCA set consists of commercial recordings by Albert Ammons and Pete Johnson, eight tunes written by both of them, and masterful gems of improvisation. Some titles are "Walkin' the Boogie," "Movin' the Boogie," "Cuttin' the Boogie," and "Foot Pedal Boogie." The other eight selections belong to Jimmy Yancey, an equally proficient barrelhouse and boogie performer (see items J6.96-J6.98) who was also in the blues tradition. His contributions included "35th and Dearborn," "Death Letter Blues," and "State Street Special."

J6.85   **They All Played Big Band Boogie.** Bandstand BS 7107.

J6.86   **Twenty-Nine Boogie Woogie Originaux.** two discs. RCA FXM2-7073 (French issue).
      Boogie woogie was advanced stride piano music, with the eight beats to the bar left-hand theme. In its transposition to "big band," it lost its verve but did acquire "swing." The Bandstand issue allows the listener to compare 15 different bands as originally recorded in 1938 through 1940. Typical titles include "Horse 'n' Boogie," "Overnight Hop," "Beat Me Daddy," "Boogie Woogie Blues," and "Wiggle Woggle," as performed by Basie, Herman, Krupa, Crosby, Will Bradley, Larry Clinton, Erskine Hawkins, and A. Lyman. The 29 selections on the French RCA set contrast the piano versions of Albert Ammons, Pete Johnson, Jimmy Yancey, Speckled Red, Big Maceo, Little Brother Montgomery, Fats Waller, Meade Lux Lewis, Roosevelt Sykes, and Memphis Slim with the orchestras of Bob Zurke, Sidney Bechet, Count Basie, Earl Hines, and Tommy Dorsey.

J6.87*   **Albert Ammons.** Boogie Woogie BW 1001.

J6.88　　**Albert Ammons. The Boogie Rocks.** Jackson 1213 (German issue).
Ammons was the most consistent of the boogie woogie pianists, and his work
has been noted elsewhere on various anthologies. These two discs present him in
small band settings, still rocking and boogieing. The first disc has seven tracks from
1939 and 1944, all piano solos, and includes "Boogie Rocks" and "Shout for
Joy"; the second side has small group performances from 1936 (with Guy Kelly on
trumpet on such as "Mile-or-Mo-Bird Rag") and from 1946. The Jackson album
covers from 1944 through 1949, with such performers as Hot Lips Page, Vic Dickenson, and Don Byas, as in "Jammin' the Boogie" and "Bottoms Up."

J6.89　　**Barrelhouse Blues and Boogie Woogie. v.1/2.** two discs. Storyville
　　　　　671.155/183 (Danish issue).

J6.90　　**Boogie Woogie Greatest Hits.** Boogie Woogie BW1000.

J6.91*　　**The Original Boogie Woogie Piano Giants.** Columbia KC 32708.
Boogie woogie is an uptempo form of piano blues, developing from the rough
barrelhouse music that was so common in southern bars and lumber camps during
the early part of this century. Its thumping is mainly an attempt to be heard over
the usually raucous noise that occurred in such drinking spots. The main characteristic of the style is a simple left hand bass pattern, eight beats to the bar. The
earliest performers in the style were Cow Cow Davenport, Jimmy Yancey, and
Pinetop Smith. The latter's 1929 recording of "Pinetop's Boogie Woogie" contained
the first recorded mention of the term, and up to that time "boogie" had the sexual
connotation later referred to as "rock and roll." It was Pinetop's recording that contained the classic line, "see that girl with the red dress on," later to crop up in many
songs right through to Ray Charles. The second line—"she boogied all night long"—
goes on in reference to sexual performance. Often, lyrics are inserted into such
songs, but the very nature of the stomping inhibits playing and singing together;
thus, a stop-time talking format was devised, with the lyrics dropped in at appropriate moments. A one-man show developed, with blues shouting and foot stomping. At the same time, depending on the situation (such as a rent party), different
moods and tempos evolved to form distinct but many patterns.
　　Another epic recording was Meade Lux Lewis's "Honky Tonk Train Blues"
(1927 and 1935), which imitated a steam locomotive and showed his great powers.
His "Yancey Special" was a tribute to Jimmy Yancey, an early influence. Yancey
was the most dextrous of the boogie woogie pianists, also being a master of the
slow blues with a left hand that would come up with notes in unexpected places.
The quickness and variety of boogie woogie fit perfectly into the blues idiom, as
the rapidity of the notes was equivalent to the bent notes on a guitar. The summit
of boogie expression was the trio of Ammons, Johnson, and Lewis (see entries
J6.82-J6.84). They rode to success on the tail of the swing jazz craze, peaking by
1940. After that, there was a short-lived success for commercial boogie woogie
in the 1940s, it being recorded by many of the big swing bands as a logical extension
of swing music. Tommy Dorsey's "Boogie Woogie" and Glenn Miller's "Beat Me
Daddy, Eight to the Bar" were monster successes, but these fully orchestrated creations soon ran their course. Although the pianistic term "boogie woogie" is the
source of the current 1970s' shout "Let's Boogie!," the meaning is actually similar

to "Let's Rock!" and thus to sexual connotations, *not* to an eight to the bar pattern.

The Boogie Woogie label is devoted to that genre, and its first offering presents the most popular selections from the past (including the tracks mentioned above). Other performers, not usually known for boogie, include Art Hodes, Louis Jordan ("Choo Choo Chi Boogie"), Joe Sullivan, and Bob Zurke. The Columbia 1938-1941 set (described in the rhythm 'n' blues section of *Black Music*) contains items from the Trio—Lewis, Ammons, and Johnson as well as Champion Jack Dupree and some small group combos led by Pete Johnson with Joe Turner vocals. The Storyville set is mostly 1960-1965 material, from Champion Jack Dupree, Memphis Slim, Speckled Red, Henry Brown, and Roosevelt Sykes, but it is also interesting for some earlier tracks from Ammons, Johnson and Lewis (1939), Lewis (1944), Dink Johnson (1947), and Jimmy Yancey (1950).

J6.92   **Pete Johnson. Boogie Woogie.** BW1003.

J6.93*   **Pete Johnson. Master of Blues and Boogie Woogie, v.1/2.** two discs. Oldie Blues OL 2801 and 2806 (Dutch issues).

The 45 tracks here come from a variety of sources and show Johnson in various configurations. Side one of the first Dutch reissue has eight items from a February 17, 1944, session, all piano solos in the boogie woogie mould. The other seven boogies, from a wide range of sources including W. C. Handy, Jimmy Yancey, and traditional material, are from 1946, 1947, and 1948. Along in most cases are Hot Lips Page, Clyde Bernhardt, Budd Johnson, Johnny Rogers, and Roy Milton. At this point, the great duos with Joe Turner's vocals and Johnson's piano, and the Ammons-Lewis-Johnson trio for boogie woogie efforts were long past. The second Dutch set is similarly arranged, but from two years only, 1939 and 1947. In his time, Johnson made over 200 recordings.

The stomping left hand produced incredibly rich rhythms, but Pete Johnson was the unsurpassed master of the moody slow blues idiom as well. His melodic inventiveness and colorful expression produced a great number of flawless gems. His right hand improvisation was not merely an automatic repetition but also a seemingly endless series of melodic changes. The *Boogie Woogie* record has nine of his solo efforts, plus two with Joe Turner and three with a small group that included Hot Lips Page on trumpet.

J6.94*   **Meade Lux Lewis.** Boogie Woogie BW1002.

Lewis was famous for his "Honky Tonk Train Blues" in the boogie woogie idiom; he was also a proficient member of the Ammons-Lewis-Johnson trio. In 1929, he recorded his train blues, a rolling imitation of a steam engine, and it soon became a classic. He devoted "Yancey Special" to Jimmy Yancey, another boogie-blues pianist, and this led to Yancey's resurgence from oblivion. He was the powerhouse behind the trio, pumping out great strength through his huge arms. Unfortunately, he was a "one genre" performer and never succeeded with small groups as Johnson or Ammons did. Other selections here include "Bear Cat Crawl," "Deep Fives," and "Boogie Woogie Prayer [parts one and two] " with Ammons and Johnson.

J6.95   **Sammy Price. Boogie Woogie and Kansas City Jazz.** Musidisc 30
CV 1230 (French issue).
Price was a latecomer to the swing craze of boogie woogie, but he was a good
interpreter nevertheless. He backed up many singers in the thirties and forties for
blues labels, and then began to lead his own group in the 1940s. He continues to
play and perform in the boogie idiom, and this disc features him with a group that
included Peanuts Holland. The six selections are fairly long, and emphasize the
Southwestern character of his music (he was born in Texas), as in "Kansas City
Blues" and "Swingin' Kansas City Style." One of the better cuts here is "Gotta
Boogie, Gotta Woogie."

J6.96*   **Jimmy Yancey. v.1/2.** two discs. Gannet GEN 5136/7.

J6.97   **Jimmy Yancey. Chicago Piano.** Atlantic SD 7229.

J6.98*   **Jimmy Yancey. Pitchin' Boogie.** Swaggie S1235 (Australian issue).
More than any of the other boogie woogie artists, Yancey was very deep into
a blues bag, and indeed, if one must categorize his music, it would be to call it
"stomps." He first began to record in 1939, and his sessions for RCA (see item
J6.82) can be regarded as masterpieces of a vigorous style. His best performances
were for the Session label, now found on the Gannet label, such as "How Long
Blues," "Yancey Special," "At the Window," "Death Letter Blues," and "Sweet
Patootie." A further session in 1950 led to the material on the Swaggie disc, while
the Atlantic has four vocals by Mama Yancey. This Patter record is a culmination
of his career. It has salutes to Albert Ammons and Pinetop Smith, and a pensive
atmosphere which might be taken as a premonition of his death from diabetes a
mere two months later. He had a profound effect on rhythm 'n' blues.

Guitar

J6.99   **Herb Ellis. Jazz/Concord.** Concord Jazz CJS 1.

J6.100   **Herb Ellis. Seven, Come Eleven.** Concord Jazz CJS 2.
Ellis was the guitarist with Oscar Peterson's drummer-less trio, 1953-1958.
During this stay, he performed a good many solos, highlighting the blues. His main
strength lies in being an accompanist, and on the above two discs (recorded in 1972
and 1973), he is partnered with an equally stunning guitarist—Joe Pass. Together
the duo set some new heights to scale in the world of jazz guitar performances.
The quartet included Jake Hanna on drums and Ray Brown on bass (who was also
with Peterson at the same time as Ellis). Duos are rather unique in jazz. Since the
Eddie Lang-Lonnie Johnson collaboration in the late 1920s, there had been none
of outstanding note. Indeed, more duos have found their way into blues, folk, and
country music (and the Lang-Johnson sessions were mostly blues).
Ellis is a Texan, with a heavy blues influence. Pass is from New Jersey, and
performs different, more sophisticated material in a more lyrical sense. However,
in collaboration, they make "sweet music," with interwoven guitar lines, shifting
from melodic lead to backup accompaniment at will, or even finger picking
together in a competitive spirit. The only consensus they had was in the format.

Ellis, as nominal leader, would begin on lead with Pass on rhythm, and then they would switch after a number of choruses. Sometimes they would break from the bass and drummer to emerge in cutting sessions and sparring, until Brown decided that they had had enough, whereupon he would cue the beginning of the ride-out choruses. The quartet was extremely tight-knit. Selections, all recorded live at concerts, contain reworked standards, such as "Look for the Silver Lining" (featuring stop-time, uptempo movements, and brilliant counterpoint), "Shadow of Your Smile," "Honeysuckle Rose," "Georgia," "Love for Sale," some Ellingtonia (such as "In a Mellotone," "Prelude to a Kiss," and "Perdido"), and of course, improvised originals. Every guitar technique ever developed is attempted (except for the obvious fuzz tones and distortion from the rock world) in this superb set of electric guitar duos.

J6.101*   **Barney Kessel. RCA 730.710 (French issue).**

J6.102   **Barney Kessel. Feeling Free.** Contemporary S7618.

J6.103   **Barney Kessel. Guitarra.** RCA Camden CAS 2404.

J6.104   **Barney Kessel. Swingin' Party at Contemporary.** Contemporary S7613.

J6.105   **Barney Kessel and Stephane Grappelli. I Remember Django.** Black Lion BL 105.

J6.106*   **Barney Kessel. Limehouse Blues.** Black Lion BL 173.

J6.107*   **Barney Kessel and Red Mitchell. Two Way Conversation.** Sonet SLP 2547 (Swedish issue).

Guitarist Kessel has been the most prolific musician from the 1940s through the early sixties. A disciple of Charlie Christian, he has other talents that he had put to good use. He recorded with Charlie Parker on the 1947 Dial sessions; he joined the Oscar Peterson trio in the early 1950s; he became house guitarist for Verve and served with Parker once again; he has done stage and film work, preferring not to travel at that point in his life. In 1960, he became more assertive, producing the hard drive of the *Swingin' Party*. His regular quartet tackled Clifford Brown's epic "Joy Spring," as well as Parker's "Now's the Time" and Milt Jackson's "Bluesology." But this was a mere break in the routine.

All the other albums here (except the Sonet) were recorded in 1969, just before and during a trip to Europe. On these discs, he consolidated several ideas that had been brewing for awhile, including some improvisations that he could not play again unless he listened to the original records. The Contemporary S7818 presents a mixture of bop and Kessel originals, with Bobby Hutcherson on vibes and Elvin Jones on drums. "The Sounds of Silence" and "This Guy's in Love with You" are balanced by the gutsy swing and single note playing of Kessel as he works out his new material.

In Europe, at two monster sessions, he created his major works. In Rome, in May, with Italian rhythm, he fashioned a set of unique originals for RCA, mostly in a Latin vein. In Paris, in June, for Black Lion, he recreated the Reinhardt swing era with Grappelli. Never have there been two contrasting sessions within such a short time span. The Kessel-Grappelli sets tear the place apart with uptempo versions of "It Don't Mean a Thing If It Ain't Got That Swing," "Tea for Two," "Limehouse Blues," "How High the Moon," "Undecided," "Willow Weep for Me," "Honeysuckle Rose," "I Can't Get Started," "It's Only a Paper Moon," and so forth, all these being classics from the swing era. On the majority of the tunes, the format is a simple statement of the melody, with both participants dueting, and then breaking apart for improvisations and chasing choruses, reaching climax after climax as both try to out-do each other before the final eight bars. In a more thoughtful vein of great beauty, the Sonet album presents a simple duo with no accompaniment from 1973, a mixture of pop and originals as the strings "talk" to each other. Simple but stunning interpretations follow "Killing Me Softly with His Song," "Alone Again (Naturally)," "Wave," and "Summertime." Great empathy exists between these two performers.

J6.108*   **Wes Montgomery. While We're Young.** two discs. Milestone M47003.
The tracks here are all that jazz listeners have available from Montgomery's jazz period—1960 and 1961. Originally out on Riverside 320 and 382, the selections include superb rhythm accompaniment only, in a quartet session with Tommy Flanagan (especially on the first disc, his most electrifying work). The most outstanding item is probably the dazzling "While We're Young" guitar solo. Montgomery never employed a pick. Instead, he used his thumb, like Barney Kessel, and doubled the octaves or block chords as the three-fingered Reinhardt did. With Verve, his commercial career expanded while his music became more slick.

J6.109   **Django Reinhardt.** five discs. Vogue COF 03 (French issue).

J6.110*   **Django Reinhardt. Best.** Capitol T 10457.

J6.111*   **Django Reinhardt. Legendary.** EMI Odeon CLP 1817 (British issue).

J6.112*   **Django Reinhardt. Swing '35-'39.** Decca Eclipse ECM 2051 (British issue).

J6.113*   **Django Reinhardt and Stephane Grappelli.** Ace of Clubs ACL 1158 (British issue).
Reinhardt was a guitar virtuoso, a gypsy who happened to play in the jazz idiom at the right place and right time. He played his own way and his own style, characterized by a three-finger method (resulting from a fire that paralyzed two fingers) of picking. He evolved a staggering technique unsurpassed to this day. In 1934, he formed the Quintet of the Hot Club of France, the first string quintet in jazz, featuring the solos of Reinhardt and Stephane Grappelli (on violin). This was one of the unique contributions that Europe made to jazz. They soon became famous outside of France, prodded on by the enormous Reinhardt talent—his mastery of the guitar, his subtle nuances, techniques, and musical imagination. The ensemble passages are basically rhythmic, without being swinging, and the unit comes to life during either the guitar or violin solos.
Scattered throughout these nine discs, surprisingly with no duplications, are 102 tracks that span 1934 through 1947 (with one from a broadcast in 1951) and these represent some of the swingiest jazz ever recorded. The widest survey

is the Vogue, with 12 tracks from 1934-1935 (his earliest recordings), and the balance from 1947. The others are from 1935-1939. Personnel changed throughout the years in the backing groups, but Reinhardt and Grappelli were the mainstays. Some solos, such as "Honeysuckle Rose" and "Sweet Georgia Brown," involve octave playing, a technique that Wes Montgomery borrowed 25 years later. Grappelli is a strong technician who can vary his moods at whim, from sad and slow to a lark's singing. With him, Reinhardt was always emotional. Typical tracks here include jazz standards ("Dinah," "Lady Be Good," "Tiger Rag," "I Got Rhythm," St. Louis Blues") and originals, which soon became standards ("Billets Doux," "Swing '39," "Souvenirs," "Daphne," "Nuages," "Vendredi 13," etc.). Throughout all these, it is plainly evident that they were not just an imitation of American jazz in either instrumentation or ideas. They were French, yet they still were jazz.

CLP 1817 is interesting for the sake of variety. Violinist Eddie South was added, for a twin fiddle effect on "Daphne"; several tracks are duets, with Grappelli and Reinhardt (the former playing piano and violin), or Reinhardt and Vola, his bassist (and here the octaval effect is clearly heard), while "Naguine" and "Echoes of Spain" are guitar solos. During the War, Reinhardt went underground, and three tracks on CLP 1817 highlight his early musical activities during the War. Grappelli was in London, and Reinhardt added Hubert Rostaing's clarinet, which really made the unit swing. In the late thirties, Reinhardt's quintet was the first jazz group to make a trans-Atlantic broadcast, and this gave him wider exposure to American audiences. After the War, Grappelli joined for the occasional session to 1947.

J6.114*   **Django Reinhardt. Django Rhythm.** Swaggie S1251 (Australian issue).

J6.115*   **Django Reinhardt. Django Swing.** Swaggie S1252 (Australian issue).

J6.116*   **Django Reinhardt. Paris, 1945.** CBS 63052 (French issue).
Reinhardt's most jazz-oriented work can be found on these three discs. The Swaggies cover 1935-1939, and Reinhardt plays here with American jazz men who happened to be in Europe (Rex Stewart, Dicky Wells, Coleman Hawkins, Benny Carter, Eddie South, Barney Bigard, and Bill Coleman). Everybody was up for these sessions, and notable tracks include the 1935 Hawkins quintet with Grappelli on a simply superb "Stardust," six stunning Dicky Wells tracks (perhaps his best performances with "Bugle Call Rag," "I Got Rhythm," "Sweet Sue, Just You," et al.), five Rex Stewart combos that produced the masterpiece "Finesse," and four duets and trios between Eddie South and Reinhardt in a rare display of tremendous empathy. In the spring of 1945, Paris was waiting for Glenn Miller to arrive to lead his band. He never came, and shortly afterwards, members of his band (Peanuts Hucko, Mel Powell, Ray McKinley, et al.) recorded with Reinhardt in another stirring session of American jazz, including "Stompin' at the Savoy," "After You've Gone," "China Boy," and "Sugar."

J6.117   **Django Reinhardt. v.1/3.** three discs. RCA 730.596, 731.042, and
          731.069 (French issue).

J6.118   **Django Reinhardt. Django in Rome, 1949-1950.** Parlophone PCS7146
          (British issue).

J6.119   **Django Reinhardt. Together Again.** World Record Club ST 1004
(British issue).
These five discs are all derived from the famous Rome sessions. In 1949,
Grappelli and Reinhardt recorded with an Italian rhythm section for a private session. This was their last time together. They were very inspired, and selections
included such modern songs as "It's Only a Paper Moon," "All the Things You
Are," "Lover Man," and "Stormy Weather," as well as jazz standards, early joint
compositions, new compositions (such as "Artillerie Lourde" and "Micro"), some
classical themes ("Bolero," "Pathétique"), and even a bop number—"Hot House,"
contained within the title "What Is This Thing Called Love?" Some 14 months
later, Reinhardt went to Rome again, this time with André Ekyan on alto sax and
clarinet. They recorded swinging selections reminiscent of wartime France, when a
clarinet was used to replace Grappelli. The big difference is that Reinhardt was now
using an *electric* guitar for crisper rhythms. Again, the types of songs remained the
same as in 1949.

VOCALS

J6.120*   **Billie Holiday. Best.** Verve V6-8808.

J6.121*   **Billie Holiday. Golden Years, v.1/2.** six discs. Columbia C3L 21 and
40.

J6.122*   **Billie Holiday. Story.** two discs. MCA 2-4006.

J6.123*   **Billie Holiday. Strange Fruit.** Atlantic SD1614.
In the opinion of many, "Lady Day" was the only successful vocalist that jazz
produced. Hers was a true jazz idiom. Her actions were intuitive rather than logical,
as jazz is; her commitment was to emotion and subjectivity. A non-returnable part
of Billie Holiday went into each and every song. She was influenced by the classic
blues singers, such as Bessie Smith and Lester Young (whose method of phrasing
was to lag behind the rest of the band). In turn, she had impact on all vocalists
after her, including Frank Sinatra. She rarely sang the blues herself, performing
popular material that was given her to record, yet she turned these tunes and other
trite items into personal statements that foreshadowed Charlie Parker in style.
Occasionally, she would accent the tune right on top of the beats for added
prominence.
Her recorded work falls neatly into about four periods. First, the Columbia
sets contain most of her recordings with Teddy Wilson, plus the discs for OKeh,
Vocalion, and Brunswick. These were her first recordings (from 1933 through
1939), beginning with some minor Goodman appearances, such as "Riffin' the
Scotch." The small group context fit her best, and with Teddy Wilson's jazzmen
(Roy Eldridge, Lester Young, Buck Clayton, Ben Webster, Johnny Hodges), she
flourished. These have now assumed legendary proportions, fixing definitive jazz
treatments of such standards as "These Foolish Things," "Pennies from Heaven,"
"I Can't Give You Anything But Love," "When You're Smiling," etc. Along with
members of the Count Basie band and others such as Red Allen, Buster Bailey,
Bunny Berigan, Chu Berry, Harry Carney, Cozy Cole, Krupa, Shaw, Teagarden—

literally anyone who was involved with jazz—Holiday made the 96 tracks on these two Columbia sets, as well as material found on Teddy Wilson sets or gap-closing anthologies.

By 1940, Holiday became attached to the cocktail club circuit and demanded a more full orchestra of ten or even more pieces. In 1942, she concluded her Columbia contract. Of all the hundred-plus tracks, the most successful were in 1937-1938 with Lester Young. Together, their similar approach led to a great deal of empathy and integration of voice and saxophone. They were literally made for each other. Each box set has a lavish 20-page booklet with text by Leonard Feather, photographs, and full discography.

The Atlantic set combines two sessions from five years apart (1939 and 1944), made for the Commodore Music Shop. Although under contract to Columbia in 1939, she wanted to record the controversial "Strange Fruit" (about Southern lynchings), which Columbia did not want but allowed her to do for another company. From these two sessions, with Eddie Heywood arrangements, came important selections such as "Lover Come Back to Me," "Embraceable You," and "My Old Flame."

From 1944-1950, Billie recorded for Decca, with arrangements largely by Bob Haggart, Camarata, and Sy Oliver. The double set features 24 selections from the entire period, with notes abstracted from her autobiography. Decca tried to make her over into a "popular" singer; hence, much of the material was over-arranged, and most of the studio musicians were white. Despite the conceptualizations here, Billie still shines, and it is all to her credit, through "Don't Explain," "Ain't Nobody's Business If I Do," "Lover Man," "Solitude," and "God Bless the Child." Her personal life during the 1940s was chaotic and bore directly on her attitude toward singing: as long as she had the security of the large band, she could perform. She fell before the white entertainer "strings" syndrome.

From 1952-1957, she worked with Norman Granz for Verve, and he put her back into the small group configuration. But it was too late, for her magic was gone, and most of what remained was a tired, loose, scratchy voice that still retained the timing and phrasing. Notable musicians included Harry Edison, Ben Webster, Benny Carter, and Charlie Shavers, performing "Travelin' Light," "I Thought about You," and "Willow Weep for Me."

J6.124   **Lambert, Hendricks and Ross. The Best.** Columbia C 32911.

Previously titled "The Hottest New Group in Jazz," this set is really a culmination of the previous fifty years of jazz history. Now and again, a few scat vocals would appear in jazz, being led by Louis Armstrong, Ella Fitzgerald, and some of the jump blues performers. With bebop, the vocal texture of jazz music became more evident. All three singers here—Jon Hendricks, Annie Ross, and Dave Lambert—associated themselves with bebop. Lambert made appearances with Parker and even recorded with him. He recorded some Keynote records with Buddy Stewart, employing scat singing. Hendricks also scatted with Parker. Annie Ross of Britain was transcribing Wardell Gray saxophone solos to vocal passages, such as "Twisted" (heard on this disc), "Farmer's Market" and "Jackie." Together, the trio has worked on Basie tunes, recorded with Brubeck, Armstrong, and Carmen McRae, and generally influenced other scat singing groups, such as Jackie and Roy Kral and the Ward Swingle Singers. This album includes the definitive version of Bobby Timmons's "Moanin' " (after the Blakey interpretation), "Sermonette" from

Cannonball Adderley, and a short version of "Summertime," based on the Miles Davis and Gil Evans recording. The three singers make good use of countermelodies and authentically reproduce the texture of bop.

POP JAZZ

J6.125*   **The Jazz/Rock/Soul Project: Great Performances That Paved the Way for Today's Pop Sound.** Riverside RS 3048.
This interesting compilation again shows the tremendous resources that can be drawn from past music. When the album came out, it was devoted to the "new" sound; in the 1970s, that sound would be called "funk," and indeed, every single cut on this album is important for determining that funk. There is Mongo Santamaria performing Herbie Hancock's "Watermelon Man," and having better success with it than Hancock did; the late Cannonball Adderley doing "This Here," the song from the fertile, creative mind of the late Bobby Timmons (who also composed "Moanin'," heard here with Wes Montgomery); Nat Adderley performs the "Work Song"; Cannonball returns for "African Waltz." This music from the early sixties laid stress on electricity and amplification, and after arriving at the simplistic rhythms and beats, produced gut songs of an uptempo jazz, with repetitive riffs that bordered between soul and rock. This is an important disc for showing influences.

J6.126*   **Cannonball Adderley. The Best of Cannonball Adderley.** Capitol SKAO 2939.
Julian "Cannonball" Adderley did proficient alto work for 20 years (1955-1975). His manner is heavy in stylization, in settings that have had wide popular appeal, and the six extended tracks here are testament to his wide base. Recording for Riverside, Capitol, and Milestone/Fantasy with the same producers (either Orrin Keepnews or David Axelrod), Adderley always preferred a "semi-live" setting with many friends in the recording studios. His uptempo performances emphasized eclectic approaches to whatever was the "in" music of the time, eventually merging into a jazz-soul form. His Capitol period was the highest in terms of popular appeal, and the best of these was "Jive Samba," the "Work Song," Joe Zawinul's "Mercy, Mercy, Mercy," and "Dat Dere." His other success, "Preacher Man," is unfortunately not available on this compilation.

J6.127   **Billy Cobham. Spectrum.** Atlantic SD 7268.
This record stresses heavy percussive drumming, for Cobham was the rock-steady ace drummer of the Mahavishnu Orchestra and a super-session man. On this, his first solo outing, he has written and produced all the material. His musical genre is eclectic, with the rock "Quadrant 4," the jazz "Searching for the Right Door/ Spectrum," and the electronic (Moog) other-worldly "Stratus." The entire job was finished within four days of recording, for as Cobham says: "I feel the music getting better and better, and just want to get there as fast as I can." A wide range of musicians and instruments are deployed (this is becoming more common in both modern jazz and rock), including pianist Jan Hammer (once with John McLaughlin), bassist Lee Sklar, and guitarist Tommy Bolin. They all cook in the Mahavishnu vein

and quite successfully. Two tracks feature the horns of Joe Farrell and Jimmy Owens. Unfortunately, in these pieces, Ron Carter's acoustic bass gets lost in the mixdown.

J6.128*   **Chick Corea. Inner Space.** two discs. Atlantic SD2-305.

J6.129   **Chick Corea. Light As a Feather.** Polydor PD 5525.

J6.130*   **Chick Corea. Piano Improvisations, v.1/3.** three discs. ECM 1014/6.
    Chick Corea was a pianist in the Miles Davis group (among his many other accomplishments). He has also been a leader in the "pretty music" school, a sort of reaction against atonality. Romanticism notwithstanding, the Atlantic issue is comprised of Tynerish material, with short melodic lines, shifting chords, and strong harmonies expressed as chamber jazz, Latin American music, ballads, and some frankly modern jazz. The entire conception is strong on rhythmic ideas. "Tones for Joan's Bones" is a contemplative piece with a superb bass solo by Steve Swallow; "Trio for Flute, Bassoon and Piano" is a coy attempt at classicism, and it features Hubert Laws on flute (drawn off his *Laws Cause* Atlantic album). The Polydor album is strictly popular, romantic material, drawn for a large audience. It introduced bassist Stanley Clarke as a force to be reckoned with in the jazz world, and the whole disc is summed up by the name of the group (and its subsequent recordings): Return to Forever. As a viable whole, the piano solos on ECM show a further excursion into soft ballads, but with the Tyner block chording. It is interesting to compare these discs with the triple set by Keith Jarrett (J6.64).

J6.131*   **Miles Davis. Bitches Brew.** two discs. Columbia GP 26.

J6.132   **Miles Davis. In a Silent Way.** Columbia PC 9875.

J6.133   **Miles Davis. Miles Smiles.** Columbia PC 6401.

J6.134   **Miles Davis. Nefertiti.** Columbia PC 9594.
    Davis had a relatively dry period (1961-1964) after Coltrane left and before Wayne Shorter arrived. After 1965, extending modes and scales with a blending of mid-sixties rock and soul sounds produced the first jazz-rock fusion, and this period found a number of technical innovations from Davis. First, he added the color of 8 beats to the bar from Afro-soul music. Second, he employed the electric fretted bass for a closed spacing of the notes, and he began to use the piano more than before, turning to the electric piano (first introduced to soul by Ray Charles on "What'd I Say?") for a harder, organ-sustained sound to reproduce the funk originated by Horace Silver. Third, he began playing around with the mixing console and introduced heavy editing to jazz (first used in the rock and roll era a decade before). With Shorter, Davis began to explore lineal, extended phrases that eschewed harmonies. His first line-up included soprano saxist Shorter, pianist Herbie Hancock, bassist Ron Carter, and drummer Tony Williams.
    On *Miles Smiles*, the sidemen create more, and in fact, Hancock and Shorter do the writing. Williams rose to pre-eminence with his rock drumming that greatly influenced Davis (as well as Sly Stone and Jimi Hendrix). Shorter and Hancock again scored *Nefertiti*. The title selection has a repeating melody throughout, and

the rhythm section improvises around it. Throughout the album, the melodies themselves are freely played with one musician echoing the other. This led to layers of sound and the recurring riffs or chords found in rock music. The next stage in the development of the "electric" Miles was *In a Silent Way*. He asked John McLaughlin, a Scottish jazz guitarist, to contribute, as well as Joe Zawinul and Chick Corea. Here, Davis employs electrified instruments, such as *three* electric pianos, bass, and guitar, for the basic rhythm. The soloists played on the beat. This was the first jazz record to be *heavily* edited from the mixing console, allowing many solos to be repeated. But this was an afterthought, else Davis would have had one keyboard performer lay down three different tracks.

Davis's jazz-rock period culminated with *Bitches Brew*, his last album with Wayne Shorter. The story here is that Clive Davis told Miles Davis that sales had dropped drastically (Davis never sold more than 50,000 units of any one album by this time), and that Miles would be let go unless he went into a rock bag. There was every indication that Davis was about to begin a new jazz venture, but he turned that aside to create the heavily soul-based *Bitches Brew* (and sold 400,000 copies of it, by the way). This was a completely electronic album, introducing the echo-plex device to provide new effects. Attached to Davis's trumpet (now heard less frequently) were a contact microphone, a wah-wah pedal, and a fuzz box—all three being normal accoutrements to a rock guitar. Most of the instruments in his group simply laid down a heavy texture of strict rhythm (one or two chords of turgid funk) and repetitive heavy percussion derived from Afro-Cuban, Latin, and primitive U.S. Southland. Davis weaved in and out with amplified whines and beats, as if cutting through the fat. These are Davis outbursts rather than lyricism.

The filtering-synthetic process had come full circle: from African roots to jazz to r 'n' b to rock to roots again. The overall texture was highly reminiscent of Ellington's "jungle music," created by plunger trumpeter Bubber Miley, except that the plunger was replaced by the wah-wah pedal. And Davis has never been that strong a trumpet player: he needs amplification and electronic devices to help his phrasing capabilities. Certainly his innovations and ideas are pure genius; he must have experienced much frustration in implementing them himself. Members of his band—particularly the later work in the 1970s—had lost all their individuality; in the past one could always pick out Dave Holland, McLaughlin, Carter, Williams, Corea, Hancock, Zawinul, Jarrett, Shorter, etc. In fact, it is highly debatable whether this is "jazz" in the strict sense of the word, and these discs are included here only because they were highly influential works that turned around the jazz and rock worlds.

J6.135   **Herbie Hancock. Sextant.** Columbia KC 32212.
Hancock, a.k.a. Mwandishi, has produced a "sound effects" record that would do Davis proud. Utilizing a wide variety of equipment (Dakha-Di-Bello, Afuche, Hum-A-Zoo, Melotrons, Guiro, from among 20 or more "instruments"), he produces a heavy textual sound. Extremely sensitive is his rendition of "Rain Dance," emulating drops of rain. Hancock is "assisted" by Benny Maupin on reeds, Eddie Henderson and Julian Priester on brass, and Buster Williams on bass. A highly developed technician, he employed all possible keyboards for input, and output was distorted by Phase Shifters, Random Resonators, ARP Synthesizers, and Echoplexes (he is the leading performer on this one). Hancock is the leading disciple of Davis at this moment, one of the few musicians who have played with Davis to actually

capitalize on the strengths of the master. Although largely an experimental album, *Sextant* does extend Davis in one possible direction. The words here are all IMAGE and IMPRESSION. The internalized feelings here overcome the digressions or pauses in life to create a harmonic whole, albeit one seen through Hancock's eyes. Music is conjured up from within the soul, and this type of music (the IMAGE part) is very difficult to reproduce live.

J6.136   **John McLaughlin. My Goal's Beyond.** Douglas 6003.

J6.137*   **John McLaughlin. The Inner Mounting Flame.** Columbia KC 31067.
        With these two discs, Mahavishnu John McLaughlin became the high priest of jazz-rock. While putting in his apprenticeship in Great Britain and then with Miles Davis, McLaughlin developed the punch and confidence needed to hold a group together. With Rick Laird on bass, Jan Hammer on piano, Billy Cobham on drums, and Jerry Goodman on violin, guitarist McLaughlin brings his fluid, dextrous skills to the forefront. Each of the eight selections on the second disc has something to say, and a lot of it is surrealistic, psychic music. McLaughlin was quite taken with Sri Chinmoy, the Indian spiritualist, and the Eastern way of life has completely pervaded his playing. (He kept his group closely disciplined, so much so that they ultimately split at the end of 1973.) The tunes alternate, slowly building to a crescendo, or perhaps utilizing progressions, on some, and tearing off at a fast pace with others. The flurry of sixteenth notes is a far cry from "Slowhand" Eric Clapton and other blues-infused players. Each of the performers here adds some concrete material, especially Hammer and Cobham, the latter with rock steady drumming that is phenomenal. The *Goal* album is mostly solo McLaughlin in a reflective mood, with reminders of his past associations with Miles Davis, the Tony Williams Lifetime, Chick Corea, and others. It is almost as if he is paying homage to the influences before saying "it is finished" and passing on to be his own man.

J6.138*   **Weather Report. I Sing the Body Electric.** Columbia KC 31352.
        Weather Report is largely composed of Joe Zawinul (ex-Adderley and ex-Davis sideman) and Wayne Shorter. Added are occasional musicians and diverse instrumentation to the basic keyboards and saxophones lineup. Making extensive use of electricity in the production of their music, this group has extended one aspect of Miles Davis' music that was apparent with the *Bitches Brew* album (and also with the *Fillmore* double set that was actually recorded prior to *Brew*). Lyricism has a place in jazz, even though many will deny it. It is the logical outgrowth of the "cool" reaction to hard bop. Employing overdubs, tape splicing, wah-wah pedals, slowdown, and speedup, plus a variety of other techniques from the recording console, Weather Report succeeds in presenting a program of surrealistic but free jazz. The key here is the second side, recorded live in Japan, where the traditional rhythm section has been developed beyond the normal pigeonhole. Zawinul's piano is playing (in Earl Hines fashion) the horn and trumpet lines, interweaving with Shorter, and denying the chords or chordal structure. Miroslav Vitous uses his bass as a third voice. No one player here has the lead—that is the secret behind improvisation. The group sounds like an organic whole—bigger than they actually are. It should be noted that Zawinul, Vitous, and Jan Hammer from the Mahavishnu Orchestra are all Eastern European in origin, and there is a hive of similar activity there.

Citations,
Directories,
Index

BOOK CITATIONS

Most of the material in this book is based on a combination of readings from both book and periodical sources. In the listing that follows, the key books of concern to students of jazz music are numbered (after being alphabetized). Taken together, the books cited in the four volumes would constitute a library detailing popular music in America. We have excluded two categories of books. Generally, *biographies* have been omitted unless they deal substantially with an innovator, concentrate on his/her stylings, and show that artist's impact and influence on other performers in the same genre. Thus, for example, we list Gray's book on Bob Dylan rather than Scaduto's largely biographical offering. Second, we have omitted *songbooks* and instructional materials that look like songbooks, unless they deal substantially with the impact and influence of the music, such as Lomax's book.

It is very difficult to separate books about different musical genres, for there is much overlapping; thus, we discuss titles in the literature survey preceding each section by referring to a designated number, which then can be followed up here for source data and comment. At the same time, many books are called "reference works" (bibliographies, discographies) and "monographic surveys." To the student of music, these terms are interchangeable. In consideration of all of the above, a numerical reference listing seems the best way to handle the matter. At any rate, this is just a source list; please refer to the musical section for comments on the literature.

1 Allen, Walter C. Hendersonia: The Music of Fletcher Henderson and His Musicians. Highland Park, NJ: 1972. 651p. illus. bibliog. discog.
   Positively the last word on Henderson and his group, their influence, and their recordings is contained in this immense "bio-discography."

2 Annual Index to Popular Music Record Reviews, 1972- . Compiled by A. Armitage and D. Tudor. Metuchen, NJ: Scarecrow, 1973- .
   This annual provides location to about 15,000 record reviews in about 55 magazines, noting for each review the reviewer's evaluation of the record. It provides a synoptic report on the year's music, pre-selecting the "best of the year" and indicating the length of each review.

3 Batcheller, John. Music in Recreation and Leisure. Dubuque, IA: W. C. Brown Co., 1972. 135p. paper.
   A short treatise on the importance of music as a social function, with chapters on how to relax through music.

4 Berendt, Joachim Ernst. The Jazz Book: From New Orleans to Rock and Free Jazz. Rev. ed. New York: Lawrence Hill, 1975. 480p. discog.
   The most popular jazz book in the world (several translations; millions of copies sold).

5   Blesh, Rudi. Combo: U.S.A.; Eight Lives in Jazz. Philadelphia: Chilton, 1971. 240p. illus.

Includes articles on Louis Armstrong, Billie Holiday, Gene Krupa, Jack Teagarden, Sidney Bechet, Eubie Blake, Charlie Christian, and Lester Young, along with significant reading notes and discographies.

6   Blesh, Rudi. Shining Trumpets: A History of Jazz. 4th ed. London, Cassell, 1958. 429p. illus. discog.

Analyses of performances by New Orleans jazzmen, along with transcriptions of 47 musical examples.

7   Blesh, Rudi, and Harriet Janis. They All Played Ragtime. 4th ed. New York: Oak, 1971. illus. bibliog. discog. music.

A pioneering work—the only one that provides a detailed history of its development as well as social commentary. The many special sections cover ragtime on record (both new and reissues), complete scores, rare photographs, and listings of performers and composers.

8   Bluestein, Gene. The Voice of the Folk: Folklore and American Literary Theory. Amherst: University of Massachusetts Press, 1972. 170p. bibliog.

Half of this book is devoted to folk music, and it includes a study of blues as a literary tradition, the black influence, and rock as poetry.

9   Boeckman, Charles. And the Beat Goes On: A Survey of Pop Music in America. Washington: R. B. Luce, 1972, 224p. illus.

10   Borretti, Rafaele, comp. Collectors' Catalog, v.2. Cosenza, Italy, 1972. 146p. discog.

This is a special issue of Collector magazine (July 1972); it is intended to be a guide to reissues in jazz and blues that were released in 1969-1972. Information furnished includes original release number and recording date. All anthologies are analyzed.

11   Buerkle, Jack V., and Danny Barker. Bourbon Street Black: The New Orleans Black Jazzman. New York: Oxford University Press, 1973. illus.

A sociological study of contemporary Dixieland performers living and playing in New Orleans.

12   Burt, Jesse, and Bob Ferguson. So You Want to Be in Music! Nashville, TN: Abingdon Press, 1970. 175p.

This career-oriented handbook does a good job of explaining the mechanics behind breaking into the business—songwriting, studio techniques, and so forth. Glossary of recording terms.

13   Chasins, Abram. Music at the Crossroads. New York: Macmillan, 1972. 240p.

An appraisal of the current state of instrumental music, both classical and popular, with consideration of the effects of jazz-rock-folk on "serious" music.

14 Chilton, John. Billie's Blues: Billie Holiday's Story, 1933-1959. New York: Stein and Day, 1975. 264p. illus. discog.

15 Chilton, John. Who's Who of Jazz: Storyville to Swing Street. Philadelphia: Chilton, 1972. 419p. illus. bibliog.
Information on over 1,000 American jazz musicians born before 1920.

16 Coker, Jerry. Improvising Jazz. Englewood Cliffs, NJ: Prentice-Hall, 1964. 115p. music.
A good textbook that covers many instruments, so as to provide for logical development in jazz improvisation.

17 Coker, Jerry. The Jazz Idiom. Englewood Cliffs, NJ: Prentice-Hall, 1975. 84p.

18 Cole, Bill. Miles Davis: A Musical Biography. New York: Morrow, 1974. 256p. illus. discog.

19 Collier, Graham. Jazz: A Student's and Teacher's Guide. New York: Cambridge University Press, 1975. 167p. illus. bibliog. discog.

20 Condon, Eddie. The Eddie Condon Scrapbook of Jazz. New York: St. Martin's Press, 1973. unpaged; chiefly illus.
Many personal recollections of other musicians by a jazz great who played with many of the finest in the Chicago, or traditional, school.

21 Connor, D. Russell, and Warren W. Hicks. BG: On the Record; a Bio-Discography of Benny Goodman. New Rochelle, NY: Arlington House, 1969. 691p. illus. bibliog. discog.
Connor published "BG: Off the Record" privately in 1958; this retitled effort is an immense updating that contains a tremendous amount of data about Goodman's recordings, his sidemen, etc.

22 Dance, Stanley. The World of Swing. New York: Scribner's, 1974. 436p. illus.
A separately available recording was issued by CBS.

23 Dankworth, Avril. Jazz: An Introduction to Its Musical Basis. New York: Oxford University Press, 1968. 91p.

24 Denisoff, R. Serge. Solid Gold: The Record Industry, Its Friends, and Enemies. New York: Transaction Books, distr. by Dutton, 1976. 350p.
Traces the steps through which a song goes to reach the public.

25 Denisoff, R. Serge, comp. The Sounds of Social Change: Studies in Popular Culture. Chicago: Rand McNally, 1972. 332p.

26 Esquire's World of Jazz. Rev. and updated. New York: Thomas Y. Crowell, 1975. 228p. illus. discog.
Reprinted articles.

27   Ewen, David. History of Popular Music. New York: Barnes and Noble, 1961.
     229p. bibliog. paper only.
     A brief introductory text to popular songs, the musical theater, and jazz in
America from Colonial times to 1960.

28   Feather, Leonard. The Book of Jazz, from Then Till Now. New York:
     Bonanza Books, 1965. 280p. discog. music.
     This revised edition attempts to answer the question, "What is jazz?" (its
nature, sources, instruments, sounds, performers, etc.). Includes musical illustrations for 17 great jazz improvisations by Armstrong, Teagarden, Coltrane,
Coleman, etc.

29   Feather, Leonard. The Encyclopedia of Jazz. Rev. ed. New York: Bonanza,
     1960. 527p. illus. bibliog. discog.
     Most of this book is biographical.

30   Feather, Leonard. The Encyclopedia of Jazz in the Sixties. New York:
     Bonanza, 1965. illus. bibliog. discog.
     An expansion of The Encyclopedia of Jazz, with emphasis on activities in the
early sixties, and with many new names among the 1,000 biographees listed.

31   Feather, Leonard. From Satchmo to Miles. New York: Stein and Day, 1972.
     258p.
     Thirteen biographical essays, most of which were published before.

32   Feather, Leonard, and Ira Gitler. The Encyclopedia of Jazz in the Seventies.
     New York: Horizon, 1976. 393p. illus. bibliog. discog.
     With 1,400 biographies, this latest edition extends the previous two editions
through 1975.

33   Ferlingere, Robert D. A Discography of Rhythm and Blues and Rock and
     Roll Vocal Groups, 1945-1965. Pittsburg, Calif.: The Author (P.O. Box 1695),
     1976. 600p.
     Twenty thousand song titles are listed in chronological order by master num-
ber, covering the output (78, 45, 33 1/3 rpm speeds, plus long-playing and extended
playing formats) of over 2,600 groups and single artists with groups. Unreleased
titles are also included, as well as recording dates.

34   Fernett, Gene. Swing Out: Great Negro Jazz Bands. Midland, MI: Pendell
     Pub., 1970. 176p.

35   Field, James J. American Popular Music, 1875-1950. Philadelphia: Musical
     Americana, 1956.

36   Foster, Pops. Pops Foster: The Autobiography of a New Orleans Jazzman,
     As Told to Tom Stoddard. Berkeley: University of California Press, 1971.
     208p. illus. bibliog. discog.
     More than half of this book provides interesting insights into the workings
of the jazz world, other musicians, and recording studios.

37 Fox, Charles. Jazz in Perspective. London: British Broadcasting Corp., 1969. 88p. paper only.

38 Fuld, James J. The Book of World Famous Music: Classical, Popular and Folk. Rev. and enl. ed. New York: Crown, 1971. 688p. bibliog.
A discussion of 1,000 songs, primarily through tracing their roots.

39 Gammond, Peter. Scott Joplin and the Ragtime Era. New York: St. Martin's Press, 1975. 223p. illus. bibliog. discog.

40 Gillett, Charlie. Making Tracks: The Story of Atlantic Records. New York: Outerbridge and Lazard, 1973.
This is probably the only book on the history of music recording, as it is a corporate history of Atlantic Records. This company was the most influential of the r 'n' b labels—and still is.

41 Gitler, Ira. Jazz Masters of the 40's. New York: Macmillan, 1966. 290p. illus. bibliog. discog.
The story of bop music, told in terms of the personalities concerned: Parker, Gillespie, Powell, Clarke, Tristano, etc.

42 Gleason, Ralph J., ed. Jam Session: An Anthology of Jazz. New York: G. P. Putnam's Sons, 1958.
A collection of Gleason's writings in the area of jazz.

43 Goldenberg, Joe. Jazz Masters of the 50s. New York: Macmillan, 1965.
One of the series edited by Martin Williams, this book surveys the 1950s decade, with listening notes.

44 Goldstein, Richard. Goldstein's Greatest Hits. Englewood Cliffs, NJ: Prentice-Hall, 1970. 258p.
His collected writings from 1966-1968, originally published in the *Village Voice*, the *New York Times*, and *New York Magazine*.

45 Gregor, Carl. International Jazz Bibliography: Jazz Books from 1919 to 1968. Strasbourg, Baden-Baden: Editions P. H. Heitz, 1969. 198p.

46 Hadlock, Richard. Jazz Masters of the 20's. New York: Macmillan, 1965. 255p. illus. bibliog. discog.

47 Herdeg, Walter, ed. Graphical Record Covers. New York: Hastings House, 1974. 192p. illus.
History and illustrations of record jacket covers.

48 Hodeir, Andre. Jazz: Its Evolution and Essence. New York: Grove Press, 1956. 295p. music.

49   Hodeir, Andre. Toward Jazz. New York: Grove Press, 1962. 224p. music.
A collection of his articles from Jazz Hot, Arts, and the Jazz Review, centered on personalities and criticism.

50   Hodeir, Andre. The Worlds of Jazz. New York: Grove Press, 1972. 288p. illus.
Covers the problems of jazz performances, composing, and evaluation.

51   Hoover, Cynthia. Music Machines—American Style: A Catalog of an Exhibition. Washington: Smithsonian Institution Press; distr. Govt. Print. Office, 1971. 139p. illus. bibliog.
The exhibition portrayed the development of music machines from cylinders and player pianos to Moog synthesizers, and the effect of technology on performers and audiences.

52   Horn, David. The Literature of American Music in Books and Folk Music Collections: A Fully Annotated Bibliography. Metuchen, NJ: Scarecrow, 1977. 556p.
A detailed listing of 1,696 books considered essential for a library on all aspects of American music: folk, country, blues, rock, musical stage, soul, jazz, etc. Strong annotations.

53   Howard, John Tasker, and George Kent Bellows. A Short History of Music in America. New York: Crowell, 1967. 496p. illus. bibliog. notes.
A brief history that surveys folk, classical, spirituals, recorded music, and musical comedy.

54   Hughes, Langston, and Milton Meltzer. Black Magic: A Pictorial History of the Negro in American Entertainment. Englewood Cliffs, NJ: Prentice-Hall, 1967. 375p.

55   Jasen, David A. Recorded Ragtime, 1897-1958. Hamden, CT: Archon, 1973. 155p. discog.
This is an index to recorded ragtime, by composer and performer, with the normal discographical information (release label number, dates, and so forth). Coverage is limited to 78 rpm records only.

56   Jepsen, Jorgen Grunnet. Jazz Records, 1942-1962. v.5-6, M-R. Copenhagen: Nordisk Tidsskrift Forlag, 1963; v.7-8, S-Z, Holte, Denmark: Knudsen, 1964-1965.

Jepsen, Jorgen Grunnet. Jazz Records, 1942-1965. v.1-3, A-El. Holte, Denmark: Knudsen, 1968.

Jepsen, Jorgen Grunnet. Jazz Records, 1942-1967. v.4b, Goo-Iwr. Copenhagen: Knudsen, 1969.

Jepsen, Jorgen Grunnet. Jazz Records, 1942-1968. v.4c, J-Ki. Copenhagen: Knudsen, 1970.

Jepsen, Jorgen Grunnet. Jazz Records, 1942-1969. v.4d, Kl-L. Copenhagen: Knudsen, 1970.
An indispensable series of discographies arranged alphabetically by artist. It continues Rust's 1897-1942 effort. It includes bluesmen, but no r 'n' b, nor some contemporary urban blues. Updated irregularly by reader contributions to Jazz Journal.

57 Jones, LeRoi. Blues People. New York: William Morrow, 1963. 244p.
The Negro experience in white America and the music that developed from it is covered here. Concentrates mostly on African origins, slave developments, and exploitation of the early jazz and bluesmen.

58 Keepnews, Orrin, and Bill Grauer, Jr. Pictorial History of Jazz. Rev. ed. London: Spring Books/Hamlyn, 1968. 297p. illus.

59 Kennington, Donald. The Literature of Jazz: A Critical Guide. Chicago: American Library Association, 1971. 142p.
All significant books as published through 1969 are listed here if they were published in English. Arrangement is by topic (e.g., biographies, reference works, periodicals), with a concluding section on films and clubs.

60 Kinkle, Roger D. The Complete Encyclopedia of Popular Music and Jazz, 1900-1950. New Rochelle, NY: Arlington House, 1974. 4v. (2644p.). discog.

61 Lang, Ian. Jazz in Perspective: The Background of the Blues. London: Jazz Book Club, 1957. 148p. illus. discog.

62 Larkin, Philip. All What Jazz?: A Record Diary, 1961-1968. New York: St. Martin's Press, 1970. 272p.
A collection of this British poet/journalist's writings (mostly from the *Observer*), reviews, and record criticisms.

63 Lawless, Ray M. Folksingers and Folksongs in America: A Handbook, Biography, Bibliography, and Discography. New ed. New York: Meredith, 1965. 750p. illus. bibliog. discog.
Evaluates some 300 songbooks and 700 albums (1948+)—with title listings, instruments, societies, and festivals.

64 Lomax, Alan. Mister Jelly Roll: The Fortunes of Jelly Roll Morton, New Orleans Creole and Inventor of Jazz. 2nd ed. Berkeley: University of California Press, 1973. 318p. illus. discog.
This biography also examines the whole ramifications of influences and styles of other performers in the jazz idiom. It also contains a chronological list of Morton's compositions.

65 Longstreet, Stephen. The Real Jazz, Old and New. New York: Greenwood Press, 1969. 202p.
Reprint of 1956 edition.

66   McCarthy, Albert. Big Band Jazz. New York: G. P. Putnam's, 1974. 368p. illus. (chiefly black and white photos). bibliog. discog.

This is a definitive history of the origins, progress, influence, and decline in the United States and elsewhere of big band and swing jazz units. Coverage extends to 550 bands plus a superb discography of over 325 records. All examples are taken from recorded material.

67   McCarthy, Albert. The Dance Band Era: The Dancing Decades from Rag-time to Swing, 1910-1950. Philadelphia: Chilton, 1972. 176p.

This is a large format book, with copious black and white photographs of the bands that English people danced to—Ray Noble, Fox, Ambrose, etc. Swing is deliberately played down as the emphasis is on dancing. The discography is excellent and comprehensive.

68   McCarthy, Albert, ed. Jazz on Records, 1917-1967. 2nd ed. New York: Oak, 1969. 416p.

Contains alphabetically arranged biographical articles with selective discog-raphies for each person. Also included are general articles, surveys by type of musi-cal appeal (e.g., "Post-War Reeds"), and geographical surveys of blues music.

69   Mattfield, Julius. Variety Music Cavalcade. 3rd ed. Englewood Cliffs, NJ: Prentice-Hall, 1971.

70   Meeker, David. Jazz in the Movies: A Tentative Index to the Works of Jazz Musicians in the Cinema. London: British Film Institute, 1972. 89p. illus.

709 film entries (American and European), cross-indexed for 270 jazz artists.

71   Mellers, Wilfrid. Music in a New Found Land. London: Barrie and Rockliff, 1964.

Here is wide coverage of the American musical tradition, relating classics to blues to jazz to pop.

72   Melly, George. Revolt into Style: The Pop Arts in Britain. London: Allen Lane, The Penguin Press, 1970. 245p.

Largely based on Melly's periodical articles, this is an analytic history of popu-lar culture in Britain in the 1960s. Its scope is wider than music and includes television, films, stage, the press, and writings.

73   Merriam, Alan P., and Robert J. Benford. A Bibliography of Jazz. Phila-delphia: The American Folklore Society, 1954; Kraus Reprint, 1970. 145p.

This contains 3,324 author entries, followed by a list of jazz magazines and various subject indexes. Coverage extends only to 1953.

74   Modern Jazz: 1945-70, the Essential Records. London: Aquarius Books, 1975. 131p. discog.

75 The Music Yearbook: A Survey and Directory with Statistics and Reference Articles. 1972- . New York: St. Martin's Press, 1973- . 750p. average length.
This annual is the most up-to-date source of information on British music and musicians. Survey articles cover all aspects of classical and popular music, with lists of books and periodicals, addresses of relevant record companies, associations, halls, museums, etc. The American equivalent is The Musician's Guide, from Music Information Service.

76 The Musician's Guide, 1954- . New York: Music Information Service, 1954- . (available every four years. Last edition: 1972).
The basic directory of music information for the United States. Sections include data on record collections, various recording awards such as the "Grammies," addresses of groups, books to read, and so forth. The British equivalent is The Music Yearbook.

77 Nanry, Charles, ed. American Music: From Storyville to Woodstock. New Brunswick, NJ: Transaction Books, 1972. 288p.
This collection of reprinted articles covers only jazz and rock.

78 National Portrait Gallery. "A Glimmer of Their Own Beauty; Black Sounds of the Twenties." Washington: Govt. Print. Office, 1971. 32p., chiefly illus. bibliog.
A catalog of an exhibition of pictures of Negro musicians.

79 New York Library Association. Children's and Young Adult Services Section. Records and Cassettes for Young Adults: A Selected List. New York, 1972. 52p. paper only. discog.
Categories include: rock, soul, blues, jazz, country and western, and various non-musical records and cassettes. Useful for the "now" sounds of 1972.

80 Ostransky, Leroy. The Anatomy of Jazz. Tacoma: University of Washington Press, 1964. 362p. music. bibliog.
Details some of the problems in jazz composition, jazz performing, and gives a general history of jazz as music.

81 Panassié, Hugues, and Madelaine Gautier. Le Dictionnaire du Jazz. Paris: Editions A. Michel, 1971. 363p. illus.
A newly expanded edition of this classic reference work, with good biographies of traditional jazz musicians.

82 Passman, Arnold. The Dee Jays. New York: Macmillan, 1971. 320p.
Passman traces the evolution of the "disc jockey" from 1909 to the underground FM stations in San Francisco, with good detail on how songs are selected for airplay.

83 Paul, Elliot. That Crazy American Music. Port Washington, NY: Kennikat Press, 1970. 317p. bibliog.
Originally published by Bobbs-Merrill in 1957.

84 Pleasants, Henry. The Great American Popular Singers. New York: Simon and Schuster, 1974. 384p. illus.
The author examines the vocal tradition in popular music, the phenomenon of imitation breeding imitation, the meaning of "art" as applied to popular music, and various evaluations of 22 innovators in the fields of jazz, musical stage, blues, gospel, country, soul, and so forth.

85 Popular Music Periodicals Index, 1973- . Comp. by Dean Tudor and Andrew Armitage. Metuchen, NJ: Scarecrow, 1974- .
An annual author-subject index to 60 or so periodicals utilizing a special thesaurus involving musical genres.

86 Propes, Steve. Golden Oldies: A Guide to 60s Record Collecting. Philadelphia: Chilton, 1974. 240p. discog.

87 Propes, Steve. Those Oldies But Goodies: A Guide to 50's Record Collecting. New York: Macmillan, 1973. 192p. bibliog. discog.
A guide to current prices, sources, and reading material devoted to collecting 78 and 45 rpm phonodiscs from the 1950-1960 period.

88 Ramsey, Frederic, Jr. Been Here and Gone. New Brunswick, NJ: Rutgers University Press, 1960. 177p. illus.
Text and photographs record the life and musical activity of black Americans in the Deep South. Their remembrances help to reveal the beginnings and development of Afro-American music in the United States.

89 Ramsey, Frederic, Jr., and Charles Edward Smith, eds. Jazzmen. New York: Harcourt, Brace, 1939. 360p. illus.
This is a classic account of American jazz told through the lives of the men who created it in the twenties and thirties. Coverage includes New Orleans, New York, Chicago, and Hot Jazz. A paperback version was issued in 1960.

90 Recording Industry Association of America. The White House Record Library. Washington: White House Historical Association, 1973. 105p.
A catalog of 2,000 records presented to the White House in March 1973. Categories include popular, classical, jazz, folk, country, gospel, and spoken word.

91 Rivelli, Pauline, and Robert Levin, eds. The Rock Giants. New York: World, 1971.
These articles have been collected from the magazine Jazz & Pop, which has since ceased publishing.

92 Roberts, John Storm. Black Music of Two Worlds. New York: Praeger, 1972. 296p. illus. bibliog. discog.
A detailed survey of black music in Africa and America.

93 Rolling Stone Magazine. The Rolling Stone Record Review. New York: Pocket Books, 1961. 556p. paper only.

Rolling Stone Magazine. The Rolling Stone Record Review. v.2. New
York: Pocket Books, 1974. 599p. paper only.

94   Rose, Al. Storyville, New Orleans. University, AL: University of Alabama Press,
     1974. 225p.

95   Rublowsky, John. Popular Music. New York: Basic Books, 1967. 164p.
     Emphasis is on country and western, rock and current popular materials.

96   Russell, Ross. Jazz Style in Kansas City and the Southwest. Berkeley: Uni-
     versity of California Press, 1971. 324p. illus. bibliog.

97   Russell, Tony. Blacks, Whites and Blues. New York: Stein and Day, 1970.
     112p. illus. bibliog. discog.
     Examines the relationships of black blues musicians and white musicians,
emphasizing their traditions and differences. In Britain, CBS released an accompanying record.

98   Rust, Brian. The American Dance Band Discography, 1917-1942. New
     Rochelle, NY: Arlington House, 1975. 2v. (2066p.).
     Some 2,373 white bands are covered (except Glenn Miller and Benny Good-
man, who have their own books); 7,141 entries in the index.

99   Rust, Brian. The Dance Bands. London: Ian Allan, 1972. 160p. illus.
     Mainly British, from 1919-1944, with many rare photographs.

100 Rust, Brian. Jazz Records, A-Z, 1897-1942. 4th ed. New Rochelle, NY:
     Arlington House, 1978. 2v.
     Similar to Jepsen's discography, this is an alphabetically arranged list of
jazz artists' records within the specified time period. Updated in a variety of
sources including Jazz Journal and Storyville.

101 Rust, Brian. The Victor Master Book, v.2 (1925-1936). Hatch End, Middlesex:
     Storyville Publications, 1969. 776p.
     A complete listing, in numerical order, of every popular music record issued
by RCA Victor between 1925-1936.

102 Sandberg, Larry, and Dick Weissman. The Folk Music Sourcebook. New
     York: Knopf, 1976. 260p. illus. bibliog. discog.
     A guide to North American folk music (blues, old time music, bluegrass, rag-
time, jazz, Canadian, ethnic): books, instruments, recordings, films, instructional
materials, societies, etc. Essentially updates Lawless's Folksingers and Folksongs in
America (New York: Meredith, 1965).

103 Schafer, William J., and Johannes Riedel. The Art of Ragtime: Form and
     Meaning of an Original Black American Art. Baton Rouge: Louisiana State
     University Press, 1972. 249p. illus. bibliog. music.
     A more formal study that duplicates to some extent the Blesh and Janis
work.

104   Schicke, C. A.   Revolution in Sound: A Biography of the Recording Industry.
        Boston: Little, Brown, 1974. 238p.
        A history of the recording industry, covering all forms of influences and
manipulation.

105   Schuller, Gunther.   Early Jazz: Its Roots and Musical Development. New
        York: Oxford University Press, 1968. 401p. bibliog. discog. music.
        Probably the most important monograph on the history of jazz up to 1932,
this is the first volume in the Oxford series, The History of Jazz.

106   Shapiro, Nat, and Nat Hentoff, eds. Hear Me Talkin' to Ya. New York:
        Dover, 1966. 429p.
        First published by Rinehart in 1955, this edition lacks the original discog-
raphy. It is the story of jazz as told by the men who made it.

107   Shapiro, Nat, and Nat Hentoff, eds. The Jazz Makers. New York: Rinehart,
        1957. 368p. discog.
        The story of 21 jazzmen (up to 1955), from Morton to Gillespie, each
written by a specialist. The individual profiles conclude with selective discographies.

108   Shaw, Arnold.   The Street That Never Slept: New York's Fabled 52nd Street.
        New York: Coward, 1971. 378p. illus. discog.
        A remarkable book that concentrates on a very small geographic area, and notes
its decline.

109   Simon, George T.   The Big Bands. 2nd ed. New York: Macmillan, 1971. 584p.
        illus.
        A complete survey of the big bands and the big names. The first edition had
a three record set (one each from Decca, RCA, and Columbia) to accompany it.

110   Simon, George T.   Simon Says: The Sights and Sounds of the Swing Era,
        1935-1955. New Rochelle, NY: Arlington House, 1971. 476p. illus.
        This is an anthology of reviews and critical pieces originally published in
Metronome, where the author was editor for 20 years.

111   Stearns, Marshall.   The Story of Jazz. New York: New American Library,
        1958. 272p. illus. bibliog.
        On a more scholarly basis, this book is similar to Ulanov and Feather. The
above edition is different from the Oxford University Press publication by virtue of
an expanded bibliography and a syllabus of 15 lectures on the history of jazz.

112   Stearns, Marshall, and Jean Stearns. Jazz Dance: The Story of American
        Vernacular Dance. New York: Macmillan, 1968. 464p. illus. bibliog. filmog.

113   Stewart, Rex.   Jazz Masters of the 30's. New York: Collier-Macmillan, 1972.
        223p.
        Previously published essays on Louis Armstrong, Duke Ellington, Count
Basie, Fletcher Henderson, and others. This is one of the Martin Williams-edited
series, covering jazz by decades.

114   Studies in Jazz Discography I. Ed. Walter C. Allen. New Brunswick, NJ:
        Institute of Jazz Studies, Rutgers University, 1971. 112p.
        Edited proceedings of the 1968 and 1969 Conference(s) on Discographical
Research. Valuable for discographers and collectors.

115   Taubman, Howard, ed. The New York Times Guide to Listening Pleasure.
        New York: Macmillan, 1968. 328p. discog.
        This is mainly a how-to guide for the novice record collector. A good two-
thirds of the book deals with classical music; the balance concentrates on folk,
jazz, Latin America, and the musical theater.

116   Toledano, Ralph de. Frontiers of Jazz. 2nd ed. New York: Frederick Ungar,
        1962. 178p.
        Originally published in 1947, this revised edition includes new material and
has dropped older articles. Sections originally appeared in mainstream magazines
such as National Review, New Republic and Saturday Evening Post. Authors include
Abbe Niles, William Russell, Hugues Panassié, Ansermet (the first jazz article!), and
Frank Norris.

117   Tudor, Dean, and Andrew Armitage. "Best of the Year." LJ/SLJ Previews,
        April and May issues, 1974-1976.
        A round-up of the year's best records, as reflected by the reviewing media.

118   Ulanov, Barry. Handbook of Jazz. New York: Viking, 1955. 248p. bibliog.
        A guide to the music, musicians, instruments, and recordings—similar to
Feather's Book of Jazz.

119   Van Eyle, William. Jazz Pearls. Oudkarspel, Holland: the Author, 1975.
        204p.
        A survey of essential jazz recordings of 3,102 tunes, listed in date order
(Joplin in 1902 to December 1974).

120   Vian, Boris. Chroniques de Jazz. Paris: Union General d' Editions, 1971.
        512p.
        Extracts from Jazz Hot and Combat.

121   Wells, Dickie. The Night People. Boston: Crescendo, 1971. 118p.
        These are personal reminiscences of Harlem, Count Basie, Ray Charles, and
so on, particularly worthwhile because of the Wellsian use and misuse of words.

122   Whitburn, Joel. Top LP Records, 1945-1972. Menomenee Falls, WI:
        Record Research, 1974.
        Artist arrangement and broad subject categories based on the Billboard
charts of jazz, rock, pop, r 'n' b, etc.

123   Whitcomb, Ian. After the Ball. London: Allen Lane, The Penguin Press,
        1972. 312p.
        The author, a singer, explores the phenomenon of popular music, from

"After the Ball" (written in 1892) through Tin Pan Alley to the Beatles. Concentration is mostly on British pop.

124   Williams, Martin, ed. The Art of Jazz: Essays on the Nature and Development of Jazz. New York: Oxford University Press, 1959.

125   Williams, Martin T. Jazz Masters in Transition, 1957-1969. New York: Macmillan, 1970. 288p.

126   Williams, Martin. Jazz Masters of New Orleans. New York: Macmillan, 1967. 287p. bibliog. discog.

127   Williams, Martin T. The Jazz Tradition. New York: Oxford University Press, 1970. 232p.
A collection of diverse writings that originally appeared as periodical articles.

128   Williams, Martin T. Where's the Melody?: A Listener's Introduction to Jazz. Rev. ed. New York: Pantheon Books, 1969. 205p.

129   Williams, Peter. Bluff Your Way in Folk and Jazz. London: Wolfe, 1969. 64p. paper only.
A sometimes funny, but unwittingly serious guide to "instant erudition." There is a checklist of techniques, heroes, names, glossaries, and recordings to mention at the next cocktail party. A very good overview.

130   Wilmer, Valerie. Jazz People. London: Allison and Busby, 1970. 167p. illus.
Wilmer is a professional photographer who has often—and most gorgeously— captured the pictorial essence of blues and jazz figures. This book mainly comprises photographs.

PERIODICAL CITATIONS

For many of the same reasons as in the Book Citations section, periodical titles here are listed alphabetically, sequentially numbered, and keyed to references in the section discussing musical genres. Periodicals come and go in the popular music world, depending on interests, finances, and subscriptions sold, and much valuable information is thereby lost. The following 18 periodicals show some stability and should at least be around when this book is two years old; consequently, prices are not noted, nor are street addresses given for foreign publications that tend to move around. The annotations give a physical description of their contents, but please refer to the music genre for more complete details on specific articles or discussions. In addition to periodicals listed, about 40 more are printed in the English language (all are indexed in *Popular Music Periodicals Index*, 1973; Scarecrow Press), about 75 more in non-English languages, and countless scores of fanzine and very specialized publications.

1   Black Music. 1974- . Monthly. 1 Throwley Way, Sutton, Surrey, England.
    A glossy but expertly edited magazine concerned with blues, rhythm 'n' blues, soul, gospel, reggae, jazz, African music—all musical fields of interest to blacks. Good reviews of records and various current awareness services.

2   Blues and Soul. 1971- . Weekly. 42 Hanway Street, London, England.
    Much the same as Black Music, with concentration on blues, jazz, soul, and reggae music.

3   Cadence. 1976- . Monthly. Rt. 1, Box 345, Redwood, NY 13679.
    An excellent source for interviews with both jazz and blues performers, this also has superb record reviews and notations. Tries to cover every single jazz album released in the world.

4   Coda. 1958- . 6x/yr. Box 87, Station J, Toronto, Canada.
    International coverage of largely modern jazz. In-depth articles and interviews, good design, and superb (and critical) jazz and blues record reviews.

5   Contemporary Keyboard. 1975- . Bimonthly. P.O. Box 615, Saratoga, CA 95070.
    Emphasizes all aspects of keyboards (piano, organ, electronic music synthesizers, etc.) with reviews, articles on personalities in both popular and classical modes of music, plus performance tips and instructions.

6   Creem. 1969- . Monthly. 187 South Woodward, Birmingham, MI 48011.
    Calls itself "America's only rock 'n' roll magazine." Articles deal with music exclusively. Good reviews.

7   Downbeat. 1934- . Biweekly. 222 W. Adams St., Chicago, IL 60606.
     The oldest continuing jazz magazine, now spreading its coverage to progressive
rock music and the new jazz personalities. Good record reviews, transcriptions of
improvised jazz solos.

8   Guitar Player. 1967- . Monthly. Box 615, Saratoga, CA 95070.
     Emphasizes all aspects of guitars (bass, pedal, acoustic, electric, etc.) with
reviews, articles on personalities in both popular and classical modes of music, plus
performance instructional guidance.

9   High Fidelity. 1951- . Monthly. ABC Leisure Magazines, Great Barrington,
     MA 02130.
     A general magazine with slight coverage of popular music.

10   Jazz Journal International. 1948- . Monthly. 7 Carnaby Street, London, England.
     Detailed articles about mainstream jazz and some few modern performers as
well. Good record reviews with added discographic descriptions. Title changed from
Jazz Journal in April 1977.

11   Journal of Jazz Studies. 1973- . Semi-annual. Transaction Periodicals
     Consortium, Rutgers University, New Brunswick, NJ 08903.
     Scholarly journal that concentrates on the social and historical aspects of
jazz music.

12   Melody Maker. 1931- . Weekly. 1 Throwley Way, Sutton, Surrey, England.
     The best of the five British weeklies devoted to popular music. News, views,
and articles on rock, jazz, folk, blues, soul, reggae, country, etc. Unusually good
record reviews.

13   Micrography. 1968- . Quarterly. Stevinstraat 14, Alphen aan den Rijn,
     Netherlands.
     A new format in 1976 led to articles and discographic details concerning the
issuance of 78 rpms and air shots in the elpee format. A good service for tracking
down rare albums and duplications of tracks on reissued albums.

14   Mississippi Rag. 1974- . Monthly. P.O. Box 19068, Minneapolis, MN 55419.
     Subtitled "The voice of traditional jazz and ragtime." Good in-depth inter-
views and reviews. Historical articles and festival coverage.

15   Popular Music and Society. 1971- . Quarterly. 318 South Grove Street,
     Bowling Green, OH 43402.
     An interdisciplinary journal "concerned with music in the broadest sense
of the term." Scholarly articles.

16   Rolling Stone. 1968- . Biweekly. 625 Third Street, San Francisco, CA
     94107.
     America's strongest youth culture magazine, describing music as a way of
life. Very opinionated, but only about one-third of it is now solely music.

17   Stereo Review. 1958- . Monthly. P.O. Box 2771, Boulder, CO 80302.
     A general magazine favoring audio equipment, classical music, and popular music about equally.

18   Storyville. 1965- . Bimonthly. 66 Fairview Drive, Chigwell, Essex, England.
     Specializes in traditional and New Orleans jazz, with some blues and subsequent reinterpretations or revivals. Articles are devoted to exploring minor performers or minor facts about famous jazzmen. Good research, copious discographies.

DIRECTORY OF LABELS AND STARRED RECORDS

This directory presents, in alphabetical order, the names and addresses of all the American manufacturers of long-playing records cited in this set of books. Similarly, the starred records from all four volumes are listed here, not simply those for the present volume. British, Japanese, Swedish, French, Danish, etc., records can be obtained from specialist stores or importers. Other information here includes some indication of the types of popular music that each firm is engaged in and a listing in label numerical order of all the starred (special importance) records as indicated in the text, along with the entry number for quick reference. For this reason, starred foreign discs are also included in this directory/listing. This directory notes the latest issuance of a disc. Some albums may have been reissued from other labels, and they will be found under the label of the latest release. In all cases, please refer to the main text. Cross-references are made here where appropriate, especially for "family" names within a label's corporate ownership. To expedite filing and ease of retrieval, this listing of records follows the numerical order of each label's issues, ignoring the alphabetical initialisms.

A & M, 1416 North LaBrea Avenue, Hollywood, CA 90028
specialty: general rock and pop

SP 4245—Herb Alpert. Greatest Hits. P3.1
SP 4251—Jimmy Cliff. Wonderful World, Beautiful People. B5.7a
SP 4257—Fairport Convention. Liege and Lief. F2.49
SP 4519—Cat Stevens. Greatest Hits. F10.90

ABC, 8255 Beverly Blvd., Los Angeles, CA 90048
specialty: general

S 371—Paul Anka. R2.15
490X—Ray Charles. A Man and His Soul. two discs. B2.40
654—Impressions. Best. B4.9
724—B. B. King. Live at the Regal. B1.296
780—Curtis Mayfield. His Early Years with the Impressions. two discs. B4.11
781/2—Ray Charles. Modern Sounds in Country and Western Music. 2 discs. B4.26
ABCX 1955-1963—Rock 'n' Soul; The History of the Pre-Beatles Decade of Rock, 1953-1963. 9 discs. R2.12

Ace of Clubs (English issue)
specialty: older popular music, jazz

ACL 1153—Spike Hughes and His All-American Orchestra. J4.47
ACL 1158—Django Reinhardt and Stephane Grappelli. J6.113

Ace of Hearts (English issue). recently deleted
specialty: MCA reissues (all forms of popular music)

AH 21—Andrews Sisters. P2.145
AH 28—Jack Teagarden. Big T's Jazz. J3.91

Ace of Hearts (cont'd)
AH 58–Carter Family. A Collection of Favourites. F5.108
AH 112–Carter Family. More Favourites. F5.111
AH 119–Jimmy Rushing. Blues I Love to Sing. B1.426
AH 135–Uncle Dave Macon. F5.31
AH 168–Jack Teagarden. "J.T." J3.92

Adelphi, P. O. Box 288, Silver Spring, MD 20907
specialty: blues, folk

Advent, P. O. Box 635, Manhattan Beach, CA 90266
specialty: blues music

2803–Johnny Shines. B1.359

Ahura Mazda (c/o Southern Record Sales)
specialty: blues

AMS 2002–Robert Pete Williams. B1.130

All Platinum, 96 West Street, Englewood, NJ 07631
specialty: blues and soul, mainly from the Chess catalog which it
purchased; see also CHESS records

2ACMB 201–Howlin' Wolf. A.K.A. Chester Burnett. two discs. B1.284
2ACMB 202–Little Walter. Boss Blues Harmonica. two discs. B1.297
2ACMB 203–Muddy Waters. A.K.A. McKinley Morganfield. two discs.
B1.303

Alligator, P.O. Box 11741, Fort Dearborn Station, Chicago, IL 60611
specialty: blues

AL 4706–Koko Taylor. I Got What It Takes. B1.407

Angel, 1750 N. Vine Street, Hollywood, CA 90028
specialty: classical and classical interpretations of popular music

S 36060–New England Conservatory Ragtime Ensemble. Scott Joplin:
The Red Back Book. J2.28

Antilles, 7720 Sunset Blvd., Los Angeles, CA 90046
specialty: folk and pop

AN 7017–Shirley Collins and the Albion Country Band. No Roses. F2.47

Apple, 1750 N. Vine Street, Hollywood, CA 90028
specialty: rock

SKBO 3403/4–The Beatles. 1962-1970. four discs. R4.3/4.

Argo (English issue)
specialty: folk (British), classical, spoken word

ZDA 66-75–Ewan MacColl and Peggy Seeger. The Long Harvest. ten discs.
F2.23

Arhoolie, 10341 San Pablo Avenue, El Cerrito, CA 94530
specialty: blues, old time music, ethnic music

1001—Mance Lipscomb, Texas Sharecropper and Songster. B1.213
1007—Mercy Dee Walton. B1.369
1008—Alex Moore. B1.228
1021—Fred McDowell. Delta Blues. B1.120
1027—Fred McDowell. volume 2. B1.119
1028—Big Mama Thornton. In Europe. B1.408
1036—Juke Boy Bonner. I'm Going Back to the Country Where They Don't
    Burn the Buildings Down. B1.146
1038—Clifton Chenier. Black Snake Blues. B1.324
1066—Earl Hooker. His First and Last Recordings. B1.279
2003—Lowell Fulson. B1.332
2004—Joe Turner. Jumpin' the Blues. B1.431
2007—Lightnin' Hopkins. Early Recordings, v.1. B1.182
2010—Lightnin' Hopkins. Early Recordings, v.2. B1.182
2011—Robert Pete Williams. Angola Prisoner's Blues. B1.131
2012—Prison Worksongs. B1.55
2015—Robert Pete Williams. Those Prison Blues. B1.134
5011—Snuffy Jenkins. Carolina Bluegrass. F6.82

Arista, 6 West 57th St., New York, NY 10019
specialty: rock, jazz, pop

B 6081—The Monkees. Re-Focus R3.20

Asch *See* Folkways

Asylum, 962 N. LaCienega, Los Angeles, CA 90069

SD 5068—Eagles. Desperado. R7.12
7E-1017—Jackson Browne. Late for the Sky. F10.3

Atco, 75 Rockefeller Plaza, New York, NY 10019
specialty: blues, rock, soul, rhythm 'n' blues

SD 33-226—Buffalo Springfield. Again. R7.6
SD33-259—Jerry Jeff Walker. Mr. Bojangles. F10.92
SD33-266—King Curtis. Best. B4.44
SD33-291—Cream. Best. R8.1
SD33-292—Bee Gees. Best, v.1. R4.22
SD33-371—The Coasters. Their Greatest Recordings: The Early Years. B2.27
SD33-372—LaVern Baker. Her Greatest Recordings. B2.71
SD33-373—Chuck Willis. His Greatest Recordings. B2.70
SD33-374—The Clovers. Their Greatest Recordings. B2.26
SD33-375—The Drifters. Their Greatest Recordings: The Early Years. B2.31
SD33-376—Joe Turner. His Greatest Recordings. B1.430
2SA-301—Otis Redding. Best. two discs. B4.28
SD2-501—Wilson Pickett. Best. two discs. B4.27
SD2-803—Eric Clapton. History. two discs. R5.16

Atlantic, 75 Rockefeller Plaza, New York, NY 10019
specialty: jazz, blues, rock, soul, rhythm 'n' blues

1224—Lennie Tristano. Line Up. J5.87
1234—Joe Turner. The Boss of the Blues. B1.428
1237—Charles Mingus. Pithecanthropus Erectus. J5.128
1238—Jimmy Giuffre. Clarinet. J5.90
1305—Charles Mingus. Blues and Roots. J5.125
1317—Ornette Coleman. The Shape of Jazz to Come. J5.112
1327—Ornette Coleman. Change of the Century. J5.108
1353—Ornette Coleman. This Is Our Music. J5.113
1357—Lennie Tristano. New. J5.88
1364—Ornette Coleman. Free Jazz. J5.109
1378—Ornette Coleman. Ornette. J5.110
SD 1429—Modern Jazz Quartet and Laurindo Almeida. Collaboration. P3.15
SD 1588—Ornette Coleman. Twins. J5.150
S 1594—Roberta Flack. Quiet Fire. B4.64
SD 1598—Gary Burton. Alone at Last. J5.143
SD 1613—Turk Murphy. The Many Faces of Ragtime. J2.26
SD 1614—Billie Holiday. Strange Fruit. J6.123
SD 1639—Art Ensemble of Chicago. J5.136
SD 1652—Modern Jazz Quartet. Blues on Bach. P3.14
SD 7200—Crosby, Stills, Nash and Young. Déjà Vu. R7.10
SD 7213—Aretha Franklin. Young, Gifted and Black. B4.67
SD 7224—Blind Willie McTell. Atlanta Twelve String. B1.125
SD 7225—Professor Longhair. New Orleans Piano. B2.67
SD 7262—Willie Nelson. Shotgun Willie. F8.119
SD 7271—Roberta Flack. Killing Me Softly. B4.63
SD 7291—Willie Nelson. Phases and Stages. F8.118
SD 8004—Ruth Brown. Rock & Roll. B2.73
SD 8020—T-Bone Walker. T-Bone Blues. B1.315
SD 8029—Ray Charles. What'd I Say. B2.41
SD 8054—Ray Charles. Greatest. B2.39
SD 8153—The Drifters. Golden Hits. B2.30
SD 8161/4—History of Rhythm 'n' Blues, v.1-4. four discs. B2.13
SD 8176—Aretha Franklin. Lady Soul. B4.66
SD 8193/4—History of Rhythm 'n' Blues, v. 5-6. two discs. B4.3
SD 8202—Booker T. and the MGs. Best. B4.8
SD 8208/9—History of Rhythm 'n' Blues. v. 7-8. two discs. B4.3
SD 8218—Sam and Dave. Best. B4.30
SD 8236—Led Zeppelin. II. R8.8
SD 8255—Champion Jack Dupree. Blues from the Gutter. B1.329
SD 8289—Marion Williams. Standing Here Wondering Which Way to Go.
  B3.66
SD 8296—John Prine. F10.82
SD 18204—Aretha Franklin. 10 Years of Gold. B4.65
SD2-305—Chick Corea. Inner Space. two discs. J6.128
SD2-306/7—The Tenor Sax: The Commodore Years. four discs. J6.8
SD2-316—Jazz Years; 25th Anniversary. two discs. J5.101

Atlantic (cont'd)
SD2-700—Cream. Wheels of Fire. two discs. R8.3
SD2-904—Carmen McRae. The Great American Songbook. two discs. P2.77
SD2-906—Aretha Franklin. Amazing Grace. two discs. B3.39
MM4-100—Mabel Mercer. A Tribute to Mabel Mercer on the Occasion of Her 75th Birthday. four discs. P2.78

Atteiram, P.O. Box 418, 2871 Janquil Drive, Smyrna, GA 30080
specialty: bluegrass

Audiofidelity, 221 W. 57th Street, New York, NY 10019
specialty: folk, jazz

Basf, 221 W. 57th Street, New York, NY 10019
specialty: jazz

Bandstand (c/o Southern Record Sales)
specialty: big bands
7106—Screwballs of Swingtime. P4.3

Barclay (France)
specialty: general
920067—Stuff Smith and Stephane Grappelli. Stuff and Steff. J4.148

Barnaby, 816 N. LaCienega Blvd., Los Angeles, CA 90069
specialty: rock and roll
BR 4000/1—Cadence Classics, v. 1-2. two discs. R2.3
BR 6006—Everly Brothers. Greatest Hits. two discs. R2.18

Barnaby/Candid (recently deleted from CBS)
specialty: jazz, blues
Z 30246—Otis Spann. Is the Blues. B1.310
Z 30247—Lightnin' Hopkins. In New York. B1.183
Z 30562—Cecil Taylor. Air. J5.132
KZ 31034—Charles Mingus. The Candid Recordings. J5.126
KZ 31290—Otis Spann. Walking the Blues. B1.311

Bear Family (West Germany)
specialty: old time music
FV 12.502—Jules Allen. The Texas Cowboy. F7.19
FV 15.507—Dock Walsh. F5.79

Bearsville, 3300 Warner Blvd., Burbank, CA 91505
specialty: rock

Bell, 6 West 57th Street, New York, NY 10019
    specialty: general pop

    1106–The Fifth Dimension. Greatest Hits on Earth. P2.137

Biograph, 16 River Street, Chatham, NY 12037
    specialty: jazz, blues, popular

    BLP C3–Boswell Sisters. 1932-1935. P2.135
    BLP C4–Mississippi John Hurt. 1928: His First Recordings. B1.190
    BLP C7/8–Ted Lewis. 1926-1933, v. 1-2. two discs. P5.13
    BLP 1008Q–Scott Jopkin. Ragtime, v. 2. J2.10
    BLP 12003–Blind Blake. v.1. B1.145
    BLP 12005–Chicago Jazz, 1923-1929, v. 1. J3.63
    BLP 12022–Ethel Waters. Jazzin' Babies Blues, v. 1. B1.411
    BLP 12023–Blind Blake. v.2. B1.145
    BLP 12026–Ethel Waters. v.2. B1.411
    BLP 12029–Skip James, Early Recordings. B1.198
    BLP 12031–Blind Blake. v.3. B1.145
    BLP 12037–Blind Blake. v.4. B1.145
    BLP 12043–Chicago Jazz, 1923-1929, v.2. J3.63
    BLP 12050–Blind Blake. v.5. B1.145

Birchmount (Canada)
    specialty: country and popular

    BM 705–Hank Williams. In the Beginning. F8.41

Black Lion, 221 West 57th Street, New York, NY 10019
    specialty: jazz and blues

    BL 173–Barney Kessel and Stephane Grappelli. Limehouse Blues. J6.106

Black Lion (England)
    specialty: jazz and blues

    BLP 30147–Jimmy Witherspoon. Ain't Nobody's Business! B1.433

Blue Goose, 245 Waverly Place, New York, NY 10014
    specialty: blues, jazz

Blue Horizon (England) recently deleted
    specialty: blues

    7-63222–Otis Rush. This One's a Good 'Un. B1.357
    7-63223–Magic Sam. 1937-1969. B1.346

Blue Note, 6920 Sunset Blvd., Hollywood, CA 90028
    specialty: jazz and blues

    BST 81201/2–Sidney Bechet. Jazz Classics, v.1-2. two discs. J3.20
    BST 81503/4–Bud Powell. Amazing, v.1-2. two discs. J5.31
    BST 81505/6–J. J. Johnson. The Eminent, v.1-2. two discs. J5.64

Blue Note (cont'd)
  BST 81518—Horace Silver with the Jazz Messengers. J5.36
  BST 81521/2—Art Blakey. A Night at Birdland. two discs. J5.9
  BST 84003—Art Blakey. Moanin'. J5.8
  BST 84008—Horace Silver. Finger Poppin'. J5.35
  BST 84067—Jackie McLean. Bluesnik. J5.66
  BST 84077—Dexter Gordon. Doin' All Right. J5.56
  BST 84163—Eric Dolphy. Out to Lunch. J5.155
  BST 84194—Wayne Shorter. Speak No Evil. J5.161
  BST 84237—Cecil Taylor. Unit Structures. J5.135
  BST 84260—Cecil Taylor. Conquistador. J5.133
  BST 84346—Thad Jones—Mel Lewis Orchestra. Consummation. J4.171
  BNLA 158/160—Blue Note's Three Decades of Jazz, v.1-3. six discs. J1.6
  BNLA 401-H—Sonny Rollins. 2 discs. J5.76
  BNLA 456—H2—Lester Young. Aladdin Sessions. two discs. J4.124
  BNLA 507—H2—Fats Navarro. Prime Source. two discs. J5.26
  BNLA 533—H2—T-Bone Walker. Classics of Modern Blues. two discs. B1.313
  BNLA 579—H2—Thelonious Monk. Complete Genius. two discs. J5.24

Blues Classics, 10341 San Pablo Ave., El Cerrito, CA 94530
  specialty: blues, gospel

  BC 1—Memphis Minnie, v.1. B1.388
  BC 2—The Jug, Jook and Washboard Bands. B1.414
  BC 3—Sonny Boy Williamson, No. 1., v.1. B1.136
  BC 4—Peetie Wheatstraw. B1.253
  BC 5/7—Country Blues Classics, v.1-3. B1.14
  BC 9—Sonny Boy Williamson, No. 2. The Original. B1.318
  BC 11—Blind Boy Fuller. B1.168a
  BC 12—Detroit Blues: The Early 1950s. B1.58
  BC 13—Memphis Minnie, v.2. B1.388
  BC 14—Country Blues Classics, v.4. B1.14
  BC 16—Texas Blues: The Early 50s. B1.101
  BC 17/19—Negro Religious Music, v.1-3. three discs. B3.17
  BC 20—Sonny Boy Williamson, No. 1., v.2. B1.136
  BC 24—Sonny Boy Williamson, No. 1., v.3. B1.136

Blues on Blues (c/o Southern Records Sales) recently deleted
  specialty: blues

Bluesville (recently deleted)
  specialty: blues

  BV 1044—Lonnie Johnson and Victoria Spivey. Idle Hours. B1.208

Bluesway *See* ABC

Boogie Disease, Box 10925, St. Louis, MO 63135
  specialty: blues

Boogie Woogie (c/o Southern Records Sales)
 specialty: jazz and blues

BW 1002—Meade Lux Lewis. J6.94

Brunswick (recently deleted); see also MCA
 specialty: jazz and soul

BL 754185—Jackie Wilson. Greatest Hits. B4.32

Buddah, 810 Seventh Ave., New York, NY 10019
 specialty: pop, soul, gospel

2009—Staple Singers. Best. B3.54
BDS 5070—Edwin Hawkins Singers. Oh Happy Day. B3.40
BDS 5665-2—Steve Goodman. Essential. two discs. F10.58

CBS, 51 West 52nd Street, New York, NY 10019
 specialty: general; formerly known as Columbia

CL 997—Count Basie. One O'Clock Jump. J4.17
CL 1098—The Sound of Jazz. J1.22
CL 1228—Jo Stafford. Greatest Hits. P2.79
CL 1230—Rosemary Clooney. Rosie's Greatest Hits. P2.96
CL 1780—James P. Johnson. Father of the Stride Piano. J6.30
CL 2604—Sophie Tucker. The Last of the Red Hot Mamas. P2.130.
CL 2639—Chick Webb. Stompin' at the Savoy. J4.52
CL 2830—Paul Whiteman. P5.19
CS 1065—Bill Monroe. 16 All Time Greatest Hits. F6.41
CS 1034—Roy Acuff. Greatest Hits. F8.17
CS 8004—Mitch Miller. Sing Along with Mitch. P2.139
CS 8158—Marty Robbins. Gunfighter Ballads and Trail Songs. F7.30
PC 8163—Miles Davis. Kind of Blue. J5.151
PC 8271—Miles Davis. Sketches of Spain. J5.85
CS 8638—Mitch Miller. Mitch's Greatest Hits. P2.138
CS 8639—Marty Robbins. Greatest Hits. R1.17
CS 8807—Barbra Streisand. P2.126
CS 8845—Lester Flatt and Earl Scruggs. Carnegie Hall. F6.28
KCS 8905—Bob Dylan. The Times They Are A-Changin'. F10.19
PC 9106—Miles Davis. My Funny Valentine. J5.153
KCS 9128—Bob Dylan. Bringing It Back Home. F10.14
PC 9428—Miles Davis. Milestones. J5.152
KCS 9463—Bob Dylan. Greatest Hits, v.1. F10.16
CS 9468—18 King Size Country Hits. F8.11
CS 9478—Johnny Cash. Greatest Hits, v.1. F8.19
G 31224—Count Basie. Super Chief. two discs. J4.18
KG 31345—Johnny Mathis. All Time Greatest Hits. two discs. P2.13
PC 31350—Simon and Garfunkel. Greatest Hits. F10.46
KC 31352—Weather Report. I Sing the Body Electric. J6.138
KG 31361—Marty Robbins. All Time Greatest Hits. two discs. F8.78
KG 31364—Ray Price. All Time Greatest Hits. two discs. F8.76

CBS (cont'd)

KG 31379—Mahalia Jackson. Great. two discs. B3.42
KG 31547—Benny Goodman. All Time Hits. two discs. J4.58
KG 31564—Eddie Condon's World of Jazz. two discs. J3.66
KG 31571—Ethel Waters. Greatest Years. two discs. P2.86
KG 31588—Percy Faith. All Time Greatest Hits. two discs. P5.79
KG 31595—The Gospel Sound, v.2. two discs. B3.9
G 31617—Teddy Wilson All Stars. two discs. J4.122
KC 31758—Earl Scruggs. Live at Kansas State. F6.124
KG 32064—Duke Ellington. Presents Ivie Anderson. two discs. P5.10
KG 32151—Precious Lord; Gospel Songs of Thomas A. Dorsey. two discs.
    B3.19
KC 32284—Clifford Brown. The Beginning and the End. J5.38
KG 32338—Luis Russell. His Louisiana Swing Orchestra. two discs. J4.85
KG 32355—A Jazz Piano Anthology. two discs. J6.12
KG 32416—Bob Wills. Anthology. two discs. F7.48
G 32593—Cab Calloway. Hi De Ho Man. two discs. P5.23
KG 32663—Gene Krupa. His Orchestra and Anita O'Day. two discs. P5.36
KC 32708—The Original Boogie Woogie Piano Giants. J6.91
KG 32822—Benny Goodman and Helen Forrest. two discs. P5.11
KG 32945—The World of Swing. two discs. J4.11
CG 33639—Johnny Cash. At Folsom Prison and San Quentin. two discs.
    F8.18
C2-33682—Bob Dylan. Basement Tapes. two discs. F10.12
C 33882—Lefty Frizzell. Remembering the Greatest Hits. F8.57
CS 9533—Leonard Cohen. Songs. F10.6
CS 9576—The Byrds. Greatest Hits. R7.7
KCS 9604—Bob Dylan. John Wesley Harding. F10.18
PC 9633—Miles Davis. Miles Ahead. J5.83
CS 9655—Art Tatum. Piano Starts Here. J6.38
CS 9660—Ballads and Breakdowns of the Golden Era. F5.1
CS 9670—The Byrds. Sweetheart of the Rodeo. R7.8
KCS 9737—Laura Nyro. New York Tendaberry. F10.80
LE 10043—Lester Flatt and Earl Scruggs. Foggy Mountain Banjo. F6.29
LE 10106—Little Jimmie Dickens. Greatest Hits. F8.53
G 30008—The Story of the Blues, v.1. two discs. B1.17
G 30009—Big Bands Greatest Hits, v.1. two discs. P5.2
C 30036—Bukka White. Parchman Farm. B1.257
G 30126—Bessie Smith. Any Woman's Blues. two discs. B1.394
KC 30130—Santana. Abraxas. R4.42
KC 30322—Janis Joplin. Pearl. R5.20
G 30450—Bessie Smith. Empty Bed Blues. two discs. B1.395
C 30466—Maynard Ferguson. M. F. Horn. J4.168
C 30496—Leroy Carr. Blues Before Sunrise. B1.107
G 30503—Great Hits of R & B. two discs. B2.12
C 30584—Earl Scruggs. Family and Friends. F6.122
G 30592—The Fifties Greatest Hits. two discs. P1.5
G 30628—Charles Mingus. Better Get It in Your Soul. two discs. J5.124
G 30818—Bessie Smith. The Empress. two discs. B1.396

CBS (cont'd)

KC 30887–Johnny Cash. Greatest Hits, v.2. F8.19
KC 31067–John McLaughlin. The Inner Mounting Flame. J6.137
G 31086–The Gospel Sound, v.1. two discs. B3.9
G 31093–Bessie Smith. Nobody's Blues But Mine. two discs. B1.397
KC 31170–Blood, Sweat, and Tears. Hits. R4.9
KG 31213–Big Bands Greatest Hits, v.2. two discs. P5.2
KC 33894–George Morgan. Remembering. F8.103
PC 34077–Leonard Cohen. Best. F10.5
KG ——–Robert Johnson. Complete. three discs. B1.110 (to be released).
C4L 18–Thesaurus of Classic Jazz. four discs. J3.86
C4L 19–Fletcher Henderson. A Study in Frustration, 1923-1938. four discs.
    J4.41
C3L 21–Billie Holiday. Golden Years, v.1. three discs. J6.121
C3L 22–Mildred Bailey. Her Greatest Performances, 1929-1946. three discs.
    P2.87
C2L 24–Joe Venuti and Eddie Lang. Stringing the Blues. two discs. J3.98
C3L 25–Woody Herman. The Thundering Herds. three discs. J4.46
C2L 29–Gene Krupa. Drummin' Man. two discs. J4.71
C3L 32–Jazz Odyssey: The Sound of Chicago. three discs. J3.67
C3L 33–Jazz Odyssey: The Sound of Harlem. three discs. J3.83
C3L 35–Original Sounds of the 20s. three discs. P1.9
C3L 40–Billie Holiday. Golden Years, v.2. three discs. J6.121
GP 26–Miles Davis. Bitches Brew. two discs. J6.131
GP 33–Bessie Smith. The World's Greatest Blues Singer. two discs. B1.393
O2L 160–Benny Goodman. Carnegie Hall Concert. two discs. J4.38
C2S 823–Tony Bennett. At Carnegie Hall. two discs. P2.2
C2S 841–Bob Dylan. Blonde on Blonde. two discs. F10.13
C2S 847–Eubie Blake. The Eighty-Six Years of Eubie Blake. two discs.
    J2.9

CBS Canada

specialty: general; formerly known as Columbia

CBS (England)

specialty: general

52538–Charlie Christian, v.1. J5.10
52648–Big Bill Broonzy. Big Bill's Blues. B1.152
52796–Blacks, Whites and Blues. F3.32
52797–Recording the Blues. B1.20
52798–Ma Rainey and the Classic Blues Singers. B1.375
63288–Screening the Blues. B1.36
66232–The Story of the Blues, v.2. two discs. B1.17

CBS (France)

specialty: general

62581–Charlie Christian, v.2. J5.10
62853–Benny Goodman. Trio and Quartet, v.1. J4.96

CBS (France) (cont'd)
    62876–Teddy Wilson. Piano Solos. J6.41
    63052–Django Reinhardt. Paris, 1945. J6.116
    63086–Benny Goodman. Trio and Quartet, v.2. J4.96
    63092–Clarence Williams Blue Five, with Louis Armstrong and Sidney Bechet. J3.50
    64218–Rare Recordings of the Twenties, v.1. B1.381
    65379/80–Rare Recordings of the Twenties, v.2-3. B1.381
    65421–Rare Recordings of the Twenties, v.4. B1.381
    66310–Miles Davis. Essential. three discs. J5.122
    67264–Duke Ellington. Complete, v.1. two discs. J4.27
    68275–Duke Ellington. Complete, v.2. two discs. J4.27
    80089–Roy Eldridge. Little Jazz. J4.25
    88000–Duke Ellington. Complete, v.3. J4.27
    88001/4–Louis Armstrong. Very Special Old Phonography. eight discs. J3.17
    88031–Buck Clayton. 1953-1955. two discs. J4.157
    88035–Duke Ellington. Complete, v.4. two discs. J4.27
    88082–Duke Ellington. Complete, v.5. two discs. J4.27
    88129–Erroll Garner. Play It Again, Erroll. two discs. P3.8
    88137–Duke Ellington. Complete, v.6. two discs. J4.27
    88140–Duke Ellington. Complete, v.7. two discs. J4.27
    J 27–New York Scene in the 1940s. J3.85

CBS (Japan)
    specialty: general
    20 AP 13/4–Stanley Brothers, v.1-2. F6.54 and F9.73

Cadence (recently deleted); most available on *Barnaby* label.
    specialty: pop
    3061–Andy Williams. Million Seller Songs. P2.67

Cadet (recently deleted); see All Platinum
    specialty: rhythm 'n' blues and soul
    S 757–Ramsey Lewis. The "In" Crowd. B4.53

Caedmon, 505 Eighth Avenue, New York, NY 10018
    specialty: spoken word, educational, folk music
    TC 1142/6–Folksongs of Britain, v.1-5. five discs. F2.9
    TC 1162/4–Folksongs of Britain, v.6-8. three discs. F2.9
    TC 1224/5–Folksongs of Britain, v.9-10. two discs. F2.9

Camden *See* RCA

Cameo (recently deleted)
    specialty: pop, rock and roll
    P 7001–Chubby Checker. Twist. R2.16

Canaan, 4800 W. Waco Drive, Waco, TX 76703
    specialty: sacred

Capitol, 1750 N. Vine Street, Hollywood, CA 90028
    specialty: general (country, rock, mood)
    SKAO 143—Ferlin Husky. Best. F8.64
    SKAO 145—Buck Owens. Best, v.3. F8.75
    ST 294—Fred Neil. Everybody's Talkin'. F10.36
    DTBB 264—Jim and Jesse. 20 Great Songs. two discs. F6.33
    DKAO 377—Peggy Lee. Greatest. three discs. P2.75
    SW 425—The Band. Stage Fright. R7.5
    SM 650—Merle Travis. The Merle Travis Guitar. F8.37
    SM 756—Tennessee Ernie Ford. Hymns. F9.39
    ST 884/6—Country Hits of the 40s, 50s, and 60s. three discs. F8.9
    SM 1061—Louvin Brothers. The Family Who Prays. F9.49
    ST 1253—Jean Shepard. This Is F8.146
    ST 1312—Rose Maddox. The One Rose. F8.140
    ST 1380—Tennessee Ernie Ford. Sixteen Tons. F8.56
    ST 1388—Les Baxter. Best. P5.78
    T 1477—Ray Anthony. Hits. P5.77
    SWBO 1569—Judy Garland. At Carnegie Hall. two discs. P2.69
    SWCL 1613—Nat "King" Cole. Story. three discs. P2.5
    ST 2089—Hank Thompson. Golden Hits. F7.47
    ST 2105—Buck Owens. Best, v.1. F8.75
    ST 2180—Kingston Trio. Folk Era. three discs. F4.11
    ST 2373—Merle Haggard. Strangers. F8.111
    ST 2422—Beatles. Rubber Soul. R4.7
    ST 2576—Beatles. Revolver. R4.6
    ST 2585—Merle Haggard. Swinging Doors. F8.112
    DT 2601—Dean Martin. Best. P2.54
    SM 2662—Merle Travis. Best. F8.36
    STFL 2814—Frank Sinatra. Deluxe Set. six discs. P2.16
    ST 2897—Buck Owens. Best, v.2. F8.75
    SKAO 2939—Cannonball Adderley. Best. J6.126
    SKAO 2946—Al Martino. Best. P2.58
    DTCL 2953—Edith Piaf. Deluxe Set. P2.113
    SKAO 2955—The Band. Music from Big Pink. R7.3
    STCL 2988—Judy Garland. Deluxe Set. three discs. P2.70
    T 10457—Django Reinhardt. Best. J6.110
    M 11026—Miles Davis. Birth of the Cool. J5.82
    M 11029—Gerry Mulligan. Tentette. Walking Shoes. J5.97
    M 11058—Duke Ellington. Piano Reflections. J6.17a.
    M 11059—Tadd Dameron. Strictly Bebop. J5.14
    M 11060—Lennie Tristano. Crosscurrents. J5.86
    ST 11082—Merle Haggard. Best of the Best. F8.110
    ST 11177—Supersax Plays Bird. J5.5
    ST 11193—Louvin Brothers. The Great Gospel Singing of the Louvin
        Brothers. F9.50
    SKC 11241—Tex Ritter. An American Legend. three discs. F7.13

Capitol (cont'd)
ST 11287—Gene Vincent. The Bop That Just Won't Stop (1956). R1.18
ST 11308—Les Paul and Mary Ford. The World Is Still Waiting for the Sunrise. P2.112
SVBO 11384—Beach Boys. Spirit of America. two discs. R3.3
ST 11440—The Band. Northern Lights. R7.4
SKBO 11537—The Beatles. Rock 'n' Roll Music. two discs. R3.4
ST 11577—Glen Campbell. Best. F8.98

Capitol (Japan)
ECR 8178—Rose Maddox. Sings Bluegrass. F6.87

Capricorn, 3300 Warner Blvd., Burbank, CA 91505
specialty: rock

2CP 0108—Duane Allman. An Anthology, v.1. two discs. R4.20
2CP 0139—Duane Allman. An Anthology, v.2. two discs. R4.20
2CP 0164—Allman Brothers Band. The Road Goes On Forever. two discs. R5.12a

Charisma (England)
specialty: folk, rock

CS 5—Steeleye Span. Individually and Collectively. F2.58

Charly (England)

CR 300-012—Yardbirds, Featuring Eric Clapton. R5.12
CR 300-013—Yardbirds, Featuring Jeff Bech. R5.12
CR 300-014—Yardbirds, Featuring Jimmy Page. R5.12

Checker (recently deleted); see All Platinum
specialty: rhythm 'n' blues, soul

3002—Little Milton. Sings Big Blues. B2.60

Chess (recently deleted, but many copies still available); see All Platinum and Phonogram
specialty: blues

1483—Muddy Waters. Folk Singer. B1.302
1514—Chuck Berry. Golden Decade, v.1. two discs. B2.37
1553—Muddy Waters. They Call Me Muddy Waters. B1.304
2CH 50027—Sonny Boy Williamson, No. 2. This Is My Story. two discs. B1.319
2CH 50030—The Golden Age of Rhythm 'n' Blues. two discs. B2.10
60023—Chuck Berry. Golden Decade, v.2. two discs. B2.37
60028—Chuck Berry. Golden Decade, v.3. two discs. B2.37

Chiaroscuro, 221 W. 57th Street, New York, NY 10019
specialty: jazz

CR 101—Earl Hines. Quintessential Recording Sessions. J6.26

Chiaroscuro (cont'd)
    CR 106–Don Ewell. A Jazz Portrait of the Artist. J6.53
    CR 108–Eddie Condon. Town Hall Concerts, 1944/5. J3.71
    CR 113–Eddie Condon. Town Hall Concerts, 1944/5. J3.71
    CR 120–Earl Hines. Quintessential Continued. J6.25

Chrysalis, 1750 N. Vine Street, Hollywood, CA 90028
    specialty: folk, rock
        CHR 1008–Steeleye Span. Below the Salt. F2.57
        CHR 1119–Steeleye Span. Please to See the King. F2.59

Classic Jazz, 43 W. 61st Street, New York, NY 10023
    specialty: jazz

Classic Jazz Masters (Denmark)
    specialty: jazz
        CJM 2/10–Jelly Roll Morton. Library of Congress Recordings. nine discs.
        J3.27

Collectors Classics (c/o Southern Record Sales)
    specialty: bluegrass
        CC 1/2–Stanley Brothers, v.1-2. two discs. F6.55
        CC 3–Lonesome Pine Fiddlers. F6.85
        CC 6–Banjo Classics. F6.2

Columbia *See* CBS

Columbia (England)
    specialty: pop, mood
    SCX 6529–Shirley Bassey. Very Best. P2.90

Concert Hall (France)
    specialty: jazz, pop
    SJS 1268–Tribute to Fletcher Henderson. J4.12

Concord Jazz, P.O. Box 845, Concord, CA 94522
    specialty: jazz

Contact (recently deleted)
    specialty: jazz
    LP 2–Earl Hines. Spontaneous Explorations. J6.27

Contemporary, 8481 Melrose Place, Los Angeles, CA 90069
    specialty: jazz

Contour (England)
specialty: pop, rock
2870.388—Dell-Vikings. Come and Go With Me. R2.31

Coral, 100 Universal City Plaza, Universal City, CA 91608
specialty: reissues of MCA material; general
CXB 6—McGuire Sisters. Best. P2.151

Coral (England)
specialty: reissues of MCA material; general
COPS 7453—Gospel Classics. B3.7
CDMSP 801—Bing Crosby. Musical Autobiography. five discs. P2.11

Coral (West Germany)
specialty: reissues of MCA material; general
COPS 6855—Roy Eldridge. Swing Along with Little Jazz. two discs. J4.26
COPS 7360—The Bands Within the Bands. two discs. J4.91

Cotillion, 75 Rockefeller Plaza, New York, NY 10019
specialty: rock, contemporary folk
SD2-400—Woodstock Two. two discs. R4.2
SD3-500—Woodstock Three. three discs. R4.2

Country Music History (West Germany)
specialty: old time music
CMH 211—Jenks "Tex" Carman. The Dixie Cowboy. F7.24

County, Box 191, Floyd, VA 24091
specialty: old time music, bluegrass
402—Delmore Brothers. Brown's Ferry Blues, 1933-1941. F8.21
404—Wade Mainer. F5.90
405—The Hillbillies. F5.85
505—Charlie Poole, v.1. F5.69
506—Gid Tanner, v.1. F5.76
509—Charlie Poole, v.2. F5.69
511—Mountain Blues, 1927-1934. F5.15
515—Mountain Banjo Songs and Tunes. F5.19
516—Charlie Poole, v.3. F5.69
518/20—Echoes of the Ozarks, v.1-3. three discs. F5.21
521—Uncle Dave Macon. Early Recordings, 1925-1935. F5.35
524—DaCosta Woltz's Southern Broadcasters. F5.61
526—Gid Tanner, v.2. F5.76
536—Kessinger Brothers. 1928-1930. F5.114
540—Charlie Poole, v.4. F5.69
541/2—Grand Ole Opry Stars. two discs. F8.13
714—Kenny Baker and Joe Greene. High Country. F6.67
729—Lilly Brothers. Early Recordings. F6.35

County (cont'd)
733—Clark Kessinger. Legend. F5.62
738—Stanley Brothers. That Little Old Country Church House. F9.76
742—Lilly Brothers. What Will I Leave Behind. F9.48
749—Springtime in the Mountains. F6.18

Creative World, 1012 S. Robertson Blvd., Los Angeles, CA 90035
specialty: progressive jazz, Stan Kenton
ST 1030—Stan Kenton. The Kenton Era. four discs. J4.173

Davis Unlimited, Route 11, 16 Bond Street, Clarksville, TN 37040
specialty: country, bluegrass, old time music
DU 33015—Fiddlin' Doc Roberts. Classic Fiddle Tunes Recorded during the Golden Age. F5.99
DU 33030—Vernon Dalhart. Old Time Songs, 1925-1930, v.1. F5.29a

Dawn Club (c/o Southern Record Sales)
specialty: jazz reissues
DC 12009—Bud Freeman. Chicagoans in New York. J3.72

Debut (Denmark)
specialty: modern jazz
DEB 144—Albert Ayler. Ghosts. J5.140

Decca *See* MCA

Delmark, 4243 N. Lincoln, Chicago, IL 60618
specialty: jazz, blues
201—George Lewis. On Parade. J3.15
202—George Lewis. Doctor Jazz. J3.12
203—George Lewis. Memorial Album. J3.14
212—Earl Hines. At Home. J6.23
DS 420/1—Anthony Braxton. For Alto. two discs. J5.105
DS 605—Curtis Jones. Lonesome Bedroom Blues. B1.338
DS 612—Junior Wells. Hoodoo Man Blues. B1.370

Deram (England)
specialty: rock, folk, pop
SMK 1117—Shirley Collins. A Favourite Garland. F2.14

Dot, 8255 Beverly Blvd., Los Angeles, CA 90048
specialty: country, pop
ABDP 4009—Mac Wiseman. 16 Great Performances. F6.112
25071—Pat Boone. Pat's Greatest Hits. R2.26
25201—Billy Vaughan. Golden Hits. P5.91
25820—Original Hits—Golden Instrumentals. R2.10

Duke, 8255 Beverly Blvd., Los Angeles, CA 90048
specialty: blues, soul

DLP 71–Johnny Ace. Memorial Album. B2.48
DLP 83–Junior Parker. Best. B1.352
DLP 84–Bobby "Blue" Bland. Best, v.1. B2.49
DLP 86–Bobby "Blue" Bland. Best, v.2. B2.49

Dunhill, 8255 Beverly Blvd., Los Angeles, CA 90048
specialty: rock, folk

DSD 50132–Jimmy Buffett. A White Sport Coat and a Pink Crustacean.
F10.54
DXS 50145–Mamas and Papas. 20 Golden Hits. two discs. R3.19

ECM, 810 Seventh Avenue, New Yorkl NY 10019
specialty: modern jazz
1014/6–Chick Corea. Piano Improvisations, v.1-3. three discs. J6.130
1018/9–Circle. Paris Concert. two discs. J5.149
1035/7–Keith Jarrett. Solo Concerts: Bremen and Lausanne. J6.64

EMI (Denmark)
specialty: general

EO 52-81004–Session at Riverside: New York. J4.164
EO 52-81005–Bobby Hackett and Jack Teagarden. Jazz Ultimate. J4.142
EO 52-81006–Session at Midnight: Los Angeles. J4.163

EMI (England)
specialty: general

Odeon CLP 1817–Django Reinhardt. Legendary. J6.111
One Up OU 2046–Big 'Uns from the 50s and 60s. R2.2
Starline SRS 5120–Wanda Jackson. R2.20
Starline SRS 5129–Johnny Otis. Pioneer of Rock. B2.64

EMI (France)
specialty: French music, general

Pathe CO 54-16021/30–Swing Sessions, 1937-1950. ten discs. J1.5
Pathe SPAM 67.092–Edith Piaf. Recital, 1962. P2.115
CO 62-80813–Jay McShann's Piano. J6.67

ESP, 5 Riverside Drive, Krumville, NY 12447
specialty: jazz

1014–Sun Ra. Heliocentric Worlds, v.1. J5.130
1017–Sun Ra. Heliocentric Worlds, v.2. J5.130

Eclipse (England)
specialty: reissues of jazz and nostalgia

ECM 2051–Django Reinhardt. Swing '35-'39. J6.112

Elektra, 962 N. LaCienega, Los Angeles, CA 90069
specialty: folk, rock

EKS 7217–Folk Banjo Styles. F3.30
EKS 7239–Bob Gibson. Where I'm Bound. F4.9
EKS 7277–Tom Paxton. Ramblin' Boy. F10.44
EKS 7280–Judy Collins. Concert. F4.6
EKS 7287–Phil Ochs. I Ain't Marching Anymore. F10.41
EKS 7310–Phil Ochs. In Concert. F10.42
EKS 74007–The Doors. R6.1
EKS 74014–The Doors. Strange Days. R6.2
EKS 75032–David Ackles. American Gothic. F10.48
EKS 75035–Judy Collins. Colors of the Day: Best. R4.27
EKL-BOX–The Folk Box. four discs. F3.7
ELK 271/2–Woody Guthrie. Library of Congress Recordings. three discs.
F10.20
EKL 301/2–Leadbelly. Library of Congress Recordings. three discs. B1.209
7E-2005–Paul Butterfield. Golden Butter. two discs. R5.8

Elektra (England)
specialty: folk, rock

K 52035–Dillards. Country Tracks: Best. F6.120

Enterprise, 2693 Union Avenue, Memphis, TN 38112
specialty: soul, gospel

1001–Isaac Hayes. Hot Buttered Soul. B4.51

Epic, 51 W. 52nd Street, New York, NY 10019
specialty: general

EE 22001–Johnny Hodges. Hodge Podge. J4.109
EE 22003–Bobby Hackett. The Hackett Horn. J4.140
EE 22005–The Duke's Men. J4.133
EE 22007–Chuck Berry and His Stomping Stevedores. J4.131
EE 22027–Gene Krupa. That Drummer's Band. J4.75
BN 26246e–The Yardbirds. Greatest Hits. R5.12
BN 26486–Tammy Wynette. Greatest Hits, v.1. F8.133
KE 30325–Sly and the Family Stone. Greatest Hits. B4.31
EG 30473–Johnny Otis Show Live at Monterey. two discs. B4.4
E 30733–Tammy Wynette. Greatest Hits, v.2. F8.133
KE 31607–Johnny Nash. I Can See Clearly Now. B4.56
KE 33396–Tammy Wynette. Greatest Hits, v.3. F8.133
PE 33409–Jeff Beck. Blow by Blow. R4.8
BG 33752–George Jones and Tammy Wynette. Me and the First Lady/We
Go Together. two discs. F8.151
BG 33779–Jeff Beck. Truth/Beck-Ola. two discs. P5.14.
BS 33782–Bob Wills/Asleep at the Wheel. Fathers and Sons. two discs.
F7.49
B2N 159–Those Wonderful Girls of Stage, Screen and Radio. two discs. P6.86

Epic (cont'd)
  B2N 164—Those Wonderful Guys of Stage, Screen and Radio. two discs.
    P6.87
  CE2E-201/2—Bing Crosby. Story. four discs. P2.8
  SN 6042—Swing Street. four discs. J4.10
  SN 6044—Jack Teagarden. King of the Blues Trombone. three discs. J3.93
  L2N 6072—Encores from the 30s, v.1 (1930-1935). two discs. P1.4 [v.2
    never released]

Epic (France)
  specialty: general

  LN 24269—Johnny Dodds and Kid Ory. J3.24
  66212—Count Basie with Lester Young. two discs. J4.19

Eubie Blake Music, 284A Stuyvesant Ave., Brooklyn, NY 11221
  specialty: ragtime and reissues

Euphonic, P.O. Box 476, Ventura, CA 93001
  specialty: piano jazz, blues

Everest, 10920 Wilshire Blvd. West, Los Angeles, CA 90024
  specialty: reissues in folk, blues, and jazz

  FS 214—Charlie Parker. v.1. J5.71
  FS 216—Otis Spann. B1.305
  FS 217—Champion Jack Dupree. B1.327
  FS 219—Charlie Christian. At Minton's. J5.11
  FS 232—Charlie Parker. v.2. J5.71
  FS 253—Fred McDowell. B1.118
  FS 254—Charlie Parker. v.3. J5.71
  FS 293—Al Haig. Jazz Will O' the Wisp. J6.56

Excello, 1011 Woodland St., Nashville, TN 37206
  specialty: blues

  DBL 28025—Excello Story. two discs. B4.2

Extreme Rarities, c/o Ken Crawford, 215 Steuben Ave., Pittsburgh, PA 15205
  specialty: jazz and soundtrack reissues

Fantasy, 10th and Parker Sts., Berkeley, CA 94710
  specialty: blues, jazz

  9432—Woody Herman. Giant Step. J4.170
  9442—Staple Singers. The Twenty-Fifth Day of December. B3.57
  CCR-2—Creedence Clearwater Revival. Chronicle. two discs. R3.6
  F 24720—Jack Elliott. Hard Travellin': Songs by Woody Guthrie and Others.
    two discs. F4.30

Fat Cat's Jazz, Box 458, Manassas, VA 22110
specialty: jazz

Flying Dutchman, 1133 Avenue of the Americas, New York, NY 10036
specialty: jazz
FD 10146–Coleman Hawkins. Classic Tenors. J4.99

Flying Fish, 3320 N. Halstead, Chicago, IL 60657
specialty: bluegrass and Western swing, blues
101–Hillbilly Jazz. two discs. F7.38

Flyright (England)
specialty: blues, r'n'b
LP 108/9–Memphis Minnie. 1934-1949. two discs. B1.389

Folk Legacy, Sharon Mt. Rd., Sharon, CT 06069
specialty: folk
FSB 20–Harry Cox. Traditional English Love Songs. F2.18
FSA 26–Sarah Ogan Gunning. A Girl of Constant Sorrow. F3.66
FSA 32–Hedy West. Old Times and Hard Times. F3.93
FSI 35–Michael Cooney. The Cheese Stands Alone. F3.62

Folklyric, 10341 San Pablo Avenue, El Cerrito, CA 94530
specialty: blues and folk reissues
9001–Son House. Legendary, 1941/42 Recordings. B1.189

Folkways, 43 W. 61st Street, New Yorkl NY 10023
specialty: folk, blues, jazz
2301/2–Jean Ritchie. Child Ballads in America. two discs. F3.84
2314–American Banjo Tunes and Songs in Scruggs Style. F6.1
2315–Stoneman Family. Banjo Tunes and Songs. F5.74
2316–Ritchie Family. F3.85
2318–Mountain Music Bluegrass Style. F6.17
2320/3–Pete Seeger. American Favorite Ballads. four discs. F4.65
2351–Dock Boggs. v.1. F5.45
2356–Old Harp Singing. F9.11
2392–Dock Boggs. v.2. F5.45
2395/9–New Lost City Ramblers. v.1-5. five discs. F5.66
2409–Country Songs–Old and New. F6.25
2426– Doc Watson and Jean Ritchie. F4.20
2431/2–Newport Folk Festival, 1959/60. v.1-2. two discs. F3.15
2433–Lilly Brothers. Folksongs from the Southern Mountains. F6.36
2445–Pete Seeger. American Favorite Ballads. F4.65

Folkways (cont'd)
2456—Pete Seeger. Broadsides. F3.89
2480—Cisco Houston. Sings Songs of the Open Road. F10.67
2492—New Lost City Ramblers. Play Instrumentals. F5.67
2501/2—Pete Seeger. Gazette, v.1-2. two discs. F3.89
2641/5—New Orleans, v.1-5. five discs. J3.2
2801/11—Jazz, v.1-11. eleven discs. J1.9
2941/2—Leadbelly. Last Sessions, v.1-2. four discs. B1.115
2951/3—Anthology of American Folk Music. six discs. F3.4
3527—Little Brother Montgomery. Blues. B1.223
3562—Joseph Lamb. A Study in Classic Ragtime. J2.11
3575—Irish Music in London Pubs. F2.35
3810—Buell Kazee. His Songs and Music. F3.71
3903—Dock Boggs. v.3. F5.45
5212—Woody Guthrie. Dust Bowl Ballads. F10.61
5264—New Lost City Ramblers. Songs of the Depression. F5.95
5272—Harry K. McClintock. Haywire Mac. F10.70
5285—Almanac Singers. Talking Union. F4.1
5801/2—American History in Ballads and Songs. six discs. F3.21
FTS 31001—Woody Guthrie. This Land Is Your Land. F10.22
FTS 31021—Watson Family. F4.19

Fontana, 1 IBM Plaza, Chicago, IL 60611
specialty: general
27560—New Vaudeville Band. P2.153

Fontana (England)
specialty: general
STL 5269—Martin Carthy. F2.13

Fountain (England)
specialty: jazz and blues reissues
FB 301—Ida Cox, v.1. B1.401
FB 304—Ida Cox, v.2. B1.401

Freedom (England)
specialty: modern jazz
FLP 40106—Cecil Taylor. D Trad That's What. J5.134

GHP (West Germany)
specialty: old time music
902—Riley Puckett. Old Time Greats. F5.39
1001—Dock Walsh. F5.81

GNP Crescendo, 9165 Sunset Blvd., Hollywood, CA 90069
specialty: jazz

GNP Crescendo (cont'd)
    S18—Max Roach-Clifford Brown. In Concert. J5.33
    9003—Coleman Hawkins. The Hawk in Holland. J4.101

Gannet (Denmark)
    specialty: jazz
    GEN 5136/7—Jimmy Yancey, v.1-2. two discs. J6.96

Good Time Jazz, 8481 Melrose Place, Los Angeles, CA 90069
    specialty: dixieland jazz, piano jazz

    10035—Luckey Roberts/Willie "The Lion" Smith. Harlem Piano. J6.34
    10043—Don Ewell. Man Here Plays Fine Piano. J6.50
    10046—Don Ewell. Free 'n' Easy. J6.49
    12001/3—Lu Watters. San Francisco Style, v.1-3. three discs. J3.59
    12004—Kid Ory. 1954. J3.42
    12022—Kid Ory. Tailgate! J3.46
    12048—Bunk Johnson. Superior Jazz Band. J3.10

Gordy, 6464 Sunset Blvd., Hollywood, CA 90028
    specialty: soul, blues

Greene Bottle (c/o Southern Record Sales)
    specialty: blues

Groove Merchant, Suite 3701, 515 Madison Avenue, New York, NY 10022
    specialty: jazz, blues

Gusto, 220 Boscobel Street, Nashville, TN 37213
    specialty: reissues of Starday and King records

Halcyon, Box 4255, Grand Central Station, New York, NY 10017
    specialty: jazz

Halcyon (England)
    specialty: reissues of jazz and nostalgia items
    HAL 5—Annette Hanshaw. Sweetheart of the Thirties. P2.104

Harmony (recently deleted); see also CBS
    specialty: budget line reissues of Columbia and Brunswick items

    HL 7191—Harry James. Songs That Sold a Million. P5.83
    HL 7233—Wilma Lee and Stoney Cooper. Sacred Songs. F9.30
    HL 7290—Bill Monroe. Great. F6.39
    HL 7299—Molly O'Day. Unforgettable. F8.131
    HL 7308—Johnny Bond..Best. F7.6
    HL 7313—Bob Atcher. Best Early American Folksongs. F7.22
    HL 7317—Sons of the Pioneers. Best. F7.16
    HL 7340—Lester Flatt and Earl Scruggs. Great Original Recordings. F6.30
    HL 7382—Gene Autry. Great Hits. F7.4

Harmony (cont'd)
   HL 7396–Carter Family. Great Sacred Songs. F9.26
   HL 7402–Lester Flatt and Earl Scruggs. Sacred Songs. F9.37
   HS 11178–Wilma Lee and Stoney Cooper. Sunny Side of the Mountain.
      F6.73
   HS 11334–Roy Acuff. Waiting for My Call to Glory. F9.15
   H 30609–Johnny Ray. Best. R2.22

Harmony (Canada)
   HEL 6004–Jazzmen in Uniform, 1945, Paris. J1.4

Herwin, 45 First Street, Glen Cove, NY 11542
   specialty: jazz and blues reissues
   101–Freddie Keppard. J3.6
   106–King Oliver. The Great 1923 Gennetts. J3.7
   202–Bessie Johnson. 1928-29. B3.43
   203–Sanctified, v.2: God Gave Me the Light, 1927-1931. B3.5
   204–Blind Joe Taggart. B3.61
   207–Sanctified, v.3: Whole World in His Hands, 1927-1936. B3.27
   208–Cannon's Jug Stompers. two discs. B1.419
   401–They All Played the Maple Leaf Rag. J2.8

Hi, 539 W. 25th Street, New York, NY 10001
   specialty: soul
   XSHL 32070–Al Green. Let's Stay Together. B4.48

Hilltop (recently deleted)
   specialty: Mercury budget reissues of country material through Pickwick
      records
   JS 6036–Louvin Brothers. F8.29
   JS 6093–Lester Flatt and Earl Scruggs. F6.27

Historical, P.O. Box 4204, Bergen Station, Jersey City, NJ 07304
   specialty: reissued jazz, blues, and country materials
   HLP 9–Benny Moten. Kansas City Orchestra, 1923-29. J4.83
   HLP 10–Chicago Southside, 1926-1932, v.1. J3.64
   HLP 24–The Territory Bands, 1926-1931, v.1. J3.103
   HLP 26–The Territory Bands, 1926-1931, v.2. J3.103
   HLP 30–Chicago Southside, 1926-1932, v.2. J3.64
   HLP 8001–Fields Ward. Buck Mountain Band. F5.101
   HLP 8004–Stoneman Family. 1927-1928. F5.73

Imperial (recently deleted); see United Artists
   specialty: blues and soul
   LP 9141–Smiley Lewis. I Hear You Knocking. B2.58

Impulse, 8255 Beverly Blvd., Los Angeles, CA 90048
specialty: jazz (modern and mainstream)

AS 6—John Coltrane. Africa Brass. J5.115
AS 10—John Coltrane. Live at the Village Vanguard. J5.120
AS 12—Benny Carter. Further Definitions. J4.24
AS 77—John Coltrane. A Love Supreme. J5.121
AS 95—John Coltrane. Ascension. J5.116
AS 9108—Earl Hines. Once Upon a Time. J4.69
AS 9148—John Coltrane. Cosmic Music. J5.117
AS 9183—Charlie Haden. Liberation Suite. J5.156
AS 9229-2—Pharoah Sanders. Nest. two discs. J5.158
ASH 9253-3—The Saxophone. three discs. J6.5
ASY 9272-3—The Drum. three discs. J6.2
ASY 9284-3—The Bass. three discs. J6.1

Increase (recently deleted); see All Platinum
specialty: rock and roll and rhythm 'n' blues in a disc jockey simulation

2000/12—Cruisin', 1955-1967. thirteen discs. R2.4

Island, 7720 Sunset Blvd., Los Angeles, CA 90046
specialty: folk and reggae music

SW 9329—The Wailers. Catch a Fire. B5.9
ILPS 9330—Toots and the Maytals. Funky Kingston. B5.8
ILPS 9334—The Chieftains. 5. F2.39

Island (England)
specialty: folk and reggae music

FOLK 1001—The Electric Muse. four discs. F2.45
HELP 25—Albion Country Band. F2.46a

Jamie (recently deleted)
specialty: rock and roll

S 3026—Duane Eddy. 16 Greatest Hits. R2.17

Jazum, 5808 Northumberland St., Pittsburgh, PA 15217
specialty: jazz and nostalgia reissues

21—Boswell Sisters. P2.136
30/1—Boswell Sisters. two discs. P2.136
43/4—Boswell Sisters. two discs. P2.136

Jazz Archives, P.O. Box 194, Plainview, NY 11805
specialty: jazz

JA 6—Charlie Christian. Together with Lester Young, 1940. J5.12
JA 18—Lester Young. Jammin' with Lester. J4.127
JA 23—Charlie Christian, with Benny Goodman's Sextet, 1939/41. J5.13

Jazz Composers' Orchestral Association, 6 West 96th Street, New York, NY 10024
specialty: modern jazz

JCOA 1001/2–Jazz Composers' Orchestra. two discs. J5.123

Jazzology, 3008 Wadsworth Mill Place, Decatur, GA 30032
specialty: jazz

Jazz Piano (Denmark)
specialty: piano jazz reissues

JP 5003–Library of Congress Sessions. J6.84

Jim Taylor Presents, 12311 Gratiot Ave., Detroit, MI 48205
specialty: mainstream jazz and blues

JTP 103–Olive Brown and Her Blues Chasers. B1.398

John Edwards Memorial Foundation, c/o Center for Study of Folklore &
Mythology, UCLA, Los Angeles, CA 90024
specialty: reissues of blues, and country and western material

Kama Sutra, 810 Seventh Ave., New York, NY 10019
specialty: rock and roll

KSBS 2010–Sha Na Na. Rock & Roll Is Here to Stay! R2.51
KSBS 2013–Lovin' Spoonful. Very Best. R3.18

Kapp (recently deleted); see also MCA
specialty: mood

3530–Roger Williams. Gold Hits. P3.24
3559–Jack Jones. Best. P2.48

Kent, 96 West Street, Englewood, NJ 07631
specialty: blues

KST 533–B. B. King. From the Beginning. two discs. B1.294
KST 534–Johnny Otis. Cold Shot. B1.351
KST 537–Jimmy Reed. Roots of the Blues. two discs. B1.232
KST 9001–Elmore James. Legend, v.1. B1.286
KST 9010–Elmore James. Legend, v.2. B1.286
KST 9011–B. B. King. 1949-1950. B1.291

Kicking Mule, P.O. Box 3233, Berkeley, CA 94703
specialty: blues, folk, and guitar albums

106–Rev. Gary Davis. Ragtime Guitar. J2.25

King, 220 Boscobel St., Nashville, TN 37213
specialty: blues, bluegrass and country music, soul

541–Hank Ballard. Greatest Jukebox Hits. B2.36
552–Don Reno and Red Smiley. F6.47

King (cont'd)
    553–Cowboy Copas. All Time Hits. F8.49
    615–Stanley Brothers. F6.58
    826–James Brown. Live at the Apollo, v.1. B4.24
    848–Don Reno and Red Smiley. F6.47
    872–Stanley Brothers. America's Finest Five String Banjo Hootenanny.
        F6.59
    919–James Brown. Unbeatable Sixteen Hits. B4.25
    1022–James Brown. Live at the Apollo, v.2. B4.24
    1059–Freddy King. Hideaway. B1.340
    1065–Don Reno. Fastest Five Strings Alive. F6.99
    1081–Little Willie John. Free At Last. B2.61
    1086–Wynonie Harris. Good Rockin' Blues. B1.423
    1110–James Brown Band. Sho Is Funky Down Here. B4.40
    1130–Roy Brown. Hard Luck Blues. B2.38

King Bluegrass, 6609 Main Street, Cincinnati, OH 45244
    specialty: bluegrass

Kudu, 6464 Sunset Blvd., Hollywood, CA 90028
    specialty: soul
    05–Esther Phillips. From a Whisper to a Scream. B4.74

Leader (England)
    specialty: folk
    LEAB 404–Copper Family. A Song for Every Season. four discs. F2.16

Lemco, 6609 Main Street, Cincinnati, OH 45244
    specialty: bluegrass
    611–J. D. Crowe. The Model Church. F9.31
    612–Red Allen and the Allen Brothers. Allengrass. F6.113

Library of Congress, Washington, D.C.
    specialty: folk and ethnic music, blues; see also Flyright
    LBC 1/15–Folk Music in America, v.1-15. fifteen discs. F3.9 [in progress]
    AAFS L 26/7–American Sea Songs and Shanties, v.1-2. two discs. F3.25
    AAFS L 62–American Fiddle Tunes. F3.16

London, 539 W. 25th Street, New York, NY 10001
    specialty: general
    NPS 4–Rolling Stones. Let It Bleed. R4.16
    PS 114–Edmundo Ros. Rhythms of the South. P5.112
    PS 483–Mantovani. Golden Hits. P5.100
    PS 492–John Mayall. Blues Breakers. R5.10
    PS 493–Rolling Stones. Got Live (If You Want It). R4.14
    PS 534–John Mayall. Alone. R5.9
    PS 539–Rolling Stones. Beggar's Banquet. R4.13

London (cont'd)

NPS 606/7–Rolling Stones. Hot Rocks, v.1. two discs. R4.15
XPS 610–Mantovani. 25th Anniversary Album. P5.101
NPS 626/7–Rolling Stones. Hot Rocks, v.2. two discs. R4.15
XPS 906–Mantovani. All Time Greatest. P5.99

MCA, 100 Universal City Plaza, Universal City, CA 91608
specialty: general; formerly known as Decca, and consequently many older
records were renumbered

DL 8044–Kansas City Jazz. J3.101
DL 8671–Gateway Singers. At the Hungry i. F4.8
DL 8731–Bill Monroe. Knee Deep in Bluegrass. F6.45
DL 8782–Sister Rosetta Tharpe. Gospel Train. B3.62
DL 9034/8–Al Jolson. Story. five discs. P2.12
DL 75326–Conway Twitty and Loretta Lynn. Lead Me On. F8.153
DS 79175–The Who. Live at Leeds. R4.17
DL 9221–Earl Hines. Southside Swing, 1934/5. J4.68
DL 9222/3–Chick Webb, v.1-2. two discs. J4.51
DL 9224–Duke Ellington, v.1: In the Beginning (1926/8). J4.28
DL 9227/8–Fletcher Henderson, v.1-2. two discs. J4.40
DL 9236–Jay McShann. New York–1208 Miles (1941-1943). J4.80
DL 79237/40–Jimmie Lunceford, v.1-4. four discs. J4.77
DL 9241–Duke Ellington, v.2: Hot in Harlem (1928/9). J4.28
DL 9242–Big Bands Uptown, 1931-1943, v.1. J3.78
DL 9243–Jan Savitt. The Top Hatters, 1939-1941. P5.44
DL 9247–Duke Ellington, v.3: Rockin' in Rhythm (1929/31). J4.28
1–Loretta Lynn. Greatest Hits, v.1. F8.130
81–Jimmy Martin. Good 'n' Country. F6.38
86–Red Foley. Songs of Devotion. F9.38
104–Bill Monroe. Bluegrass Instrumentals. F6.43
110–Bill Monroe. The High, Lonesome Sound. F6.44
115–Jimmy Martin. Big 'n' Country Instrumentals. F6.37
131–Bill Monroe. A Voice from On High. F9.61
420–Loretta Lynn. Greatest Hits, v.2. F8.130
527–Bill Monroe. I Saw the Light. F9.60
2106–Neil Diamond. His 12 Greatest Hits. P2.33
2128–Elton John. Greatest Hits. R4.10
DEA 7-2–Those Wonderful Thirties. two discs. P1.14
DXS 7181–Webb Pierce. Story. two discs. F8.30
2-4001–Bill Anderson. Story. two discs. F8.44
2-4005–Inkspots. Best. two discs. B2.22
2-4006–Billie Holiday. Story. two discs. J6.122
2-4008–Fred Waring. Best. two discs. P2.141
2-4009–Buddy Holly. two discs. R1.8
2-4010–Bill Haley and His Comets. Best. two discs. R1.7
2-4018–A Jazz Holiday. two discs. J3.82
2-4019–Art Tatum. Masterpieces. two discs. J6.36
2-4031–Kitty Wells. Story. two discs. F8.132
2-4033–Four Aces. Best. two discs. P2.149

MCA (cont'd)
2-4038—Patsy Cline. Story. two discs. F8.129
2-4039—Mills Brothers. Best. two discs. P2.140
2-4040—Ernest Tubb. Story. two discs. F8.38
2-4041—Guy Lombardo. Sweetest Music This Side of Heaven. two discs. P5.37
2-4043—Bert Kaempfert. Best. two discs. P5.85
2-4047—Ella Fitzgerald. Best. two discs. P2.68
2-4050—Count Basie. Best. two discs. J4.13
2-4052—The Weavers. Best. F4.21
2-4053—Red Foley. Story. two discs. F8.101
2-4056—Carmen Cavallaro. Best. two discs. P5.106
2-4067—The Who. A Quick One (Happy Jack). two discs. R4.19
2-4068—The Who. Magic Bus. two discs. R4.18
2-4071—Eddie Condon. Best. two discs. J3.68
2-4072—Xavier Cugat. Best. two discs. P5.107
2-4073—Jimmy Dorsey. Best. two discs. P5.26
2-4076—Glen Gray and the Casa Loma Orchestra. Best. two discs. P5.32
2-4077—Woody Herman. Best. two discs. J4.43
2-4079—Louis Jordan. Best. B2.45
2-4083—Bob Crosby. Best. two discs. J3.54
2-4090—Bill Monroe. Best. two discs. F6.42
2-8001—American Graffiti. two discs. R2.1
2-11002—That's Entertainment! two discs. P6.85

MCA (England)
specialty: general; formerly Decca American

MCFM 2720—Dick Haymes. Best. P2.45
MCFM 2739—Connie Boswell. Sand in My Shoes. P2.68a

MCA (France)
specialty: general; jazz reissues from American Decca

510.065—Lucky Millinder. Lucky Days, 1941-1945. B2.22a
510.071—The Swinging Small Bands, v.1. J4.93
510.085—James P. Johnson. J6.29
510.088—The Swinging Small Bands, v.2. J4.93
510.090—Kings and Queens of Ivory, v.1. J6.15 (set in progress)
510.111—The Swinging Small Bands, v.3. J4.93
510.123—The Swinging Small Bands, v.4. J4.03

MCA (West Germany)
specialty: general; reissued Decca material

628.334—Tex Ritter. The Singing Cowboy. two discs. F7.14

MGM, 810 Seventh Ave., New York, NY 10019
specialty: general

GAS 140—Osborne Brothers. F6.93
SE 3331—Hank Williams. I Saw the Light. F9.85

MGM (cont'd)
SE 4946—Tompall and the Glaser Brothers. Greatest Hits. F8.128

MGM (England)
specialty: general; reissues of American MGM product

2353.053—Hank Williams. Greatest Hits, v.1. F8.40
2353.071—Billy Eckstine. Greatest Hits. P2.34
2353.073—Hank Williams. Greatest Hits, v.2. F8.40
2353.118—Hank Williams. Collector's, v.1. F8.39
2683.016—Hank Williams. Memorial Album. two discs. F8.42
2683.046—Hank Williams. On Stage! two discs. F8.43

MPS (West Germany)
specialty: jazz

20668—Oscar Peterson. Exclusively for My Friends, v.1. J6.69
20693—Oscar Peterson. Exclusively for My Friends, v.6. J6.69
206696—Oscar Peterson. Exclusively for My Friends, v.2. J6.69
206701—Oscar Peterson. Exclusively for My Friends, v.3. J6.69
206718—Oscar Peterson. Exclusively for My Friends, v.4. J6.69

Magpie (England)
specialty: blues

PY 18000—Robert Wilkins. Before the Reverence, 1928-1935. B1.129a

Mainstream, 1700 Broadway, New York, NY 10019
specialty: jazz and blues

MRL 311—Lightnin' Hopkins. The Blues. B1.181
MRL 316—Maynard Ferguson. Screamin' Blues. J4.169
MRL 399—Andy Kirk. March, 1936. J4.70

Mamlish, Box 417, Cathedral Station, New York, NY 10025
specialty: blues

S3804—Mississippi Sheiks. Stop and Listen Blues. B1.220

Master Jazz Recordings, 955 Lexington Avenue, New York, NY 10024
specialty: jazz

MJR 8116—Billy Strayhorn. Cue for Saxophone. J4.150

Matchbox (England)
specialty: blues

SDR 213—Little Brother Montgomery. 1930-1969. B1.222

Melodeon, 16 River Street, Chatham, NY 12037
specialty: blues, jazz, bluegrass reissues

MLP 7321—Skip James. Greatest of the Delta Blues Singers. B1.199
MLP 7322—Stanley Brothers. Their Original Recordings. F6.57

Melodeon (cont'd)
  MLP 7323–Blind Willie McTell. The Legendary Library of Congress Session,
    1940. B1.127
  MLP 7324–Part Blues. B1.34
  MLP 7325–Red Allen. Solid Bluegrass Sound of the Kentuckians. F6.21

Mercury, 1 IBM Plaza, Chicago, IL 60611
  specialty: general
  MG 20323–Carl Story. Gosepl Quartet Favorites. F9.81
  60232–Dinah Washington. Unforgettable. B4.79
  60587–Frankie Laine. Golden Hits. P2.50
  60621–George Jones. Greatest Hits. F8.26
  60645–Sarah Vaughan. Golden Hits. P2.83
  SR 61268–Dave Dudley. Best. F8.121
  SR 61369–Tom T. Hall. Greatest Hits, v.1. F8.113
  SRM 1-1044–Tom T. Hall. Greatest Hits, v.2. F8.113
  SRM 1-1078–Johnny Rodriguez. Greatest Hits. F8.105
  SRM 1-1101–Bachman-Turner Overdrive. Best. R8.11
  SRM 20803–Jerry Lee Lewis. The Session. two discs. R2.49
  SRM 2-7507–Rod Stewart. Best. R4.44

Milestone, 10th and Parker Streets, Berkeley, CA 94710
  specialty: jazz and blues; reissues from the Riverside catalog
  M 2012–Earl Hines. A Monday Date, 1928. J6.21
  47002–Bill Evans. Village Vanguard Session. two discs. J6.55
  47003–Wes Montgomery. While We're Young. two discs. J6.108
  47004–Thelonious Monk. Pure Monk. two discs. J6.32
  47007–Sonny Rollins. Freedom Suite, Plus. two discs. J5.77
  47018–Jelly Roll Morton. 1923-1924. two discs. J6.33
  47019–Bix Beiderbecke and the Chicago Cornets. two discs. J3.53
  47020–New Orleans Rhythm Kings. two discs. J3.57
  47021–Ma Rainey. two discs. B1.392

Monmouth/Evergreen, 1697 Broadway, Suite 1201, New York, NY 10019
  specialty: jazz, reissued stage and show soundtracks, reissued nostalgia-pop
    music
  MES 6816–Ray Noble and Al Bowlly, v.1. P5.102
  MES 6917–Maxine Sullivan and Bob Wilber. The Music of Hoagy Carmichael.
    P2.82
  MES 7021–Ray Noble and Al Bowlly, v.2. P5.102
  MES 7024/5–Claude Thornhill. two discs. P5.89 and P5.90
  MES 7027–Ray Noble and Al Bowlly, v.3. P5.102
  MES 7033–Jack Hylton, v.1. P5.98
  MES 7039/40–Ray Noble and Al Bowlly, v.4-5. two discs. P5.102
  MES 7055–Jack Hylton, v.2. P5.98
  MES 5056–Ray Noble and Al Bowlly, v.6. P5.102

Monument, 51 W. 52nd Street, New York, NY 10019
  specialty: country music

  18045—Roy Orbison. Very Best. R2.21
  Z 30817—Kris Kristofferson. Me and Bobby McGee. F10.24
  Z 32259—Arthur Smith. Battling Banjos. F6.105

Motown, 6255 Sunset Blvd., Hollywood, CA 90028
  specialty: soul

  663—The Supremes. Greatest Hits. two discs. B4.12
  702-S2—Gladys Knight and the Pips. Anthology. two discs. B4.68
  MS5-726—Motown Story; The First Decade. five discs. B4.5
  782-A3—The Temptations. Anthology. three discs. B4.18
  793-R3—Smokey Robinson and the Miracles. Anthology. three discs. B4.29

Muse, Blanchris, Inc., 160 W. 71st Street, New York, NY 10023
  specialty: jazz and blues

  MR 5087—Elmore James/Eddie Taylor. Street Talkin'. B1.368

Muskadine, Box 635, Manhattan Beach, CA 90266
  specialty: blues reissues

Nonesuch, 962 N. LaCienega, Los Angeles, CA 90069
  specialty: mainly classical, but here includes ragtime music

  H 71305—Joshua Rifkin. Joplin Piano Rags, v.3. J2.23
  HB 73026—Joshua Rifkin. Joplin Piano Rags, v.1/2. J2.23.

Ode, 1416 North LaBrea, Hollywood, CA 90028
  specialty: popular

  SP 77009—Carole King. Tapestry. R3.15

Odeon *See* EMI Odeon (England)

Old Homestead, P.O. Box 100, Brighton, MI 48116
  specialty: bluegrass, old time music, sacred music, and reissues

  OH 90001—Wade Mainer. Sacred Songs of Mother and Home. F9.54
  OHCS 101—Molly O'Day. A Sacred Collection. F9.63

Old Masters, Max Abrams, Box 76082, Los Angeles, CA 90076
  specialty: jazz and pop reissues

  TOM 23—Ted Weems. 1928-1930. P5.46a

Old Timey, 10341 San Pablo Ave., El Cerrito, CA 94530.
  specialty: reissues of old time music and western swing

  OT 100/1—The String Bands, v.1-2. two discs. F5.24
  OT 102—Ballads and Songs. F5.3

Old Timey (cont'd)
    OT 103/4—Cliff Carlisle, v.1-2. two discs. F8.48
    OT 105—Western Swing, v.1. F7.36
    OT 106/7—J. E. Mainer's Mountaineers, v.1-2. two discs. F5.65
    OT 112—Tom Darby and Jimmy Tarlton. F5.113
    OT 115—Allen Brothers. The Chattanooga Boys. F5.117
    OT 116/7—Western Swing, v.2-3. two discs. F7.36

Oldie Blues (Holland)
    specialty: blues reissues

    OL 2801—Pete Johnson, v.1. J6.93
    OL 2806—Pete Johnson, v.2. J6.93

Onyx, Blanchris, Inc., 160 W. 71st Street, New York, NY 10023
    specialty: jazz reissues

    ORI 204—Red Rodney. The Red Arrow. J5.75
    ORI 205—Art Tatum. God Is in the House. J6.35
    ORI 207—Hot Lips Page. After Hours in Harlem. J5.67
    ORI 208—Don Byas. Midnight at Minton's. J5.42
    ORI 221—Charlie Parker. First Recordings! J5.28

Origin Jazz Library, Box 863, Berkeley, CA 94701
    specialty: blues and gospel reissues

    OJL 12/3—In the Spirit, No. 1-2. two discs. B3.13

Pablo, 1133 Avenue of the Americas, New York, NY 10036
    specialty: mainstream jazz

    2625.703—Art Tatum. Solo Masterpieces. thirteen discs. J6.39
    2625.706—Art Tatum. Group Masterpieces. eight discs. J4.155

Paltram (Austria)
    specialty: blues and gospel

    PL 102—Texas Blues. B1.97

Paramount, 8255 Beverly Blvd., Los Angeles, CA 90048
    specialty: popular, rock

    PAS 6031—Commander Cody and His Lost Planet Airmen. Hot Licks, Cold Steel, and Truckers' Favorites. F8.108

Parlophone (England)
    specialty: general, jazz reissues

    PMC 7019—Lonnie Johnson and Eddie Lang. Blue Guitars, v.1. B1.207
    PMC 7038—The Chocolate Dandies. 1928-1933. J4.55
    PMC 7082—The Territory Bands, 1926-1929. J3.104
    PMC 7106—Lonnie Johnson and Eddie Lang. Blue Guitars, v.2. B1.207

Parrot, 539 W. 25th Street, New York, NY 10001
specialty: general
XPAS 71028–Tom Jones. This Is P2.49

Peacock, 8255 Beverly Blvd., Los Angeles, CA 90048
specialty: gospel
136–Mighty Clouds of Joy. Best. B3.48
138–Dixie Hummingbirds. Best. B3.33
139–Five Blind Boys of Mississippi. Best. B3.36
140–Golden Gems of Gospel. B3.6

Philadelphia International, 51 W. 52nd Street, New York, NY 10019
specialty: soul

Philips, 1 IBM Plaza, Chicago, IL 60611
specialty: general; see also Phonogram
PHS 600.298–Nina Simone. Best. B4.70

Philo, The Barn, North Ferrisburg, VT 05473
specialty: folk music

Phoenix, 7808 Bergen Line Ave., Bergenfield, NJ 07047
specialty: jazz and blues reissues
LP 7–Wynonie Harris. Mister Blues Meets the Master Saxes. B1.424

Phonogram (England)
specialty: general, reissues of Philips and Chess materials
6414.406–Alan Stivell. Renaissance of the Celtic Harp. F2.61
6467.013–Memphis Country. F8.12
6467.025/7–Sun Rockabillies, v.1-3. three discs. R1.5
6467.306–Muddy Waters. At Newport. B1.300
6641.047–Genesis, v.1. four discs. B1.275
6641.125–Genesis, v.2. four discs. B1.276
6641.174–Genesis, v.3. four discs. B1.277
6641.180–The Sun Story, 1952-1968. two discs. R1.6

Pickwick, 135 Crossways Park Drive, Woodbury, Long Island, NY 11797
specialty: reissues of Mercury and Capitol material, all fields

Piedmont (c/o Southern Record Sales)
specialty: blues
PLP 13157–Mississippi John Hurt. Folksongs and Blues, v.1. B1.191
PLP 13161–Mississippi John Hurt. Folk Songs and Blues, v.2. B1.191

Pine Mountain, Box 584, Barbourville, KY 40906
specialty: reissues of old time material
PM 269–The Blue Sky Boys. Precious Moments. F9.22

Polydor, 810 Seventh Avenue, New York, NY 10019
specialty: general pop and soul

PD 4054–James Brown. Hot Pants. B4.39
104.678–James Last. This Is P5.86

Polydor (England)
specialty: pop and soul

2310.293–Charlie Feathers/Mac Curtis. Rockabilly Kings. R1.14
2384.007–Oscar Peterson. Exclusively for My Friends, v.5. J6.69
2424.118–Jerry Butler. Best. B4.42

Prestige, 10th and Parker Streets, Berkeley, CA 94710
specialty: jazz, blues and folk music

7159–Thelonious Monk. Monk's Mood. J5.25
7326–Sonny Rollins. Saxophone Colossus. J5.79
7337–Stan Getz. Greatest Hits. J5.89c
7593–Dickie Wells. In Paris, 1937. J4.156
7643–Benny Carter. 1933. J4.20
7827–Lee Konitz. Ezz-thetic. J5.92
PR 24001–Miles Davis. two discs. J5.16
PR 24020–Clifford Brown. In Paris. two discs. J5.40
PR 24024–The Greatest Jazz Concert Ever. two discs. J5.6
P 24030–Dizzy Gillespie. In the Beginning. two discs. J5.22
PR 24034–Miles Davis. Workin' and Steamin'. two discs. J5.21
P 24039–Eddie "Lockjaw" Davis. The Cookbook. two discs. P3.6
P 24040–Buck Clayton and Buddy Tate. Kansas City Nights. two discs.
    J4.161
P 24044–Sonny Stitt. Genesis. two discs. J5.80
PR 24045–25 Years of Prestige. two discs. J5.104
P 34001–Charles Mingus. The Great Concert. three discs. J5.127

Puritan, P.O. Box 946, Evanston, IL 60204
specialty: bluegrass

Pye (England)
specialty: general

502–Donovan. History. F10.8

RBF, 43 W. 61st Street, New York, NY 10023
specialty: jazz, blues and old time music reissues

RF 3–A History of Jazz: The New York Scene, 1914-1945. J3.80
RBF 8/9–The Country Blues, v.1-2. two discs. B1.11
RBF 10–Blind Willie Johnson. B3.45
RBF 11–Blues Rediscoveries. B1.10
RBF 15–Blues Roots: The Atlanta Blues. B1.63
RBF 19–Country Gospel Song. F9.5
RBF 51–Uncle Dave Macon. F5.32

RBF (cont'd)
    RBF 202—The Rural Blues. two discs. B1.22
    RBF 203—New Orleans Jazz: The Twenties. two discs. J3.5

RCA, 1133 Avenue of the Americas, New York, NY 10036
    specialty: general; formerly known as Victor
    LSPX 1004—Guess Who. Best. R3.10
    LPM 1121—Rosalie Allen. Queen of the Yodellers. F8.134
    LPM 1183—Eartha Kitt. That Bad Eartha. P2.109
    LPE 1192—Glenn Miller. Plays Selections from "The Glenn Miller Story."
        P5.15
    LPM 1223—Eddy Arnold. All Time Favorites. F8.88
    LPM 1241—Artie Shaw's Gramercy Five. J4.146
    LPM 1246—Fats Waller. Ain't Misbehavin'. J4.117, P2.65
    LPM 1295—Muggsy Spanier. The Great Sixteen. J3.58
    LPM 1364—Duke Ellington. In a Mellotone. J4.32
    LPM 1649—Jelly Roll Morton. King of New Orleans Jazz. J3.26
    LPM 2078—Bunny Berigan. P5.5
    LPM 2323—Bix Beiderbecke. Legend. J3.88
    LPM 2398—Dizzy Gillespie. The Greatest. J5.53
    LSP 2587—Lena Horne. Lovely and Alive. P2.72
    LSP 2669—Elton Britt, v.1. F8.47
    LSP 2887—Chet Atkins. Best. F8.90
    LSP 2890—Jim Reeves. Best, v.1. F8.92
    LSC 3235—Spike Jones. Is Murdering the Classics. P4.8
    LSP 3377—Glenn Miller. Best. P5.14
    LSP 3476—Sons of the Pioneers. Best. F7.17
    LSP 3478—Hank Snow. Best, v.1. F8.32
    LSP 3482—Jim Reeves. Best, v.2. F8.92
    LSP 3766—Jefferson Airplane. Surrealistic Pillow. R6.7
    LSP 3956—Nilsson. Aerial Ballet. F10.75
    LSP 3957—Jose Feliciano. P2.40
    LSP 3988—Gary Burton. A Genuine Tong Funeral. J5.144
    LSP 4187—Jim Reeves. Best, v.3. F8.92
    LSP 4223—Charley Pride. Best, v.1. F8.104
    LSP 4289—Harry Nilsson. Nilsson Sings Newman. F10.77
    LSP 4321—Porter Wagoner. Best, v.2. F8.83
    LSP 4374—Nina Simone. Best. B4.69
    LSP 4459—Jefferson Airplane. Worst. R6.9
    LSP 4682—Charley Pride. Best, v.1. F8.104
    LSP 4751—Waylon Jennings. Ladies Love Outlaws. F8.11
    LSP 4798—Hank Snow. Best, v.2. F8.32
    LSP 4822—Elton Britt, v.2. F8.47
    LSP 4854—Waylon Jennings. Lonesome, On'ry, and Mean. F8.115
    ARL1-0035—Arthur Fiedler and the Boston Pops. Greatest Hits of the 20s.
        P5.81
    ARL1-0041/5—Arthur Fiedler and the Boston Pops. Greatest Hits of the
        30s, 40s, 50s, 60s, and 70s. five discs. P5.81

RCA (cont'd)
    KPM1-0153—Elvis Presley. The Sun Sessions. R1.11
    APL1-0240—Waylon Jennings. Honky Tonk Heroes. F8.116
    CPL1-0374—John Denver. Greatest Hits. F10.56
    APL1-0455—George Hamilton IV. Greatest Hits. F8.61
    APL1-0928—Neil Sedaka. His Greatest Hits. R2.42
    ANL1-1035—Spike Jones. Best. P4.7
    ANL1-1071—Carter Family. 'Mid the Green Fields. F5.110
    ANL1-1083e—The Browns. Best. F8.97
    APL1-1117—Dolly Parton. Best. F8.143
    ANL1-1137—Perry Como. I Believe. F9.28
    ANL1-1140—Vaughan Monroe, Best. P2.59
    ANL1-1213—Porter Wagoner. Best, v.1. F8.83
    CPL1-1756e—Russ Columbo. A Legendary Performer. P2.29
    CPL1-2099—Woody Guthrie. Dust Bowl Ballads. F10.62
    CPL1-5015—Cleo Laine. Live!! At Carnegie Hall. P2.74
    CPL2-0466—Stars of the Grand Ole Opry, 1926-1974. two discs. F8.8
    ADL2-0694—Wilf Carter. Montana Slim's Greatest Hits. two discs. F7.10
    VPS 6014—Hank Snow. This Is My Story. two discs. F8.33
    LSP 6016—Willie "The Lion" Smith. Memoirs. two discs. J6.74
    VPS 6027—Sam Cooke. This Is. . . . two discs. B2.42
    VPS 6032—Eddy Arnold. This Is. . . . two discs. F8.89
    VPM 6040—Benny Goodman. This Is. . . . , v.1. two discs. J4.62
    VPM 6042—Duke Ellington. This Is. . . . two discs. J4.33
    VPM 6043—This Is the Big Band Era. two discs. P5.4
    VPM 6056—Gene Austin. This Is. . . . two discs. P2.1
    VPM 6063—Benny Goodman. This Is. . . . , v.2. J4.62
    VPSX 6079—Chet Atkins. Now and . . . Then. two discs. F8.91
    VPM 6087—Tommy Dorsey. Clambake Seven. two discs. P5.9

RCA Bluebird (series devoted to reissues)
    AXM2-5501—Tampa Red. two discs. B1.242
    AXM2-5503—Bill Boyd. Country Ramblers, 1934-1950. two discs. F7.39
    AXM2-5506—Big Maceo. Chicago Breakdown. two discs. B1.283
    AXM2-5507—Fletcher Henderson. Complete, 1923-1936. two discs. J4.39
    AXM2-5508—Earl Hines. The Father Jumps. two discs. J4.65
    AXM2-5510—Monroe Brothers. Feats Here Tonight. F5.115
    AXM2-5512—Glenn Miller. Complete, v.1. two discs. P5.39 (in progress,
        about 20 discs)
    AXM2-5517—Artie Shaw. Complete, v.1. two discs. P5.45 (in progress, about
        12 discs)
    AXM2-5518—Fats Waller. Piano Solos, 1929-1941. two discs. J6.40a
    AXM2-5521—Tommy Dorsey. Complete, v.1. two discs. P5.8 (in progress,
        about 12 discs)
    AXM2-5525—Blue Sky Boys. two discs. F5.105
    AXM2-5531—The Cats and the Fiddle. I Miss You So. two discs. B2.24
    AXM2-55??—Grand Ole Opry Stars. two discs. F8.14 (forthcoming)
    AXM2-55??—Patsy Montana. two discs. F7.11 (forthcoming)
    AXM6-5536—Lionel Hampton. Complete, 1937-1941. six discs. J4.97

RCA Camden (reissues)

2460—Pee Wee King. Biggest Hits. F7.44

RCA Vintage (jazz and blues and folk reissues; series recently deleted)
LPV 501—Coleman Hawkins. Body and Soul. J4.98
LPV 504—Isham Jones. P5.12
LPV 507—Smoky Mountain Ballads. F5.7
LPV 513—John Jacob Niles. Folk Balladeer. F3.79
LPV 519—The Bebop Era. J5.2
LPV 521—Benny Goodman. Small Groups. J4.95
LPV 522—Authentic Cowboys and Their Western Folksongs. F7.1
LPV 532—The Railroad in Folksong. F3.40
LPV 533—Johnny Hodges. Things Ain't What They Used to Be. J4.112
LPV 548—Native American Ballads. F5.5
LPV 551—Charlie Barnet, v.1. P5.21
LPV 552—Early Rural String Bands. F5.22
LPV 554—Fred Waring. P2.143
LPV 555—Paul Whiteman, v.1. P5.18
LPV 558—Johnny Dodds. J3.22
LPV 565—Leo Reisman, v.1. P5.17
LPV 566—Barney Bigard/Albert Nicholas. J4.132
LPV 567—Charlie Barnet, v.2. P5.21
LPV 569—Early Bluegrass. F6.15
LPV 570—Paul Whiteman, v.2. P5.18
LPV 581—Bunny Berigan. His Trumpet and Orchestra, v.1. P5.7
LPV 582—Artie Shaw. J4.86

RCA (England)
specialty: general

SD 1000—Frank Sinatra, with Tommy Dorsey. six discs. P2.14
INTS 1072—Gene Krupa. Swingin' with Krupa. J4.74
INTS 1343—Rudy Vallee Croons the Songs He Made Famous. P2.22
DPS 2022—Jimmy Driftwood. Famous Country Music Makers. two discs.
    F10.9
LSA 3180—Hoagy Carmichael. Stardust. P2.26
LPL1-5000—Cleo Laine. I Am a Song. P2.73
LFL4-7522—Perry Como. The First Thirty Years. four discs. P2.6

RCA (France)
specialty: jazz and blues reissues

730.549—Jelly Roll Morton, v.1. J3.25
730.561—Boogie Woogie Man. J6.82
730.581—Memphis Slim. B1.349
730.605—Jelly Roll Morton, v.2. J3.25
730.703/4—Original Dixieland Jazz Band. two discs. J3.51
730.708—Erskine Hawkins, v.1. J4.64
730.710—Barney Kessel. J6.101

RCA (France) (cont'd)

731.051/2—Louis Armstrong. Town Hall Concert, 1947. two discs. J3.38

731.059—Jelly Roll Morton, v.3. J3.25

741.007—Ethel Waters. 1938/1939. P2.85

741.040—Jelly Roll Morton, v.4. J3.25

741.044—Benny Goodman. The Fletcher Henderson Arrangements, v.1. J4.37

741.054—Jelly Roll Morton, v.5. J3.25

741.059—Benny Goodman. The Fletcher Henderson Arrangements, v.2. J4.37

741.061—Don Redman. 1938/1940. J4.50

741.070—Jelly Roll Morton, v.6. J3.25

741.073—Benny Carter. 1940/1941. J4.21

741.080—McKinney's Cotton Pickers. Complete, v.1. J4.48

741.081—Jelly Roll Morton, v.7. J3.25

741.087—Jelly Roll Morton, v.8. J3.25

741.088—McKinney's Cotton Pickers. Complete, v.2. J4.48

741.089—The Greatest of the Small Bands, v.1. J4.92

741.103—The Greatest of the Small Bands, v.2. J4.92

741.106—The Greatest of the Small Bands, v.3. J4.92

741.107—New Orleans, v.1. J3.3

741.109—McKinney's Cotton Pickers. Complete, v.3. J4.48

741.116—Erskine Hawkins, v.2. J4.64

741.117—The Greatest of the Small Bands, v.4. J4.92

DUKE 1/4—Duke Ellington. Integrale. J4.31

FPM1-7003—New Orleans, v.2. J3.3

FPM1-7059—McKinney's Cotton Pickers. Complete, v.4. J4.48

FPM1-7014—The Greatest of the Small Bands, v.5. J4.92

FPM1-7024—Erskine Hawkins, v.3. J4.64

FPM1-7059—McKinney's Cotton Pickers. Complete, v.5. J4.48

FXM1-7060—Henry "Red" Allen, v.1. J3.33

FXM1-7090—Henry "Red" Allen, v.2. J3.33

FXM1-7124—The Greatest of the Small Bands, v.6. J4.92

FXM1-7136—Jean Goldkette. 1928-1929. P5.28

FXM1-7323—Big Joe Williams. B1.259

FXM3-7143—History of Jazz Piano. three discs. J6.10

FXM1-7192—Henry "Red" Allen, v.3. J3.33

RCA (Japan)

specialty: jazz, blues, and country

RA 5459/66—Jimmie Rodgers. 110 Collection. eight discs. F8.31

RA 5641/50—Carter Family. The Legendary Collection, 1927-1934, 1941. ten discs. F5.109

RSO, 75 Rockefeller Plaza, New York, NY 10019

specialty: rock music

RSO 3016—Blind Faith. R8.12

Radiola Records

> 2MR 5051—The First Esquire All-American Jazz Concert, January 18, 1944. two discs. J1.19

Ranwood, 9034 Sunset Blvd., Los Angeles, CA 90069
specialty: mood music

Rebel, Rt. 2, Asbury, WV 24916
specialty: bluegrass

> 1497—Country Gentlemen. Gospel Album. F9.29
> 1506—Country Gentlemen. Award Winning. F6.23
> 1511—Seldom Scene. Act One. F6.126
> 1514—Ralph Stanley. Plays Requests. F6.52
> 1520—Seldom Scene. Act Two. F6.126
> 1528—Seldom Scene. Act Three. F6.126
> 1530—Ralph Stanley. A Man and His Music. F6.51
> 1547/8—Seldom Scene. Recorded Live at the Cellar Door. two discs. F6.128

Red Lightnin' (England)
specialty: blues reissues

> RL 001—Buddy Guy. In the Beginning. B1.337
> RL 006—When Girls Do It. two discs. B1.274
> RL 007—Junior Wells. In My Younger Days. B1.371
> RL 009—Earl Hooker. There's a Fungus Amung Us. B1.281
> RL 0010—Clarence "Gatemouth" Brown. San Antonio Ballbuster. B1.322

Reprise, 3300 Warner Blvd., Burbank, CA 91505
specialty: general, troubador music

> FS 1016—Frank Sinatra. A Man and His Music. two discs. P2.17
> 6199—Tom Lehrer. An Evening Wasted. P4.10
> 6216—Tom Lehrer. Songs. P4.11
> 6217—The Kinks. Greatest Hits. R4.11
> 6261—Jimi Hendrix. Are You Experienced? R8.4
> 6267—Arlo Guthrie. Alice's Restaurant. F10.60
> 6286—Randy Newman. F10.38
> 6341—Joni Mitchell. Clouds. F10.30
> 6383—Neil Young. After the Gold Rush. R7.19
> 6430—Pentangle. Cruel Sister. F2.53
> 2RS 6307—Jimi Hendrix. Electric Ladyland. two discs. R8.5
> MS 2025—Jimi Hendrix. Greatest Hits. R8.6
> MS 2038—Joni Mitchell. Blue. F10.29
> MS 2064—Randy Newman. Sail Away. F10.39
> MS 2148—Maria Muldaur. R4.35

Rimrock, Concord, AR 72523
specialty: sacred, bluegrass

> 1002—The Family Gospel Album. F9.2

Rome, 1414 E. Broad St., Columbus, OH 43205
specialty: bluegrass

1011—Don Reno and Red Smiley. Together Again. F6.49

Roots (Austria)
specialty: blues and gospel reissues; old time music reissues

RL 301—Blind Lemon Jefferson, v.1. B1.112
RL 306—Blind Lemon Jefferson, v.2. B1.112
RL 317—Lucille Bogan and Walter Roland. Alabama Blues, 1930-1935. B1.386
RL 322—Memphis Jug Band, v.1. B1.421
RL 330—Tommy Johnson/Ishman Bracey. Famous 1928 Sessions. B1.113
RL 331—Blind Lemon Jefferson, v.3. B1.112
RL 337—Memphis Jug Band, v.2. B1.421
RL 701—Riley Pickett. Story, 1924-1941. F5.40

Roulette, 17 W. 60th Street, New York, NY 10023
specialty: general and jazz

RE 124—Count Basie. Echoes of an Era: Kansas City Suite/Easin' It. two discs. J4.166

Roulette (England)
specialty: general and jazz

SRCP 3000—Count Basie. The Atomic Mr. Basie. J4.165

Rounder, 186 Willow Avenue, Somerville, MA 02143
specialty: blues, old time music, bluegrass

001—George Pegram. F5.96
0011—Tut Taylor. Friar Tut. F5.44
0014—Don Stover. Things in Life. F6.109
0017—Almeda Riddle. Ballads and Hymns from the Ozarks. F3.83
1001—Blind Alfred Reed. How Can a Poor Man Stand Such Times and Live? F5.41
1002—Aunt Molly Jackson. Library of Congress Recordings. F3.68
1003—Fiddlin' John Carson. The Old Hen Cackled and the Rooster's Gonna Crow. F5.29
1004—Burnett and Rutherford. A Rambling Reckless Hobo. F5.118
1005—Gid Tanner. "Hear These New Southern Fiddle and Guitar Music." F5.78
1006—Blue Sky Boys. The Sunny Side of Life. F5.106
1007—Frank Hutchison. The Train That Carried My Girl from Town. F5.30
1008—Stoneman Family. 1926-1928. F5.72
1013/20—Early Days of Bluegrass, v.1-8. eight discs. F6.16
2003—Martin, Bogan and Armstrong. Barnyard Dance. B1.218
3006—Boys of the Lough. Second Album. F2.10

Rural Rhythm, Box A, Arcadia, CA 91006
specialty: bluegrass

Sackville (Canada)
specialty: jazz

2004—Willie "The Lion" Smith and Don Ewell. Grand Piano Duets. J6.76

Savoy, 6 West 57th Street, New York, NY 10019
specialty: jazz; in the process of being reissued by Arista

MG 12020—Dizzy Gillespie. Groovin' High. J5.54
MG 12106—J. J. Johnson. Boneology. J5.63
MG 14006—Clara Ward Singers. Lord Touch Me. B3.64
MG 14014—Great Golden Gospel Hits, v.1. B3.11
MG 14019—Sonny Terry and Brownie McGhee. Back Country Blues. B1.248
MG 14069—Great Golden Gospel Hits, v.2. B3.11
MG 14076—James Cleveland, v.1. B3.29
MG 14131—James Cleveland, v.2. B3.29
MG 14165—Great Golden Gospel Hits, v.3. B3.11
MG 14252—James Cleveland, v.3. B3.29
SJL 2201—Charlie Parker. Bird: The Savoy Recordings. two discs. J5.30
  [in progress]
SJL 2202—Lester Young. Pres. two discs. J4.126
SJL 2211—Dexter Gordon. Long Tall Dexter. two discs. J5.55
SJL 2214—Billy Eckstine. Mr. B and the Band. two discs. P2.35
SJL 2216—Fats Navarro. Savoy Sessions: Fat Girl. two discs. J5.27

Scepter, 254 W. 54th Street, New York, NY 10019
specialty: pop

Shandar (France)
specialty: modern jazz

SR 10000—Albert Ayler, v.1. J5.139
SR 10004—Albert Ayler, v.2. J5.139

Shelter, 100 Universal City Plaza, Universal City, CA 91608
specialty: rock

SW 8901—Leon Russell. R4.41

Sire, 8255 Beverly Blvd., Los Angeles, CA 90048
specialty: rock

SAS 3702—The History of British Rock, v.1. two discs. R4.1
SAS 3705—The History of British Rock, v.2. two discs. R4.1
SAS 3712—The History of British Rock, v.3. two discs. R4.1
SASH 3715—Fleetwood Mac. In Chicago. two discs. R5.18

Solid State, 6920 Sunset Blvd., Hollywood, CA 90028
specialty: jazz
18048—Thad Jones-Mel Lewis Orchestra. Monday Night. J4.172

Sonet (Sweden)
  specialty: jazz and blues

  SLP 2547–Barney Kessel and Red Mitchell. Two Way Conversation. J6.107

Sonyatone Records (c/o Southern Record Sales)

  STR 201–Eck Robertson. Master Fiddler, 1929-1941. F5.41a

Smithsonian Classic Jazz, P.O. Box 14196, Washington, D.C. 20044
  specialty: jazz reissues

Speciality, 8300 Santa Monica Blvd., Hollywood, CA 90069
  specialty: rhythm 'n' blues, blues, soul, gospel music

  2113–Little Richard. Greatest 17 Original Hits. B2.46
  2115–Ain't That Good News. B3.1
  2116–Soul Stirrers and Sam Cooke, v.1. B3.53
  2126–Percy Mayfield. Best. B2.62
  2128–Soul Stirrers and Sam Cooke, v.2. B3.53
  2131–Don and Dewey. B2.53
  2177/8–This Is How It All Began, v.1-2. two discs. B2.4

Spivey, 65 Grand Ave., Brooklyn, NY 11205
  specialty: blues

  2001–Victoria Spivey. Recorded Legacy of the Blues. B1.405

Spotlite (England)
  specialty: reissues of bop jazz

  100–Billy Eckstine. Together. J5.49
  101/6–Charlie Parker. On Dial. six discs. J5.29
  119–Coleman Hawkins and Lester Young. J4.106
  131–Howard McGhee. Trumpet at Tempo. J5.23

Springboard, 947 U.S. Highway 1, Rahway, NJ 07601
  specialty: reissues of jazz and rock 'n' roll

Stanyan, 8440 Santa Monica Blvd., Hollywood, CA 90069
  specialty: mood

  SR 10032–Vera Lynn. When the Lights Go On Again. P2.76

Starday, 220 Boscobel St., Nashville, TN 37213
  specialty: country and western, bluegrass and sacred materials

  SLP 122–Stanley Brothers. Sacred Songs from the Hills. F9.75
  SLP 146–Bill Clifton. Carter Family Memorial Album. F6.71
  SLP 150–George Jones. Greatest Hits. F8.28
  SLP 161–Lewis Family. Anniversary Celebration. F9.46
  SLP 174–Country Gentlemen. Bluegrass at Carnegie Hall. F6.24
  SLP 250–Diesel Smoke, Dangerous Curves, and Other Truck Driver
    Favorites. F8.10

Starday (cont'd)
SLP 303—Preachin', Prayin', Singin'. F9.14
SLP 398—Moon Mullican. Unforgettable Great Hits. F8.72
SLP 482—New Grass Revival. F6.121
SLP 772—Stanley Brothers. Sing the Songs They Like Best. F6.61
SLP 953—Stanley Brothers. Best. F6.60
SLP 956—Carl Story. Best. F9.80
SLP 961—Don Reno and Red Smiley. Best. F6.48

Starline *See* EMI Starline (England)

Stash, Record People, 66 Greene Street, New York, NY 10012
specialty: jazz and blues reissues [thematic: drugs and alcohol]
100—Reefer Songs. P4.4

Stax, 2693 Union Ave., Memphis, TN 38112
specialty: soul

Storyville (Denmark)
specialty: jazz and blues
670.184—Boogie Woogie Trio. J6.83
671.162—Lonnie Johnson. B1.203

Strata East, 156 Fifth Avenue, Suite 612, New York, NY 10010
specialty: modern jazz

String (England)
specialty: old time music, western swing
801—Beer Parlor Jive. F7.33

Sun, 3106 Belmont Blvd., Nashville, TN 37212
specialty: rock 'n' roll, rhythm 'n' blues, blues, country; see also Phonogram
and Charly for English reissues
100/1—Johnny Cash. Original Golden Hits, v.1-2. two discs. R1.13
102/3—Jerry Lee Lewis. Original Golden Hits, v.1-2. two discs. R1.9
106—Original Memphis Rock & Roll. R1.4
128—Jerry Lee Lewis. Original Golden Hits, v.3. R1.9

Sunbeam, 13821 Calvert St., Van Nuys, CA 91401
specialty: big band reissues, Benny Goodman
SB 101/3—Benny Goodman. Thesaurus, June 6, 1935. three discs. J4.61

Sussex, 6255 Sunset Blvd., Suite 1902, Hollywood, CA 90028
specialty: soul

Swaggie (Australia)
specialty: jazz and blues reissues

Swaggie (cont'd)

S 1219/20—Sleepy John Estes, v.1-2. two discs. B1.164
S 1225—Lonnie Johnson. B1.204
S 1235—Cripple Clarence Lofton/Jimmy Yancey. B1.216, J6.98
S 1242—Bix Beiderbecke. Bix and Tram, 1927/8, v.1. J3.87
S 1245—Bob Crosby's Bob Cats. 1937-1942, v.1. J3.56
S 1251/2—Django Reinhardt. two discs. J6.114/5
S 1269—Bix Beiderbecke. Bix and Tram, 1927/8, v.2. J3.87
S 1275—Count Basie. Swinging the Blues, 1937/39. J4.14
S 1288—Bob Crosby's Bob Cats. 1937-1942, v.2. J3.56

Swing Era (c/o Southern Record Sales)
specialty: reissues of big band material

LP 1001—Themes of the Big Bands. P5.3

Takoma, P.O. Box 5369, Santa Monica, CA 90405
specialty: folk guitar and blues

B 1001—Bukka White. Mississippi Blues. B1.256
C 1002—John Fahey, v.1: Blind Joe Death. F4.32
C 1024—Leo Kottke. 6 and 12 String Guitar. F4.37

Tamla, 6464 Sunset Blvd., Hollywood, CA 90028
specialty: soul

S 252—Marvin Gaye. Greatest Hits, v.1. B4.46
S 278—Marvin Gaye. Greatest Hits, v.2. B4.46
S 282—Stevie Wonder. Greatest Hits, v.1. B4.62
T 308—Stevie Wonder. Where I'm Coming From. B4.34
T 313—Stevie Wonder. Greatest Hits, v.2. B4.62
T 326—Stevie Wonder. Innervisions. B4.37

Tangerine, 8255 Beverly Blvd., Los Angeles, CA 90048
specialty: soul

Tax (Sweden)
specialty: jazz reissues

m8000—Lester Young. The Alternative Lester. J4.125
m8005—Cootie Williams. The Boys from Harlem. J4.87
m8009—The Territory Bands. J3.107
m8011—Cootie Williams. The Rugcutters, 1937-1940. J4.88

Testament, 577 Lavering Avenue, Los Angeles, CA 90024
specialty: blues

T 2207—Chicago Blues: The Beginning. B1.270
T 2210—Muddy Waters. Down on Stovall's Plantation. B1.301
T 2211—Otis Spann. Chicago Blues. B1.307
T 2217—Johnny Shines and Big Walter Horton. B1.361
T 2219—Fred McDowell. Amazing Grace. B3.46
T 2221—Johnny Shines. Standing at the Crossroads. B1.235

The Old Masters *See* Old Masters

Tishomingo (c/o Southern Record Sales)
specialty: western swing

2220—Rollin' Along. F7.34

Topic (England)
specialty: folk music

12 T 118—Bert Lloyd. First Person. F2.21
12 T 136—The Watersons. Frost and Fire. F2.31

Tradition, 10920 Wilshire Blvd., Los Angeles, CA 90024
specialty: folk

2050—The Clancy Brothers and Tommy Makem. Best. F2.40
2053—Oscar Brand. Best. F4.5

Trip, 947 U.S. Highway 1, Rahway, NJ 07065
specialty: reissues of Emarcy jazz catalog (Mercury)

TLP 5501—Sarah Vaughan. 1955. P2.84

Truth (Austria)
specialty: gospel music

1002/3—Guitar Evangelists, v.1-2. two discs. B3.12

Twentieth Century, 8255 Sunset Blvd., Los Angeles, CA 90046
specialty: general

Union Grove (c/o Southern Record Sales)
specialty: material from the Union Grove Fiddlers' Convention

United Artists, 6920 Sunset Blvd., Hollywood, CA 90028
specialty: general

UAS 5596—Country Gazette. A Traitor in Our Midst. F6.117
UAS 5632—Duke Ellington. Money Jungle. J6.18
UA 6291—George Jones. Best. F8.23
UAS 9801—Will the Circle Be Unbroken? three discs. F8.16
UAS 9952—Miles Davis. two discs. J5.15
UALA 089-F2—Vicki Carr. The Golden Songbook. two discs. P2.93
UALA 127-J3—John Lee Hooker. Detroit. three discs. B1.175
UALA 233G—Fats Domino. two discs. B2.44
UALA 243-G—Gordon Lightfoot. The Very Best. F10.27

United Artists (England)
specialty: general

UAS 29215—Sound of the City: New Orleans. B2.19
UAS 29898—Slim Whitman, Very Best. 2 discs. F8.94

United Artists (England) (cont'd)
UAD 60025/6—The Many Sides of Rock 'n' Roll, v.1. two discs. R2.8
UAD 60035/6—The Many Sides of Rock 'n' Roll, v.2. two discs. R2.8
UAD 60091/2—Lena Horne. Collection. two discs. P2.71
UAD 60093/4—The Many Sides of Rock 'n' Roll, v.3. two discs. R2.8

Vanguard, 71 W. 23rd Street, New York, NY 10010
specialty: folk music and blues

2053/5—Newport Folk Festival. three discs. F3.15
2087/8—Newport Folk Festival. two discs. F3.15
6544—Bert Jansch and John Renbourn. Jack Orion. F2.50
VSD 79144/9—Newport Folk Festival. six discs. F3.15
VSD 79180/6—Newport Folk Festival. seven discs. F3.15
VSD 79216/8—Chicago/The Blues/Today! three discs. B1.266
VSD 79219/25—Newport Folk Festival. seven discs. F3.15
VSD 79306/7—Joan Baez. Any Day Now. two discs. F10.1
VSD 79317—Greenbriar Boys. Best. F6.80
VSD 5/6—Ian and Sylvia. Greatest Hits, v.1. two discs. F4.35
VSD 9/10—Doc Watson. On Stage. two discs. F4.18
VSD 15/16—The Weavers. Greatest Hits. two discs. F4.22
VSD 23/24—Ian and Sylvia. Greatest Hits, v.2. two discs. F4.35
VSD 35/36—The Greatest Songs of Woody Guthrie. two discs. F3.37
VSD 39/40—Max Morath. The Best of Scott Joplin and Other Rag Classics.
    two discs. J2.17
VSD 41/42—Joan Baez. Ballad Book. two discs. F4.3
VSD 43/44—Odetta. Essential. two discs. F4.45
VSD 47/48—From Spirituals to Swing, 1938/39. two discs. J4.2
VSD 49/50—Joan Baez. Contemporary Ballad Book. two discs. F10.2
VSD 65/66—Jimmy Rushing. Best. two discs. B1.425
VSD 79/80—Joan Baez. Lovesong Album. two discs. F4.4
VSD 99/100—Vic Dickenson. Essential. two discs. J4.137
VSDB 103/4—Buck Clayton. Essential. two discs. J4.158

Vanguard (England)
specialty: jazz, blues and folk

VRS 8502—Mel Powell. Thinamagig. J4.114
VRS 8528—Mel Powell. Out on a Limb. J4.113

Verve, 810 Seventh Ave., New York, NY 10019
specialty: jazz

FTS 3008—Blues Project. Projections. R5.6
VC 3509—Charlie Parker. J5.69
V6-8412—Stan Getz. Focus. J5.89b
V6-8420—Oscar Peterson. Trio Live from Chicago. F6.71
V6-8526—Bill Evans. Conversations with Myself. J6.54
V6-8538—Oscar Peterson. Night Train. J6.72
V6-8808—Billie Holiday. Best. J6.120

Verve (England)
specialty: jazz, reissues of American Verve

2304.074–Stan Getz. Greatest Hits. P3.9
2304.169–Coleman Hawkins and Ben Webster. Blue Saxophones. J4.105,
    J4.119
2317.031–Woody Herman. At Carnegie Hall, March 25, 1946. J4.42
2610.020–Jazz at the Philharmonic, 1944-1946. two discs. J1.12
2682.005–Johnny Hodges. Back to Back/Side by Side. two discs. J4.107
2683.023–Ben Webster and Oscar Peterson. Soulville. two discs. J4.120
2683.025–Teddy Wilson and Lester Young. Prez and Teddy. two discs.
    J4.123, J4.128
2683.049–Ben Webster. Ballads. two discs. P3.21

Vetco, 5828 Vine Street, Cincinnati, OH 45216
specialty: old time music reissues

101–Uncle Dave Macon. The Dixie Dewdrop, v.1. F5.33
105–Uncle Dave Macon. The Dixie Dewdrop, v.2. F5.33

Vocalion, 100 Universal City Plaza, Universal City, CA 91608
specialty: reissues of MC material

VL 3715–Sons of the Pioneers. Tumbleweed Trails. F7.18
VL 73866–Jo Stafford. Sweet Singer of Songs. P2.80

Virgin, 75 Rockefeller Plaza, New York, NY 10019
specialty: rock

Viva, 6922 Hollywood Blvd., Hollywood, CA 90028
specialty: reissues of nostalgia materials

Vogue (France)
specialty: reissues of jazz and blues

SB 1–Sidney Bechet. Concert à l'Exposition Universelle de Bruxelles, 1958.
    J3.19
LAE 12050–Gerry Mulligan. J5.95

Volt, 2693 Union Ave., Memphis, TN 38112
specialty: soul

Voyager, 424 35th Avenue, Seattle, WA 98122
specialty: old time music

VRLP 303–Gid Tanner. A Corn Licker Still in Georgia. F5.77

Wand (recently deleted)
specialty: rhythm 'n' blues

653–Isley Brothers. Twist and Shout. B2.34

Warner Brothers, 3300 Warner Blvd., Burbank, CA 91505
  specialty: general

  2WS 1555–Peter, Paul and Mary. In Concert. two discs. F4.13
  WS 1749–Grateful Dead. Anthem of the Sun. R6.5
  WS 1765–Petula Clark. Greatest Hits. P2.95
  WS 1835–Van Morrison. Moondance. F10.33
  WS 1843–James Taylor. Sweet Baby James. F10.47
  WS 1869–Grateful Dead. Workingman's Dead. R6.6
  BS 2607–Deep Purple. Machine Head. R8.17
  BS 2643–Bonnie Raitt. Give It Up. R4.39
  2LS 2644–Deep Purple. Purple Passages. two discs. R8.15
  BS 2683–Eric Weissberg. Dueling Banjos. F6.63
  3XX 2736–Fifty Years of Film Music. three discs. P6.79
  2SP 9104–Phil Spector's Greatest Hits. two discs. R2.11a

World Jazz, 221 West 57th Street, New York, NY 10019
  specialty: jazz

World Pacific Jazz (recently deleted)
  specialty: jazz

  1211–Cy Touff and Richie Kamuca. Having a Ball. J4.115

World Records (England)
  specialty: nostalgia, jazz, British dance bands; formerly World Record Club

  F 526–The Anatomy of Improvisation. J5.1
  SH 118/9–Golden Age of British Dance Bands. two discs. P5.93
  SH 146–Al Bowlly. P2.4
  SH 220–Original Dixieland Jazz Band. London Recordings, 1919-1920.
    J3.52
  SHB 21–Ambrose. two discs. P5.94

Xanadu, 3242 Irwin Ave., Knightsbridge, NY 10463
  specialty: reissues of jazz

Yazoo, 245 Waverly Place, New York, NY 10014
  specialty: blues

  L 1001–Mississippi Blues, 1927-1941. B1.84
  L 1002–Ten Years in Memphis, 1927-1937. B1.76
  L 1003–St. Louis Town, 1927-1932. B1.94
  L 1005–Blind Willie McTell. The Early Years, 1927-1933. B1.126
  L 1011–Big Bill Broonzy. Young. B1.155
  L 1013–East Coast Blues, 1926-1935. B1.65
  L 1016–Guitar Wizards, 1926-1935. B1.41
  L 1017–Bessie Jackson and Walter Roland. 1927-1935. B1.387
  L 1020–Charley Patton. Founder of the Delta Blues. two discs. B1.129
  L 1022–Ten Years of Black Country Religion, 1926-1936. B3.23
  L 1023–Rev. Gary Davis. 1935-1949. B3.31

Yazoo (cont'd)

L 1024—Mister Charlie's Blues. F5.14
L 1025—Cripple Clarence Lofton/Walter Davis. B1.215
L 1033—Roosevelt Sykes. The Country Blues Piano Ace. B1.238
L 1036—Leroy Carr. Naptown Blues, 1929-1934. B1.108
L 1037—Blind Willie McTell. 1927-1935. B1.124
L 1041—Georgia Tom Dorsey. Come on Mama, Do That Dance. B1.162
L 1050—Furry Lewis. In His Prime, 1927-1929. B1.211

DIRECTORY OF SPECIALIST RECORD STORES

The record stores listed here handle orders for hard-to-find and rare items (primarily covering blues, country, ethnic, folk, and jazz). In fact, where many labels are concerned, record stores will be the only means of distribution. The following stores are highly recommended because of the superior service they give in obtaining issues from small, independent labels. Request a current catalog. (Note: These stores *may* offer library discounts, but since they are *not* library suppliers per se, this should be clarified at the outset of any transaction.)

UNITED STATES

County Sales
Box 191
Floyd, VA 24091

Roundhouse Record Sales
P.O. Box 474
Somerville, MA 02144

Rare Record Distributing Co.
417 East Broadway
P.O. Box 10518
Glendale, CA 91205

Southern Record Sales
5101 Tasman Drive
Huntington Beach, CA 92649

CANADA

Coda Jazz and Blues Record Centre
893 Yonge Street
Toronto M4W 2H2

GREAT BRITAIN (INCLUDING EUROPE)

Dave Carey—The Swing Shop
18 Mitcham Lane
Streatham, London SW16

Flyright Records
18 Endwell Rd.
Bexhill-on-Sea
East Sussex

Collet's Record Centre
180 Shaftesbury Ave.
London WC2H 8JS

Peter Russell Record Store
24 Market Avenue
Plymouth PL1 1PJ

Dobell's Record Shop
75 Charing Cross Road
London WC 2

ARTISTS' INDEX

Every performing artist in this book is listed alphabetically, and immediately following the name is a series of alphanumeric codes referring the reader to the appropriate annotation in the main text. Included are references to those annotations in which the artist is noted as having been influential or influenced, but does not necessarily appear on the relevant phonodisc. Also, in the case of annotations covering several offerings by one performer or group, the alphanumeric code here listed refers only to the *first* code of a series in which that first code is obviously the first entry of a combined review. The code numbers in boldface type refer to an artist or group's major main entry phonodiscs (those items starred in text).

Ervin, Booker, J5.124, J5.165
Eureka Brass Band, **J3.8**
Europe, Jim, J3.78
Evans, Bill, J5.86, J5.99, J5.122, J5.170,
  J6.9, **J6.54, J6.55**
Evans, Gil, J3.78, J5.82, J5.122, J5.151,
  J5.174, J6.124
Evans, Herschel, J4.13
Ewell, Don, J2.8, J3.42, J3.94, **J6.49-53,**
  J6.76

Faddis, Jon, J4.171
Farlow, Tal, J5.46
Farmer, Art, J5.59, J5.167
Farrell, Joe, J4.167, J6.127
Fatool, Nick, J1.121, J4.151, J6.77
Favors, Malachi, J5.136
Fazola, Irving, J3.54, J3.56
Ferguson, Maynard, **J4.167-69**, J5.38,
  J5.99
Fields, Greechy, J3.26
Fields, Herbie, J5.67
Fitzgerald, Ella, J1.9, J1.13, J4.27, J4.51,
  J4.122
Five Pennies, J3.86
Flanagan, Tommy, J1.13, J5.75, J5.177,
  J6.108
Flores, Chuck, J4.115
Floyd, Troy, J3.99
Fol, Raymond, J4.111
Foster, Frank, J4.166
Foster, Pops, J3.20, J3.21, J3.73, J4.4, J4.85,
  J6.49
Freeman, Bud, J1.1, J1.7, J1.16, J3.61,
  J3.66, **J3.72**, J3.75, J3.86, J3.90, J4.6,
  J4.92
Friars Society, J3.61
  See also New Orleans Rhythm Kings
Fuller, Blind Boy, J2.7
Fuller, Curtis, J5.177
Fuller, Walter, J4.65
Fuzzy Wuzzies, J3.99

Gaillard, Slim, J4.10
Garland, Ed, J3.42
Garland, Red, J5.15
Gates, Rev. J. M., J1.7
Gentle Giant, J5.122
Gershwin, George, J6.62
Getz, Stan, J1.1, J1.13, J4.42, J4.173, J5.51,
  J5.55, **J5.89a-89b**, J5.99, J6.57
Gillespie, Dizzie, J1.7, J1.12, J1.13, J3.78,
  J3.98, J4.25, J4.42, J4.65, J4.92,
  J4.97, **J4.139**, J5.1, J5.6, J5.10, **J5.22**,
  J5.28, J5.33, J5.38, J5.45, J5.48,
  J5.50, **J5.51-54**, J5.67
Giuffre, Jimmy, J1.22, J4.42, **J5.90**, J5.99,
  J5.166, J5.168, J5.169

Goldkette, Jean, J3.88, J3.97
Golson, Benny, J5.51
Gonsalves, Paul, J4.27, J6.3
Gonzales, Babs, J5.1
Goodman, Benny, J1.7, J1.10, J1.20, J3.22,
  J3.78, J3.86, J3.93, J3.96a, J4.1, J4.2,
  J4.6, **J4.37, J4.38**, J4.39, **J4.58-62**,
  J4.71, J4.91, **J4.95, J4.96**, J4.97, J5.13,
  J6.77, J6.121
Goodman, Jerry, J6.135
Goodrick, Michael, J5.143
Gordon, Bobby, J3.99
Gordon, Dexter, J1.1, J5.1, J5.14, J5.22,
  J5.28, J5.48, **J5.55-58**, J5.59, J5.99,
  J6.3
Gramercy Five, J4.86
Grand Terrace Club Band, J4.65
Grappelli, Stephane, J1.1, **J4.148, J6.105**,
  J6.109, **J6.113**, J6.114, J6.117
Gray, Glen, J1.7, J1.10
Gray, Wardell, **J5.59**, J6.3, J6.124
Green, Freddie, J4.13, J4.157, J4.166
Green, Lil, J4.135
Green, Urbie, J3.49, J4.157
Greer, Sonny, J1.7, J4.8, J4.27, J4.97,
  J4.107
Grey, Al, J1.13, J1.18, J4.166, J5.51
Grimes, Henry, J5.147
Grimes, Tiny, J4.162, J5.67, J6.36
Grossman, Stefan, J2.4
Gryce, Gigi, J5.51
Guarnieri, Johnny, J1.21, J4.9, J4.124,
  J4.146, J5.10
Gunther, Paul, J6.68
Guy, Joe, J5.67, J5.68

Hackett, Bobby, J3.68, J3.90, J4.38, J4.81,
  J4.140-42
Haden, Charlie, J5.106, J5.123, J5.150,
  J5.156, J5.171
Haggart, Bob, J3.54, J3.56, J6.122
Haig, Al, J5.22, J5.26, J5.28, J5.51, J5.59,
  J5.71, J5.82, J5.89, **J6.56, J6.57**
Haines, Paul, **J5.171**
Hall, Edmond, J1.6, J3.34, J4.137, **J4.143**,
  J5.7
Hall, Herb, J4.144
Hall, Jim, J5.91, J5.170
Hall, Minor, J3.42, J3.46, J6.49
Hamilton, Chico, **J5.91**
Hammer, Jan, J6.127, J6.136, J6.138
Hampton, Lionel, J1.10, J4.20, J4.58,
  J4.63, J4.91, J4.95, **J4.97**, J4.98, J4.155,
  J5.10, J5.60
Hampton, Slide, J4.167
Hancock, Herbie, J5.61, J5.122, J5.153,
  J5.161, J5.163, J5.164, J6.125, J6.131,
  J6.135
Handy, John, J5.124
Handy, W. C., J2.8, J3.36, J6.59, J6.92